scholarship. Among all the details, the reality of the King's coming to take his rightful place shines through. It's a great encouragement to see the contribution of this author and his writing to both biblical scholarship and Bible translation!"
—**Andy Warren-Rothlin**, Global Translation Advisor, United Bible Societies; former Professor of Hebrew, Theological College of Northern Nigeria

I0804725

"What a delight it is to watch my former students who continue their education and distinguish themselves as Christian scholars in their own right! This is what Chris Tachick has done with his Th.M. thesis concerning the use of Zephaniah 3 in John's Gospel. He demonstrates insightful capability in the languages of both Testaments. Therefore, I heartily commend his careful, skillful, and convincing exegetical work that advances our insights and understanding of the apostle John's uses of the Old Testament by way of verbal links and evocative allusions, imageries, and figures drawn from Holy Scripture as he testifies that Israel's prophesied Messiah is Jesus of Nazareth."
—**Ardel B. Caneday**, Professor of New Testament & Greek, University of Northwestern—St. Paul

"I am delighted to see Christopher Tachick's thorough and competent study of the use of Zephaniah in the New Testament. This Minor Prophet has been mostly overlooked and deserves the serious attention given it here. Tachick's methodology is sound, his research is thorough, and his argumentation is careful. He makes a compelling case for his 'Zephaniah proposal' and at the same time provides important insights into the study of both Zephaniah and John's Gospel. I heartily recommend his work."
—**E. Ray Clendenon**, Senior Editor of Bible and Reference Publishing, B&H Publishing Group

"Christopher Tachick's exploration of the evocative use of Zephaniah 3 in the triumphal entry account in John's Gospel exemplifies best practices in intracanonical, intertextual studies. It is thoroughly researched, cogently argued, and keenly sensitive to the broader literary-theological contexts of both the Old Testament source(s) and the interpretation offered by the inspired New Testament author."
—**Dennis E. Johnson**, Professor of Practical Theology, Westminster Seminary California

"In this thoroughly researched and well-written study, the author makes a very plausible case for the use of Zephaniah 3 in John 12. Tachick clearly articulates and capably defends his thesis, excelling in both in-depth analysis and theological synthesis. I highly recommend this exemplary piece of scholarship."
—**Andreas J. Köstenberger**, Senior Research Professor of New Testament and Biblical Theology, Southeastern Baptist Theological Seminary; Founder, Biblical Foundations (www.biblicalfoundations.org)

"This is an exemplary study of the use of the Old Testament in the New that sheds fresh light on Jesus's triumphal entry in John. Christopher Tachick carefully and persuasively argues that an under-appreciated allusion to Zephaniah 3 informs John's presentation of Jesus as 'King of Israel.' I warmly recommend this book to theological students, scholars, and pastors."
—**Brian J. Tabb**, Academic Dean, Bethlehem College & Seminary

"This carefully argued thesis makes important contributions to our understanding the Fourth Gospel's use of the OT and of the book of Zephaniah alike. The author's expertise in discourse linguistics lends methodological clarity and nuance to his exegesis, which interacts capably with an impressive range of scholarship. Together with his keen theological eye, this makes it an excellent example of solidly grounded whole-Bible interpretation."
—**Daniel C. Timmer**, Professor of Biblical Studies, Doctoral Program, Puritan Reformed Theological Seminary

"This is a very detailed analysis of the arguments for reading the entry narrative in John as referencing Zephaniah and the theological consequences of such a reading. The author uses a wide range of data and skills in textual criticism, Hebrew grammar, linguistics, discourse analysis, exegesis, intertestamental literature, and New Testament theology, resulting in an exemplary piece of biblical

"King of Israel" and "Do Not Fear, Daughter of Zion"

Reformed Academic Dissertations

A Series

Series Editor
John J. Hughes

"King of Israel" and "Do Not Fear, Daughter of Zion"

The Use of Zephaniah 3 in John 12

Christopher S. Tachick

P&R
P U B L I S H I N G
P.O. BOX 817 • PHILLIPSBURG • NEW JERSEY 08865-0817

"King of Israel" and "Do Not Fear, Daughter of Zion": The Use of Zephaniah 3 in John 12. Christopher S. Tachick, Th.M., M.A., B.A. Submitted to Bethlehem College & Seminary, May 2015, in partial fulfillment for the award of a Th.M. degree. Supervisor: Jason S. DeRouchie. Examiners: Andreas J. Köstenberger and Brian J. Tabb.

Printed in the United States of America

ISBN: 978-1-62995-411-0 (pbk)

To Elizabeth, my excellent and praiseworthy wife
(Prov. 12:4; 31:10–31),
and Toph, Judah, and Hadassah, my beloved arrows (Ps. 127:3–4)

Contents

Analytical Outline

Series Introduction

P&R Publishing has a long and distinguished history of publishing carefully selected, high-value theological books in the Reformed tradition. Many theological books begin as dissertations, but many dissertations are worthy of publication in their own right. Realizing this, P&R has launched the Reformed Academic Dissertation (RAD) program to publish top-tier dissertations (Ph.D., Th.D., D.Min., and Th.M.) that advance biblical and theological scholarship by making distinctive contributions in the areas of theology, ethics, biblical studies, apologetics, and counseling.

Dissertations in the RAD series are curated, which means that they are carefully selected, on the basis of strong recommendations by the authors' supervisors and examiners and by our internal readers, to be part of our collection. Each selected dissertation will provide clear, fresh, and engaging insights about significant theological issues.

A number of theological institutions have partnered with us to recommend dissertations that they believe worthy of publication in the RAD series. Not only does this provide increased visibility for participating institutions, it also makes outstanding dissertations available to a broad range of readers while helping to introduce promising authors to the publishing world.

We look forward to seeing the RAD program grow into a large collection of curated dissertations that will help to advance Reformed scholarship and learning.

John J. Hughes
Series Editor

Foreword

Preaching around A.D. 33 and having recently witnessed Jesus Christ's triumphal entry into Jerusalem, his week of passion, his resurrection, his ascension, and then the birth of his church at Pentecost, the Apostle Peter daringly proclaimed from Jerusalem's Temple Mount that "God foretold by the mouth of *all* the prophets that his Christ would suffer" and that "*all* the prophets . . . proclaimed these days" of the church's rise (Acts 3:18, 24). Indeed, Peter would later declare that "to [Christ] *all* the prophets bear witness" (10:43). In Wittenberg, Germany, a millennium and a half later, in lectures dated to 13 August 1525, Martin Luther asserted of the prophet Zephaniah, "Among the minor prophets, he makes the clearest prophecies about the kingdom of Christ" (*Minor Prophets I: Hosea–Malachi*, Luther's Works 18, 319). What is so striking about these statements from both the apostle and Luther is that God's prophetic mouthpiece Zephaniah never explicitly mentioned the promised Messiah, whether with reference to his tribulation or triumph. Nevertheless, those reading his book through the light and lens of Christ, assert that they find within it God predicting both Christ's suffering and sovereignty.

The study before you by Christopher Tachick helps clarify how the assertions by both the apostle and Luther are true. It does so by adding to the significant wrestling done over the last five decades on how the New Testament authors cite, allude to, or echo the Old Testament. Tachick's formal training as a linguist, exegete, and theologian, his grasp of the biblical languages, along with English, French, and German, and his years of service with Wycliffe Bible Translators have supplied him with key skills for this task. But even more, he knows the God of Scripture, and he is convinced of the Bible's overarching unity and of the way the whole progresses, integrates, and climaxes in Christ. This study is both careful and thoughtful, and engages the best scholarship on both Zephaniah and the Fourth Gospel. Tachick persuasively argues that John's narrative of Jesus' triumphal entry alludes at two different points (John 12:13, 15) to Zephaniah 3:14–15, and the study helpfully unpacks the significance of this fact for the message of John's Gospel.

Interpreters commonly recognize the citations of Psalm 118:25–26 and Zechariah 9:9 in John 12:13–15, where we read:

> So they took branches of palm trees and went out to meet him, crying out, "Hosanna! Blessed is he who comes in the name of the Lord, even the *King of Israel*!" And Jesus found a young donkey and sat on it, just as it is written, "*Fear not, daughter of Zion*; behold, your king is coming, sitting on a donkey's colt."

However, as Tachick rightly observes, the psalmist did not include the phrase "King of Israel," and Zechariah's opening charge is actually "rejoice" rather than "fear not." What, therefore, is John doing in these citations? Tachick suggests that he is intentionally alluding to Zephaniah 3:14–15, which is the only place in the Old Testament where we find the grouping of "King of Israel," "Fear not," and "daughter of Zion":

> Sing aloud, O *daughter of Zion*; shout, O Israel! Rejoice and exult with all your heart, O daughter of Jerusalem! The Lord has taken away the judgments against you; he has cleared away your enemies. The *King of Israel*, the Lord, is in your midst; you shall *never* again *fear* evil.

To guide his study, Tachick employs the rigorous methodology set forth in works like G. K. Beale and D. A. Carson, eds.,

Commentary on the New Testament Use of the Old Testament (Baker, 2007) and G. K. Beale, *Handbook on the New Testament Use of the Old Testament: Exegesis and Interpretation* (Baker, 2012). In chapter 1, he surveys the various proposals to the sources of "King of Israel," "fear not," and "daughter of Zion," and lays out his methodology. Chapter 2 carefully assesses the literary context of John 12:9–19, examines the chief arguments for what he tags "the Zephaniah Proposal," and compares the texts Psalm 118, Zechariah 9, Zephaniah 3, and John 12. Chapter 3 supplies the heart of the study, engaging in a rigorous textual assessment of Zephaniah 3:8–20. Here Tachick is at his best, carefully tracing Zephaniah's flow of thought and faithfully articulating the prophet's vision of global renewal growing out of the arrival of the day of the Lord. Chapter 4 surveys the reception of Zephaniah 3 in Jewish literature, and then Chapter 5 assesses both the hermeneutical and theological use of Zephaniah 3 in John 12. Tachick argues that John's primary hermeneutical use of Zephaniah was to highlight the initial direct fulfillment of the prophet's predictions, but that John also drew on Zephaniah to support his application of narrative irony and to serve as a structural blueprint for his narrative. Tachick also identifies that John's theological use highlights the very close association between Yahweh and King Jesus, incorporates Zephaniah's teaching on both the Gentile ingathering and warrior-king motifs, and stresses that Zephaniah's eschatological "day" of the Lord has dawned. Chapter 6 summarizes the whole.

The prophet Zephaniah envisioned a global renewal arising from the arrival of the day of the Lord. At that time, the warrior-king Yahweh would deliver his city Jerusalem and all the humble gathered there, including some transformed worshippers from the nations. By his allusions to Zephaniah 3, John portrays Jesus' triumphal entry unto death and victorious resurrection as inaugurating Zephaniah's day of the Lord and the eschatological reign of Yahweh associated with it. In Christ, the end of the ages has dawned, and through him we gain both a light for seeing what the Old Testament anticipated and a lens for guiding us to a proper assessment that magnifies him as the one to whom all the Old Testament points and as the one from whom all fulfillment comes. I celebrate the publication of this work, which faithfully engages in the discipline of biblical theology for the glory of Christ and the good of his church.

Jason S. DeRouchie
Professor of Old Testament and Biblical Theology
Bethlehem College & Seminary
Elder, Bethlehem Baptist Church

Preface

This book on Zephaniah 3 in John 12 is a revision of my Master of Theology (Th.M.) thesis completed in May 2015. Although the process of researching, writing, revising, and editing has demanded much time and energy, it has also deepened my joy in the Lord. As I wrap up the final editing, celebrations of the 500th anniversary of the commencement of the Reformation are taking place all over the world. My heart's cry resonates with the Reformers as I offer this work to God and proclaim: *Soli Deo gloria*!

The genesis for this study was a paper written for Dr. DeRouchie's exegetical course "Zephaniah: A Summons to Satisfaction" in January 2014 at Bethlehem College & Seminary in Minneapolis, Minnesota. DeRouchie required each student to complete an exegetical/biblical-theological paper on a select portion of Zephaniah, and I wrote on Zephaniah 3:14–16 due to a comment DeRouchie made in class. He observed that the Entry Narrative in John 12 was unique among the Synoptic Gospels at several points, but John's title for Jesus at the entry (i.e., "King of Israel") was particularly intriguing since Zephaniah 3 has the same title, for Yahweh. Those comments launched me into writing an exegetical paper that assessed the arguments for the Zephaniah Proposal. Although several scholars conclude that the Zephaniah Proposal is viable, few examine the OT context, none chart Zephaniah 3's use in Jewish literature, and none write more than a few pages on the topic. So, that short paper grew into my Th.M. thesis and then this book.

I translated Zephaniah (Hebrew into English), completed a

text hierarchy, and prepared an exegetical arc of the book, based on observing Zephaniah's logical/clause connectors, verb forms (e.g., *weqatal, qatal*), etc.[1] In my exegetical work on the Hebrew text of Zephaniah, I concluded that the number and significance of the participant references come to a climax in Zephaniah 3 and that 3:14–15 is the peak of the book. I also argued that imperatives provide the structure of Zephaniah. Initially, I had speculated that the imperatives in 3:14 simply stand in a series with the imperatives of 2:1–3 and 3:8, but after more fully recognizing the significance of the *qatal* verbs in 3:15 and the structural indicators in Zephaniah 3, I saw the evidence weighed in favor of interpreting 3:14–15 as an eruptive, parenthetical outburst of joy (following DeRouchie's argument; see chap. 3).

I also researched how the FG uses the OT. Having translated (Greek into English) and arced John 12, I considered the role that Zephaniah 3 plays alongside other major OT backgrounds in John 12: Psalm 118, Zechariah 9, and Isaiah 52–53. To better understand why John 12 would use Zephaniah 3, I undertook a study of Zephaniah in Jewish literature and discovered that a strand of Jewish interpretation joined Zephaniah 3 and Zechariah 9, and considered them as containing messianic expectations. After conducting this background research, I applied those findings to probe the chief hermeneutical and theological implications for the Zephaniah Proposal in John 12. John's Entry Narrative beckons the disciple to behold Jesus, the King of Israel, and to follow him without fear.

In my role with Wycliffe Bible Translators, I serve as a translation consultant in the OT and NT with a particular focus on the OT.

[1] For recent discussions on text hierarchy, arcing, bracketing, and phrasing, see Jason S. DeRouchie, *How to Understand and Apply the Old Testament: Twelve Steps from Exegesis to Theology* (Phillipsburg, NJ: P&R Publishing, 2017), 237–68; Andrew David Naselli, *How to Understand and Apply the New Testament: Twelve Steps from Exegesis to Theology* (Phillipsburg, NJ: P&R Publishing, 2017), 121–61; Thomas R. Schreiner, *Interpreting the Pauline Epistles*, 2nd ed. (Grand Rapids: Baker Academic, 2011), 97–124.

Preface

This book is rooted in an intense desire for the bibleless to access the Word of God and to better understand how the OT points forward to Jesus in the NT. Just as this study has caused me to more deeply delight in King Jesus, my prayer is that it also bears fruit in the lives of many people and many peoples.

Note: All references of this type—see § 2.4.2—refer to corresponding sections in the analytical outline.

Christopher S. Tachick
St. Paul, Minnesota
Reformation Day 2017

Acknowledgements

All praise and thanksgiving for this project first and foremost goes to God. "For from him and through him and to him are all things. To him be glory forever. Amen" (Rom. 11:36).

This monograph is a slightly revised and updated version of my Th.M. thesis submitted to Bethlehem College & Seminary in 2015. Many people and institutions have a part in helping to make this book a reality, but I can only name a few here.

I would like to express my sincere gratitude to Cameroon Association for Bible Translation and Literacy (CABTAL), which released me to the Th.M. study program where this book took shape. I am also thankful for SIL's and Wycliffe's commitment to academic excellence and for having granted me the time necessary to complete my Th.M. thesis. Thanks is likewise due to Seed Company which granted me time and provided encouragement for working on this book. During this season of research, my family's prayer and financial partners have faithfully "held the ropes" of support, and I am incredibly thankful to God for each of you. It is my honor and privilege to serve the African church in Bible translation together with you.

Many people had a more direct influence on this monograph. Daniel Brendsel read my thesis and provided substantive yet gracious feedback, for which I am profoundly grateful. Thank you for your eye for detail and for engaging with my arguments. Many thanks also to Andy Warren-Rothlin who provided several substantive and editorial comments in order to improve and strengthen the work. In addition, James Scott copyedited the footnotes and bibliography, and John Muether compiled the Index of Subjects and Names; I thank God for your help with this project. Thank you also to the editors of RAD for accepting this monograph for publication in the series, and John Hughes, Julia Craig, and Amanda Martin at P&R Publishing for your kind assistance in publishing this work. A special word of thanks goes to John for answering my many questions and guiding this project's publication from start to finish.

To my thesis committee members, Andreas Köstenberger and Brian Tabb, thank you for your scholarly analyses, constructive critiques, and words of affirmation. At least three times, Brian, meeting with you enabled me to persevere in this endeavor. I would like to particularly thank my thesis supervisor, Jason DeRouchie, for your Christ-exalting friendship, humility, admonitions, and academic rigor. Your academic guidance, exemplary scholarship, pastoral care, and encouragement have greatly increased my joy in the King.

Finally, I am profoundly thankful for my beloved wife Elizabeth and three children Toph, Judah, and Hadassah, to whom this book is dedicated. You have all joyfully sacrificed so that I could focus on researching and writing, and together with you, I rejoice in God's kindness that led us to complete this project. Words would fail to express how much your love, prayers, patience and encouragement buoyed me in the study. We are a team, and I am a deeply blessed husband and father because of you.

Abbreviations

1 Apol.	*Apologia i* (*First Apology*, Justin)
1CS	first common singular
1QPZEPH (1Q15)	*Pesher* on Zephaniah from Qumran, Cave 1
1QS	*Rule of the Community* from Qumran, Cave 1
2FS	second feminine singular
2MP	second masculine plural
3CP	third common plural
3FS	third feminine singular
3MS	third masculine singular
3MP	third masculine plural
4QPZEPH (4Q170)	Pesher on Zephaniah from Qumran, Cave 4
4QXIIA (4Q76)	Minor Prophets[a] (frags.) from Qumran, Cave 4
4QXIIB (4Q77)	Minor Prophets[b] (frags.) from Qumran, Cave 4
4QXIIG (4Q82)	*The Greek Minor Prophets Scroll* from Qumran, Cave 4
4Q464	*Exposition on the Patriarchs* from Qumran, Cave 4

4QMMT	*Miqṣat Maʿaśê ha-Torah*, "Some of the Torah Observations," from Qumran, Cave 4
8ḤevXII gr (8Ḥev 1)	The Greek Minor Prophets Scroll from Naḥal Ḥever, Cave 8
AB	Anchor Bible
ABD	*The Anchor Bible Dictionary*. Edited by David Noel Freedman. 6 vols. New York, 1992
AbrNSup	Abr-Nahrain Supplement Series
Adj	adjective
Adv	adverb
AnBib	Analecta Biblica
Ag. Ap.	*Against Apion* (Josephus)
AGJU	Arbeiten zur Geschichte des antiken Judentums und des Urchristentums
AIL	Ancient Israel and Its Literature
Ant.	*Jewish Antiquities* (Josephus)
ArBib	The Aramaic Bible
ASBF	Analecta (Studium Biblicum Franciscanum)
ASNU	Acta Seminarii Neotestamentici Upsaliensis
ASOR	American Schools of Oriental Research
ATSAT	Arbeiten zu Text und Sprache im Alten Testament
b. ʿAbod. Zar.	Babylonian (Talmud) ʿAbodah Zarah
b. ʿArak.	Babylonian (Talmud) ʿArakin
b. B. Meṣ.	Babylonian (Talmud) Baba Meṣiʿa

b. Ber.	Babylonian (Talmud) Berakot
b. Pesaḥ.	Babylonian (Talmud) Pesaḥim
b. Qidd.	Babylonian (Talmud) Qiddušin
b. Sanh.	Babylonian (Talmud) Sanhedrin
b. Šabb.	Babylonian (Talmud) Šabbat
b. Sukkah	Babylonian (Talmud) Sukkah
BBC	Blackwell Bible Commentaries
BBR	*Bulletin for Biblical Research*
BCOTWP	Baker Commentary on the Old Testament Wisdom and Psalms
BDAG	Danker, Frederick W., Walter Bauer, William F. Arndt, and F. Wilbur Gingrich. *Greek-English Lexicon of the New Testament and Other Early Literature*. 3rd ed. Chicago, 2000
BECNT	Baker Exegetical Commentary on the New Testament
BETL	Bibliotheca Ephemeridum Theologicarum Lovaniensium
BHS	*Biblia Hebraica Stuttgartensia*. Edited by Karl Elliger and Wilhelm Rudolph. Stuttgart, 1983
BHQ	*Biblia Hebraica Quinta*. Edited by Adrian Schenker et al. Stuttgart, 2004–
Bib	*Biblica*
BibOr	Biblica et orientalia
BIOSCS	*Bulletin of the International Organization for Septuagint and Cognate Studies*

BIS	Biblical Interpretation Series
BJS	Brown Judaic Studies
BLS	Bible and Literature Series
BNTC	Black's New Testament Commentaries
BS	Biblical Studies
BSac	*Bibliotheca Sacra*
BTNT	Biblical Theology of the New Testament
BZAW	Beihefte zur Zeitschrift für die alttestamentliche Wissenschaft
BZNW	Beihefte zur Zeitschrift für die neutestamentliche Wissenschaft
CAT	Commentaire de l'Ancien Testament
CBC	Cambridge Bible Commentary
CBET	Contributions to Biblical Exegesis and Theology
CBQ	*Catholic Biblical Quarterly*
CBQMS	Catholic Biblical Quarterly Monograph Series
CIET	Collection d'Institut d'Études Théologiques
CJB	Complete Jewish Bible
CRINT	Compendia Rerum Iudaicarum ad Novum Testamentum
CurBR	*Currents in Biblical Research*
CurBS	*Currents in Research: Biblical Studies*
DATIM	Das Alte Testament im Dialog

Did.	Didache
DJG	*Dictionary of Jesus and the Gospels*. Edited by Joel B. Green and Scot McKnight. Downers Grove, IL, 1992
DOTP	*Dictionary of the Old Testament Prophets*. Edited by Mark J. Boda and J. Gordon McConville. Downers Grove, IL, 2012
EBib	*Etudes bibliques*
EBS	Encountering Biblical Studies
ECC	Eerdmans Critical Commentary
Eccl. Rab.	Ecclesiastes Rabbah
EstAg	*Estudio Agustiniano*
ESV	English Standard Version
ETS	Erfurter theologische Studien
EvQ	*Evangelical Quarterly*
FFNT	Foundations and Facets: New Testament
FG	The Fourth Gospel (Gospel of John)
FOTL	Forms of the Old Testament Literature
FS	feminine singular
FP	feminine plural
GD	Georgias Dissertations
Gen. Rab.	Genesis Rabbah
GNS	Good News Studies
Greg	*Gregorianum*

HALOT	Koehler, L., W. Baumgartner, and J. J. Stamm. *The Hebrew and Aramaic Lexicon of the Old Testament.* Translated and edited under the supervision of M. E. J. Richardson. 5 vols. Leiden, 1994–2000
HBM	Hebrew Bible Monographs
HCOT	Historical Commentary on the Old Testament
HMS	Hearing the Message of Scripture: A Commentary on the Old Testament
HNT	Handbuch zum Neuen Testament
HS	*Hebrew Studies*
HSM	Harvard Semitic Monographs
HSS	Harvard Semitic Studies
HT	Helps for Translators
IBC	Interpretation: A Bible Commentary for Teaching and Preaching
IBHS	Bruce K. Waltke and Michael O'Connor. *An Introduction to Biblical Hebrew Syntax.* Winona Lake, IN, 1990
ICC	International Critical Commentary
IDB	*Interpreter's Dictionary of the Bible.* Edited by G. A. Buttrick. 4 vols. Nashville, 1962
Imv	imperative
Inf	infinitive construct
Interj	interjection

ISBE	*The International Standard Bible Encyclopedia*. Edited by G. W. Bromiley. 4 vols. Grand Rapids, 1979–88
ISBL	Indiana Studies in Biblical Literature
ITC	International Theological Commentary
J.W.	*Jewish War* (Josephus)
JBL	*Journal of Biblical Literature*
JOTT	*Journal of Translation and Textlinguistics*
JQR	*Jewish Quarterly Review*
JSJ	*Journal for the Study of Judaism in the Persian, Hellenistic, and Roman Periods*
JSNT	*Journal for the Study of the New Testament*
JSNTSup	Journal for the Study of the New Testament Supplement Series
JSOTSup	Journal for the Study of the Old Testament Supplement Series
JTS	*Journal of Theological Studies*
KAT	Kommentar zum Alten Testament
KJV	King James Version
Lev. Rab.	Leviticus Rabbah
LHBOTS	Library of Hebrew Bible/Old Testament Studies
LNTS	Library of New Testament Studies
LOBS	Library of Biblical Studies
LSTS	Library of Second Temple Studies

LXX	Septuagint, following *Septuaginta* (Rahlfs, 2006 ed.)
m. Pesaḥ.	Mishnah Pesaḥim
m. Sukkah	Mishnah Sukkah
Mart. Isa.	Martyrdom of Isaiah
MBPS	Mellen Biblical Press Series
Midr. Pss.	Midrash Psalms
MS	masculine singular
MP	masculine plural
MT	Masoretic Text, following Biblia Hebraica Quinta
MUR88	Minor Prophets Scroll (MurXII) from Murabbaʿat
NA^{27}	*Novum Testamentum Graece*. Edited by Barbara Aland, Kurt Aland, Johannes Karavidopoulos, Carlo M. Martini, Bruce M. Metzger. 27th ed. Stuttgart, 1993
NA^{28}	*Novum Testamentum Graece*. Edited by Barbara Aland, Kurt Aland, Johannes Karavidopoulos, Carlo M. Martini, Bruce M. Metzger. 28th ed. Stuttgart, 2012
NAB	New American Bible
NAC	New American Commentary
NCB	New Century Bible
NDBT	*New Dictionary of Biblical Theology*. Edited by T. D. Alexander and B. S. Rosner. Downers Grove, IL, 2000

NET	New English Translation
NETS	*A New English Translation of the Septuagint: And the Other Greek Translations Traditionally Included Under That Title*. Edited by Albert Pietersma and Benjamin G. Wright. Oxford, 2007
NIB	*The New Interpreter's Bible*. Edited by L. E. Keck. 12 vols. Nashville, 1996
NIBCOT	New International Biblical Commentary on the Old Testament
NICNT	New International Commentary on the New Testament
NICOT	New International Commentary on the Old Testament
NIDB	*The New Interpreter's Dictionary of the Bible*. Edited by Katharine D. Sakenfeld. 5 vols. Nashville, 2009
NIDOTTE	*New International Dictionary of Old Testament Theology and Exegesis*. Edited by Willem A. VanGemeren. 5 vols. Grand Rapids, 1997
NIV	New International Version
NIVAC	NIV Application Commentary
NJB	New Jerusalem Bible
NLT	New Living Translation
NovT	*Novum Testamentum*
NovTSup	Supplements to Novum Testamentum
NRSV	New Revised Standard Version

NT	New Testament
NTD	Das Neue Testament Deutsch
NTOA	Novum Testamentum et Orbis Antiquus
NTS	*New Testament Studies*
OG	Old Greek (the first Greek OT translation)
OT	Old Testament
ÖTKNT	Ökumenischer Taschenbuchkommentar zum Neuen Testament
OTG	Old Testament Guides
OTL	Old Testament Library
OTM	Old Testament Message
PiNTC	Pillar New Testament Commentary
Prep	preposition
Pro	pronoun
Pss. Sol.	Psalms of Solomon
Ptc	participle
PTL	*PTL: A Journal for Descriptive Poetics and Theory of Literature*
PTMS	Pittsburgh Theological Monograph Series
RB	*Revue biblique*
REBC	Revised Expositor's Bible Commentary
RNT	Regensburger Neues Testament
RST	Regensburger Studien zur Theologie
RSV	Revised Standard Version

RTL	*Revue théologique de Louvain*
SAIS	Studies in the Aramaic Interpretation of Scripture
SBL	Studies in Biblical Literature
SBLDS	Society of Biblical Literature Dissertation Series
SBLSS	Society of Biblical Literature Semeia Studies
SBLSymS	Society of Biblical Literature Symposium Series
SD	Studies and Documents
SHBC	Smyth & Helwys Bible Commentary
Sib. Or.	Sibylline Oracles
SJ	Studia Judaica
SJT	*Scottish Journal of Theology*
SNTSMS	Society for New Testament Studies Monograph Series
Somn. 2	*De somniis* II (Philo)
SP	Sacra Pagina
SPHS	Homage Series (Scholars Press)
SSEJC	Studies in Scripture in Early Judaism and Christianity
StBL	Studies in Biblical Literature
S. Eli. Rab.	Seder Eliyahu Rabbah
t. Ber.	Tosefta Berakot
T. Naph.	Testament of Naphtali

TDNT	*Theological Dictionary of the New Testament*. Edited by G. Kittel and G. Friedrich. Translated by G. W. Bromiley. 10 vols. Grand Rapids, 1964–76
TDOT	*Theological Dictionary of the Old Testament*. Edited by G. J. Botterweck, H. Ringgren, and H.-J. Fabry. Translated by J. T. Willis, G. W. Bromiley, D. W. Stott, and D. E. Green. 15 vols. Grand Rapids, 1974–2006
THKNT	Theologischer Handkommentar zum Neuen Testament
TJ	Targum Jonathan
TL	*Theology and Life*
TLL	Topics in Language and Linguistics
TLOT	*Theological Lexicon of the Old Testament*. Edited by Ernst Jenni, with assistance from Claus Westermann. Translated by Mark E. Biddle. 3 vols. Peabody, MA, 1997
TOTC	Tyndale Old Testament Commentaries
TSAJ	Texte und Studien zum antiken Judentum
TUGAL	Texte und Untersuchungen zur Geschichte der altchristlichen Literatur
TynBul	*Tydale Bulletin*
VT	*Vetus Testamentum*
VTSup	Supplements to Vetus Testamentum
VULG.	Vulgate
WBC	Word Biblical Commentary

WEC	Wycliffe Exegetical Commentary
WMANT	Wissenschafliche Monographien zum Alten und Neuen Testament
WUNT	Wissenschaftliche Untersuchungen zum Neuen Testament
YJS	Yale Judaica Series
YLT	Young's Literal Translation
y. ʻAbod. Zar.	Jerusalem (Talmud) ʻAbodah Zarah
ZBK	Zürcher Bibelkommentare
ZECOT	Zondervan Exegetical Commentary on the Old Testament

Symbols for Septuagint textual witnesses follow *Septuaginta: Id est Vetus Testamentum graece iuxta LXX interpretes*, ed. Alfred Rahlfs and Robert Hanhart, rev. ed. (Stuttgart: Deutsche Bibelgesellschaft, 2006). Symbols for Greek New Testament textual witnesses follow those explained in NA^{28}. All other references to ancient (incl. Jewish and Roman literature, and Josephus) and modern sources follow the conventions and abbreviations set forth in SBL Press, *The SBL Handbook of Style: For Biblical Studies and Related Disciplines*, 2nd ed. (Atlanta: SBL Press, 2014).

1

Introduction

The Zephaniah Proposal: Zephaniah 3 in John 12

According to the Zephaniah Proposal, John's Gospel[1] plausibly uses Zephaniah. All four Gospels document Jesus's entry into Jerusalem,[2] but this book focuses on the account related in John's Gospel.

[1] In this work we refer to the FG indiscriminately as "John" or "John's Gospel" due to convenience and scholarly convention. By using these terms synonymously, we refer to the final form of the text as we have it today. While we affirm the unity of the book and Johannine authorship (for a defense of this, see D. A. Carson, *The Gospel according to John*, PiNTC [Grand Rapids: Eerdmans, 1991], 40–49, 68–81), our approach is not dependent on this view.

[2] The Entry Narrative is significant (Matt. 21:1–9; Mark 11:1–10; Luke 19:28–38; John 12). Brent Kinman notes that it starts Jesus's "final week in Jerusalem," and is "potentially his most self-consciously messianic act . . . . [which was] open to great misunderstanding" ("Jesus' Royal Entry into Jerusalem," *BBR* 15 [2005]: 223). He further argues that the "basic shape of the Entry . . . is historically reliable" (257). Also, while Jesus does not technically enter Jerusalem in the narrative of the FG (though that seems implied in John 12:12), the Synoptic narratives make it explicit that he enters the city with the Entry Narrative episode (Matt. 21:10; Mark 11:11; Luke 19:41, 45). In saying that this was Jesus's entry *to Jerusalem*, we are not making a claim regarding John's relationship to the Synoptics, but only highlighting the implication that the Synoptics and the FG narrated the same event. There is sufficient content of the entry common between all four Gospels (e.g., Jesus on a donkey near Jerusalem, a crowd using Psalm 118) to indicate that they all refer to the same

John 12:12–19 quotes the OT both in John 12:13 (Ps. 118:26) and 12:15 (Zech. 9:9), and some propose that between those two references, John also used Zephaniah 3.[3]

At least two expressions of the Entry Narrative may come from Zephaniah 3. In the first, John 12:13, a "large crowd" met Jesus with palm branches and shouted a phrase that precisely matches Psalm 118(117):26 in the LXX:[4] εὐλογημένος ὁ ἐρχόμενος ἐν ὀνόματι κυρίου (cf. Matt. 21:9; 23:39; Mark 11:9; Luke 13:35). Immediately following this phrase is an expression that describes Jesus (ὁ βασιλεὺς τοῦ Ἰσραήλ [12:13])[5] but is not found in Psalm 118 nor in the

---

situation; but put negatively, John differs with the Synoptics "in every point where it is possible to differ in relating the same event" (C. H. Dodd, *Historical Tradition in the Fourth Gospel* [Cambridge: Cambridge University Press, 1963], 155). Finally, while the Entry Narrative was reported in all four NT Gospels, this book only analyzes John's unique record. Note that, for example, John's entry expressions ὁ βασιλεὺς τοῦ Ἰσραήλ and μὴ φοβοῦ are not found in the Synoptics, and John narrates Jesus riding the donkey *after* the crowd shouts Psalm 118:25 (the Synoptics have the opposite order). For a discussion surveying the relationship of John and the Synoptics, see D. Moody Smith, *John among the Gospels*, 2nd ed. (Columbia, SC: University of South Carolina Press, 2001). For our purposes, we follow the recent, coherent defense for the position, that "John knew and was influenced by Mark's gospel" (literarily or orally), articulated by Daniel J. Brendsel in six arguments (*"Isaiah Saw His Glory": The Use of Isaiah 52–53 in John 12*, BZNW 28 [Berlin: de Gruyter, 2014], 23–27): overlapping pericopes, verbal agreements, shared sequencing, narrative parenthesis (John 3:24; 11:2), historical and theological details, and historical connections. So, the most important comparison with John is Mark, without necessarily denying that John knew other Synoptics.

[3] As a starting point, note that the margin of NA^{28} at John 12:13d lists Zephaniah 3:15 (LXX) as a direct quotation, and at John 12:15 identifies Zephaniah 3:14–16 (with Isa. 35:4; 40:9) as an allusion.

[4] J. Ramsey Michaels, *The Gospel of John*, NICNT (Grand Rapids: Eerdmans, 2010), 676.

[5] Scholars debate whether the phrase in John 12:13 represents a Johannine narrative comment (C. K. Barrett, *The Gospel according to St. John*, 2nd ed. [Philadelphia: Westminster, 1978], 418), or even whether the crowd actually uttered the phrase (Leon Morris, *The Gospel according to John*, NICNT, rev. ed. [Grand Rapids: Eerdmans, 1995], 520). Even if it was the crowd's declaration, John has repeated it verbatim for his own purposes which we must discern.

other Entry Narratives. Scholars debate the source of that acclamation, and some argue that it comes from Zephaniah 3:15. A second verse in the same Entry Narrative (John 12:15) used the OT (Zech. 9:9), this time in connection with Jesus's finding and sitting on a donkey. Immediately following the introductory formula καθώς ἐστιν γεγραμμένον, however, the opening imperative (μὴ φοβοῦ [John 12:15a]) is absent from Zechariah 9:9.[6] Scholars have made various proposals for the source and meaning of this imperative, and some hold that John used Zephaniah 3:16.

Past Research on Zephaniah in John 12

Scholars have produced many studies on the use of the OT in the NT[7] and show no signs that their production will decrease. Andreas Obermann used three domains to synthesize the scholarly work on the use of the OT in John's Gospel (FG): (1) Scripture in the light of John's theology and structure, (2) investigation into

John's text is unique here; we interpret the statement to declare Jesus as royalty, perhaps as an addition to Psalm 118 (see Andreas J. Köstenberger, *John*, BECNT [Grand Rapids: Baker, 2004], 370). Lastly, Raymond E. Brown noted that John used "king" and the verb "to come" for a similar event juxtaposed in 6:14–15: "There the people designate Jesus as 'the Prophet *who is to come* into the world,' and Jesus recognizes that this means they will attempt to make him king" (*The Gospel according to John*, AB [Garden City, NY: Doubleday, 1966–70], 1:462, italics original).

[6] M. J. J. Menken, "The Quotations from Zech 9,9 in Mt 21,5 and in John 12,15," in *John and the Synoptics*, ed. A. Denaux, BETL 101 (Leuven: Leuven University Press, 1992), 575. Scholars have identified several other differences between Zechariah 9:9 and the citation in John 12:15 (ibid., 575–77; Menken, *Old Testament Quotations in the Fourth Gospel: Studies in Textual Form*, CBET 15 [Kampen: Kok Pharos, 1996], 79–97; Brown, *John*, 1:458), but we presently focus on only the ending of John 12:13 and the beginning of John 12:15.

[7] For an introduction to the debates on the NT use of the OT, see, e.g., Jonathan Lunde, "An Introduction to Central Questions in the New Testament Use of the Old Testament," in *Three Views on the New Testament Use of the Old Testament*, ed. Kenneth Berding and Jonathan Lunde (Grand Rapids: Zondervan, 2008), 7–39.

John's sources and their usage, and (3) John's theological motivations in his use of Scripture.[8] In this field, early scholarship tended to focus on explicit OT quotations in the FG (2),[9] studying John's citation methodology, his sources, the citation formulae, or the citation's function (e.g., theological, rhetorical, or social).[10]

Past Scholars Considering the Zephaniah Proposal in John 12

Modern scholars have debated for over 55 years whether John 12 uses Zephaniah 3. What follows is a survey of the interpretation of the Zephaniah Proposal.

Barnabas Lindars

In 1961, Barnabas Lindars proposed that the words "do not fear" (John 12:15) are "probably" from the MT of Zephaniah 3:16 as a *pesher* "commentary" on colt-riding, and he later speculated that Zephaniah 3:14 supplied John 12:13 with "king of Israel."[11] Lindars's brief discussions included two observations: (1) the LXX version of Zephaniah 3:14 matches Zechariah 9:9's first words, and

[8] Andreas Obermann, *Die christologische Erfüllung der Schrift im Johannesevangelium: Eine Untersuchung zur johanneischen Hermeneutik anhand der Schriftzitate*, WUNT, 2nd ser., 83 (Tübingen: Mohr Siebeck, 1996), 34. He lists Thoma, Franke, Barrett, Schnackenburg, Hengel, Hanson, and Schuchard as representative of the first category; Faure, Goodwin, Noack, and Reim for the second; and Longenecker, Hengel, Hanson, Schuchard, and Menken in the third.

[9] See Edwin D. Freed, *Old Testament Quotations in the Gospel of John*, NovTSup 11 (Leiden: Brill, 1965); Menken, *Quotations*; G. Reim, *Studien zum Alttestamentlichen Hintergrund des Johannesevangeliums*, SNTSMS 22 (Cambridge: Cambridge University Press, 1974); Bruce G. Schuchard, *Scripture within Scripture: The Interrelationship of Form and Function in the Explicit Old Testament Citations in the Gospel of John*, SBLDS 133 (Atlanta: Scholars Press, 1992).

[10] Ruth Sheridan, *Retelling Scripture: 'The Jews' and the Scriptural Citations in John 1:19–12:15*, BIS 110 (Leiden: Brill, 2012), 12.

[11] Barnabas Lindars, *New Testament Apologetic: The Doctrinal Significance of the Old Testament Quotations* (Philadelphia: Westminster, 1961), 113–15; Lindars, *The Gospel of John*, NCB (Grand Rapids: Eerdmans, 1972), 423–24.

(2) Justin Martyr cited the text of Zechariah 9:9 but attributed it to Zephaniah (*1 Apol.* 35:11). Lindars concludes, "Justin's mistaken attribution is thus due to the influence of the exegetical work of correlating these 'salvation' texts, which was also known to John,"[12] speculating that John was aware of a pre-FG linkage of Zechariah 9 and Zephaniah 3.

Edwin D. Freed

Paralleling Lindars, Edwin Freed understands John 12:15's "do not fear" to indicate a joint use of Zephaniah 3:14 with Zechariah 9:9. After analyzing the possible sources for John's four terms "do not fear" (μὴ φοβοῦ) and "daughter of Zion" (θυγάτηρ Σιών), Freed argued that only the MT of Zephaniah 3:14–17 combined all four.[13] He then observed that John's narrative agrees with the MT but does not have Zephaniah's LXX renderings of the verb θάρσει and the vocative θύγατερ. This led him to postulate that "perhaps Jn translated the Heb. of Zeph" which he considered "more likely because it contains the phrase 'king of Israel' [see John 12:13]."[14] However, in discussing the "quotation" of "king of Israel" (John 12:13), Freed parted from Lindars by concluding that John depended on the Synoptics, even though these words are not in his Synoptic sources. John altered the Synoptic material in order to connect the Lazarus miracle with the Jesus-as-king motif, thus John's μὴ φοβοῦ (John 12:15) is "the equivalent of χαῖρε in Zeph 3:14 or Zech 9:9. The coming of the messianic king is a time for rejoicing without fear [of Jesus's miracles]."[15]

Freed's discussion largely centers on identifying the OT reference and text source of John's narrative (e.g., MT, LXX), along with

[12] Lindars, *Apologetic*, 115.

[13] Freed, *Quotations*, 78.

[14] Ibid.

[15] Ibid., 79. Freed's focus included responding to those who claimed John depended solely on the Hebrew OT for his quotations, and so he argued that John's main source for his quotations was the Synoptics (ibid., 130; Freed, "The Entry into Jerusalem in the Gospel of John," *JBL* 80 [1961]: 329–38, esp. 336–38).

some basic treatment of its meaning in John. But his consideration of the Zephaniah Proposal is relatively brief and introductory, and he regrettably does not engage the OT in its original context.[16] In addition, few follow his conclusions about Johannine dependence on the Synoptics as the best explanation for John's source(s).[17]

Raymond E. Brown

In the most extensive discussion to his time of both the original context of Zephaniah and the Johannine significance for the proposed usage of Zephaniah, Raymond Brown argued that the MT of Zephaniah 3:15–16 functions as a reasonable source for both FG expressions "do not be afraid" and "King of Israel."[18] Brown examined the context of Zephaniah 3:9–17, noting that the chief thematic connections between Zephaniah and the FG include: (1) the arrival of Yahweh to Jerusalem (Zeph. 3:9–10), which plays out as the entry of Jesus in John 12:12–19; and (2) a "universalistic," all-nations thrust (Zeph. 3:9–10, 17, 19), which colors not only the context of the Entry Narrative but also its climax with the coming of the Greeks (John 12:20).[19] Brown's analysis, though brief, included not only identifying the source(s) of the two expressions in the FG as the text of Zephaniah but also noting the OT context with a view to

[16] For example, in a footnote without further comment, he briefly notes the difference between Zephaniah's and John's contexts: "Although in Zephaniah 'king' refers to Yahweh himself rather than to the messiah as 'king of Israel'" (Freed, *Quotations*, 78n4).

[17] Many do not agree with Freed's assessment (e.g., Smith, *John among the Gospels*, 195–241; Dodd, *Historical Tradition*, 154–55; Rudolf Bultmann, *The Gospel of John*, ed. R. W. N. Hoare and J. K. Riches, trans. G. R. Beasley-Murray [Philadelphia: Westminster, 1971], 417; Brown, *John*, 1:459–61; Kiyoshi Tsuchido, "Tradition and Redaction in John 12.1–43," *NTS* 30 [1984]: 611–13, 615; J. A. T. Robinson, *The Priority of John* [London: SCM, 1985], 229–38; Wayne A. Meeks, *The Prophet-King: Moses Traditions and the Johannine Christology*, NovTSup 14 [Leiden: Brill, 1967], 83–87; Schuchard, *Scripture*, 71).

[18] Brown, *John*, 1:458–63, who also notes that "O daughter of Zion" occurs in 3:14 (1:458).

[19] Ibid., 1:462–63.

forwarding serious proposals about the theological implications its use might have on John's Entry Narrative.

Günter Reim

In contrast to scholars who treated John's explicit quotations and only incidentally noted non-quotational material, Günter Reim's historical-critical work in 1974 was dedicated not only to examining the source(s) of the FG citations but also to considering the OT allusions and themes that form the Gospel's "Hintergrund."[20] He argued that Isaiah 40–66 (in particular, the Servant texts) was the only *written* text available to the FG,[21] and so he proposed that John 12 used only Isaiah 40:9 and 62:11 (coupled to Zech. 9:9 tradition) as the written sources for John 12:15.[22] Some have critiqued Reim's overall thesis as over-reaching the evidence, for it only shows that the FG *often* used Isaiah.[23] Whether that general critique applies to the specific instance of the "do not fear" at the beginning of Zechariah 9:9 requires additional study, but Reim's early contribution does show the importance of not ignoring non-quoted OT material in the FG.

M. J. J. Menken

M. J. J. Menken's work on OT citations in the FG exhibited Obermann's second and third categories of study. Though Menken does not argue that Zephaniah 3 is the exclusive source that stands behind John 12's μὴ φοβοῦ, he does discuss the possibility. He sought to analyze "the problem of the textual form of the OT quotations in the Fourth Gospel" by determining (1) the exact OT source(s) of a given quotation in the FG and (2) the reason(s) for the changes made by the FG's final form, if there are alterations.[24]

[20] Reim, *Studien*, 97–188.

[21] Ibid., 162–82, 260–61.

[22] Ibid., 30–31. For a German response to Reim, see Obermann, *Erfüllung*, 16–18.

[23] See, e.g., Sheridan, *Retelling*, 19.

[24] Menken, *Quotations*, 13. That work re-publishes and translates some of

Scholarship ante-dating Menken largely focused on determining the source of a quotation and presumed that John forgot textual details of his quoted sources. By contrast, Menken welded together the work of source and redaction criticism. He explains, "Many deviations in [the FG's OT] scriptural quotations and in the transmission of the biblical text are the result not of a defective memory, but of a conscious application of exegetical techniques and devices."[25] Changes reflect authorial intentionality.

In Menken's chapter entitled, "'Do Not Fear, Daughter Zion . . .' (John 12:15)," he notes that Jesus's sitting on a donkey is said to fulfill Zechariah 9:9.[26] After surveying the possible OT versions of John 12:15's quotation, Menken concluded that though "Zech 9:9 is quoted in a recognizable way, it is impossible to decide whether the Hebrew text or the LXX has been used."[27] His main argument is that John and/or pre-Johannine redactors of John 12:15 "have made use of this exegetical technique [referring to analogous scriptural passages] to adjust the quotation from Zech. 9:9 as well as possible to the present literary and theological context."[28] He noted and discussed four deviations from Zechariah 9:9: (1) μὴ φοβοῦ, instead of "rejoice"; (2) exclusion of σοι (but retention of ὁ βασιλεύς σου); (3) καθήμενος, rather than "riding"; and (4) a unique description of Jesus's mount (i.e., πῶλον ὄνου), not matching any version of Zechariah 9.

As for the first deviation, Menken posited that the source of μὴ φοβοῦ may come from Isaiah 35:4; 40:9; 41:10; 44:2; or Zephaniah 3:16. But due to lack of verbal agreement in the other options, he reduced that list to both Isaiah 40:9 and Zephaniah 3:16. In adjudicating between these two options, he argued that one cannot nor need not decide between them. On the one hand, "Zeph. 3:15 has

---

his articles from 1985 to 1996.

[25] Ibid., 14.

[26] Ibid., 79: "There can be no doubt about the source of this quotation being Zech. 9:9."

[27] Ibid., 82–83.

[28] Ibid., 97.

with John 12:13 the title 'the King of Israel' in common," while on the other hand, "in early Christianity Isa. 40:1–11 was generally considered as a significant piece of Scripture, and . . . it was easy for John to apply God's action in Isa. 40:11 to Jesus [e.g., John 10:1–18, 26–29; 11:52; 21:15–17]."[29] Menken proposed that John redacted this Zephanian-Isaianic OT phrase to correct the Lazarus-observing crowd's (John 11:1–44; 12:9, 12, 17–18) kingly expectations of Jesus (John 12:13): "They misunderstand Jesus as a national king who does frightening things."[30] For Menken, John provides evidence for such a conclusion: (1) the crowd considered Jesus's miraculous raising of Lazarus an indication of "Jesus' divine power" (i.e., someone to be feared); (2) the crowd's actions exhibited national-political hopes; and (3) the pericope parallels 6:14–15, indicating that the crowd expected Jesus's kingship.[31]

Regarding limitations in Menken's argument, he did not explore the OT context of John's sources, since he aimed to discern John's source(s) and rationale for the "changes." Thus, while he proposed that Isaiah 40 and Zephaniah 3 stand behind John 12:15's "do not fear," he did not further examine Zephaniah's literary context. Though his early work in John 12:15 narrowly focused on Zechariah 9:9, in a recent article he broadened his scope to include allusions to the Minor Prophets in the FG. That article briefly argued that John 1:47 alludes to Zephaniah 3:13.

In John 1, Jesus considered Nathanael to be "an Israelite in whom there is no deceit (δόλος)" (cf. Zeph. 3:13).[32] Though Menken did not explicitly forge a connection between a Zephanian "king of Israel" in John 1:49 and John 12:13–15, the Zephaniah Proposal in John 12 could be strengthened if John 1:47 shows awareness of

[29] Ibid., 84.
[30] Ibid., 86.
[31] Ibid., 85.
[32] Menken, "The Minor Prophets in John's Gospel," in *The Minor Prophets in the New Testament*, ed. M. J. J. Menken and Steve Moyise, LNTS 377 (London: T&T Clark, 2009), 83, 92.

Zephaniah 3. Thus, despite its general lack of OT exegesis, Menken's work serves as a helpful foundation for further studying the Entry Narrative's use of Zephaniah.

Bruce G. Schuchard

Bruce Schuchard's work extends Menken's project, with some minor differences. He follows Menken's fundamental critique of past scholarly work on the FG's citations, that John intentionally deviated from his OT sources and purposefully modified them to suit his literary and theological program. Additionally, his method builds upon Menken's by examining each citation in the FG (i.e., noting the OT context, the citation form, the text traditions, and explanations for John's changes to the OT text) and by observing the "interrelationship of form and function" by John.[33] Schuchard differs from Menken, however, in his tallies and interpretations of the explicit citations in John. In addition, Schuchard uniquely proposes the thesis that John leveraged "one and only one textual tradition, the OG" (referring to the first Greek OT translation rather than the more imprecise term LXX).[34] Schuchard concludes that the quotation of Zechariah 9:9 (and even John's changes to it) in John 12:15 "recalls the OG."[35]

Schuchard's treatment of the Entry Narrative focused on the form and function of the citation of Zechariah 9:9 in John 12:15. As part of the analysis, he admitted that many hold that Zephaniah

[33] Schuchard, *Scripture*, xiv–xvi.

[34] Ibid., xvii. Also, Schuchard (xviin28) cited L. Greenspoon ("The Use and Abuse of the Term 'LXX' and Related Terminology in Recent Scholarship," *BIOSCS* 20 [1987]: 21–29) as evidence of the misuse of the term LXX; cf. Emanuel Tov, "The Septuagint," in *Mikra: Text, Translation, Reading and Interpretation of the Hebrew Bible in Ancient Judaism and Early Christianity*, ed. Martin Jan Mulder, CRINT 2.1 (Assen: Van Gorcum; Philadelphia: Fortress, 1988), 161–88. Schuchard (*Scripture*, xiii) tallied 13 explicit OT quotations in the FG (1:23; 2:17; 6:31, 45; 10:34; 12:14–15, 38, 40; 13:18; 15:25; 19:24, 36, 37), while Menken (*Quotations*, 12) tallied 17 (1:23; 2:17; 6:31, 45; 7:38, 42; 8:17; 10:34; 12:15, 34, 38, 40; 13:18; 15:25; 19:24, 36, 37). However, the difference seems largely because their definitions of *quotation* are not the same.

[35] Schuchard, *Scripture*, 84.

3:15 is the source for John 12:13's ὁ βασιλεὺς τοῦ 'Ισραήλ, but he concluded that John used Isaiah 44:6, because it is the only place in the OG where the identical expression occurs.[36] Then, based on that positive identification for "king of Israel," he argued that the source for μὴ φοβοῦ is not Isaiah 40:9 or Zephaniah 3:14–17, but rather the same paragraph as the "king of Israel" reference: Isaiah 44:2. Isaiah 44 is thus a connective "bridge" between the "king" and Zechariah 9:9.[37] Its common points with Zechariah 9:9 and the context of John's Entry Narrative confirmed this for Schuchard. John 12 records the Isaiah 44-language to revere Jesus as "God-King," and then John uses more Isaiah 44-language (i.e., the prohibition "do not fear") with Zechariah 9:9 in order to affirm and correct the crowd's nationalistic kingly hopes for Jesus.[38]

Though Schuchard challenged the Zephaniah Proposal, he mentioned its arguments and recognized its possibility. His alternative proposal of Isaiah 44 included surveying the sources and their function in John, but he did not research the OT context(s) of Isaiah or Zephaniah.

Conclusion on Past Research on the Zephaniah Proposal

As a sample survey from the last 50 years shows, several scholars have produced monographs on the use of the OT in the FG and have focused on a diverse spectrum of OT texts—e.g., the FG's use of Genesis, Deuteronomy (or Moses), Esther, Psalms, Song of Songs, Isaiah, Ezekiel, Zechariah, and Wisdom literature.[39] Despite

[36] Ibid., 77–78.

[37] Ibid., 76, 78. Isaiah 44:2's phrase (אַל־תִּירָא עַבְדִּי יַעֲקֹב), however, does not match John 12:15's addressee, and textual criticism casts doubt on the presence of articles in John 12:13 and Isaiah 44:6 (LXX; see Menken, *Quotations*, 84n21).

[38] Schuchard, *Scripture*, 78–80.

[39] On the FG's use of Genesis, see Dan Lioy, *The Search for Ultimate Reality: Intertextuality between the Genesis and Johannine Prologues* (New York: Lang, 2005). For its use of Deuteronomy or Moses, see Severino Pancaro, *The Law in the Fourth Gospel: The Torah and the Gospel, Moses and Jesus, Judaism and*

this, lacking still is an extended study on the proposed usage of Zephaniah in any part of the NT, let alone the FG. Over the last few decades, a growing number of scholars have joined Lindars, Freed and Brown in favoring the existence (whether termed simply possible or likely) of Zephaniah 3 in John 12,[40] based at least in part

---

Christianity according to John, NovTSup 42 (Leiden: Brill, 1975). For its use of Esther, see John Bowman, *The Fourth Gospel and the Jews: A Study in R. Akiba, Esther, and the Gospel of John*, PTMS 8 (Pittsburgh: Pickwick, 1975), but for a response to Bowman, see Luc Devillers, *La fête de l'envoyé: La section johannique de la fête des tentes (Jean 7,1–10,21) et la christologie*, *EBib* 49 (Paris: Gabalda, 2002), 12, 262–64. For its use of the Psalms, see Margaret Daly-Denton, *David in the Fourth Gospel: The Johannine Reception of the Psalms*, AGJU 47 (Leiden: Brill, 2000), and note also two monographs that examine one Psalm in the FG, with the latter focusing on John 12: G. W. Vander Hoek, "The Function of Ps 82 in the Fourth Gospel and History of the Johannine Community: A Comparative Midrash Study" (PhD diss., Claremont Graduate School, 1988); A. C. Brunson, *Psalm 118 in the Gospel of John: An Intertextual Study on the New Exodus Pattern in the Theology of John*, WUNT, 2nd ser., 158 (Tübingen: Mohr Siebeck, 2003). For its use of Song of Songs, see Ann Roberts Winsor, *A King Is Bound in the Tresses: Allusions to the Song of Songs in the Fourth Gospel*, StBL 6 (New York: Lang, 1999). For the use of Isaiah, see Brendsel, *Isaiah*. For its use of Ezekiel, see William G. Fowler, "The Influence of Ezekiel in the Fourth Gospel: Intertextuality and Interpretation" (PhD diss., Golden Gate Baptist Theological Seminary, 1995) and G. T. Manning, *Echoes of a Prophet: The Use of Ezekiel in the Gospel of John and in Literature of the Second Temple Period*, JSNTSup 270 (London: T&T Clark, 2004). For its use of Zechariah, see Adam Kubiś, *The Book of Zechariah in the Gospel of John*, *EBib* 64 (Pendé: Gabalda, 2012). For its use of Wisdom literature, see Martin Scott, *Sophia and the Johannine Jesus*, JSOTSup 71 (Sheffield: JSOT Press, 1992); Michael E. Willett, *Wisdom Christology in the Fourth Gospel* (San Francisco: Mellen Research University Press, 1992); and Frédéric Manns, *L'évangile de Jean et la sagesse*, ASBF 62 (Jerusalem: Franciscan Printing Press, 2003).

[40] P. C. Mateos, "Uso e interpretación de Zacarías 9,9–10 en el Nuevo Testamento," *EstAg* 7 (1972): 475; 8 (1973): 3–10; M.-É. Boismard and A. Lamouille, *Synopse des quatre évangiles en français* (Paris: Cerf, 1977), 3:309; Jürgen Becker, *Das Evangelium nach Johannes*, ÖTKNT (Gütersloh: Mohn, 1979–81), 2:444; L. A. Losie, "Triumphal Entry," in *DJG*, 858; Peter W. Ensor, *Jesus and His 'Works': The Johannine Sayings in Historical Perspective*, WUNT, 2nd ser., 85 (Tübingen: Mohr Siebeck, 1996), 62; Yves Simoens, *Selon Jean*, CIET 17 (Brussels: Éditions de l'Institut d'Études Théologiques,

on the strong verbal and thematic parallels between the two texts.[41] Still, most scholars who consider the usage of Zephaniah in John 12's Entry Narrative either relegate it to a footnote or do not dedicate more than two or three pages to the discussion.[42] Three exceptions to this pattern are the recent treatments of A. C. Brunson, Ruth Sheridan, and Adam Kubiś on the FG.[43]

Three Recent Studies Favoring the Zephaniah Proposal

A. C. Brunson

In 2001, Brunson published a dissertation on Psalm 118:25 in John, arguing: "the [FG's] citation of a verse or phrase from Ps 118

1997), 2:482; Ulrich Wilckens, *Das Evangelium nach Johannes*, NTD 4 (Göttingen: Vandenhoeck & Ruprecht, 1998), 189; Christian Dietzfelbinger, *Das Evangelium nach Johannes*, ZBK (Zürich: Theologischer Verlag, 2001), 1:384; Klaus Wengst, *Das Johannesevangelium*, THKNT (Stuttgart: Kohlhammer, 2001), 2:56; Andrew T. Lincoln, *The Gospel according to Saint John*, BNTC (Peabody, MA: Hendrickson, 2005), 343–44; Hartwig Thyen, *Das Johannesevangelium*, HNT (Tübingen: Mohr Siebeck, 2005), 555–56. Several list the Zephaniah Proposal as possible, e.g., E. C. Hoskyns, *The Fourth Gospel*, ed. F. N. Davey, 2nd ed. (London: Faber & Faber, 1956), 422; F.-M. Braun, *Jean le théologien: Les grandes traditions d'Israël et l'accord des Écritures, selon le Quatrième Évangile, EBib* (Paris: Gabalda, 1964), 2:19; Bultmann, *John*, 418n4; Claus-Peter März, *"Siehe, dein König kommt zu dir . . . ": Eine traditionsgeschichtliche Untersuchung zur Einzugsperikope*, ETS 43 (Leipzig: St. Benno-Verlag, 1980), 161.

[41] For Zephaniah Proposal advocates who argue that John was "conflating" Zephaniah 3:15–16 and Zechariah 9:9, see O. Palmer Robertson, *The Books of Nahum, Habakkuk, and Zephaniah*, NICOT (Grand Rapids: Eerdmans, 1990), 338; Rudolf Schnackenburg, *The Gospel according to St John*, trans. K. Smyth et al., HTKNT (New York: Crossroad, 1980–82), 2:375–76; and Craig R. Koester, *Symbolism in the Fourth Gospel: Meaning, Mystery, Community*, 2nd ed. (Minneapolis: Fortress, 2003), 125. Alternatively, some think that John used Zephaniah 3:16 "midrashically" with Zechariah 9 (e.g., Craig S. Keener, *The Gospel of John: A Commentary* [Peabody, MA: Hendrickson, 2003], 2:870n22).

[42] For example, Brendsel noted the possibility of the Zephaniah Proposal, but he preferred Isaiah 52:7–53:12 as a more likely source for John and as part of John's larger Isaianic blueprint (*Isaiah*, 183–84n117).

[43] Brunson, *Psalm 118*; Sheridan, *Retelling*; Kubiś, *Zechariah*.

points beyond that single verse to its immediate context, and further to the entire psalm, which is its larger literary unit."[44] He examined Psalm 118 in its original, Jewish setting as well as Second Temple, non-Jewish, and rabbinic literature, arguing that a liturgical Tabernacles (and Dedication) usage of Psalm 118 predominated by A.D. 70 and that John 12 incorporates that background. Since the only explicit citation of Psalm 118 in the FG is the Entrance Narrative, Brunson paid particular attention to John 12 throughout the work. As evidence that Psalm 118 played a role in shaping John's narrative, he discovered Psalm 118's "new exodus" themes (i.e., return from exile, defeat of enemies, and Yahweh's presence) in John 12's use of the OT (e.g., Ps. 118:26; Zeph. 3; Zech. 9:9).[45]

In part of that discussion, Brunson argued that John likely referenced Zephaniah 3 in the words "do not fear" and "king of Israel." Regarding the latter, he listed serious candidates for its OT source and favored Zephaniah 3:15–16 due to its strong verbal parallels with John 12.[46] For the former expression, he read "do not fear" as exultative, and *not*—against the scholarly consensus—as Jesus's correction of the crowd's nationalistic misunderstanding.[47] Jesus was praised as king, so "the allusion to Zeph 3.16 [to not fear Yahweh] then clarifies that the king of Israel is none other than Yahweh."[48]

In keeping with Psalm 118 (and its Tabernacles usage) and Zechariah 9, the Entry Narrative is then an enthronement of Jesus

[44] Brunson, *Psalm 118*, 20.

[45] Ibid., 20, 153–79, 378–86.

[46] Ibid., 225–36, 258, 277. Discussing John 12:15, Brunson writes, "Because of the phrase that it ['do not fear'] shares with Zech 9.9 ('rejoice daughter of Zion'), and because of its explicit use of 'king of Israel' which connects it to the quotation of Ps 118 in John 12.12, Zephaniah is to be preferred" (ibid., 236). He also observed that all five seriously proposed OT sources for "do not fear" (Isa. 35:4; 40:9; 41:10; 44:2; Zeph. 3:16) share the "new exodus" themes noted above (ibid., 234–38, 277).

[47] Ibid., 277.

[48] Ibid., 238, who further considers Zephaniah 3's import for John (see, e.g., ibid., 236–39).

as king, with the Zechariah 9 quote supporting and expanding on the principal ideas already planted in the Psalm 118 citation: the coming one, the Tabernacles language of salvation (e.g., *hosanna*) and symbols (e.g., *lulab* branch), and the warrior-king of Israel.[49] Zephaniah 3 featured this last theme and confirmed for Brunson that John intended to display the divine warrior motif in the Entrance Narrative. Brunson's work highlights the need to consider how Psalm 118 and Zechariah 9 link to Zephaniah.[50]

Ruth Sheridan

Second, Sheridan examined the seven explicit OT quotations in John 1:19–12:15 with a reader-oriented, intertextual methodology. She argued that "the rhetorical design of John's Gospel [i.e., his citations with the formula ἐστιν γεγραμμένον] encourages an ideal reader to construct a particular characterization of 'the Jews' in light of the OT citations . . . . [Regarding the citations' function, they] *witnessed* to Jesus in his public ministry before 'the Jews.'"[51] That witness in John "is at once 'Jewish' and 'anti-Jewish,'" she holds, since the content of the citations is the hope-giving Jewish OT, but the Jews ultimately rejected Jesus.[52] In John 12, she observed that three groups reacted to Jesus's entry—the disciples, Pharisees, and the crowd—but only the disciples understood it properly, albeit post-glorification (12:16).

She briefly considered the OT context of Zechariah 9:9, which John cited "in order to draw attention to Jesus as the royal savior."[53]

[49] Ibid., 278.

[50] In passing, we note that another work on the Psalms in John mentioned the Zephaniah Proposal as possible but opted for a different conclusion than Brunson. Daly-Denton holds that "the king of Israel" "reinforces" the Jewish rabbinical practice of *gezerah shawah*; "to come" links Psalm 118:25 and Zechariah 9:9 (*David*, 178–79).

[51] Sheridan, *Retelling*, 235. The quotations (7) are in John 1:23; 2:17; 6:31, 45; 7:37–39; 10:34; 12:15.

[52] Ibid., 241.

[53] Ibid., 224.

Many themes from Zechariah 9's context, including post-exilic ones, find ready expression in John 12. She then explored the Zephaniah Proposal, the "conflated" texts Zechariah 9:9 and Zephaniah 3:16, ultimately deeming this "a tenable hypothesis, as Zeph 3:16 contains a number of verbal parallels with John's citation."[54] In addition to listing several parallels between Zephaniah 3 and John 12, she noted themes from Zephaniah that aligned and were relevant to John's context, e.g., the "ingathering," the King-of-Israel-in-your-midst, and some post-exilic redemption motifs.[55] John 12 highlights Zephaniah 3, Sheridan argued. The first citation of John (1:19) serves as an *inclusio* with this last citation in the Book of Signs (12:15) allowing the reader to easily link "the one who comes" to the Messiah-King Jesus. She adds, "But Jesus is more than a king: he is the 'Lord' in their midst (Cf. Zeph 3:15, 17a)."[56] Lastly, Jesus was in the crowd's midst to deliver a "word of salvation," not to calm their fears as a result of his miracles (e.g., raising of Lazarus). For her, the salvation announcement sufficiently explains why John's "do not fear" alludes to Zephaniah 3:16.[57]

Adam Kubiś

Third, Kubiś studied "the Johannine reception of a single biblical book, to wit the prophecy of Zechariah, in its multi-faceted traditions (Masoretic text, Septuagint, DSS, Targums, etc.) and forms (quotations, allusions and echoes) . . . [and] their interconnection."[58] His published dissertation is thorough and recent (2012), advancing the thesis that Zechariah plays a significant role in the FG. He devotes substantial ink to Zechariah 9:9 in John 12:15.

In surveying the three strongest proposals for the source of the expression "do not fear" (Isa. 40:9–10; 44:2; Zeph. 3:16), Kubiś

[54] Ibid., 222, 226.
[55] Ibid., 226–28.
[56] Ibid., 227–28.
[57] Ibid., 228, countering Menken (*Quotations*, 86).
[58] Kubiś, *Zechariah*, 16.

summarized the four strongest arguments regarding Zephaniah 3:16's "contents" and "textual form" in its relation to Zechariah 9:9 and John 12:15: Zephaniah 3:14–15 and Zechariah 9:9–10 (1) begin identically in the Old Greek, (2) emphasize the king's presence, (3) describe defeat of enemies, and (4) share deliverance "lexemes."[59] In concluding with the Zephaniah Proposal, he acknowledged the difficulties inherent in determining John's source: "Even if the choice between Zephaniah, Isaiah or Zechariah is hardly possible, and moreover does not really seem to be necessary, still *the overall weight of argumentation favors the prophecy of Zephaniah as the source for the introduction of* μὴ φοβοῦ into the Johannine quotation of Zec 9:9."[60]

After indicating he preferred the Zephaniah Proposal for John's μὴ φοβοῦ, Kubiś discussed six scholarly explanations for its insertion in John 12: "king of peace," "divinity of Jesus," "universalism," "the context of the passion," and the "raising of Lazarus."[61] Rather than select one of these six, he proposed a seventh, more general, reason that subsumed most of those options: "the announcement of coming salvation" (i.e., Jesus's coming as Savior).[62]

Conclusion on Three Studies Favoring the Zephaniah Proposal

These three contributions on the use of the OT in the FG—Brunson on Psalm 118, Sheridan on "the Jews," and Kubiś on Zechariah—all advanced arguments in favor of the Zephaniah Proposal, while considering it from different angles. Despite the absence of significant exegesis of Zephaniah, Brunson argued that John integrated Zephaniah 3 with Zechariah 9, Psalm 118, and several other themes in the FG—e.g., the coming of Yahweh, the warrior-king, and a "new exodus." Similarly, Sheridan cited verbal parallels, examined thematic proposals, and proposed contextual links in the FG

[59] Ibid., 82. For a discussion of these connections, see § 2.4.2.

[60] Ibid., 91, italics ours.

[61] Ibid., 86–92.

[62] Ibid., 92, not indicating awareness of Sheridan's similar conclusion (*Retelling*, 228).

with Zephaniah, though the constraints of her thesis did not permit a refutation of competing proposals on OT source(s), a satisfactory examination of the OT context(s), or a more detailed exegesis of John 12. As for Kubiś, his work is the most thorough and up-to-date regarding the Zephaniah Proposal, yet Zechariah was his focus. He did not extensively examine Zephaniah's OT context or explore its use in John.

Conclusion

As the foregoing survey has demonstrated, many scholars argue for the possible and even plausible use of Zephaniah 3 in John 12, yet previous treatments of John's Entry Narrative have largely ignored Zephaniah's literary, historical and canonical context.[63] Most notably, there are no major monographs on the use of Zephaniah in the NT. Discussion of Zephaniah is either brief or only a few pages in length, and the text of Zephaniah is routinely pillaged for select Johannine themes. As such, Zephaniah's text and the potential role it plays in John is frequently muted or ignored. Therefore, there is a substantive need for exegetical sensitivity to the OT context of this tiny prophetic book, as it relates to the FG. This book attempts to play a role in reversing that trend, by testing the Zephaniah Proposal and by examining both the OT contexts (Zephaniah, and to a limited extent, the other OT quotations in the Entry Narrative) and John 12.

Theoretical Framework

Defining Quotation, Allusion, and Echo

Definitions of quotation, allusion, echo, and other similar terms have not often received careful attention, and much of the scholarly disagreement on how a text is classified may be due to the definitions

[63] These three contexts correspond to the three interpretive contexts outlined by Edmund Clowney (*Preaching and Biblical Theology* [Grand Rapids: Eerdmans, 1961], 16) and Richard Lints (*The Fabric of Theology: A Prolegomenon to Evangelical Theology* [Grand Rapids: Eerdmans, 1993], 293–310).

of terms. Scholars, for example, have tallied the number of explicit quotations in the FG differently, based on different definitions and criteria.[64] And the lack of a consensus on the objective criteria used to discern a quote greatly complicates this area of study.[65]

Some scholars have narrowly required that an explicit quotation formula accompany cataloged quotations;[66] when formulae are absent, all texts clearly drawn from previous material should at best be termed allusions. However, some NT uses of the OT do not have a citation formula and yet include unique and "obviously parallel" connections,[67]

[64] Schuchard (*Scripture*, xiii–xiv) and D. A. Carson ("John and the Johannine Epistles," in *It Is Written: Scripture Citing Scripture: Essays in Honor of Barnabas Lindars*, ed. D. A. Carson and H. G. M. Williamson [Cambridge: Cambridge University Press, 1988], 246) count 13 OT quotations; Obermann, 14 (*Erfüllung*, 76); Daly-Denton, 16 (*David*, 34); Brunson, 17 (*Psalm 118*, 141–42; i.e., John 1:23/Isa. 40:3; John 2:17/Ps. 69:9; John 6:31/Ps. 78:24; John 6:45/Isa. 54:13; John 7:37–38/?; John 7:42/?; John 10:34/Ps. 82:6; John 12:14–15/Zech. 9:9; John 12:38/Isa. 53:1; John 12:39–40/Isa. 6:10; John 13:18/Ps. 41:9; John 15:25/Ps. 35:19 and/or Ps. 69:4; John 17:12/?; John 19:24/Ps. 22:18; John 19:28/?; John 19:36/Ex. 12:46 or Ps. 34:20 or Num. 9:12; John 19:37/Zech. 12:10, excl. the quotation without a formula in John 12:13/Ps. 118:25–26); John Painter ("The Quotation of Scripture and Unbelief in John 12:36b–43," in *The Gospels and the Scriptures of Israel*, ed. C. A. Evans and W. R. Stegner, JSNTSup 104, SSEJC 3 [Sheffield: Sheffield Academic Press, 1994], 429–30) and Freed (*Quotations*, xii), 18; Martin Hengel, 19 ("The Old Testament in the Fourth Gospel," in *The Gospels and the Scriptures of Israel*, ed. C. A. Evans and W. R. Stegner, JSNTSup 104, SSEJC 3 [Sheffield: Sheffield Academic Press, 1994], 392); and C. F. Burney, 20 (*The Aramaic Origin of the Fourth Gospel* [Oxford: Clarendon, 1922], 114–25). In comparison to the other Gospels, C. K. Barrett observes that the FG includes fewer OT citations than the Synoptics: 124 in Matthew, 70 in Mark, 109 in Luke, but 27 in John ("The Old Testament in the Fourth Gospel," *JTS* 48 [1947]: 155).

[65] Kubiś, *Zechariah*, 20.

[66] See Menken, *Quotations*, 11; Freed, *Quotations*, xii.

[67] G. K. Beale, *Handbook on the New Testament Use of the Old Testament: Exegesis and Interpretation* (Grand Rapids: Baker, 2012), 29. Note that though Beale indicated that slight differences in the proposed source text cited and the NT text might be due to any number of factors (e.g., different *Vorlage* of the Hebrew or Greek text, intentional modification of the original text, etc.), "most commentators agree on the vast majority of what should be recognized

thus allowing scholars to count John 12:13 as an informal quotation of Psalm 118:26.[68] So we adopt G. K. Beale's definition of *quotation*, that it includes formal and informal markers: "a direct citation of an OT passage that is easily recognizable by its clear and unique verbal parallelism."[69] Most conclude that John's Entry Narrative quotes the OT twice: John 12:13 (Ps. 118:26) and 15 (Zech. 9:9).[70]

Allusions are more difficult to discern and define.[71] Added to the challenges with allusions, there is great debate about echoes and how they relate to allusions. Precision in definition is difficult to achieve as many scholars define an allusion in a continuum or even "a spectrum of being virtually certain, probable, or possible, the latter being essentially equivalent to 'echoes.'"[72] So, discerning both allusion and echo includes some subjectivity.

---

as quotations from the OT" (29). Nevertheless, scholars have proposed varying numbers of quotations in the NT: 295 quotations of the OT in the NT, including those with and without introductory formulas (Roger Nicole, "The New Testament Use of the Old Testament," in *The Right Doctrine from the Wrong Texts? Essays on the Use of the Old Testament in the New*, ed. G. K. Beale [Grand Rapids: Baker, 1994], 13), while another writer has counted 401 based on the United Bible Societies's 1966 Greek New Testament (Klyne Snodgrass, "The Use of the Old Testament in the New," in *The Right Doctrine from the Wrong Texts? Essays on the Use of the Old Testament in the New*, ed. G. K. Beale [Grand Rapids: Baker, 1994], 35).

[68] Brunson, *Psalm 118*, 141–42; Obermann, *Erfüllung*, 70–76.

[69] Beale, *Handbook*, 29.

[70] See, e.g., Andreas J. Köstenberger, "John," in *Commentary on the New Testament Use of the Old Testament*, ed. G. K. Beale and D. A. Carson (Grand Rapids: Baker, 2007), 470–74. Freed notes, "This [John 12:13] is the only direct quotation in John not introduced or followed by a formula" ("Entry into Jerusalem," 332).

[71] This is immediately evident in the greatly varying totals of allusions that scholars have counted in the New Testament: from 613 to 4,105 (see Nicole, "New Testament Use," 14). Also note the count made by Walter C. Kaiser Jr., "A rough count of the references in Nestle's Greek Testament yields about 950 quotations and allusions, and the United Bible Society's Greek text lists over 2,500 NT passages from nearly 1,800 OT passages" (*The Uses of the Old Testament in the New* [Chicago: Moody, 1985], 2).

[72] Beale, *Handbook*, 31.

As a starting point for *allusion*, we once more note Beale's definition and explanation:

> In contrast to a quotation of the OT, which is a direct reference, allusions are indirect references (the OT wording is not reproduced directly as in a quotation). Some believe that an allusion must consist of a reproduction from the OT passage of a unique combination of at least three words. . . . The telltale key to discerning an allusion is that of recognizing an *incomparable or unique parallel in wording, syntax, concept, or cluster of motifs in the same order or structure.*[73]

From the detected combinations between the proposed source and John, it stands to reason that the more uniqueness shared between that text and John in those categories (vocabulary, syntax, theme, etc.),[74] the stronger the case can be made for John's use of that source as an allusion.

At least a few difficulties with Beale's proposed criteria for allusion are apparent as it relates to our work in John. First, it is not clear what we are to do if two or more competing sources are identical (or nearly identical) to John, share John's unique wording, and in general, are plausible sources. Should only one of those sources be permitted, or might a given text in John have been based upon several sources or even the collective "tradition" of those proposed texts?[75] In this book, we consider it possible that John may have conjoined two OT texts in an allusion, detectable by their similar placement on the spectrum of allusion (as highly probable). However, the higher one text rises above the other(s) particularly in important literary features (i.e., in verbal parallels of unique combinations, thematic

[73] Ibid., italics original.

[74] Ibid., 31–32; cf. Christopher A. Beetham, *Echoes of Scripture in the Letters of Paul to the Colossians*, BIS 96 (Leiden: Brill, 2008), 17–20.

[75] Kaiser refers to the NT's use of multiple sources as the *ḥaraz* method (*Uses of the Old Testament*, 4).

parallels of similar motifs stressed, and structural parallels),[76] the greater the argument for it as the chief allusion.

Second, a three-word minimum seems quite arbitrary, but should only serve as a "rule of thumb" when individual cases are examined and exceptions to the rule are found.[77] We must not discard a source simply because it does not abide by the three-word rule, though it should undergo greater scrutiny as the proposed allusion. With this understanding, we retain the three-word minimum as a generalized principle, positing that a one-word connection between John and a proposed source is *typically* insufficient as clear justification that an allusion exists.[78]

And finally, we achieve a more precise definition for *allusions* by also defining *echoes*. Beale holds that OT allusions are regularly intentional (or done consciously) by a NT author.[79] Some further argue that echoes are less explicit (or, less clear) allusions, or even that allusions are authorially intended whereas echoes may or may not be intentional.[80] However, this distinction puts an almost impossible

[76] Here we follow the points made in Brendsel, *Isaiah*, 33.

[77] Beale, *Handbook*, 31–32.

[78] Cf. Kenneth Duncan Litwak, *Echoes of Scripture in Luke-Acts: Telling the History of God's People Intertextually*, JSNTSup 282 (London: T&T Clark, 2005), 64. John 19:28 may be an exception to this general rule (see Brian J. Tabb, "Jesus's Thirst at the Cross: Irony and Intertextuality in John 19:28," *EvQ* 85 [2013]: 338–51).

[79] Beale, *Handbook*, 31. Beetham argues for this as the distinguishing feature between allusions and echoes (*Echoes*, 20). Beale does not make clear distinctions between the two (*Handbook*, 32) and speculates that both allusions and echoes can be either intended or unintended by the author (Beale, "Revelation," in *It Is Written: Scripture Citing Scripture: Essays in Honor of Barnabas Lindars*, ed. D. A. Carson and H. G. M. Williamson; [Cambridge: Cambridge University Press, 1988], 319–21). Benjamin D. Sommer has identified intentional echoes (*A Prophet Reads Scripture: Allusion in Isaiah 40–66* [Stanford, CA: Stanford University Press, 1998], 15–17).

[80] John Hollander, *The Figure of Echo: A Mode of Allusion in Milton and After* (Berkeley: University of California Press, 1981), 63–64; Richard B. Hays, *Echoes of Scripture in the Letters of Paul* (New Haven: Yale University Press, 1989), 19–29; and Beetham, *Echoes*, 15–24.

onus on the interpreter to arbitrate the grey line between allusion and echo or to discern authorial intention. Someone today may say, "All's well that ends well," but does he necessarily signal a reference to Shakespeare's 1601 play by the same name and intend for the hearer to find elements from that play in his speech? That is possible, but the speaker may simply have used a stock expression, historically derived from Shakespeare but now used quite apart from the meaning of the expression in the play.

For reasons like the above, some abandon this version of the distinction between echo and allusion. Instead, they discuss an evoking text's "marker" and the "marked" feature(s) of the source. A "marker" entails "technical, phonological, or semantic repetition" of the feature(s) from the source text,[81] but the evoking text's "marker" and the "marked" feature(s) in the source text might not exactly correspond (e.g., grammatical or other differences).[82] Both allusions and echoes have these two dimensions, but only allusions affect the meaning of the evoking text, according to Benjamin Sommer: "The meaning of an alluding text is affected by the content of the source text, while echoes do not suggest any altered understanding of the passage in which they appear."[83] To test the Zephaniah Proposal, then, we attempt to discern an allusion by examining the NT passage's markers and the impact the OT passage(s) makes on the NT's meaning—the absence of which may indicate an echo.

A constellation of textual indicators (criteria) can be helpful for this study. Beale's criteria significantly overlaps Richard Hays's helpful rubric for determining an allusion to a source: "availability,"

[81] Carmela Perri, "On Alluding," *Poetics* 7 (1978): 300.

[82] Brendsel, *Isaiah*, 31.

[83] Sommer, *Prophet*, 30–31; see also Kubiś (*Zechariah*, 21–25). Brendsel (*Isaiah*, 31) follows Sommer's argument in preferring "functional over formal definitions of allusion and echo" (Brendsel, personal comments to author, June 12, 2015); in an allusion, the evoked text affects the meaning of the evoking text. Ziva Ben-Porat ("The Poetics of Literary Allusion," *PTL* 1 [1976]: 107–8) and Perri ("On Alluding," 295, 300) further explain the phenomenon of "marked" features from the source text(s).

"volume," "recurrence," "thematic coherence," "historical plausibility," "history of interpretation," and "satisfaction."[84] Scholars have critiqued each point of Hays's approach.[85] Brawley has argued that only Hays's first two criteria are essential (the other five criteria overlap),[86] and Beale reduced the list to five also due to overlapping.[87] By applying Hays's criteria to John rather than Paul, noting the overlapping categories, and removing the secondary criteria, three main criteria remain. The criteria of availability, volume, and thematic coherence are the strongest indicators of an allusion to another source.[88]

According to Hays, availability refers to testing the likelihood that John's proposed source was "available to the author and/or original readers," while the criterion of volume refers to testing several things (read in concert with Beale above): "The degree of explicit repetition of words or syntactical patterns, but other factors may also be relevant: how distinctive or prominent is the precursor text within

[84] Hays, *Echoes*, 29–31. He produced these "tests" to determine echoes of Scripture in Paul, but at points Hays treats synonymously the terms "allusion" and "echo" (18–21, 30–31, and 119). We use the criteria for allusions in John, assessing whether the evidence points to the evoked text affecting the meaning of the evoking text.

[85] Stanley Porter, "Allusions and Echoes," in *As It Is Written: Studying Paul's Use of Scripture*, ed. S. E. Porter and C. D. Stanley, SBLSymS 50 (Atlanta: Society of Biblical Literature, 2008), 29–40; David A. Shaw, "Converted Imaginations? The Reception of Richard Hays's Intertextual Method," *CurBR* 11 (2013): 234–45.

[86] Robert L. Brawley, *Text to Text Pours Forth Speech: Voices of Scripture in Luke-Acts*, ISBL (Bloomington: Indiana University Press, 1995), 13–14.

[87] Beale, *Handbook*, 34–35.

[88] The criterion of "recurrence" was valid for the Pauline Epistles but not for John's one Gospel (arguments for Johannine authorship of the epistles of John and Revelation are not undertaken in this book), and within John's Gospel this criterion (i.e., usage of the proposed source elsewhere in the book) overlaps with availability. The last three ("historical plausibility," "history of interpretation," and "satisfaction") involve overlapping and secondary indicators for determining an allusion (Beale, *Handbook*, 35). Richard B. Hays's recently published work explores the broad use of Scripture in each Gospel, focusing on three themes: Israel, Jesus, and the church (*Echoes of Scripture in the Gospels* [Waco, TX: Baylor University Press, 2016]).

Scripture, and how much rhetorical stress does the echo receive in Paul's discourse?"[89] Both availability and high volume must be present to make a strong case for identifying the source of an allusion. But thematic coherence has its relevance also, since it entails analyzing John's contextual indicators (e.g., structural and "thematic link[s]") to validate the OT source, a practice that "does shade into interpretation."[90]

In summary, for our work in John, we propose a constellation of tests for a proposed allusion. In synthesizing Beale's criteria with Hays's and applying them to John's Gospel, we will determine credible allusions primarily with the following three criteria:

1. Source arguably *available* to the author.
2. Parallel's *volume* (in general, three-word linguistic or grammatical verbal coherence).
3. *Thematic coherence* (linguistic, thematic and/or structural confirmatory evidence).

This proposal of three criteria permits us to have a simple but relatively objective way to test claims that an author alluded to a source. These criteria are meant, on the one hand, to avoid complete ambiguity and lack of definition in identification of sources, while also refusing to shackle John with chains of detailed requirements that render inadmissible actual allusions.

Methodology

The methodology for this study of the FG's use of Zephaniah is guided by the six-fold organizational scheme outlined in Beale and Carson's *Commentary*.[91]

[89] Hays, *Echoes*, 30.

[90] Beale, *Handbook*, 35.

[91] G. K. Beale and D. A. Carson, "Introduction," in *Commentary on the New Testament Use of the Old Testament*, ed. G. K. Beale and D. A. Carson (Grand Rapids: Baker, 2007), xxiv–xxvi; cf. Beale's nine steps (*Handbook*, 42–54).

1. *NT context*. On the one hand, the purpose of this step is broad: "to establish the topic of discussion, the flow of thought, and, where relevant, the literary structure, genre, and rhetoric of the passage."[92] But on the other hand, the step is narrow, since we need to "identify the OT reference" and to discern whether it is "a quotation or allusion."[93] The Zephaniah Proposal is debated, so we will undertake a fresh look at the evidence for it.
2. *OT context*. Similar to step one, this step includes an analysis of "the OT context both broadly and immediately, especially thoroughly interpreting the paragraph in which the quotation or allusion occurs."[94] Attention may need to be given to the use of the OT in the OT as well, since Zephaniah may itself have used another OT text, for example.
3. *OT text in Jewish literature*. "Survey the use of the OT text in early and late Judaism that might be of relevance to the NT appropriation of the OT text."[95]
4. *Textual comparison*. This step includes textual criticism of the NT, LXX, MT, Targums and Jewish citations, then a comparison between these texts. This may clarify the NT's source.
5. *The NT author's textual and hermeneutical use of the OT*. Many possibilities exist for the NT's hermeneutical use of the OT (e.g., incidental language connection, NT fulfillment of OT prophecy). In the latter possibility, we ask, Has God sovereignly "established patterns that, rightly read, anticipate a recurrence of God's actions? Or are they claiming . . . that the OT texts themselves point forward in some way to the future? . . . . [Also,] do the NT writers appeal to the OT

[92] Beale and Carson, "Introduction," xxiv.

[93] Beale, *Handbook*, 42–43, 29–40. The reader will notice that this collapses the first two steps listed in Beale's more detailed *Handbook* with the first step from Beale and Carson's *Commentary*.

[94] Ibid., 42.

[95] Ibid.

using exactly the same sorts of exegetical techniques and hermeneutical assumptions that their unconverted Jewish contemporaries display"?[96]

6. *The NT author's theological and rhetorical use of the OT*. Beale and Carson note, "In one sense, this question is wrapped up in all the others, but it is worth asking separately as it highlights things that may otherwise be overlooked" (e.g., "YHWH" as Jesus).[97]

Since in articles, monographs, and dissertations, many scholars have exemplarily implemented the outline presented by Beale and Carson, this method for studying the OT in the NT is well-established.[98]

Thesis and Outline

The present work, on the one hand, examines the Zephaniah Proposal in the Entry Narrative of John 12, and on the other hand, handles Zephaniah 3 through the basic steps indicated above. *Our thesis is that John 12 alludes to Zephaniah 3:14–15 and that Zephaniah 3 has a greater impact on John's Entry Narrative than many scholars hold.* Due to the dearth of studies on the OT text of Zephaniah as it relates to the Entry Narrative, our particular focus is on an exegesis of Zephaniah 3, which affords new insights into the text of John 12.

[96] Beale and Carson, "Introduction," xxv. This combines steps 6 and 7 from Beale (*Handbook*, 42, 50–52). Since we are only testing a proposal, rather than accomplishing all the parts of the OT in the NT program, we do not examine all the other potential citations or allusions to Zephaniah in the NT or even in the FG. An exception to this is the proposed allusion in John 1 which may connect to the Zephaniah Proposal in John 12.

[97] See Beale and Carson, "Introduction," xxv–xxvi. We combine Beale's steps 8–9 (*Handbook*, 43, 52–54).

[98] E.g., the 18 scholars contributing to the volume edited by Beale and Carson (*Commentary*); Andrew David Naselli, *From Typology to Doxology: Paul's Use of Isaiah and Job in Romans 11:34–35* (Eugene, OR: Pickwick, 2012); Brendsel, *Isaiah*.

To argue this thesis and test the Zephaniah Proposal, this book employs the above scheme, slightly modifying it for our purposes, in the following chapters:

1. *Introduction*.
2. *Steps 1 and 4*:[99] Context of John 12:9–19. After surveying the proposals for the OT source(s) of the expressions "do not fear"[100] and "king of Israel," we examine the chief arguments for the Zephaniah Proposal, investigate another potential Zephaniah allusion in John, and compare Zechariah 9, Psalm 118 and Zephaniah 3 to John 12.
3. *Step 2*: Literary Context of Zephaniah 3. This is the heart of the book. After discussing introductory issues of Zephaniah's prophecy, we de-limit the text of Zephaniah 3 and undertake a paragraph-by-paragraph analysis of Zephaniah 3:8–20.
4. *Step 3*: Jewish Reception of Zephaniah 3. We survey the reception of Zephaniah 3 in early Jewish literature including its translation in Targum Zephaniah.
5. *Steps 5–6*: Hermeneutical and Theological Use of Zephaniah 3 in John 12. We undertake a detailed exegetical examination of John 12's Entry Narrative, hermeneutical assumptions and theological use of Zephaniah 3, in relation to Psalm 118 and Zechariah 9. We also discuss John 12's thematical links with Zephaniah.
6. *Conclusion*. We summarize our findings of John 12's use of Zephaniah 3 and identify potential areas for further research.

[99] We examine textual issues at this point in the book, because many contest the use of Zephaniah in John 12's Entry Narrative. As Naselli notes, the order of the steps can be adjusted as long as steps one through four are accomplished before advancing to steps five and six (*Typology to Doxology*, 5).

[100] Brunson (*Psalm 118*, 234) identifies only five sources seriously defended by commentators (Isa. 35:4; 40:9; 41:10; 44:2; and Zeph. 3:16). We add Zechariah 8–9, due especially to the discussions by Kubiś (*Zechariah*, 85–86) and Frédéric Manns ("Exégèse rabbinique et exégèse johannique," *RB* 92 [1985]: 533).

2

John 12 and the Zephaniah Proposal

Literary and Thematic Context of John's Entry Narrative

In this chapter, we study John 12:9–19 in its literary context and consider its relationship to Zephaniah 3:14–15. First, we outline the broad literary context of the FG before narrowly focusing on the Entry Narrative. We next examine the most significant textual issues in John 12:13 and 15 related to ὁ βασιλεὺς τοῦ Ἰσραήλ and μὴ φοβοῦ. Then, after assessing the Zephaniah Proposal for those words, we proceed to address textual issues in the MT and LXX of Zephaniah 3:14–16. In a final step, we compare the MT and LXX of Zephaniah 3 with John 12.

Broader Literary Context of John's Entry Narrative

The FG claims to be written for the following purpose: "that you may believe that the Christ, the Son of God, is Jesus, and that by believing you may have life in his name" (20:31).[1] According to this statement, the main themes of the book include belief in Jesus, his

[1] For a defense of the translation "the Christ, the Son of God, is Jesus" based on the syntax of the construction and for the interpretation that this verse serves as the FG's purpose statement, see D. A. Carson, "The Purpose of the Fourth Gospel: John 20:31 Reconsidered," *JBL* 106 (1987): 639–51; Carson, *The Gospel according to John*, PiNTC (Grand Rapids: Eerdmans, 1991), 660–63.

being the Son of God, and having life in him. The prologue (John 1:1–18) contains similar themes, declaring Jesus Christ to be the living Word-become-flesh.

Some commentators outline the major sections of the FG as the Book of Signs (1:19–12:50) and the Book of Glory (13:1–20:31), aside from the introductory Prologue (1:1–18) and the Epilogue (21:1–25).[2] This structuring usually depends on the observation that John used the word σημεῖον at key junctures and only in chapters 2–12 (excl. 20:30). The "first of his signs" occur when Jesus turned the water into wine at the wedding part of Cana (John 2:11), and the (seventh) climactic sign occurs with the raising of Lazarus (John 11:47; 12:18).[3]

This outline is attractive due to its simplicity, but we must account for the word "signs" in John's summary statement (20:30–31), which "makes it clear that from the Evangelist's perspective the *entire* Gospel is a book of signs."[4] Also, Jesus's passion narrative does not properly begin until chapter 18, after the intimate last supper discourse(s) of chapters 13–17. And the language of "signs" is absent in 1:19–51, whereas John 2–12 already used terminology about Jesus's "glory" and "glorification" (e.g., 2:11; 11:3; 12:23).[5] Dividing

[2] Raymond E. Brown, *The Gospel according to John*, AB (Garden City, NY: Doubleday, 1966–70), 1:cxxxviii–cxxxix; cf. C. H. Dodd, *The Interpretation of the Fourth Gospel* (Cambridge: Cambridge University Press, 1953), 289, who refers to John 13–21 as the "Book of the Passion."

[3] Many note that Jesus accomplished seven signs in John: water to wine (2:1–11); official's son's healing (4:46–54); paralytic's healing (5:1–15); loaves multiplied (6:1–15); walking on Sea of Galilee (6:16–21); blind man's healing (9); Lazarus's raising from the dead (11) (see, e.g., Brown, *John*, 1:cxxxix; Andreas J. Köstenberger, "John," in *Commentary on the New Testament Use of the Old Testament*, ed. G. K. Beale and D. A. Carson [Grand Rapids: Baker, 2007], 467). John used the word σημεῖον seventeen times, sometimes in the singular and other times in the plural form (2:11, 18, 23; 3:2; 4:48, 54; 6:2, 14, 26, 30; 7:31; 9:16; 10:41; 11:47; 12:18, 37; 20:30).

[4] Carson, *John*, 103, italics original.

[5] George Mlakuzhyil, *The Christocentric Literary Structure of the Fourth Gospel*, AnBib 117 (Rome: Pontifical Biblical Institute, 1987), 82.

the book into Signs and Glory is broadly true, but it does not account for all the data and so cannot be rigidly maintained.

This is particularly true when considering the literary context of John 12:9–19, which we read as part of the book's hinge. R. Alan Culpepper sums up the literary function of John 12: "In many ways chapter 12 is a transitional chapter. It brings Jesus's public ministry to a close, describes the preliminary steps towards his arrest and death, and forms a solid link between chapters 11 and 13."[6] Others, however, draw together chapters 11 and 12 as the book's hinge, due to about 70 shared terms, themes, and literary connections between these two chapters. They note the sustained narration and reflection on the Lazarus sign together with the foreshadowing of Jesus's death.[7] Jesus heals Lazarus in John 11, but then chapter 12 refers to this event, interweaving it with Jesus's entry. These observations underline the pivotal role that chapter 12 plays in the FG, and the important literary context of the Lazarus sign (John 11).

In John 11:1–44,[8] Jesus heals Lazarus but delays doing so

[6] R. Alan Culpepper, *Anatomy of the Fourth Gospel: A Study in Literary Design*, FFNT (Philadelphia: Fortress, 1983), 171.

[7] E.g., Mlakuzhyil argues, "11,1–54 is parallel to 11,55–12,50" (*Christocentric*, 220). Several structurally outline John 11–12 together (e.g., Andreas J. Köstenberger, *A Theology of John's Gospel and Letters: Biblical Theology of the New Testament*, BTNT [Grand Rapids: Zondervan, 2009], 168–70; Brown, *John*, 1:cxli; Carson, *John*, 106–7; Francis J. Moloney, *The Gospel of John*, SP [Collegeville, MN: Liturgical, 1998], 24, 322; Gary M. Burge, *John*, NIVAC [Grand Rapids: Zondervan, 2000], 42; Craig S. Keener, *The Gospel of John: A Commentary* [Peabody, MA: Hendrickson, 2003], 2:833; Andrew T. Lincoln, *The Gospel according to Saint John*, BNTC [Peabody, MA: Hendrickson, 2005], 4; Carson, *John*, 105–8; D. A. Carson, Douglas J. Moo, and Leon Morris, *An Introduction to the New Testament*, 2nd ed. [Grand Rapids: Zondervan, 2005], 225–29), and this book takes the same approach.

[8] We find ample evidence that John 10:42 ends a section, and 11:1 marks a fresh start. 11:1 shifts to a new location (i.e., from the Jordan to Bethany), new participants (i.e., Jesus and many, then Lazarus and his sisters), different discourse (i.e., reported speech and summary statement, then information and action). The postpositive δέ functions as a discourse marker to introduce background material about Lazarus's illness and his sisters, who become the feature

until after four days postmortem for God and the Son of God to be glorified. This was Jesus's central concern, since Jesus states that purpose at the beginning and end of the pericope (11:4, 40). But Jesus's delayed healing of Lazarus was calculated not only to get greater glory for himself and his Father, but also to stimulate the disciples, Martha, and the crowd (ὄχλον) to respond in faith to the Son-Sent-by-the-Father (John 11:15, 24–27, 40, 42). Jesus prayed before calling out Lazarus from the tomb (11:44),[9] and in this way accomplished the Lazarus "sign" (John 12:18). Verse 44's graveside healing of Lazarus satisfactorily ends the tension created in 11:1–3.

John 11:45–54 form the next unit. Verse 45's postpositive οὖν signals a new stage in the discourse, and the scene shifts from Jesus at Lazarus's grave to the Jews's responses: some believed in Jesus (11:45), but others rejected him (11:46–53). The rejection culminates in the narrator's ominous report, "From that day on they made

participants in the ensuing narrative. Of Stephen H. Levinsohn's two types of Johannine backgrounding δέ functions, 11:1 best fits the category "*presentational* articulation . . . . to introduce participants or props that will feature in the ongoing story" (*Discourse Features of New Testament Greek: A Coursebook on the Information Structure of New Testament Greek*, 2nd ed. [Dallas: SIL International, 2000], 90, italics original; cf. John 3:1).

[9] Similar to A. C. Brunson's thesis that Psalm 118 influences the text of the FG before John 12:13 (*Psalm 118 in the Gospel of John: An Intertextual Study on the New Exodus Pattern in the Theology of John*, WUNT, 2nd ser., 158 [Tübingen: Mohr Siebeck, 2003], 385), several argue for an allusion to Psalm 118:21 in Jesus's prayer in John 11:41 (cf. John 11:27, ὁ εἰς τὸν κόσμον ἐρχόμενος): Anthony T. Hanson ("The Old Testament Background to the Raising of Lazarus," in *Studia Evangelica*, ed. E. A. Livingstone, TUGAL 112 [Berlin: Akademie-Verlag, 1973], 6:255; Hanson, *The New Testament Interpretation of Scripture* [London: SPCK, 1980], 210n21); Max Wilcox ("The 'Prayer' of Jesus in John XI.41b–42," *NTS* 24 [1977]: 131–32); Wendy Sproston North ("Jesus' Prayer in John 11," in *The Old Testament in the New Testament: Essays in Honour of J. L. North*, ed. Steve Moyise, JSNTSup 189 [Sheffield: Sheffield Academic Press, 2000], 164–80), the latter scholar reading the allusion as linked with John 12:13's Psalm 118:25 (i.e., "the coming one") quotation.

plans to kill [Jesus]" (11:53).[10] Jesus then removes himself from public ministry (11:54) to minister to his disciples.

With the previous verses providing the harbinger about the Jewish leaders' murderous intentions that provoked Jesus to withdraw, John 11:55–57 function as part of a turning point in the narrative of the FG. They introduce the Passover setting, which is the time period for chapter 12. The chief priests and Pharisees planned to arrest Jesus during Passover (11:57), setting their murderous intent in motion (11:53). But Jesus's attendance was uncertain (11:56).

Then, in three pericopes John 12:1–36 narrates Jesus approaching Jerusalem, and the chapter ends with the theological motif of unbelief (12:37–50).[11] In John 12's first narrative, verses 1–8 relate the story about Jesus dining in Bethany with Lazarus and Mary anointing Jesus's feet. This event was not entirely festive, since Jesus's death is again foreshadowed in at least two points: Judas Iscariot is identified for the reader as the future betrayer of Jesus (12:4), and Jesus states that Mary kept the oil "for the day of my burial. . . . You [disciples] will not always have me!" (12:7–8). In the second pericope, John 12:9–19 narrates Jesus's Entry Narrative. And third, John 12:20–36 portray Greeks coming to see Jesus and the arrival of Jesus's "hour" (12:23).

Jesus's death was indeed near. Jesus spends time with his disciples (John 13–16) and prays to the Father (John 17) before the FG details the events of Jesus's trial and glorification at the cross (John 18–20). An epilogue relates Jesus's final post-resurrection appearance (John 21).

Textual Limits of John's Entry Narrative: John 12:9–19

Focusing more narrowly on Jesus's entry, we now de-limit the text. John 12:12–14 relates the action sequence proper, for the day

[10] C. K. Barrett notes that this section (vv. 45–54) "raises the dramatic tension of the gospel to a climax which is resolved only in the passion narrative" (*The Gospel according to St. John*, 2nd ed. [Philadelphia: Westminster, 1978], 404).

[11] Ibid., 14; Carson, *John*, 107; Carson, Moo, and Morris, *Introduction*, 228.

of Jesus's entry. To be specific, John 12:12a opens as a new day (τῇ ἐπαύριον) and includes the new information that Jesus was in fact coming to Jerusalem for Passover and that the large crowd (ὁ ὄχλος πολὺς) learned of it.[12] The day continued with the crowd taking branches, meeting him and crying out words from Psalm 118. Then, Jesus found and sat on a donkey, according to Zechariah 9:9's prophecy (John 12:14–15).

Though John 12:16–19 do not include events that happened on the same day as Jesus's entry, they sustain reflection on the Entry Narrative: the disciples recall Jesus's entry (12:16), the entry crowd bears witness (12:18), and Jesus's fame increases (12:19). 12:19 records the Pharisees's assessment (οὖν), "the world has gone after [Jesus]," but then 12:20 begins a new section since it shifts to new participants (i.e., Greeks) and focus (i.e., *request to see* Jesus).[13]

Commentators debate where John's Entry Narrative begins. John 12:9–11 relate how the large crowd of Jews who witnessed Lazarus's resurrection came to Jesus and that the Jews planned to kill Lazarus in addition to Jesus. Does this passage go with what precedes or what follows? Some connect John 12:9–11 with Jesus's anointing in Bethany (12:1–8) since John 12:9 indicates that the crowd went to Jesus "there" (ἐκεῖ) with Lazarus.[14] And the "large

[12] People celebrated "the feast" (τὴν ἑορτήν). The Passover setting is mentioned three times in John 11:55–56 and 12:1 (for a defense of Passover, not Tablernacles, as John 12's setting, see Brunson, *Psalm 118*, 191–93).

[13] Contra Ernst Haenchen, who argues that the mention of "the whole world" (v. 19) constitutes the conceptual link to the Greeks (v. 20), and that therefore a hard break does not exist between 12:19–20 (*John*, ed. R. W. Funk and U. Busse, trans. R. W. Funk, Hermeneia [Philadelphia: Fortress, 1984], 2:93). We agree that 12:20 conceptually builds on 12:19 (see § 5.3.2), but verse 20 introduces new participants with an imperfect verb and postpositive δὲ. These grammatical and discourse considerations warrant a paragraph break.

[14] R. H. Lightfoot, *St. John's Gospel*, ed. C. F. Evans (Oxford: Clarendon, 1956; repr., London: Oxford University Press, 1963), 233; Rudolf Schnackenburg, *The Gospel according to St John*, trans. K. Smyth et al., HTKNT (New York: Crossroad, 1980–82), 2:370; Carson, *John*, 431; Ulrich Wilckens, *Das Evangelium nach Johannes*, NTD 4 (Göttingen: Vandenhoeck & Ruprecht,

crowd" (ὄχλος πολὺς) came to see Lazarus whom Jesus raised from the dead (12:9), a narrative recall to the events of chapter 11. Others link verses 9–11 with 12:12 where the entry proper begins.[15]

We join verses 9–11 to the entry (vv. 12–19) for the following reasons. (1) The FG names Lazarus only in chapters 11–12 for a total of eleven times, but the final mentions of Jesus's raising of Lazarus occur before and after the entry events (John 12:9–11, 17). In an important way, then, Lazarus's resurrection contributes to John's structuring of the entry and yet refers back to chapter 11's events.[16] (2) The sub-units of John 12:9–11 and 17–19 have many other parallels (e.g., "the crowd," Lazarus's being "raised from the dead," Jesus's antagonists "the chief priests" and "the Pharisees," and the mention of Jesus's followers) that lead many scholars to read them as indicating an *inclusio*-like "literary frame"[17] around the Entry Narrative (vv. 12–16). When read with this framing device, the entry describes

1998), 187; Klaus Wengst, *Das Johannesevangelium*, THKNT (Stuttgart: Kohlhammer, 2001), 2:46.

[15] Brown, *John*, 1:456, 459; Leon Morris, *The Gospel according to John*, NICNT, rev. ed. (Grand Rapids: Eerdmans, 1995), 516–23; George R. Beasley-Murray, *John*, 2nd ed., WBC (Nashville: Thomas Nelson, 1999), 209; Daniel J. Brendsel, *"Isaiah Saw His Glory": The Use of Isaiah 52–53 in John 12*, BZNW 28 (Berlin: de Gruyter, 2014), 162–63.

[16] Andreas J. Köstenberger, *John*, BECNT (Grand Rapids: Baker, 2004), 320; Köstenberger, "John," 470; cf. John 11:1, 2, 5, 11, 14, 43; 12:1, 2, 9, 10, 17.

[17] Brendsel, *Isaiah*, 162; see also Brown, *John*, 1:456, 463–64; Moloney, *John*, 350; R. Alan Culpepper, *The Gospel and Letters of John* (Nashville: Abingdon, 1998), 193; Köstenberger, *John*, 372–73. Judith M. Lieu posits that the narratorial intrusion of John 12:16 forms an *inclusio* with the remembering of John 2:17, and that this shows the "primacy of an omniscient narrator over his characters" ("Narrative Analysis and Scripture in John," in *The Old Testament in the New Testament: Essays in Honour of J. L. North*, ed. Steve Moyise, JSNTSup 189 [Sheffield: Sheffield Academic Press, 2000], 151–52). Several argue that the "remembering" in John 12:16 "provide[s] the rationale for the Gospel and its distinctive presentation of Jesus—a remembering through the mediation of the Scriptures and through the spirit (14.26; cf. 15.26–27; 16.14)" (ibid., 152; cf. Culpepper, *Anatomy*, 28–30; Anthony T. Hanson, *The Prophetic Gospel: A Study of John and the Old Testament* [Edinburgh: T&T Clark, 1991], 246–53).

the crowd wanting to see Lazarus and thus Jesus's life was in danger as he approached Jerusalem.[18] (3) Aside from the geographic connection in 12:9 (i.e., Bethany), verses 9–11 do not share many links with verses 1–8, and verses 9–11 interrupt the event sequence.[19] Jesus's entry occurred the next day (τῇ ἐπαύριον, 12:12), assumedly the day after Jesus's Bethany anointing (12:1–8), but when exactly the actions of verses 10–11 occurred (i.e., Jews trusting in Jesus and the chief priests' decision to kill Lazarus) is uncertain. Verses 9–11 do contain important and ominous background about Lazarus and Jesus leading up to the entry proper (12:12–19). We thus read 12:9–19 as a textual unit.

Textual Issues

Important Textual Issues in John 12:13 and 15

We first examine the textual issues in John 12:13 and 15, the verses that most directly relate to the Zephaniah Proposal. Most importantly for our work, the words βασιλεὺς τοῦ 'Ισραήλ (John 12:13) are textually stable as are μὴ φοβοῦ in John 12:15 (e.g., both expressions are found in 𝔓[66, 75] ℵ A B L). We do not find notable alternative readings in early Greek manuscripts for either expression, so we do not doubt the text's integrity here.[20] Textual issues do

[18] Brendsel posits two reasonable explanations for the *inclusio* of John's Entry Narrative: the *inclusio* "situates the entry squarely within the opposition to Jesus and his impending death" and "helps put into focus what the crowds are really excited about at the entry (John 12:9, 17–18)" (*Isaiah*, 162–63). Some redaction-critical scholars looking for signs material in John suppose that John 12:12–16 was inserted into pre-existing Lazarus-signs material, John 12:9–11 and 18–19 (Urban C. von Wahlde, *The Earliest Version of John's Gospel: Recovering the Gospel of Signs*, GNS 30 [Wilmington, DE: Glazier, 1989], 128–29). Our objective is not to recover original signs material, but Wahlde rightly observes that John tightly connects verses 9–11 and 18–19.

[19] Brendsel, *Isaiah*, 162–63.

[20] Fragmentary manuscripts with lacunae provide the only deviations from these two expressions. Though there is no competing Greek textual tradition for John 12's "king of Israel," the only legible part of the fragmentary papyrus

remain in these verses, however, and they may impact the Zephaniah Proposal.

John 12:13

We examine three textual issues in John 12:13. First, the crowd's cry ὡσαννά· εὐλογημένος ὁ ἐρχόμενος ἐν ὀνόματι κυρίου is well-attested and has minimal textual issues. For example, one Greek uncial (D) has the reading εὐλογητός, a rare Greek NT adjective that may mean either "blessed" or "praised."[21] But Codex Bezae seems to represent a singular reading, against the otherwise well-attested εὐλογημένος (e.g., 𝔓[66, 75] B 33).[22] John's text here is stable.

Important manuscripts are, however, split on whether to read the καί following the quoted words of Psalm 118:25–26. Many strong witnesses support reading it (e.g., א B L W 579, and various versions), while the weightiest evidence against including the καί is 𝔓[66] and א[2a] along with some Coptic versions, later Greek uncials, and the Majority Text.[23] Turning to internal considerations, the grammar of John's clause can sustain either reading. Without the καί, the expression ὁ βασιλεὺς τοῦ Ἰσραήλ directly follows ὁ ἐρχόμενος ἐν ὀνόματι κυρίου, and would likely function epexegetically

---

𝔓[2] in 12:13c is οὗ Ἰσραήλ. As for John 12:15, the fragmentary Miniscule 33 lacks the first half of verse 15.

[21] See BDAG, s.v. εὐλογητός.

[22] D. C. Parker observes that this codex's "many unique readings only very rarely deserve serious consideration if one is trying to establish the best available text" (*Codex Bezae: An Early Christian Manuscript and Its Text* [Cambridge: Cambridge University Press, 1992], 1).

[23] Gordon D. Fee argued that 𝔓[66] was a "basically Neutral text" in John 1–5 and generally accurate there, but then it is freer in the later chapters of the FG, often aligning with Byzantine and Western texts (*Papyrus Bodmer II [P66]: Its Textual Relationships and Scribal Characteristics*, SD 34 [Salt Lake City: University of Utah Press, 1968], 35). If he is correct, the textual tradition that does not read the καί is somewhat weakened here. For a discussion of singular readings, see Eldon Jay Epp, *Perspectives on New Testament Textual Criticism: Collected Essays, 1962–2004*, NovTSup 116 (Leiden: Brill, 2005), 101–24.

to more precisely identify the coming one as the king of Israel.[24] On the other hand, scholars who read the καί after the Psalm 118 quotation propose a variety of syntactical uses for it here: (1) ascensive (i.e., "even"),[25] (2) epexegetical (i.e., "that is") to coordinate "the two titles in one,"[26] or (3) continuative (i.e., "and"), reading "the king of Israel" as a second acclamation.[27] Regarding the καί as original is uncertain but possible.

In a related issue in this verse, we understand that following the καί, the original text likely read ὁ. The evidence of textual witnesses strongly favors including the article (𝔓[66, 75] ℵ B L, and some ancient versions),[28] and the earliest textual evidence against its inclusion dates much later, from the fifth century. Without the article, the expression would better match the anarthrous expression βασιλεὺς εἶ τοῦ Ἰσραήλ in John 1:49, so scribal assimilation to that passage may explain the readings that exclude it. While there is some textual doubt, reading the article as original is warranted. Following the καί, the text likely reads, "*the* king of Israel."

John 12:15

We examine two noteworthy textual issues in John 12:15. First, despite textual diversity in the spelling of "daughter," manuscript and grammatical evidence favor the nominative form. Most

[24] For an explanation, defense, and further specification of this broad syntactical usage of the article and its eight sub-uses, see Daniel B. Wallace, *Greek Grammar beyond the Basics: An Exegetical Syntax of the New Testament* (Grand Rapids: Eerdmans, 1996), 216–27. If the article is not read with "king," the anarthrous king still provides specificity for the coming one/the Lord. Scholars debate whether the crowd (F. F. Bruce, *The Gospel of John: Introduction, Exposition and Notes* [Grand Rapids: Eerdmans, 1983], 259), narrator, or someone else "uttered" the words "(and) the king of Israel." See discussion in § 5.2.3.1 and Brendsel, *Isaiah*, 168n42.

[25] E.g., Morris, *John*, 520n44.

[26] Barrett, *John*, 418; Brunson, *Psalm 118*, 223.

[27] J. F. Coakley, "Jesus' Messianic Entry into Jerusalem (John 12:12–19 par)," *JTS* 46 (1995): 477.

[28] Morris, *John*, 520.

of the important, early manuscripts read it as θυγάτηρ (e.g., 𝔓[66] A B 579), whereas the best case for reading the vocative θύγατερ rests on Codex Alexandrinus (see also later uncials, manuscripts, and the Majority Text). On the grammatical level, the vocative form may be the harder reading, but we favor the nominative form; in the NT the singular imperative μὴ φοβοῦ addresses a person's name in the vocative (e.g., Luke 1:13, 30; Acts 27:24) but uses the nominative for an impersonal form of address (Luke 12:32). In John 12:15, "daughter" supplies the imperative's only named, singular addressee, so the nominative likely functions as a vocative.[29]

Second, the reading ἰδοὺ ὁ βασιλεύς σου ἔρχεται καθήμενος ἐπὶ πῶλον ὄνου has strong manuscript support (e.g., 𝔓[66, 75] B VULG.), and we find Greek textual differences to it only in late and minority readings. One late uncial (A) removes the second person pronoun altogether, another one instead reads σοι (Π), a later miniscule reads σου but adds a pronoun (i.e., σοι) after ἔρχεται (565), and two late miniscules read a postpositive γὰρ (579, 1424). None of these textual differences mount a significant textual challenge to the above expression's authenticity, and they are explainable as interpretive maneuvers or assimilation to the OT (Zech. 9:9).

Summarizing the Textual Issues in John 12:13 and 15

While the textual integrity of βασιλεὺς τοῦ Ἰσραήλ and μὴ φοβοῦ in John 12:13 and 15 is unassailable, some textual doubt remains for other terms. Most notably, we provisionally include the καί in John 12:13 following the quote from Psalm 118:26, but this is

[29] For an explanation and defense of the vocative syntactical option for the articular and anarthrous nominative, see Wallace, *Greek Grammar*, 56–59. Only a couple manuscripts include the FS article η with the nominative "daughter" (𝔓[75] B[2]). If the article is included, though highly unlikely given its poor attestation, the text may emphasize the addressee. John 12:15 likely most directly draws this word from Zechariah 9:9 in the quotation, so the locus of the textual issue may reside there (James Hamilton, "The Influence of Isaiah on the Gospel of John," *Perichoresis* 7 [2007]: 145n15, though he holds that John 12:15a depends on Isaiah 35:4 and 40:9).

uncertain. We do, however, have stronger manuscript and grammatical evidence for reading the first article in ὁ βασιλεὺς τοῦ Ἰσραήλ, and for reading the nominative form θυγάτηρ.

Important Textual Issues in Zephaniah 3:14–15 and 16

We proceed to examine the textual issues in Zephaniah 3:14–16. Verses 14–15 form a sub-unit by themselves and provide all the vocabulary relevant for John 12:13–15.[30] Zephaniah 3:16 nevertheless restates 3:15's negative expression, so our analysis includes verse 16.[31]

Zephaniah 3:14

In verse 14, there are two minor variations among the textual witnesses, both related to the addressee(s). First, immediately following the first imperative in this verse, the MT reads בַּת־צִיּוֹן, and the

[30] We discuss the units of Zephaniah 3 below (see § 3.2.2), but here we make some initial observations to argue that Zephaniah 3:14–15 stands as a coherent, discrete sub-unit. (1) The imperatives and fresh set of vocatives in 3:14 mark verses 14–15 as "syntactically independent from the preceding block of material" (Marvin A. Sweeney, *Zephaniah: A Commentary*, ed. Paul D. Hanson, Hermeneia [Minneapolis: Fortress, 2003], 194). (2) Verse 15 follows the imperatives of verse 14 with a couple asyndetic phrases in the *qatal*, whose function most naturally is to "support" the imperatives (Duane A. Garrett and Jason S. DeRouchie, *A Modern Grammar for Biblical Hebrew* [Nashville: Broadman & Holman, 2009], 74). (3) Verse 16 signals a new unit withe בַּיּוֹם הַהוּא (see, e.g., Ehud Ben Zvi, *A Historical-Critical Study of the Book of Zephaniah*, BZAW 198 [Berlin: de Gruyter, 1991], 238, 245).

[31] Zephaniah 3:15d's לֹא + *yiqtol* construction (MT) can be a predictive (e.g., LXX, Peshitta, VULG.) or a directive (see Garrett and DeRouchie, *Modern Grammar*, 296 and 331). As for Zephaniah 3:16b's אַל־תִּירָאִי, both external (LXX, Peshitta, VULG.) and internal evidence favor a directive reading (e.g., note the parallel exhortation [v. 16c]), though Zephaniah may intend the "reassurance formula" in both verses 15d and 16c, a standard component of "oracles of salvation" (Sweeney, *Zephaniah*, 201; cf. Ben Zvi, *Zephaniah*, 244). Whether or not verses 15 and 16 share such a formula, our point here is that the grammatical form in the MT of verse 15 could read as a directive. John 12:15's exhortation to not fear could then correspond to either Zephaniah 3:15 or 16.

final addressee in the verse is identified as בַּת יְרוּשָׁלָם. Most of the ancient versions match the Hebrew's addressees here (LXX, Peshitta, Vulg.).[32] Targum Jonathan alone, however, translated "daughter" both times as כְּנִשְׁתָּא, a word often used in Mishnaic and Talmudic times to refer to Israel gathered as a "congregation."[33] It is noteworthy that the Targums also translated "daughter" as "congregation" in the similar passages of Zechariah 2:14 and 9:9, but as "people" in TJ Isaiah 23:12.[34] The interpretational emphasis of the Aramaic translation is apparent and so does not challenge the MT's reading.

In a second minor textual issue in this verse, the MT (see also Mur88)[35] names the second addressee as יִשְׂרָאֵל (see Peshitta, Vulg., TJ), but of the ancient versions only LXX manuscripts render this as θυγατερ Ιερουσαλημ. Many scholars explain the LXX's

[32] The main variation among the LXX manuscripts is orthographic. The LXX spelling of "daughter" (in both occurrences in v. 14) was either θυγάτηρ or θύγατερ (a nominative or vocative), with perhaps a slight preference for the latter as being original. There is good textual support for reading θύγατερ (e.g., Codex Vaticanus) in both occurrences, and we follow some eclectic LXX editions in preferring the vocative (e.g., Alfred Rahlfs and Robert Hanhart, eds., *Septuaginta: Id est Vetus Testamentum graece iuxta LXX interpretes*, rev. ed. [Stuttgart: Deutsche Bibelgesellschaft, 2006], 541; Joseph Ziegler, ed., *Duodecim Prophetae*, vol. 13, *Septuaginta: Vetus Testamentum Graecum Auctoritate Academiae Scientiarum Gottingensis Editum* [Göttingen: Vandenhoeck & Ruprecht, 1943], 283).

[33] Ahuva Ho found that Jewish literature sometimes read "daughter" as כְּנִשְׁתָּא דִירְוּשְׁלַם ("congregation of Israel") (*The Targum of Zephaniah: Manuscripts and Commentary*, SAIS 7 [Leiden: Brill, 2009], 380).

[34] Ho notes that this could be due to different translations, translators, or redactions (ibid., 381); cf. Kevin J. Cathcart and Robert P. Gordon, *The Targum of the Minor Prophets: Translated, with a Critical Introduction, Apparatus, and Notes*, ArBib 14 (Wilmington, DE: Glazier, 1989), 173n32.

[35] Marvin A. Sweeney dates this scroll from Murabba'at to the second century A.D. and cautiously accepts its witness ("Synchronic and Diachronic Concerns in Reading the Book of the Twelve Prophets," in *Perspectives on the Formation of the Book of the Twelve: Methodological Foundations, Redactional Processes, Historical Insights*, ed. Rainer Albertz, James D. Nogalski, and Jakob Wöhrle, BZAW 433 [Berlin: de Gruyter, 2012], 26).

unique reading here in terms of scribal error: dittography[36] or assimilation to the final addressee in the verse.[37] The latter explanation is the simplest one, but we cannot be certain. Noting several possible explanations for the LXX reading and strong textual evidence for the reading "Israel," most scholars do not see warrant for emending the MT text to the LXX.[38]

Zephaniah 3:15

There are a few textual issues in this verse.[39] But we examine only the two relevant expressions: "king of Israel" (מֶלֶךְ יִשְׂרָאֵל [MT]) and "you will/shall not fear" (לֹא־תִירְאִי [MT]).

In the first textual issue, the MT reads מֶלֶךְ יִשְׂרָאֵל, but several Septuagint manuscripts (including Lucian's Recension) render the expression as a verb (βασιλευσει). This textual evidence of the

[36] Ivan J. Ball Jr. writes, "The LXX translation was probably due to vertical dittography or to the use of a text which had been subject to Judaising reworking" (*A Rhetorical Study of Zephaniah* [Berkeley, CA: Bibal Press, 1988], 179, citing Gillis Gerleman, *Zephanja: Textkritisch und Literarisch Untersucht* [Lund: Gleerup, 1942], 61).

[37] Anthony Gelston, *The Twelve Minor Prophets*, ed. Adrian Schenker et al., *BHQ* 13 (Stuttgart: Deutsche Bibelgesellschaft, 2010), 110. Also, Sweeney postulates that "the inconsistency in gender appears to have agitated the LXX translator, who renders 'Israel' here as 'Daughter Jerusalem' in keeping with the concluding reference to the addressee in the verse" (*Zephaniah*, 198). He also notes that Zephaniah 3:14d may have referred to Jerusalem due to his envisioning centralized worship in the temple.

[38] Sweeney, *Zephaniah*, 198; John M. P. Smith, "Zephaniah," in *Micah, Zephaniah, Nahum, Habakkuk, Obadiah and Joel*, ICC (New York: Scribner's, 1911), 255; cf. Jer. 17:13; 50:17; Ezek. 4:3, 13; 6:2; Mic. 2:12.

[39] We do not here examine the following issues: (1) Some Hebrew witnesses do not have either an open or closed Hebrew marker dividing verses 15 and 16 (MUR88, Leningrad Codex and Cairo Codex), while the Aleppo Codex has an open marker. (2) Several LXX manuscripts read λελύτρωταί σε ("he has redeemed you") perhaps reading MT's פנה as פדך מנ. Smith thinks the LXX reading (cf. Peshitta, VULG., TJ) "is a legitimate and natural development of the primary meaning, 'turn'" ("Zephaniah," 261). In successive lines in *BHQ*, we also find textual issues with (3) אֹיְבֵךְ and (4) מִשְׁפָּטַיִךְ (see discussion in § 3.3.3).

Septuagint, combined with metrical considerations in Zephaniah 3, causes some scholars to emend the text based on ימלך rather than מלך ישראל (cf. Mic. 4:7).[40] But there are several reasons for not following that reading here: (1) The textual tradition is strong for reading the original text as מֶלֶךְ יִשְׂרָאֵל (e.g., MT, Peshitta, TJ, VULG.), a reading that even important Septuagint witnesses follow (e.g., B S* Q C). (2) We do not consider metrical considerations as determinative for textual criticism,[41] but if we admit Ivan Ball Jr.'s strophic analysis, reading "king of Israel" makes metrical sense in its line.[42] (3) According to Micah 4:7's vowel pointing in the MT, מלך in וּמָלַךְ יְהוָה reads as a verb (cf. Ex. 15:18; Ps. 146:10); scribal assimilation to that similar prophetic passage can explain the verbal vowel pointing in some of Zephaniah's Greek manuscripts.[43] Yahweh as king (noun), however, does occur in a select number of passages (e.g., 1 Sam. 8:7; 12:12; Ps. 29:10; Isa. 44:6).[44] Based on this external and internal evidence, with many scholars we read the original text as מֶלֶךְ יִשְׂרָאֵל יְהוָה ("the king of Israel, Yahweh").[45]

[40] Hubert Irsigler, *Gottesgericht und Jahwetag: Die Komposition Zef 1,1–2, 3, untersucht auf der Grudlage der Literarkritik des Zefanjabuches*, ATSAT 3 (Sankt Ottilien: EOS-Verlag, 1977), 191, as cited by Ben Zvi, *Zephaniah*, 245n815.

[41] Douglas K. Stuart notes, "Emendation may rarely be attempted *metri causa* alone. One must satisfy the demands of coherence and appropriateness before changing what has been received" (*Studies in Early Hebrew Meter*, HSM 13 [Missoula, MT: Scholars Press, 1976], 22).

[42] Ball, *Rhetorical Study*, 181–82. He argues that this line (Zeph. 3:15c) parallels verse 17.

[43] Gelston, *Twelve Minor Prophets*, 111.

[44] Smith posits that "the awkwardness of the syntax and the undue length of the line" demonstrate that an MT "glossator" "inserted" Yahweh's name to ensure a correct interpretation of "king of Israel" ("Zephaniah," 256). But this introduces an unsubstantiated reading of the text.

[45] Ball, *Rhetorical Study*, 181–82; M. O'Connor, *Hebrew Verse Structure* (Winona Lake, IN: Eisenbrauns, 1997), 260; H. W. M. van Grol, "Classical Hebrew Metrics and Zephaniah 2–3," in *The Structural Analysis of Biblical and Canaanite Poetry*, ed. W. van der Meer and J. C. de Moor, JSOTSup 74 (Sheffield: JSOT Press, 1988), 186–206; Smith, "Zephaniah," 256; Liudger Sabottka, *Zephanja: Versuch einer Neuübersetzung mit philogischen Kommentar*,

In a second issue in this verse, the textual evidence divides over reading the expression as *you shall not fear* (many Hebrew versions, e.g., Leningrad Codex, Aleppo Codex; cf. TJ,[46] VULG.) or *you shall not see/experience* evil (2 medieval Hebrew manuscripts, LXX, Peshitta). Both readings likely posit the form תִּירְאִי as original but based on different verbal roots; the former reading supposes ירא ("to fear") while the latter reading likely supposes ראה ("to see"; e.g., ὄψῃ [LXX]) and finds support in Habakkuk 1:13 (i.e., the expression ראה רע ["see evil"]).[47] But note that Habakkuk's clause is grammatically different than Zephaniah 3:15 and uses the term עֵינַיִם; Zephaniah does not include any such visual vocabulary in his verse. Additionally, the LXX-posited understanding of תִּירְאִי occurs only once in the Hebrew OT (Isa. 60:5) according to the Masorah Parva,[48] and even that one occurrence is textually uncertain.

We argue that the "fear" reading of לֹא־תִירְאִי is original due to the following reasons. (1) It may be considered more grammatically difficult. Outside this verse, Hebrew does not pair "to not fear" and "evil" (רע), except for the idiom לא־ירא רע attested in Psalm 23:4

BibOr 25 (Rome: Pontifical Biblical Institute, 1972), 128. Note that TJ closes this verse with a longer, interpretive clause (i.e., "the Lord, *has promised to make his Shekinah dwell* in your midst" [Cathcart and Gordon, *Minor Prophets*, 173, italics original]) perhaps reflecting "doubts about the presence of the Shekinah in the Jerusalem temple, though the possibility of a future earthly manifestation might still be allowed" (ibid., 173n36).

[46] Scholars debate the TJ's evidence at this point. Some scholars interpret the expression as "you will not be alarmed at the sight of evil," arguing that the Aramaic combines and "compromises" (e.g., Smith, "Zephaniah," 256) the readings found in the MT ("be afraid") and in the LXX and Peshitta ("see"). Others note that the Targums here used *mn qdm* together with "be afraid," and this "standard" use (cf. v. 7) signals a genitive construction that should be translated as "no longer be afraid of evil" (Cathcart and Gordon, *Minor Prophets*, 173n37). The *verb* "to see" does not occur in TJ, so we classify TJ's witness with the MT.

[47] Ben Zvi, *Zephaniah*, 244 (cf. Gen. 44:34; Num. 11:15; Esth. 8:6; Ps. 90:15; Prov. 22:3; 27:12; Isa. 33:15).

[48] Ibid.

(cf. Ps. 49:6; Prov. 14:16).[49] לא־תיראי elsewhere takes a personal object (Isa. 54:14) or occurs as a stand-alone expression (Isa. 57:11; cf. אַל־תִּירָא, Gen. 15:1; Isa. 7:4). (2) Many commentators note the one-letter, orthographic and limited aural difference between the roots ירא ("to fear") and ראה ("to see").[50] Scribes could easily have confused them, especially if their interpretations are complementary or in this context approximate "peace."[51] (3) The root ירא occurs in the prohibitive of the following verse. Some scholars claim that juxtaposed verses would not repeat the verb form תיראי with the same root (ירא),[52] but the evidence in this prophetic book challenges that interpretation. Zephaniah repeated verbal roots in successive lines as a standard literary feature (e.g., 1:2–3, 8–9; 2:1, 3).[53] Furthermore, the grammatical constructions of the two forms in 3:15–16 are not identical; verse 15 prefaced the verb with the negative לֹא, and verse 16 used אַל in addressing Zion/Jerusalem. In preferring the "fear" reading in 3:15, it is likely that the text develops this verbal idea in 3:15–16 by deploying similar negative expressions.[54]

Zephaniah 3:16

We comment on only two textual issues in this verse, both of which are minor. Most of the LXX's versions read the first verb as ἐρεῖ κύριος, but they seem to interpret the MT's יֵאָמֵר (see Mur88,

[49] Ibid.

[50] E.g., Adele Berlin, *Zephaniah*, AB (New York: Doubleday, 1994), 143; Sweeney, *Zephaniah*, 200.

[51] Ho, *Zephaniah*, 382n786; cf. Ball, *Rhetorical Study*, 182; Ben Zvi, *Zephaniah*, 244; Smith, "Zephaniah," 256.

[52] Donald Leigh Williams, "Zephaniah: A Re-interpretation" (PhD diss., Duke University, 1962), 281, as cited by Ball, *Rhetorical Study*, 182.

[53] Ball, *Rhetorical Study*, 182.

[54] See the chiasm in § 3.2.2. We argue, however, that 3:16 returns to 3:11's future day. For further internal evidence for reading ירא here, see Sabottka, *Zephanja*, 128; cf. Larry L. Walker, "Zephaniah," in *Daniel–Malachi*, ed. Tremper Longman III and David E. Garland, REBC (Grand Rapids: Zondervan, 2008), 695.

VULG., Peshitta, TJ).[55] We believe that the MT's reading best preserves the original, since the LXX is the only ancient version that reads a subject. Furthermore, a theological agenda or scribal error could readily explain the LXX's insertion of κύριος: it "may have taken the prefix י as an abreviation [sic] for יהוה."[56] In the MT's reading and Masoretic pointing, the niphal verb is likely passive, since the context does not explicitly state a subject.[57]

The expression אַל־תִּירָאִי is well-attested; the MT (cf. MUR88) includes it, and it stands behind other ancient witnesses (e.g., Peshitta, VULG., TJ). The LXX rendered it as θάρσει ("take courage"), but this does not necessarily reflect a different textual tradition. The LXX may simply have put "the negative Hebrew expression into a positive equivalent."[58] And the LXX sometimes translated אַל־תִּירָאִי as θάρσει (e.g., Gen. 35:17; 1 Kings 17:13), so its presence here is not unusual.

Summarizing the Textual Issues in Zephaniah 3:14–16

In 3:14, the external and internal evidence favors the addressees as read in the MT tradition (i.e., בַּת־צִיּוֹן and יִשְׂרָאֵל). As for 3:15, we argue that the nominal construct form מֶלֶךְ יִשְׂרָאֵל and

[55] 3:16 (MT) does not name a subject, but a lamed-prefixed noun (לִירוּשָׁלַם) follows the verb. Jerusalem most naturally functions as the verb's indirect object (cf. Berlin, *Zephaniah*, 141, 144, who reads the verse as two balanced lines of poetry). Ball (*Rhetorical Study*, 183) reads it as a vocative due to the *athnach* under תִּירָאִי.

[56] Ibid., following Gerleman, *Zephanja*, 61.

[57] The verb אמר occurs in the niphal form 19 times in the OT. It can always read as a passive, and often the literary context prohibits the active sense (e.g., Gen. 22:14, 32:29; Num. 23:23). Assuming the passive reading, Ben Zvi argues that it "not only projects the announcement into an undetermined future but also adds to the vagueness of the picture by using a passive verbal form that points to the identity of the addressee, Jerusalem, but leaves entirely undefined the identity of the future speaker or speakers" (*Zephaniah*, 245; cf. Berlin, *Zephaniah*, 143).

[58] Ball, *Rhetorical Study*, 183. The LXX translation is "ordinary" (Gerleman, *Zephanja*, 61).

the MT's "fear" reading of לֹא־תִּירְאִי are original. The textual issues in Zephaniah 3:16 are not major: the original speech verb was likely the niphal passive יֵאָמֵר, and the LXX's θάρσει does not challenge the well-attested verbal construction אַל־תִּירָאִי.

Comparing the OT Quotations in John 12:13 and 15

The Zephaniah Proposal asserts that the FG uses Zephaniah between two OT quotations in John 12 (Ps. 118[117]:25–26 and Zech. 9:9). Table 1 below compares those quotations.

John 12:13 Quoting Psalm 118(117):25–26

In John 12:13, the crowd shouts to Jesus ὡσαννά· εὐλογημένος ὁ ἐρχόμενος ἐν ὀνόματι κυρίου, words that informally quote Psalm 118(117):25–26. We find that exact expression only in Psalm 117:26 (LXX) and the Entry Narratives of all four Gospels (see NA28).[59] Most commentators identify John 12:13 as a quotation due to (1) a precise and unique correspondence of the six words εὐλογημένος ὁ ἐρχόμενος ἐν ὀνόματι κυρίου with Psalm 118(117):26, (2) a lack of textual issues in John's text here, and (3) the LXX corresponding to the MT (Ps. 118:25–26).[60] This may be the only time in the FG where John informally quotes the OT.[61]

The two most significant differences between the MT, LXX and NA28 here are the following: (1) The NT reads ὡσαννά, while

[59] Hans Hübner, *Vetus Testamentum in Novo*, vol. 1.2, *Evangelium secundum Iohannem* (Göttingen: Vandenhoek & Ruprecht, 2003), 438–39; Gleason L. Archer and Gregory Chirichingo, *Old Testament Quotations in the New Testament: A Complete Survey* (Chicago: Moody, 1983), 89. The exception to this is Matthew 23:39, which likely refers back to the entry (Matt. 21:9) and thus to the same OT reference (Ps. 118[117]:25–26).

[60] Archer and Chirichingo categorize John 12:13's quotation of Psalm 118:26 with an (A) rating (*Quotations*, 89) to signal that the MT and LXX in relation to John 12:13 are "virtually equivalent in meaning and therefore free from problems" (xi).

[61] See, e.g., Köstenberger, "John," 470.

Table 1: Textual Comparison of Psalm 118(117):25–26; Zechariah 9:9; John 12:13c and 15

BHQ	LXX, NETS	NA[28]
Ps. 118(117):25–26		John 12:13c
25 אָנָּא יְהוָה הוֹשִׁיעָה נָּא אָנָּא יְהוָה הַצְלִיחָה נָּא 26 בָּרוּךְ הַבָּא בְּשֵׁם יְהוָה בֵּרַכְנוּכֶם מִבֵּית יְהוָה	25 ὦ κύριε σῶσον δή ὦ κύριε εὐόδωσον δή 26 εὐλογημένος ὁ ἐρχόμενος ἐν ὀνόματι κυρίου εὐλογήκαμεν ὑμᾶς ἐξ οἴκου κυρίου	13c καὶ ἐκραύγαζον• ὡσαννά• εὐλογημένος ὁ ἐρχόμενος ἐν ὀνόματι κυρίου, [καὶ] ὁ βασιλεὺς τοῦ Ἰσραήλ.
25 Yahweh, please save! Yahweh, please give success! 26 Blessed is the one who comes in the name of Yahweh. We bless you from the house of Yahweh.	25 Ah Lord, do save! Ah Lord, do give success! 26 Blessed is the one who comes in the name of the Lord. We bless you from the house of the Lord.	13c and they cried out, "Hosanna; Blessed is the one who comes in the name of the Lord, that is, the king of Israel."

BHQ	LXX, NETS	NA[28]
Zech. 9:9		John 12:15
9 גִּילִי מְאֹד בַּת־צִיּוֹן הָרִיעִי בַּת יְרוּשָׁלַםִ הִנֵּה מַלְכֵּךְ יָבוֹא לָךְ צַדִּיק וְנוֹשָׁע הוּא עָנִי וְרֹכֵב עַל־חֲמוֹר וְעַל־עַיִר בֶּן־אֲתֹנוֹת	9 χαῖρε σφόδρα θύγατερ Σιων κήρυσσε θύγατερ Ιερουσαλημ ἰδοὺ ὁ βασιλεύς σου ἔρχεταί σοι δίκαιος καὶ σῴζων αὐτός πραΰς καὶ ἐπιβεβηκὼς ἐπὶ ὑποζύγιον καὶ πῶλον νέον	15 μὴ φοβοῦ, θυγάτηρ Σιών• ἰδοὺ ὁ βασιλεύς σου ἔρχεται, καθήμενος ἐπὶ πῶλον ὄνου.
9 Rejoice greatly, daughter of Zion! Shout, Daughter Jerusalem! Behold, your king comes to you, righteous and vindicated, humble and riding on a donkey, and/even on a colt, the foal of a donkey.	9 Rejoice greatly, O daughter Sion! Proclaim, O daughter Ierousalem! Behold, your king comes to you, just and salvific is he, meek and riding on a beast of burden and a young foal.	15 Do not fear, O daughter of Zion! Behold, your king comes, sitting on the colt of a donkey.
*Double underline indicates MT, LXX and NA[28] agreement; single underline, agreement between NA[28] and MT alone; and highlighted text, disagreement between MT and LXX.		

the LXX (Ps. 117:25) reads σῶσον δή. Since Psalm 118:25 (MT) includes the expression that linguistically approximates ὡσαννα (הוֹשִׁיעָה נָּא), scholars debate whether John used the Hebrew OT here.[62] And (2) John 12:13 continues with the following expression missing from the Psalm: [καὶ] ὁ βασιλεὺς τοῦ 'Ισραήλ.[63]

Some scholars conclude that these words were simply the invention of the crowd at the moment of the entry or a later editorial addition, and so we need not discern an OT source behind them.[64] However, we see warrant for investigating the OT for the expression "the king of Israel." The expression (1) immediately follows an established OT quotation (Ps. 118) in John and (2) occurs often in the OT, providing a ready bank of source possibilities that the crowd, narrator, and/or editor of the FG could have employed.[65] Below, we consider the Zephaniah Proposal for this expression.

John 12:15 Quoting Zechariah 9:9

In John 12:15, Zechariah 9:9 was introduced by a quotation formula (John 12:14) and so was formally quoted. Among the OT texts, only Zechariah 9:9 combines the unique elements in John 12:15b–d,[66] yet the differences between those two texts are noteworthy.

[62] Scholars debate whether the source version was Aramaic or Hebrew, and whether the words derive from the crowd, the OT, or John the narrator. For bibliography and discussion, see Brunson, *Psalm 118*, 203–14.

[63] Brunson persuasively argues that even though Psalm 118(117) does not anywhere include the word βασιλεύς/מֶלֶךְ, the psalm has royal associations. (1) The person leading the procession (Ps. 118:19–27) exercises the royal role as head of the nation defeating the enemies (Ps. 118:10–13), (2) the language of the psalm as a whole configures with the structure of a royal psalm, and (3) post-exilic evidence (e.g., rabbinic traditions and the Targums) associates the psalm with King David and the Festival of Tabernacles (ibid., 34–45).

[64] E.g., Morris, *John*, 521n48; Douglas J. Moo, *The Old Testament in the Gospel Passion Narratives* (Sheffield: Almond, 1983), 180. Moo ponders whether the expression is "stereotyped."

[65] Brunson, *Psalm 118*, 225–38.

[66] Archer and Chirichingo categorize John 12:15's quotation of Zechariah 9:9 with an (A) rating to signal that John 12:15b–c (incl. "daughter of Zion")

There are four main differences between John 12:15 and Zechariah 9:9. John (1) is much shorter, (2) reads καθήμενος ("sitting") instead of "riding," (3) describes the mount unlike any version we have of Zechariah 9:9 (πῶλον ὄνου), and (4) starkly contrasts Zechariah's "Rejoice!" (גִּילִי/χαῖρε)[67] with the words μὴ φοβοῦ ("Do not fear!").[68] Zechariah 9 does not have "Do not fear!" in either the MT or LXX.

Albert William Martin Jr. speculates that John casually changed the text of Zechariah 9:9a to μὴ φοβοῦ, and the change is not theologically significant.[69] This is possible but unlikely. Since John's text is not textually doubted at this point, we must consider the "change" from Zechariah 9:9 in John's own literary context. First, given the celebratory setting of the entry, John's choice of the negative imperative μὴ φοβοῦ rather than the expected positive imperative "Rejoice!" from Zechariah 9:9 suggests that something more is going on than simply incidental changes.[70] Second, John introduces

---

reasonably represents the MT and LXX, which are themselves in large agreement. They also argue that John's "καθήμενος (rather than LXX's ἐπιβεβηκώς) is an acceptable rendering for רֹכֵב 'riding,'" and Isaiah 35:4 supplied him with μὴ φοβοῦ (*Quotations*, 130–31; cf. M. J. J. Menken, *Old Testament Quotations in the Fourth Gospel: Studies in Textual Form*, CBET 15 [Kampen: Kok Pharos, 1996], 82–97).

[67] Menken, *Quotations*, 79–80; Menken, "The Quotations from Zech 9,9 in Mt 21,5 and in John 12,15," in *John and the Synoptics*, ed. A. Denaux, BETL 101 (Leuven: Leuven University Press, 1992), 575; cf. Bruce G. Schuchard, *Scripture within Scripture: The Interrelationship of Form and Function in the Explicit Old Testament Citations in the Gospel of John*, SBLDS 133 (Atlanta: Scholars Press, 1992), 72: "The precise form of John 12.15 is unlike any other extant form of this Old Testament passage either in the versions or elsewhere in Jewish or early Christian literature."

[68] *HALOT* suggests rendering ירא as, "to be afraid" (2:433). English versions prefer "do not be afraid" (e.g., CJB, NET, NIV, NJB, NLT) or the more archaic-sounding "fear not" (e.g., ESV, KJV, YLT).

[69] Albert William Martin Jr., *Interpretation of the Triumphal Entry in the Early Church* (Ann Arbor, MI: University Microfilms, 1971), 206.

[70] Schuchard, *Scripture*, 74–75; Edwin D. Freed, *Old Testament Quotations in the Gospel of John*, NovTSup 11 (Leiden: Brill, 1965), 78; Menken, *Quotations*,

John 12:15 with the same formula that he used to quote the OT in John 6:31 (καθώς ἐστιν γεγραμμένον) to make a significant theological point there (see John 6:32). John's departure from Zechariah's text is likely theologically pregnant.

Since John did not likely draw μὴ φοβοῦ from Zechariah 9:9, John's stark deviation from the Zechariah text leads us to consider the Zephaniah Proposal.

Assessing the Zephaniah Proposal (Zeph. 3:14–15 in John 12:13c and 15a)

Zephaniah's Volume in John 12

We argue that we should consider Zephaniah 3:14–15 a plausible source for the expressions in John 12:13c and 15a. An allusion to Zephaniah in John 12 is possible based on the OT's statistical evidence. Zephaniah 3 shares a unique combination of markers in John 12.

(1) John 12:13d's string "king of Israel" occurs in the same OT verse (מלך ישׂראל/ὁ βασιλεὺς τοῦ 'Ισραήλ, with or without articles) only two times when it bears an explicit identification with Yahweh (יהוה [MT]; κύριος [LXX]): Isaiah 44:6 and Zephaniah 3:15.[71] By contrast, the OT never directly identifies "the king of Israel" as "the coming one" as does John 12:13. Instead, the LXX string ὁ βασιλεὺς τοῦ 'Ισραήλ (with or without articles) and the MT string מלך ישׂראל occur in an OT verse with ἔρχομαι/בוא only to relate events (e.g., "king came") but not to establish the king's identity.[72] Furthermore, the clause βασιλεὺς (τοῦ) 'Ισραήλ

83–84; Brunson, *Psalm 118*, 234.

[71] Isaiah 43:15 and Psalm 89(88):19 come close but include pronominal suffixes, have different grammar than John 12:13's text, and do not use the full title "king of Israel." These significant differences render Psalm 89:19 and Isaiah 43:15 as unlikely parallels (and sources) to John 12. We do not insist on precisely matching verbal parallels, but a more precise match surely increases its likelihood as the source (see § 1.3.1).

[72] 1 Kings 20(21):43; 22:30; 2 Kings 14:13; 15:29; 2 Chron. 18:29; 25:23.

occurs in the LXX in a number of passages but never to designate Israel's messianic king.[73]

Scholars who argue in favor of Isaiah 44:6 as the source note that it is the only LXX text that reads identical to the two-article expression (ὁ βασιλεὺς τοῦ Ἰσραήλ) in John 12:13d, and they find μὴ φοβοῦ in the context (Isa. 44:2; cf. John 12:15).[74] But those are the only two "explicit connection[s]" shared by Isaiah 44:1–8 and John's entry,[75] and the position heavily depends on affirming textually doubted articles, the ὁ in John 12:13 and τοῦ in Isaiah

[73] Aside from Zephaniah 3:15 and Isaiah 44:6, they all refer to kings of the united kingdom, divided northern kingdom, or even the divided southern kingdom (see Jason S. DeRouchie, *Zephaniah*, ZECOT [Grand Rapids: Zondervan, forthcoming]; 1 Sam. 26:20; 2 Sam. 6:20; 1 Kings 15:17; 16:28; 21:4, 7, 11, 21, 40, 41, 43; 22:3, 4, 6, 8, 9, 10, 18, 26, 29, 30, 32, 33; 2 Kings 3:9, 10, 12, 13; 5:7, 8; 6:10, 21, 26, 30; 7:6, 14; 9:16, 21; 13:14; 14:9, 11, 13; 16:5; 21:3; 23:13; 24:13; 2 Chron. 16:1; 18:3, 5, 7, 8, 9, 17, 25, 28, 29, 31, 32, 34; 25:18, 21, 23; 28:6; Ezra 5:11; Neh. 13:26; Isa. 7:1; Hos. 10:15; Tob. [S] 1:5). If considering occurrences where the two nouns do not stand in construct/genitival relationship, then the field widens considerably to several texts referring to either a divine or human king (e.g., 1 Sam. 15:17; 2 Sam. 5:12; 12:7; 1 Kings 14:14; 2 Kings 9:3, 12; 1 Chron. 11:3; 14:2; 28:4). Richard Bauckham holds that the title is messianic based in part on messianically-interpreted, OT "king" passages (e.g., Pss. 2:6; 72:1; Jer. 23:5; Ezek. 37:24; Zech. 9:9; "Messianism according to the Gospel of John" in *Challenging Perspectives on the Gospel of John*, ed. John Lierman, WUNT, 2nd ser., 219 [Tübingen: Mohr Siebeck, 2006], 59), but none of those OT passages contain the full title "king of Israel." In addition, the full title designating a Davidic Messiah appears in a limited set of extra-canonical literature (i.e., Pss. Sol. 17:21, 32, 42; cf. Sib. Or. 5:108). Furthermore, John 12 does not mention Davidic kingship, which reduces the probability that John intends to mark the phrase in the Entry Narrative as *exclusively* having a Davidic (messianic) sense (for the OT title's divine sense, see Brunson, *Psalm 118*, 225–34; § 5.3.1).

[74] Schuchard, *Scripture*, 78; cf. Rudolf Bultmann, *The Gospel of John*, ed. R. W. N. Hoare and J. K. Riches, trans. G. R. Beasley-Murray (Philadelphia: Westminster, 1971), 418n4 (with Isa. 41:10 and possibly Zeph. 3:16); Charles Goodwin, "How Did John Treat His Sources?" *JBL* 73 (1954): 68.

[75] Adam Kubiś, *The Book of Zechariah in the Gospel of John*, *EBib* 64 (Pendé: Gabalda, 2012), 84. As for explicit verbal correspondences with this text and John, we could perhaps add the references to "Yahweh" (Isa. 44:2, 5, 6).

44:6 (LXX).[76] Zephaniah 3 remains at least as strong a candidate for John 12's expressions as Isaiah 44, especially if the literary context of Zephaniah 3 parallels the context of John 12 (see § 2.4.2).

Scholars have proposed a few other possible sources for the expression, most notably Isaiah 52:7's coming king (מָלַךְ אֱלֹהָיִךְ אֹמֵר לְצִיּוֹן [MT]; λέγων Σιων βασιλεύσει σου ὁ θεός [LXX]).[77] They plausibly argue that interest in Isaiah 52 dominates the latter part of John 12 which explicitly names the prophet and quotes from him at least twice (John 12:38–41). Daniel J. Brendsel recently traced Isaiah 52's textual progression, vocabulary and themes throughout John 12, the most notable link being Jesus's messianic claims and his Isaianic Servant-like suffering to death.[78]

[76] Menken, *Quotations*, 84n21.

[77] Brendsel, *Isaiah*, 174–81; Catrin H. Williams, "The Testimony of Isaiah and Johannine Christology," in *"As Those Who Are Taught": The Interpretation of Isaiah from the LXX to the SBL*, ed. C. Mathews McGinnis and P. K. Tull, SBLSymS 27 (Atlanta: Society of Biblical Literature, 2006), 119; Craig A. Evans, "Obduracy and the Lord's Servant: Some Observations on the Use of the Old Testament in the Fourth Gospel," in *Early Jewish and Christian Exegesis: Studies in Memory of William Hugh Brownlee*, ed. Craig A. Evans and William F. Stinespring, SPHS 10 (Atlanta: Scholars Press, 1987), 235–36. Hübner lists three possible sources (i.e., Isa. 44:6; 52:7; Zeph. 3:15) for John 12:13's "king of Israel" (*Vetus Testamentum*, 438–39). Brunson adds Isaiah 41:21 (*Psalm 118*, 236). But such additions require expanding the search to the verb form of "king" or equating "Jacob" with "Israel."

[78] Brendsel, *Isaiah*, 184n117. He also detects a structural progression shared between John 12:12–19 and Isaiah 52:8–10: the return of the king, joyful shouts at arrival, and the nations seeing God's salvation. This structural patterning may continue through John 12:20–36 (Isa. 52:13–15) and John 12:38 (Isa. 53:1) (180–81). For more on the use of Isaiah in John 12, see Evans, "Obduracy," 235–46; Williams, "Testimony," 107–24; Hamilton, "Influence of Isaiah," 139–62; Carson, *John*, 450; Carson, "John and the Johannine Epistles," in *It Is Written: Scripture Citing Scripture: Essays in Honor of Barnabas Lindars*, ed. D. A. Carson and H. G. M. Williamson (Cambridge: Cambridge University Press, 1988), 249. However, we consider the possibility that Zephaniah played some role, perhaps even complementary to Isaiah, in structuring John's entry, if Zephaniah shares a textual progression similar to Isaiah 52 and John 12 (see § 5.2.3.3).

Such observations lead Brendsel to conclude that Isaiah 52:7–12 serves as "the more likely influence in the entry scene,"[79] when compared to Zephaniah 3:14–16.

At the level of vocabulary, however, Isaiah 52:7 (LXX) renders "king" as a verb and does not include the full title "king of Israel." Furthermore, it does not explicitly associate the king with Yahweh, though those dots could be connected through the next verse (Isa. 52:8). By contrast, Zephaniah 3:15 contains the full title identified as Yahweh. Isaiah 52 may play a larger role in the structure and themes of John 12, and perhaps even in the entry. But this need not exclude the possibility that Zephaniah 3 provides vocabulary, structure, and themes for John 12.

Zephaniah 3 is one of a few texts that explicitly and compactly join John 12's three terms "Lord, king of Israel," so the Zephaniah Proposal for John 12:13c is at least possible.

(2) Edwin D. Freed notes, "The four words, 'fear not, daughter of Zion,' occur nowhere in the same context in the LXX. They do occur in the MT of Zeph 3:14–17."[80] Indeed, John 12:15a's command μὴ φοβοῦ occurs 32 times in the Protestant canon of the LXX, but none also include the address θύγατερ Σιων in the same verse to match the first two lines of John 12:15. Excluding times when μὴ φοβοῦ occurs in an LXX verse that has a textual dispute in the MT (i.e., Gen. 28:13; Prov. 7:1), the LXX always translated μὴ φοβοῦ from אל־תירא (MT). In the MT that expression occurs in 46 more verses to total 78 times in the OT.[81] אל־תירא בת ציון never occurs,

[79] Brendsel, *Isaiah*, 184n117, who devoted a chapter to examining John's entry (161–86).

[80] Freed, *Quotations*, 78.

[81] Μὴ φοβοῦ occurs 32 times in the LXX (Gen. 15:1; 21:17; 26:24; 28:13; 46:3; Deut. 31:6, 8; Judg. 4:18; 6:23; Ruth 3:11; 1 Sam. 4:20; 22:23; 23:17; 28:13; 2 Sam. 9:7; 2 Kings 6:16; 1 Chron. 22:13; 28:20; Ps. 48:17; Prov. 7:1; Isa. 7:4; 10:24; 41:10, 13; 43:1, 5; 44:2; 54:4; Jer. 26:28; Lam. 3:57; Dan. 10:12, 19), and the MT's parallel expression אל־תירא is found in all of those passages, plus 46 others (Gen. 35:17; 43:23; 50:19, 21; Ex. 14:13; 20:20; Num. 14:9; 21:34; Deut. 1:21; 3:2; 20:3; Josh. 8:1; 10:8, 25; 11:6; 1 Sam. 12:20;

but that negative imperative explicitly addresses צִיּוֹן twice: Isaiah 40:9 and Zephaniah 3:16.

Many scholars prefer understanding the source for John 12:15a to at least include Isaiah 40:9–11, which contains the expression אַל־תִּירָאִי (MT; μὴ φοβεῖσθε [LXX]).[82] They add other arguments. First, in the LXX, Isaiah 40:9–11 and Zechariah 9:9 share the following words which represent "an adequate translation of the Hebrew text": Σιών, Ἰερουσαλήμ, and ἰδοὺ introducing ἔρχεταί.[83] Second, the content is similar to John 12 since Isaiah 40:9 is "addressed to the one who brings good tidings to Zion."[84] Third, John applied Isaiah 40:11's imagery of the sheep-feeding shepherd for Jesus (John 10:1–18, 26–29; 11:52; 21:15–17) and applied Isaiah 40:3–5 to John the Baptist (John 1:23),[85] so the passage was available to the FG.

---

2 Sam. 13:28; 1 Kings 17:13; 2 Kings 1:15; 19:6; 25:24; 2 Chron. 20:15, 17; 32:7; Neh. 4:8; Job 5:22; Prov. 3:25; Isa. 35:4; 37:6; 40:9; 41:14; 51:7; Jer. 1:8; 10:5; 30:10; 40:9; 42:11; 46:27, 28; Ezek. 2:6; Joel 2:21, 22; Zeph. 3:16; Hag. 2:5; Zech. 8:13, 15).

[82] F. F. Bruce, *The New Testament Development of Old Testament Themes* (Grand Rapids: Eerdmans, 1968), 106–7; Robert G. Bratcher, ed., *Old Testament Quotations in the New Testament*, HT (London: United Bible Societies, 1967), 23; Hamilton, "Influence of Isaiah," 144–45 (with Isa. 35:4); Menken, *Quotations*, 84 (with Zeph. 3:16); D. Moody Smith, *Johannine Christianity: Essays on Its Setting, Sources, and Theology* (Columbia, SC: University of South Carolina Press, 1984), 103; G. Reim, *Studien zum Alttestamentlichen Hintergrund des Johannesevangeliums*, SNTSMS 22 (Cambridge: Cambridge University Press, 1974), 30 (conflated with Isa. 62:11); R. N. Longenecker, *Biblical Exegesis in the Apostolic Period*, 2nd ed. (Grand Rapids: Eerdmans; Vancouver: Regent College Publishing, 1999), 138; Barrett, *John*, 418; Carson, *John*, 433; Köstenberger, *John*, 371 (cf. Isa. 44:2; Zeph. 3:16); Bruce, *New Testament*, 106; Williams, "Testimony," 119. Brendsel sees (1) Isaiah 52–53 influencing John 12's structure and (2) John 12 reading Isaiah 52–53 as the climax to the promises which stretch back to Isaiah 40, so that (3) Isaiah 40:9 is possibly in John 12:15a (*Isaiah*, 185–86).

[83] Menken, *Quotations*, 84.

[84] Carson, *John*, 433; Köstenberger, *John*, 371; cf. Williams, "Testimony," 119.

[85] For the former connection, see Menken, *Quotations*, 84; Kubiś, *Zechariah*, 83; Schuchard, *Scripture*, 74. For John's use of Isaiah 40:3–5, see Brunson, *Psalm 118*, 235.

Fourth, Isaiah 40:1–11 was important for the early church, evident by how often the NT quoted and alluded to it.[86]

Isaiah 40:9–11 presents a good case as a source behind John 12:15a. But there are two main issues with adopting it as the unique source behind the expression. First, in Isaiah 40:9 (LXX) it is grammatically plural (μὴ φοβεῖσθε), but in John 12, the imperative is grammatically singular. If the FG used Isaiah 40 in an LXX version we access today, then he transformed the plural into a singular, which is a possible but significant adjustment.[87] Commentators propose other texts as John's source for the expression (e.g., Isa. 35:4;[88] Zech. 8:13, 15[89]), but this same critique of the plural-singular difference applies.[90] It should be noted, however, that similar to

[86] Menken, *Quotations*, 84. Also, NA[28] lists quotations and allusions to Isaiah 40 in the NT, and Kubiś adds a possible allusion to Isaiah 40:6–8 in John 1:14 (*Zechariah*, 83).

[87] Schuchard, *Scripture*, 74; Morris, *John*, 512n48.

[88] Archer and Chirichingo, *Quotations*, 131; Krister Stendahl, *The School of St. Matthew, and Its Use of the Old Testament*, ASNU 20 (Uppsala: Gleerup, 1954), 119–20 (with Isa. 40:9); NA[27] (with Isa. 40:9; Zeph. 3:14); Hübner, *Vetus Testamentum*, 438–43 (with Isa. 40:9–10; Zeph. 3:14–15); Hamilton, "Influence of Isaiah," 144–45 (with Isa. 40:9).

[89] Kubiś proposed that John 12:15 borrowed μὴ φοβοῦ from the literary context of Zechariah 9, without denying that John also referenced other "do not fear" passages. He noted the "do not fear" expressions in Zechariah 8:13, 15 (אַל־תִּירָאוּ [MT]; θαρσεῖτε [LXX]) and provided evidence that Zechariah 8 and 9 embody similar vocabulary and themes which could have led a NT author to read them together. In both chapters: (1) God or his appointed king comes to deliver salvation which leads the people to not fear, (2) Jerusalem is addressed, (3) both Judah and Jerusalem experience salvation (Zech. 8:13; 9:10), and (4) the similar theme of "universal peace (8:12–13 and 9:10; cf. 8:16.19)," occurs. After noting the connections between Zechariah 8–9, and the similar texts in Isaiah and Zephaniah, Kubiś concludes, "Zec 8 can be understood as belonging to the same 'fear not!' proclamations as the texts taken from Dtr-Is [41:8–13, 14–16; 43:1b–4; 43:5–7; 44:2b–5] and Zep. It might then be argued that the author of the FG, by the use of μὴ φοβοῦ, referred to all of these passages at once" (*Zechariah*, 85–86). A textual fusion is indeed possible, and we argue that at least Zephaniah 3 should be included in this set.

[90] Some argue that Isaiah 35:4 additionally has poor thematic correspondence

Isaiah 40:9, Zephaniah 3:16's verb in the LXX does not match John 12:15a, but neither text's MT rendering causes any such problems. In a second issue with proposing Isaiah 40 as the sole source for John, Isaiah 40 only addresses "Zion" and not "daughter of Zion."[91] This same critique applies to other proposed sources, where the OT text does not address (daughter of) Zion at all (e.g., Isa. 41:10;[92] Zech. 8:13, 15[93]). Zephaniah 3:14 does explicitly include the full address θυγάτηρ Σιών/בַּת־צִיּוֹן, so in this way, Zephaniah 3 makes up for what Isaiah 40 lacks in relation to John 12. John 12:15a may allude to both Isaiah 40 and Zephaniah 3 in textual fusion, as some conclude.[94]

---

with John 12. Archer and Chirichingo probably overstate the case when they indicate that the only correspondence with John 12:15 and Isaiah 35:4 is the expression "Do not fear" (*Old Testament Quotations*, 131), since they neglect to note its expression "behold God comes" (הִנֵּה אֱלֹהֵיכֶם יָבוֹא/ἰδοὺ ὁ θεὸς ἥξει). In context, Isaiah 35:6 also includes the exodus motif of water streaming into the desert, which could have provided a parallel for Jesus as the living water in John 7:37–38 (Brunson, *Psalm 118*, 235). But the water imagery is not relevant to Jesus's entry in John 12.

[91] See Freed, *Quotations*, 78.

[92] Some scholars mention but do not often defend Isaiah 41:10 as a possible source for John 12:15: Bultmann, *John*, 418n4 (with Isa. 44:2 and Zeph. 3:16 [possible]); Menken, *Quotations*, 83 (in a list of other OT occurrences of μὴ φοβοῦ); cf. Kubiś, *Zechariah*, 85–86. For a critique of this proposal, see Brunson, *Psalm 118*, 235.

[93] See Kubiś, *Zechariah*, 85–86. Without denying the Zephaniah Proposal, he posits that Zechariah 8:13, 15 supply the expression to John and labels five Isaianic occurrences of "do not fear" (Isa. 41:8–13, 14–16; 43:1b–4; 43:5–7; 44:2b–5), "war oracles" that may have influenced John to change Zechariah 9:9a to μὴ φοβοῦ (84–85). Terry Collins similarly discerns OT "do not fear" proclamations ("The Literary Contexts of Zechariah 9:9," in *The Book of Zechariah and Its Influence*, ed. C. Tuckett [Burlington, VT: Ashgate, 2003], 35–37).

[94] Menken, for example, argues that a decision between Isaiah 40:9 and Zephaniah 3:16 is impossible and unnecessary (*Quotations*, 84). According to Carson, "It is not uncommon for New Testament quotations from the Old Testament to derive from two or more passages" (*John*, 433; cf. Matt. 27:9–10; Mark 1:2–3). Some of John's formal quotations do not match any single OT source but may depend on a textual combination: John 6:31 (Ps. 78[77]:24;

To clarify, Zephaniah 3:15 uses the similar expression לֹא־תִירְאִי without specifying the addressee, yet in these verses only two named addressees match the verb's FS form, one of which is 3:14a's בַּת־צִיּוֹן. 3:14a exhorts her, and 3:14d similarly exhorts בַּת יְרוּשָׁלָםִ. Now, since Jerusalem and Zion often occur in synonymous parallelism for poetic effect,[95] perhaps we need not choose between them as the addressee even in 3:15. Also, Zephaniah 3:16's אַל־תִּירָאִי ostensibly addresses צִיּוֹן, paralleling the only other "Zion" occurrence: 3:14a's בַּת־צִיּוֹן.

Zechariah 9:9 includes the address "daughter of Zion," so requiring this address in John 12:15a's OT source may be unnecessary: the occurrence in John likely comes from Zechariah 9:9 and not the other OT source(s).[96] Zechariah 9:9 may indeed supply John 12:15's addressee, but since Zephaniah 3:14–16 matches John's imperative (μὴ φοβοῦ; cf. אל־תירא/לא־תירא) *and* addressee—a rare combination—this surely increases its likelihood as a source for John 12.

Ex. 16:4?); 19:36 (Ex. 12:46; Num. 9:12; Ps. 34:20?); and 7:38 (Cf. Menken, *Quotations*, 47–65, 147–66, 187–203; Schuchard, *Scripture*, 33–57). Brendsel judges that "an awareness of John's practice of fusing biblical texts may prove fruitful for exegesis" (*Isaiah*, 218; cf. ibid., 67–134, where he explores John 12:37–43's use of Isaiah 6. The expression above ["textual fusion"] draws on his label of the same phenomenon, "interpretive fusion" [183]). Some scholars favor an allusion to several "do not fear" passages (incl. Zeph. 3:14–16; see O. Palmer Robertson, *The Books of Nahum, Habakkuk, and Zephaniah*, NICOT (Grand Rapids: Eerdmans, 1990), 338; M. Theobald, *Das Evangelium nach Johannes: Kapitel 1–12*, RNT [Regensburg: Friedrich Pustet, 2009], 789; cf. Kubiś, *Zechariah*, 82–86).

[95] "Daughter of Zion" and "daughter of Jerusalem" occur in synonymous parallelism in poetic or prophetic texts (e.g., 2 Kings 19:21; Isa. 37:22; Lam. 2:13; Mic. 4:8; Zech. 8:3; 9:9; cf. Pss. 51:20; 147:12; Isa. 4:4; 10:32; 33:20; 40:9; 52:1, 2; 62:1; 64:9; Jer. 51:35; Lam. 2:10), and other texts identify Jerusalem as Zion (e.g., 2 Chron. 5:2), so a hard distinction between them may be superfluous. Indeed, "Jerusalem" parallels "Zion" in Zephaniah 3:16.

[96] Hamilton, "Influence of Isaiah," 145n15. בַּת־צִיּוֹן occurs in the MT 26 times, uniquely "in texts which are prophetic and/or poetic" (Johannes Vlaardingerbroek, *Zephaniah*, HCOT [Leuven: Peeters, 1999], 208).

(3) In combining the data sets from point one and two, we note that Zephaniah 3:14–16 (MT) is the only OT text that includes *both* combinations of phrases in John 12:13d and 15a:[97]

- The title "king of Israel" linked to "Yahweh" (i.e., coming in the name of the *Lord*), and
- The command "Do not fear!" addressed to "daughter of Zion."

Each exact combination is rare enough. And given such a uniquely shared set of terms, many find warrant for arguing that Zephaniah 3 at least partly stands behind John 12:13c and 15a.[98]

Zephaniah's Thematic Coherence with John 12

The second argument for concluding that John 12 alluded to Zephaniah 3 is that Zephanian themes seem present in John's narrative. These observations depend on exegetical decisions in Zephaniah and John 12, and related texts. Since the rest of this book examines such connections, we here only outline the main considerations.

Zephaniah 3:14–17 shares several points of overlap with Zechariah 9:9 (quoted in John 12:15), in both thematic content and textual form. The LXX of both texts begins identically with the following seven words: χαῖρε σφόδρα θύγατερ Σιων κήρυσσε θύγατερ Ιερουσαλημ. No other LXX text includes even the expression χαῖρε σφόδρα, so this makes the unique, seven-word verbal correspondence between Zephaniah and Zechariah even more

[97] P. C. Mateos, "Uso e interpretación de Zacarías 9,9–10 en el Nuevo Testamento," *EstAg* 8 (1973): 4; cf. Brunson, *Psalm 118*, 236; Menken, *Quotations*, 84; Ruth Sheridan, *Retelling Scripture: 'The Jews' and the Scriptural Citations in John 1:19–12:15*, BIS 110 (Leiden: Brill, 2012), 227–28. We posit that Zephaniah 3:14–15 (excl. v. 16) supplies these sets to John 12:13–15 (see § 3.2).

[98] For a list of scholars following the Zephaniah Proposal (or at least considering the proposal viable), see § 1.2.1.7. Of note, NA[28] lists a direct quotation of Zephaniah 3:15 (LXX) in John 12:13d and an allusion to Zephaniah 3:14–16 (with Isa. 35:4; 40:9) in John 12:15a.

remarkable (esp. if σφόδρα is read).[99] Those two texts exhibit fewer, unique points of verbal correspondence in the MT. Yet, (1) Zephaniah 3:14–17 (MT) makes the short list of texts that have the imperative summons to joy (רנן/רוע) addressed to בת ציון (Zech. 2:14[10]) and בת ירושלם (Zeph. 3:14; Zech. 9:9).[100] (2) "The emphasis of both texts is on the royal figure (Zep 3:15, מֶלֶךְ יִשְׂרָאֵל/βασιλεὺς Ισραηλ) who comes or stays in the midst of his people."[101] (3) Both explicitly refer to defeating enemies/peace (Zeph. 3:15; Zech. 9:9–10). (4) In Zephaniah 3:17 God brings about salvation (גִּבּוֹר יוֹשִׁיעַ/δυνατὸς σώσει) in terms "likewise reflected in Zec 9:9 by the use of the same lexemes (ישע/σῴζω)."[102]

(5) Furthermore, some scholars argue for a "textual dependence" between the final forms of Zechariah 9:9a–b and Zephaniah 3:14–17, as well as a few other OT texts (e.g., Isa. 12:6; Zech. 2:14[10]).[103]

[99] Kubiś, *Zechariah*, 82. The reading σφόδρα is textually uncertain in Zephaniah 3:14 (LXX; e.g., absent in Codices Vaticanus, Sinaiticus and Alexandrinus). Some explain its attestation among other manuscripts as "the result of the connection of analogous scriptural texts" (Menken, *Quotations*, 84n19), Zechariah 9:9 in particular (e.g., מְאֹד; see Kubiś, *Zechariah*, 41).

[100] Ben Zvi, *Zephaniah*, 239–40; Rex Mason, "The Use of Earlier Biblical Material in Zechariah 9–14: A Study in Inner Biblical Exegesis," in *Bringing Out the Treasure: Inner Biblical Allusion in Zechariah 9*–14, ed. Mark J. Boda and Michael H. Floyd, JSOTSup 370 (Sheffield: Sheffield Academic Press, 2003), 30–34, 42–45; Collins, "Zechariah 9:9," 35–37. Risto Nurmela includes Isaiah 12:6 in this list (*Prophets in Dialogue: Inner-Biblical Allusions in Zechariah 1–9 and 9–14* [Åbo: Åbo Akademi University Press, 1996], 57, 214–17), but there the addressee is only "Zion," not "daughter of Zion."

[101] Kubiś, *Zechariah*, 82; cf. Sheridan, *Retelling*, 227–38; Menken, *Quotations*, 84.

[102] Kubiś, *Zechariah*, 82; cf. Sheridan, *Retelling*, 227–38. Other scholars argue that Zephaniah 3:14–15 basically conforms to the genre "hymn of praise" (e.g., Ben Zvi, *Zephaniah*, 238–39).

[103] Nurmela argues that Zephaniah 3:14–17 depends on both Isaiah 12:6 and Zechariah 9:9 (*Prophets in Dialogue*, 217). Mason argues the other direction, that Zephaniah 3:14 and Zechariah 2:14 influenced Zechariah 9:9 ("Zechariah 9–14," 30–34, 42–45). The latter view is certainly more faithful to the historical time frame associated with each biblical prophet as the biblical text itself testifies. Richard L. Schultz surveys and critiques the methods

For our purposes, we need to neither establish a textual dependency nor determine the nature or direction of such a supposed dependency, in order to argue for a Johannine allusion to Zephaniah 3 in combination with a quotation from Zechariah 9:9. Whether or not a textual dependence exists between them, these two texts contain uniquely shared content in the LXX and share rare content in the MT, especially with the imperative summons for the daughter of Zion to rejoice.[104] John could easily have read Zephaniah 3:14–17 with the very similar Zechariah 9:9.

Turning to a comparison of Zephaniah 3:14–16 and John 12:9–19, we already noted the following expressions: "king of Israel," "Yahweh"/"lord," "do not fear," and "daughter of Zion." Beyond this shared vocabulary, we can outline the most salient themes to examine in this book.

1. While the text of Zephaniah does not use the verb ερχομαι/בוא to describe the activity of Israel's king, Zephaniah 3:15 and 17 describe him in the midst of Jerusalem similar to King Jesus nearing Jerusalem (John 12:12).[105] Both texts describe Israel's present or returning king.
2. Zephaniah refers to Yahweh's ingathering of the peoples he

commonly employed to discern verbal parallels and prophetic quotation (*The Search for Quotation: Verbal Parallels in the Prophets*, ed. David J. A. Clines and Philip R. Davies, JSOTSup 180 [Sheffield: Sheffield Academic Press, 1999], 62–114).

[104] Collins thinks that Zechariah 9:9–10 functions as part of the literary form "proclamations of the coming of the Lord" with a seven-part structure to the proclamation. The first and second parts are (1) the command "Rejoice" made (2) to the addressee "Daughter Zion, daughter Jerusalem," and in his text comparison, these are both included only in Zechariah 2:14(10); Zephaniah 3:14–15, and 16–17 ("Zechariah 9:9," 36). He identifies several texts that display this literary form (Isa. 30:27; 35:4; 40:9–11; 62:11; Zeph. 3:14–15, 16–17; Zech. 2:14[10]; 9:9).

[105] Barnabas Lindars, *The Gospel of John*, NCB (Grand Rapids: Eerdmans, 1972), 423–24; Kubiś, *Zechariah*, 82; Sheridan, *Retelling*, 227–38; Menken, *Quotations*, 84; Brown, *John*, 1:462–63; Robertson, *Zephaniah*, 337–38.

delivers (3:9–10, cf. 3:19–20), and John 12 signals a similar theme with the Greeks (e.g., 12:19–23).[106]

3. Zephaniah 3:15 details Yahweh's removal of enemies, and in John 12:31 Jesus moves to defeat Satan (cf. enemies who plotted Jesus's death [12:9–11, 17–19]).[107]
4. Zephaniah 3:12 describes a remnant taking refuge "in the name of Yahweh" (בְּשֵׁם יְהוָה/ἀπὸ τοῦ ὀνόματος κυρίου), while John 12:13 describes a crowd acclaiming Jesus as coming "in the name of the Lord" (ἐν ὀνόματι κυρίου).[108]
5. Zephaniah 3:11 refers to what will be said "on that day" (בַּיּוֹם הַהוּא; cf. Zeph. 3:16), and in John 12:7 Jesus foretells the "day" (ἡμέραν) of his burial.

The themes are ostensibly not unique to Zephaniah 3 but also occur in other OT texts, including Isaianic ones noted above. But if John 12:13c and 15a alludes to Zephaniah 3, then we would expect these two texts to demonstrate such congruent themes.

Zephaniah's Availability to John

At first glance, the criterion of availability may be the weakest link for the Zephaniah Proposal.[109] John does not explicitly quote or name the prophet, though he frequently quoted other prophets (e.g., Isaiah in John 1:23; 12:38, 39, 41). Despite John's relative silence on

[106] Sheridan focuses on Zephaniah's ingathering themes shared by John 12 (*Retelling*, 226–29), Brunson relates these ideas to the ingathering themes to the "new exodus" (*Psalm 118*, 378–86), and Brown expounds on a "universalistic," all-nations motif in John 12 (*John*, 1:462–63).

[107] Brunson, *Psalm 118*, 236.

[108] See Brown, *John*, 1:462–63; Robertson, *Zephaniah*, 337–38. The remnant in Zephaniah 3:13 are told that "none shall make them afraid (מַחֲרִיד/ὁ ἐκφοβῶν)." The vocabulary in the LXX here is similar to John 12:15a. Note, however, that in Zephaniah 3:12b the MT focuses on taking refuge (וְחָסוּ), but the LXX refers to revering (εὐλαβηθήσονται) the Lord's name.

[109] We consider the criteria of availability and recurrence together in this section (cf. § 1.3.1).

Zephaniah, we forward two arguments to claim that this short prophetic book was available.

First, John quoted to and/or alluded to the Book of the Twelve which includes Zephaniah. We find evidence that the Twelve were read during the NT era as *one literary unit of twelve prophetic compositions* (incl. Zeph.).[110] The Twelve's *individuality* is internally detectable since nine of the prophets begin with a superscription, placing each in a historical setting.[111] The chief evidence that these 12 individual prophets were considered a *unit* in the NT era comes from the book of Acts and Josephus. Acts quotes Amos 5:25–27 as what "is written in the book of the prophets" (7:42), Habakkuk 1:5 regarding "what the prophets said" (13:40), and Amos 9:11–12 as part of "the words of the prophets" (15:15). And Josephus counts thirteen prophetic books in his listing of Jewish holy books (*Ag. Ap.* 1.38–41), which at least indicates an awareness of these (twelve) books as a unit.[112] The literary unity of the Twelve is confirmed by (1) Sirach 49:10 (ca. 150 B.C.) with the phrase

[110] Though the placement varies somewhat among the lists, Zephaniah is included among the Twelve in every major listing of OT books (e.g., in the MT [Cairo Codex, Jerome's Latin Vulgate] and LXX traditions [Codices Vaticanus, Sinaiticus, Alexandrinus]). For evidence and discussion, see Sweeney, "Reading the Book of the Twelve Prophets," 26–31; Sweeney, "Twelve, Book of the," in *DOTP*, 788–806.

[111] Hos. 1:1; Joel 1:1; Amos 1:1; Obad. 1; Mic. 1:1; Nah. 1:1; Hab. 1:1; Zeph. 1:1; Mal. 1:1. See Aaron Schart, "Putting the Eschatological Visions of Zechariah in Their Place: Malachi as a Hermeneutical Guide for the Last Section of the Book of the Twelve," in *Bringing Out the Treasure: Inner Biblical Allusion in Zechariah 9–14*, ed. Mark J. Boda and Michael H. Floyd (Sheffield: Sheffield Academic Press, 2003), 333–34.

[112] M. J. J. Menken discusses the Acts evidence and Josephus's count ("The Minor Prophets in John's Gospel," in *The Minor Prophets in the New Testament*, ed. M. J. J. Menken and Steve Moyise, LNTS 377 [London: T&T Clark, 2009], 79); cf. Clay Alan Ham, "The Minor Prophets in Matthew's Gospel," in *The Minor Prophets in the New Testament*, ed. Maarten J. J. Menken and Steve Moyise, LNTS 377 (London, New York: T&T Clark, 2009), 39; Jason T. LeCureux, *The Thematic Unity of the Book of the Twelve*, HBM 41 (Sheffield: Sheffield Phoenix Press, 2012), 2–5.

τῶν δώδεκα προθητῶν, (2) Masoretes who marked the middle verse of the Twelve (Mic. 3:12) when their normal practice was to signal the middle of each biblical book, and (3) evidence from spacing practices in Qumran scrolls. Indeed, several modern scholars affirm the Twelve as a literary unit yet comprised of 12 writings (incl. Zephaniah).[113]

John formally quotes from the Book of the Twelve at least twice: Zechariah 9:9 in the Entry Narrative (John 12:15), and Zechariah 12:10 (John 19:37).[114] This evidence provides awareness of at least Zechariah, and given the quoted Zechariah 9:9 in our pericope, it would hardly be a surprise for John to use two similar passages from the Twelve alongside each other.

As for allusions in John, they are by nature more difficult to defend and establish. Our argument does not depend on defending particular Johannine allusions to other Minor Prophets. But scholars observe allusions to the Twelve in John (e.g., Zechariah, Jonah,

[113] For additional evidence and bibliography see Ham, "Minor Prophets," 39; Richard J. Coggins, "The Minor Prophets: One Book or Twelve?" in *Crossing the Boundaries: Essays in Biblical Interpretation in Honour of Michael D. Goulder*, ed. M. D. Goulder et al., BIS 8 (Leiden: Brill, 1994), 63–64; Paul R. House, *The Unity of the Twelve*, JSOTSup 97, BLS 27 (Sheffield: Sheffield Academic Press, 1990). Many notice unifying theme(s) in the Twelve (e.g., LeCureux, *Thematic Unity*, 2–5). The Twelve seem to be written together on one scroll at Qumran (4QXIIa–b) which dates to about 150 B.C. (Russell Fuller, "The Form and Formation of the Book of the Twelve," in *Forming Prophetic Literature: Essays on Isaiah and the Twelve in Honor of John D. W. Watts*, ed. James W. Watts and Paul R. House, JSOTSup 235 [Sheffield: Sheffield Academic Press, 1996], 86–101). But note Ehud Ben Zvi's arguments against affirming the literary collection of the Twelve at the expense of observing the particular contributions of each individual book ("Twelve Prophetic Books or 'The Twelve': A Few Preliminary Considerations" in *Forming Prophetic Literature: Essays on Isaiah and the Twelve in Honor of John D. W. Watts*, ed. James W. Watts and Paul R. House, JSOTSup 235 [Sheffield: Sheffield Academic Press, 1996], 125–56).

[114] Carson, *John*, 433, 627; Köstenberger, *Theology*, 306–9; Menken, "Minor Prophets," 79–80. Many list a third occurrence in John 7:38 (Zech. 14:8) (see, e.g., Kubiś, *Zechariah*, 18, 219–315).

Micah, Malachi), based on specific term(s)—not just theme(s)—uniquely shared by the FG and the OT text.[115]

Second, John 1:47 may contain an allusion to Zephaniah 3:13, a connection Menken has recently defended.[116] We briefly assess the arguments for this contested allusion.

Jesus labels Nathanael as "an Israelite indeed, in whom there is no deceit (δόλος)" (John 1:47). Many commentators understand John to allude to Jacob's deceit in getting Esau's birthright and blessing (Gen. 27:35–36; cf. 32:28–30), which requires equating the name "Jacob" in Genesis 27 with his name change "Israel" a few chapters later.[117] In a later part of Jesus's conversation with Nathanael (John 1:51), John likely makes reference to Jacob's ladder (Gen. 28:12), so an allusion to Genesis 27's Jacob in John 1:47 has added credibility.[118] Still other scholars read this as an allusion to the Suffering Servant (e.g., Isa. 53:9; cf. 44:3–7).[119]

Now, the LXX occasionally uses the word δόλος (and the related term δόλιος) positively to describe a good person without deceit, and this usage most often occurred in the Psalms (Pss. 15:3; 17:1; 23:4; 32:2; 34:14; 120:2; Isa. 53:9; Zeph. 3:13). Menken notes

[115] Menken discusses many allusions (Zech. 14:8 in John 7:38; Mal. 4:5 [3:23] in John 1:21; Zeph. 3:13 in John 1:47; Zech. 14:21 in John 2:16; Mal. 3:1 in John 3:28; Mic. 5:1 in John 7:42; Mal. 2:10 in John 8:41; Zech. 1:5 in John 8:52; Jonah 1:12–15 in John 11:50 and Zech. 13:7 in John 16:32) ("Minor Prophets," 80–96; cf. Köstenberger, *Theology*, 304–9; Köstenberger, "John," 418–20). For the FG's quotes and allusions to Zechariah, see Kubiś, *Zechariah*.

[116] Menken briefly argues for Zephaniah 3:13 as the chief OT allusion ("Minor Prophets," 92); cf. NA[28] (Zeph. 3:13 with Ps. 32:2). James Bruckner (*Jonah, Nahum, Habakkuk, Zephaniah*, NIVAC [Grand Rapids: Zondervan, 2004], 338) and Brown (*John*, 1:87) mention Zephaniah 3:13.

[117] Carson, *John*, 160–62; J. Ramsey Michaels, *The Gospel of John*, NICNT (Grand Rapids: Eerdmans, 2010), 129–30; Morris, *John*, 145–50; Barrett, *John*, 185; Köstenberger, *John*, 82; Brown, *John*, 87.

[118] Barrett, *John*, 185. For a defense of the use of Genesis 28 in John 1:51, see Morris, *John*, 149–50; Carson, *John*, 163–65; Köstenberger, *John*, 85–86.

[119] Brown discusses the Suffering Servant proposal but considers this reading "tenuous" (*John*, 1:87–88).

that Zephaniah 3:13 stands out as the only (i.e., "unique") OT text combining "no deceit" and "Israel": "a deceitful tongue [will not] be found in their [i.e., remnant Israel's] mouths."[120] In addition to this unique combination of terms, Menken sees an allusion to Zephaniah confirmed by the combination's thematic coherence in John 1: "Nathanael represents 'the remnant of Israel'; more generally, Jesus' disciples constitute the nucleus of the eschatological Israel, of which Jesus is king (see 1.31, 47; 12.13)."[121] Nathanael says that Jesus is "the king of Israel" (John 1:49), a title found in the FG only here and the entry narrative.[122] And that title is likewise found in Zephaniah (3:15),[123] adding justification for reading an allusion to Zephaniah in John 1:47.

Strong vocabulary connections between John 1:47 and Zephaniah 3:13 (LXX) register an allusion to Zephaniah as possible, despite the evidence from Genesis 27 and Isaiah 53. Even if one does not accept an allusion to Zephaniah 3 here, Zephaniah was likely available to the FG. It is included in the literarily unified Book of the Twelve, and the FG quoted Zechariah.

Conclusion: Validity of the Zephaniah Proposal

Our data analysis above demanded quotation-level verbal correspondence, yet we posit that John 12:13d and 15a do not quote Zephaniah. The "missing" expressions are too brief to be considered quotations but long enough to qualify as allusions: two to four

[120] Menken, "Minor Prophets," 92; cf. Kubiś, *Zechariah*, 103.

[121] Menken, "Minor Prophets," 92. We consider this interpretation of "Israel" to be unlikely from Nathanael's perspective, but John may still allude to Zephaniah here and then develop the remnant theme later in the FG (see § 5.2).

[122] Several scholars note this *inclusio* between John 1:49 and John 12:13 (e.g., Wayne A. Meeks, *The Prophet-King: Moses Traditions and the Johannine Christology*, NovTSup 14 [Leiden: Brill, 1967], 83; Margaret Daly-Denton, *David in the Fourth Gospel: The Johannine Reception of the Psalms*, AGJU 47 [Leiden: Brill, 2000], 178; Kubiś, *Zechariah*, 103).

[123] Sheridan, *Retelling*, 227; Köstenberger, *Theology*, 307 (note also the title "Son of God"; cf. Ps. 2:7; 2 Sam. 7:14).

words ([ὁ] βασιλεὺς [τοῦ] Ἰσραήλ) and two words (μὴ φοβοῦ). Also, many alternative proposals come from other texts, most notably Isaiah, and they too, along with Zephaniah 3, present verbal and thematic similarities with John 12:13d and/or 15a. But our position is that Zephaniah 3's *unique vocabulary combination* shared with John 12 presents the Zephaniah Proposal as a strong candidate for John's set of markers (i.e., allusions). We find Zephanian themes present in John 12 and argue that the Twelve was available to John (e.g., John 12 quotes Zech. 9:9). We thus consider the Zephaniah Proposal as viable.

Comparing the Texts of Zephaniah 3:14–16 and John 12:13c and 15

The three words מֶלֶךְ יִשְׂרָאֵל יְהוָה, and the expression לֹא־תִירְאִי addressed to בַּת־צִיּוֹן, all occur together in a span of two verses in the OT only in Zephaniah 3:14–15. Table 2 below compares Zephaniah 3:14–15 and 16 (MT and LXX) with John 12.

At least four observations stand out in this textual comparison. First, similar to the earliest manuscript witnesses of John 12:13d (ὁ βασιλεὺς τοῦ Ἰσραήλ), the MT of Zephaniah 3:15 has the corresponding words מֶלֶךְ יִשְׂרָאֵל as definite. Both nouns in that construct chain are definite since the governing head noun "Israel" is a proper noun.[124] By contrast, the LXX manuscripts that read the noun phrase, treat it as an anarthrous construction (βασιλεὺς Ισραηλ).

It is certainly possible that, since John's text included at least the genitive article and since the LXX of Zephaniah 3:15 had no articles, John accessed the MT rather than the LXX for the expression βασιλεὺς τοῦ Ἰσραήλ. But Ἰσραήλ is an indeclinable proper noun, and when a genitival relationship with another word was clearly intended, the LXX sometimes inserts the genitive article (e.g., Ex. 24:10; 2 Sam. 6:19) and other times did not (e.g., "sons [of] Israel"

[124] Garrett and DeRouchie, *Modern Grammar*, 74.

[Gen. 32:32]). The FG always included an article with 'Ισραήλ, but like the LXX, other NT writers treated the article as optional. Johannine preference may explain the article in John 12.[125]

Second, Zephaniah 3:15 (MT) includes the name יְהוָה which corresponds to the LXX's rendering κύριος. John 12:13 uses the same word found in Zephaniah 3:15 (κυρίου [LXX; see also Zeph. 3:12]), but John most directly draws that word from the OT quotation (Ps. 118).[126]

Third, the LXX does not render either occurrence of negative + תיראי in Zephaniah 3 as μὴ φοβοῦ (cf. John 12:15). Instead, most LXX manuscripts use a future verb form of "to see" (i.e., ὄψῃ) in 3:15, which may interpret the MT as promising that Israel will not experience any evil. And in Zephaniah 3:16 the LXX chose the imperative form of "to take courage!" (θάρσει). This leads some scholars to conclude that if John 12 used Zephaniah 3, he referenced the MT.[127] But others speculate that John could have referenced the Old Greek form θάρσει and negativized it into μὴ φοβοῦ, due to at least three observations.[128] (1) Whenever the LXX reads μὴ φοβοῦ, the MT almost always reads אַל־תִּירָא or אַל־תִּירְאִי.[129] But the LXX also translates the Hebrew expression as θαρσέω, indicating that

[125] The FG uses the article in all four occurrences of the word 'Ισραήλ (1:31, 49; 3:10; 12:13), but other NT writers sometimes included the article (Matt. 2:20; Acts 28:20) and other times did not (Matt. 15:24; Acts 2:36; 7:23). Of course, an allusion need not slavishly follow the grammar of the alluding source.

[126] See § 2.3.1. John 12 seems to identify the one coming in the name of the Lord as the king of Israel, so Zephaniah may provide a bridge to the Psalm 118 quote.

[127] Menken, *Quotations*, 84; Brown, *John*, 1:458.

[128] See Freed, *Quotations*, 78–80; Kubiś, *Zechariah*, 82–83.

[129] Gen. 15:1; 21:17; 26:24; 46:3; Judg. 4:18; 6:23; Ruth 3:11; 1 Sam. 4:20; 22:23; 23:17; 28:13; 2 Sam. 9:7; 2 Kings 6:16; 1 Chron. 22:13; 28:20; Ps. 48:17; Isa. 7:4; 10:24; 41:10, 13; 43:1, 5; 44:2; 54:4; Jer. 26:28; Lam. 3:57; Dan. 10:12, 19. The exceptions are two occurrences where the Hebrew text is uncertain (Gen. 28:13; Prov. 7:1) and the two Deuteronomy occurrences (Deut. 31:6 [אַל־תִּירְאוּ], 8 [לֹא תִירָא]).

Table 2: Textual Comparison of Zephaniah 3:14–16 and John 12:13c–d and 15

BHQ	LXX, (NETS)	NA28
Zeph. 3:14–16		John 12:13c, 15
14 רָנִּי בַּת־צִיּוֹן	14 χαῖρε σφόδρα θύγατερ Σιων	13c ἐκραύγαζον• ὡσαννά•
הָרִיעוּ יִשְׂרָאֵל	κήρυσσε θύγατερ Ιερουσαλημ	
שִׂמְחִי וְעָלְזִי בְּכָל־לֵב	εὐφραίνου καὶ κατατέρπου	
בַּת יְרוּשָׁלָםִ	ἐξ ὅλης τῆς καρδίας σου	
	θύγατερ Ιερουσαλημ	
15 הֵסִיר יְהוָה מִשְׁפָּטַיִךְ	15 περιεῖλεν κύριος τὰ ἀδικήματά σου	εὐλογημένος ὁ ἐρχόμενος
פִּנָּה אֹיְבֵךְ	λελύτρωταί σε ἐκ χειρὸς ἐχθρῶν σου	ἐν ὀνόματι κυρίου,
מֶלֶךְ יִשְׂרָאֵל יְהוָה בְּקִרְבֵּךְ	βασιλεὺς Ισραηλ κύριος ἐν μέσῳ σου	[καὶ] ὁ βασιλεὺς τοῦ Ἰσραήλ.
לֹא־תִירְאִי רָע עוֹד	οὐκ ὄψῃ κακὰ οὐκέτι	15 μὴ φοβοῦ, θυγάτηρ Σιών•
		ἰδοὺ ὁ βασιλεύς σου
16 הַהוּא יֵאָמֵר בַּיּוֹם	16 ἐν τῷ καιρῷ ἐκείνῳ ἐρεῖ κύριος	ἔρχεται,
לִירוּשָׁלַםִ אַל־תִּירָאִי צִיּוֹן	τῇ Ιερουσαλημ θάρσει Σιων	καθήμενος ἐπὶ πῶλον ὄνου.
אַל־יִרְפּוּ יָדָיִךְ	μὴ παρείσθωσαν αἱ χεῖρές σου	

BHQ	LXX, (NETS)	NA[28]
Zeph. 3:14–16		John 12:13c, 15
14 Shout for joy, daughter of Zion! Shout, Israel! Rejoice and exult with all your heart, daughter of Jerusalem! 15 The Lord has taken away your judgments; he has turned back your enemy. The king of Israel, Yahweh, is in your midst; you may not fear evil any longer. 16 On that day it will be said to Jerusalem, "Do not fear, Zion; do not let your hands go limp."	14 Rejoice, O daughter Sion! Proclaim, O daughter Ierousalem! Be glad, and be delighted with your whole heart, O daughter Ierousalem! 15 The Lord has taken away your injustices; he has redeemed you from the hand of your enemies. The king of Israel, the Lord, is in your midst; you shall see disaster no more. 16 At that time the Lord will say to Ierousalem, "Courage, O Sion; do not let your hands grow weak."	13c and they cried out, "Hosanna; Blessed is the one who comes in the name of the Lord, [that is,] the king of Israel." 15 Do not fear, daughter of Zion! Behold, your king comes, sitting on the colt of a donkey.
*Double underline indicates MT, LXX and NA[28] agreement; single underline, agreement between NA[28] and MT alone; and highlighted text, disagreement between MT and LXX.		

θαρσέω and a negated φοβέω significantly overlap in meaning in classical Greek.[130] (2) Based on how often John uses the verbs, he has a slight preference for the negated φοβέω (6:20; 12:15; cf. 6:19, 20, 22; 12:15; 19:8) over θαρσέω (16:33; cf. φόβος in 7:13; 19:38; 20:19). (3) Some OT texts juxtapose joy and lack of fear (e.g., Joel 2:21; cf. Zeph. 3:14–16), so this may "suggest the interchangeability of the phrases and hence the possibility of their mutual replacement."[131]

If John used the LXX of Zephaniah 3:16 (i.e., θάρσει), he could have transformed it to the negative expression μὴ φοβοῦ, which matches the MT (אַל־תִּירָאִי). But if he did reference the LXX and re-transform it into a negative, he likely drew only from Zephaniah 3:16, since it would be difficult to arrive at μὴ φοβοῦ solely based on Zephaniah 3:15's ὄψῃ. Alternatively, if John referenced the MT, he could have translated μὴ φοβοῦ from Zephaniah 3:15 or 16; both exhibit the negativized "fear" verb. Verse 15 is in Zephaniah's peak (see § 3.2.3), but a verdict on John's OT version must remain tentative. He may have referenced either (or both) the MT or the LXX, or some version thereof.

Fourth, we argued above that the nominative form θυγάτηρ best represents John 12:15a's original text, whereas Zephaniah 3:14 (LXX) has the vocative θύγατερ, and Hebrew does not mark nouns morphologically. This does not cause an interpretive dilemma for the following two reasons. (1) John probably draws the addressee most directly from his Zechariah 9:9 quotation, yet both Zechariah and Zephaniah have the same spellings for this word in their LXX and MT renderings. (2) James Hamilton correctly notes that John may have referenced a different version: "Since John could be quoting from Hebrew, from a Targum, or from another Greek text [perhaps his own translation], this difficulty [vocative θύγατερ in OT sources;

[130] Kubiś, *Zechariah*, 82–83 (cf. Gen. 35:17; Ex. 14:13; 20:20; 1 Kings 17:13; Zech. 8:13, 15).

[131] Ibid., 82. But Zephaniah's argument does not replace joy with fearlessness (see § 3.3.5).

nominative form in John 12:15] is by no means insuperable."[132] This form does not cause OT in the NT issues.

In summary, the phrase following John 12's Psalm 118 quotation ("king of Israel") and the phrase missing from the Zechariah 9:9 quotation ("do not fear") are adequately found in Zephaniah 3:14–15. But that is not all. Zephaniah 3:14–15 identify the king as the Lord (i.e., Yahweh), and in John 12:13 King Jesus comes in the name of the Lord. Also, Zephaniah 3 exhorts the "daughter of Zion," as does Zechariah 9:9/John 12:15. If John used a Hebrew text comparable to the MT of Zephaniah 3:14–15 (or v. 16), John's allusions closely correspond with Zephaniah. On the other hand, John may have referenced Zephaniah 3:16 in the LXX and transformed it, or accessed a different *Vorlage* than we have today.

Conclusion

John's entry (12:9–19) quotes the OT twice in order to affirm the kingship of Jesus (Ps. 118:25–26) as he sat on a donkey in accordance with Scripture (Zech. 9:9). Sandwiched between these two OT quotations, we conclude that John plausibly alluded to Zephaniah 3:14–15 with both brief expressions βασιλεὺς τοῦ Ἰσραήλ and μὴ φοβοῦ, but we leave open the possibility of a textual fusion with a select few OT texts in both places. The OT quotations are closely related textually to Zephaniah 3, so John renders the linkage between them intelligible. When textually compared, John 12 and Zephaniah 3 exhibit uniquely shared expressions and do not have insurmountable textual issues to restrict the FG's appropriation of Zephaniah 3.

[132] Hamilton, "Influence of Isaiah," 145n15. He speculates whether John 12:15 "conflates" Zechariah 9:9's "daughter of Zion" and the coming King, with Isaiah 35:4 and 40:9, "where God comes as King, as part of his presentation of Jesus as God (cf. Jn 1:1, 18; 20:28; and 18:5)."

3

Literary and Thematic Context of Zephaniah 3:14–15

Similar to our methodology in chapter 2 for John 12, in this chapter on Zephaniah 3, we first examine the broad context before narrowly focusing on the immediate context of the Zephaniah Proposal (3:14–15). This includes discerning Zephaniah's audience, purpose, text type, and argument before exegeting 3:14–15 and their role in 3:8–20.[1]

Zephaniah Introduction

Zephaniah and His Original Audience

In the main ancient versions available, Zephaniah is the ninth book in the Twelve.[2] Like other prophetic addresses Zephaniah

[1] Chapter 3 distinctly benefits from extended personal correspondence with Jason S. DeRouchie. For example, he reads 2:1–3 and 3:8 as Zephaniah's main exhortations, concludes 3:14–15 is a parenthetical outburst of joy, and finds that parallel sections of בַּיּוֹם הַהוּא (3:11–13, 16–20) provide structure to 3:8–20 (*Zephaniah*, ZECOT [Grand Rapids: Zondervan, forthcoming]).

[2] Marvin A. Sweeney noted that in ancient versions (see the MT, LXX, MUR88, TJ, Peshitta, VULG., and likely also Naḥal Ḥever) Zephaniah consistently follows Habakkuk and precedes Haggai as the ninth book in the Minor Prophets. Thus, despite different sequencing among these traditions, Zephaniah seems to play a similar role in each of them. Read after Habakkuk's description of Neo-Babylon's domination over Judah (seventh century B.C.; cf. Hab. 3:16) and before Haggai's exhortation to rebuild the temple (i.e., early Persian era), Zephaniah is the historical-canonical hinge between "Babylonian

reports Yahweh's word, given in the days of King Josiah of Judah (Zeph. 1:1). The audience is thus Judah: the "shameless nation" (ESV), "the remnant of the house of Judah" (2:7), the "humble of the land" (2:3), and its capital city Jerusalem (1:4, 12; 3:14, 16). Zephaniah addresses Judah's inhabitants with his chief imperatives (2:1–3; 3:8, 14),[3] includes them in judgment, calls them to rejoice and motivates them to do so.[4] Yet, the book condemns nations (cf. "Cush," 2:12) and gives them glimmers of hope in chapters 2–3, so they may be an important, secondary audience.

Dating Zephaniah's Prophetic Activity and Written Composition

Scholars debate the date for Zephaniah's proclamation(s). But the book's superscription (1:1), the most direct statement about its date, declares that Zephaniah carried out his prophetic ministry to

---

destruction" and sixth century Judean "exile" (*Zephaniah: A Commentary*, ed. Paul D. Hanson, Hermeneia [Minneapolis: Fortress, 2003], 1–2; cf. James Nogalski, *Literary Precursors to the Book of the Twelve*, BZAW 217 [Berlin: de Gruyter, 1993], 198–200).

[3] The plural imperatives suggest "the prophets were actually appealing to the individual members of the nation and not to the corporate entity itself" (Jason S. DeRouchie, "Who Should Seek the Lord Together? Identifying the Addressees in Zephaniah 2:1, 3," forthcoming). Also, Zephaniah does not seem to exclude Judah's sinful leaders from judgment (1:8–13; 3:1–4; Willem A. VanGemeren, *Interpreting the Prophetic Word: An Introduction to the Prophetic Literature of the Old Testament* [Grand Rapids: Zondervan, 1990], 176). VanGemeren observes that Zephaniah "spoke to the people in the second person, and his oracles of judgment against the leaders are in the form of indirect speech" (473n64). The הוֹי-oracle in 3:1–4 may appear at first to address Nineveh, but verses 3–4 show that the woe targets Jerusalem, by using these terms: city of leaders, judges, prophets, and priests that violate the torah (חָמְסוּ תּוֹרָה; cf. 1:4–12).

[4] Zephaniah may indeed be "a brief exemplar of prophetic rhetoric" (Barry A. Jones, "Zephaniah, Book of," in *NIDB*, 5:977). Jones lists Zephaniah's "unique expressions" as 1:12; 1:15–16; and 3:17 (see discussion in Richard J. Coggins and Jin H. Han, *Six Minor Prophets through the Centuries: Nahum, Habakkuk, Zephaniah, Haggai, Zechariah, and Malachi*, BBC [Malden, MA: Wiley-Blackwell, 2011], 95; Sweeney, *Zephaniah*, 1).

Judah during King Josiah's reign (640–609 B.C.).[5] Josiah undertook a massive reform movement wherein he destroyed pagan idolatry and returned Judah to Yahweh-worship (2 Kings 23:19). The lost book of Deuteronomy was "found" (2 Kings 22:9; 2 Chron. 30), Josiah sought Yahweh in his 8th year (632 B.C.), and he carried out campaigns of idolatry destruction in his 12th (628 B.C.) and 18th years (622 B.C.) (2 Kings 22:3; 2 Chron. 34:3, 8).[6]

Though Zephaniah most likely prophesied sometime during King Josiah's reign, either before or after the reforms, most date the final composition of some or all of Zephaniah 3:14–20 to the exilic or post-exilic period. For many, this section includes features and terms that reflect a late outlook: the vision of universal restoration, the call for the remnant to rejoice at their return following judgment, and the reassurance of salvation.[7]

[5] See Nogalski's overview (*Literary Precursors*, 178–80). Zephaniah's genealogy in the superscription (1:1) outlines four generations, the longest of any prophet. It may include the reformer, King Hezekiah of Judah, perhaps to forge "a natural as well as theological tie to the piety of previous generations to which Zephaniah was calling for a return" (David W. Baker, "Zephaniah: Theology of," in *NIDOTTE*, 4:1309; cf. John S. Kselman, "Zephaniah: Book of," *ABD*, 6:1077). Mark J. Boda argues for Zephaniah's "royal descent" ("Zephaniah, Book of," in *DOTP*, 899–901). Gene Rice proposes that he had African ancestors (i.e., בֶּן־כּוּשִׁי, 1:1; "The African Roots of the Prophet Zephaniah," *JRT* 36 [1979]: 21–31). In the OT, the name Zephaniah sometimes refers to a priest (Jer. 21:1; 29:25), but elsewhere to other personages (e.g., Zech. 6:10, 14). Zephaniah includes what some consider priestly vocabulary (e.g., 1:4–5, 7–9; 3:4, 18), but this does not definitively show the author was a priest.

[6] For the reckoning of these dates, see Sweeney, *Zephaniah*, 15–16; cf. Jack Finegan, *Handbook of Biblical Chronology: Principles of Time Reckoning in the Ancient World and Problems of Chronology in the Bible*, rev. ed. (Peabody, MA: Hendrickson, 1998), 252–54. Finegan notes that King Josiah's death in Megiddo during his 31st year at the hands of Pharaoh Necho II (609–595 B.C.; 2 Kings 23:29; 2 Chron. 35:21) configures with Assyria and Egypt's datable military activity recorded in British Museum Tablet No. 21901. Josiah thus died in Duzu/Tammuz 609 B.C. (ibid., 252), providing the latest date for Zephaniah's prophetic activity. This means that prophets contemporary to Zephaniah may include Jeremiah (Jer. 1:2), Nahum (Nah. 3:7), and Habakkuk (Hab. 1:6).

[7] E.g., Mária Eszenyei Széles, *Wrath and Mercy: A Commentary on the Books*

However, a growing number of scholars challenge the presuppositions commonly employed in the post-exilic redaction position and argue for Zephaniah's literary unity. (1) We do not find a scrap of manuscript evidence that indicates Zephaniah 3:14–15 were ever excluded from the book.[8] (2) Zephaniah 3:14–15 include vocabulary and themes from the rest of the book, arguing for the book's literary integrity.[9] Indeed, Zephaniah 3:14–15 manifests not only lexical

---

of Habakkuk and Zephaniah, trans. George A. F. Knight, ITC (Grand Rapids: Eerdmans, 1987), 106; John M. P. Smith, "Zephaniah," in *Micah, Zephaniah, Nahum, Habakkuk, Obadiah and Joel*, ICC (New York: Scribner's, 1911), 173. See also bibliography and discussion in Marvin A. Sweeney, "Zephaniah: A Paradigm for the Study of the Prophetic Books," *CurBS* 7 (1999): 119–45; Nogalski, *Literary Precursors*, 201–4; Boda, "Zephaniah," 900. As Ehud Ben Zvi logically notes, if these words were not authentic to the prophet but are simply those of later redactors, Zephaniah had offered little (or almost no) hope of deliverance to his original audience (*A Historical-Critical Study of the Book of Zephaniah*, BZAW 198 [Berlin: de Gruyter, 1991], 35; but note Zeph. 2:3).

[8] Adele Berlin, *Zephaniah*, AB (New York: Doubleday, 1994), 22–23. E. Ray Clendenen considers it hermeneutically prudent to presume that each book of the Twelve "came directly or indirectly from the prophet and was produced with a coherent structure. Whether or not there were later additions to the books is impossible to prove" ("Textlinguistics and Prophecy in the Book of the Twelve," *JETS* 46 [2003]: 398; cf. Paul R. House, *The Unity of the Twelve*, JSOTSup 97, BLS 27 [Sheffield: Sheffield Academic Press, 1990], 11–16).

[9] Arvid S. Kapelrud, *The Message of the Prophet Zephaniah: Morphology and Ideas* (Oslo: Universitetsforlaget, 1975), 70–71; Sweeney, "Paradigm," 119–45; O. Palmer Robertson, *The Books of Nahum, Habakkuk, and Zephaniah*, NICOT (Grand Rapids: Eerdmans, 1990), 335; Lawrence Boadt, *Jeremiah 26–52, Habakkuk, Zephaniah, Nahum*, OTM (Wilmington, DE: Glazier, 1982), 228; Carl-A. Keller, "Sophonie," in *Michée, Nahoum, Habacuc, Sophonie*, CAT (Neuchâtel: Delachaux & Niestlé, 1971), 212–13. Ivan J. Ball Jr. finds nine terms shared between Zephaniah 2:5–7 and 3:1–20 (*A Rhetorical Study of Zephaniah* [Berkeley, CA: Bibal Press, 1988], 281–87; Ball, "The Rhetorical Shape of Zephaniah," in *Perspectives on Language and Text: Essays and Poems in Honor of Francis I. Andersen's Sixtieth Birthday, July 28, 1985*, ed. Francis I. Andersen, Edgar W. Conrad, and Edward G. Newing [Winona Lake, IN: Eisenbrauns, 1987], 163–65). Even some form critics reluctantly observe literary connections with the previous units (e.g., Ben Zvi, *Zephaniah*, 241–42; Nogalski, *Literary Precursors*, 203). Clendenen correctly observes that assigning textual oddities as redactional additions denies the possibility of analyzing the text's

coherence but also rhetorical cohesion, as it plays a role in the whole prophecy.[10]

Zephaniah may indeed have composed 3:14–15 before the exile, around the time of King Josiah (1:1). (1) Historically-speaking, Babylon did exile Judah, but before that event, Assyria presented Judah as a threat and a paradigm of impending exile since they destroyed Israel and dominated the region during King Josiah's reign. And (2) King Josiah's religious reform could have provided an occasion for hoping in Jerusalem's restored glory, so the judgments and salvation in Zephaniah may have *foretold the future* (i.e., not regurgitated the past).[11] In other words, nothing requires a post-exilic date for our text, and a pre-exilic date corresponding to the superscription is

---

structural logic ("Textlinguistics and Prophecy," 398).

[10] We follow Robert E. Longacre's definitions: "By 'cohesion' I refer especially to surface structure devices such as grammatical forms and conjunctions, while 'coherence' is reserved for lexical and referential continuity" (*Joseph, A Story of Divine Providence: A Text Theoretical and Textlinguistic Analysis of Genesis 37 and 39–48* [Winona Lake, IN: Eisenbrauns, 1989], 18). Some lump these together as "coherence" (e.g., internal, structural, perspectival and thematic coherence; cf. Kenneth H. Cuffey, "Remnant, Redactor, and Biblical Theologian: A Comparative Study of Coherence in Micah and the Twelve," in *Reading and Hearing the Book of the Twelve*, ed. James D. Nogalski and Marvin A. Sweeney, SBLSymS 15 [Atlanta: Society of Biblical Literature, 2000], 186–87).

[11] Marvin A. Sweeney, "Dating Prophetic Texts," *HS* 48 (2007): 55–73; Sweeney, *Zephaniah*, 17, 196–97; Sweeney, "A Form-Critical Reassessment of the Book of Zephaniah," *CBQ* 53 (1991): 390; Michael H. Floyd, *Minor Prophets: Part 2*, FOTL 22 (Grand Rapids: Eerdmans, 2000), 177–78, though he remains open on a pre- or post-exilic date. Duane L. Christensen argues that the historical allusions in 2:4–15 (e.g., Nineveh, before its destruction in 612 B.C.) fit King Josiah's reign, and we need not rely on a Scythian invasion as the background for what also fits Zephaniah's text as Assyrian threats to Judah ("Zephaniah 2:4–15: A Theological Basis for Josiah's Program of Political Expansion," *CBQ* 46 [1984]: 669–82). The actions condemned in Zephaniah 1:4–6 may best fit the period preceding Josiah's last reform of 622 B.C. (see Kenneth L. Barker and D. Waylon Bailey, *Micah, Nahum, Habakkuk, Zephaniah*, NAC [Nashville: Broadman & Holman, 1998], 396, who accept the superscription and date Zephaniah's prophetic activity to pre-626 B.C.).

defendable. We thus read Zephaniah as composed in King Josiah's reign and reflecting hopes of that period.

Text Type of Zephaniah and Zephaniah 3:14–15

We turn now to situate the literary text of Zephaniah as prose or poetry. Scholars categorize books in the Twelve similar to Zephaniah (e.g., Hag., Zech., and Mal.) as "oracular prose"[12] due to their preponderance of narrative features. Zephaniah 1:1 does place the prophetic book in a narrative framework, but the book does not leverage the standard narrative verb form *wayyiqtol* to advance a linear, historical progression (cf. 2:8–10).[13] Most scholars thus take the opposite position, arguing it is fundamentally poetry and labeling it as "prophetic verse," since the prophet uses an "elevated rhetorical style."[14] Adele Berlin is skeptical about the presence of formal meter

[12] Carol L. Meyers and Eric M. Meyers, *Haggai, Zechariah 1–8*, AB (Garden City, NY: Doubleday, 1987), lxiv; Andrew E. Hill, *Malachi*, AB (Garden City, NY: Doubleday, 1998), 26.

[13] Norman K. Gottwald, "Poetry, Hebrew," in *IDB*, 3:829; cf. Paul R. House, *Zephaniah: A Prophetic Drama*, JSOTSup 69, BLS 16 (Sheffield: Almond, 1988), 30. House argues that Zephaniah manifests prophet-Yahweh dialogues, logically-progressive plot, and other features typical of and identifying its genre as a "prophetic drama" (94–116). However, this genre classification is unlikely for several reasons. (1) In Israel's literature and history we do not find any other examples of such a genre (J. J. M. Roberts, *Nahum, Habakkuk, and Zephaniah: A Commentary*, OTL [Louisville: Westminster John Knox, 1991], 161; Ernst R. Wendland and David J. Clark, "Zephaniah: Anatomy and Physiology of a Dramatic Prophetic Text," *JOTT* 16 [2003]: 15; Berlin, *Zephaniah*, 12). (2) Oracular speech often blurred the speakers of prophet and Yahweh (Floyd, *Minor Prophets*, 166–67; Roberts, *Zephaniah*, 161; Berlin, *Zephaniah*, 12–13). (3) House's literary analysis of Zephaniah sometimes ignores structural features (e.g., the הוֹי-oracle in 3:1 starts a new sub-unit, but he overlooks this by seeing one speech in 2:13–3:5 [House, *Zephaniah*, 123–24; cf. Roberts, *Zephaniah*, 161–62]). Lastly, we note that directive speech (e.g., much of Zephaniah) may be *non-narratival* prose, so Zephaniah's hortatory discourse could take the form of prose or poetry. Since many classify the book as exclusively or even predominantly poetic, we devote space to the issue.

[14] Berlin, *Zephaniah*, 11; cf. House, *Zephaniah*, 30–37; Kapelrud, *Zephaniah*, 25; the poetic structuring of Zephaniah in *BHS*; Robert A. Bennett, "The Book

in Zephaniah, yet finds that his poetry often adds vividness: e.g., poetic phrases ("elated with pridefulness" [3:11]), wordplays (2:4), and anaphora (1:3; 3:2).[15]

Having noted the two extreme positions, we argue that Zephaniah should be read as prophetic prose-poetry, located somewhere on the cline between prose and poetry. It is prophetic since Zephaniah purports to be the word of Yahweh (e.g., 1:1; 3:20; 3:8 [נְאֻם־יְהוָה]; cf. Deut. 18:18; 2 Kings 17:13).[16] And using Andersen and Freedman's analysis of prose particles (i.e., the particles אֵת, אֲשֶׁר, and הַ)—a low percentage of prose particle saturation (<5%) typifies poetry, and a high percentage (<15%) typifies prose[17]—a computer search finds that Zephaniah is in the middle

of Zephaniah: Introduction, Commentary, and Reflections," in *NIB*, 7:666; Barker and Bailey, *Zephaniah*, 391. Rightly emphasizing the prophetic nature of Zephaniah, Wendland and Clark classify the book as "dramatic prophecy" ("Zephaniah," 15). Others see Zephaniah as poetic and argue for the presence of meter (e.g., M. O'Connor, *Hebrew Verse Structure* [Winona Lake, IN: Eisenbrauns, 1997], 240–62; H. W. M. van Grol, "Classical Hebrew Metrics and Zephaniah 2–3," in *The Structural Analysis of Biblical and Canaanite Poetry*, ed. W. van der Meer and J. C. de Moor, JSOTSup 74 [Sheffield: JSOT Press, 1988], 186–206, though Grol excludes several sections from his analysis [1:1–2:12; 2:15–18; 3:9–13, 18–20], which are coincidentally the more prosaic sections in the book).

[15] Berlin, *Zephaniah*, 11–13; cf. Ball's list of Zephaniah's poetic features (*Rhetorical Study*, 6–11, though he does not label the book as exclusively poetic); Wendland and Clark, "Zephaniah," 1–44. Kapelrud finds prose only in 1:1 and 2:10–11, but like Berlin, he rightly notes that Zephaniah does not follow a rigid metrical schema (*Zephaniah*, 25–27).

[16] House, *Zephaniah*, 110–14. He observes in Zephaniah the seven features common to prophetic literature ("Thus says Yahweh," election and covenant, rebellion, judgment, compassion, redemption, and consummation; 113–14). For the prophetic genre in the Twelve and their function as covenant "enforcers," see Clendenen, "Textlinguistics and Prophecy," 385–87.

[17] Francis I. Andersen and A. Dean Forbes, "'Prose Particle' Counts of the Hebrew Bible," in *The Word of the Lord Shall Go Forth*, ed. Carol L. Meyers and M. O'Connor, ASOR 1 (Winona Lake, IN: Eisenbrauns, 1983), 165–83. Such statistical analysis led to the following general guidelines: "practically everything with a reading of 5% or less will be poetry," "practically everything with a

of the spectrum: a total average of 12.3% for the book.[18] Zephaniah 1's Day of Yahweh judgments are more prosaic, while the last two chapters are more poetic. Zephaniah fits comfortably between both poles, a characteristic of elevated prophetic oratory (e.g., Hosea).[19]

That said, Zephaniah 3:14–15 does read as a more poetic section. Ivan Ball Jr. argues that Zephaniah erupts climactically "into 'pure' poetry" at both 1:15–16 and 3:14–17, the latter as a "Zion hymn of YHWH's kingship."[20] Ball's "hymn" contains only one full prose particle in the expression בַּיּוֹם הַהוּא (3:16; 1.8% prose in 55 words) compared to four prose particles in 3:8–13. Verses 14–15 do configure to the low prose particle counts typical of poetic texts and contain poetic features (e.g., a chiasm; see § 3.2.2), but we do not classify this section as a *pure hymn*.

---

reading above 15% will be prose," and those between 5–15% may be "elevated speech, which we call prophetic discourse" (David N. Freedman, "Another Look at Biblical Hebrew Poetry," in *Poetry and Orthography*, ed. John R. Huddleston, vol. 2, *Divine Commitment and Human Obligation: Selected Writings of David Noel Freedman* [Grand Rapids: Eerdmans, 1997], 215, 217). Scholars commonly admit these criteria as generally helpful in discerning prose-poetry boundaries.

[18] The percentages are 21.19% in Zeph. 1 (269 words, 57 prose particles), 7.658% in Zeph. 2 (222 words, 17 prose particles), and 7.246% in Zeph. 3 (276 words, 20 prose particles) (Andersen and Forbes, "'Prose Particle' Counts," 175). Byron G. Curtis recently confirmed these results ("The Zion-Daughter Oracles: Evidence on the Identity and Ideology of the Late Redactors of the Book of the Twelve," in *Reading and Hearing the Book of the Twelve*, ed. J. D. Nogalski and M. A. Sweeney, SBLSymS 15 [Atlanta: Society of Biblical Literature, 2000], 176).

[19] Francis I. Andersen and David Noel Freedman, *Hosea*, AB (Garden City, NY: Doubleday, 1980), 57–66. For this conclusion specific to Zephaniah, see Ball, *Rhetorical Study*, 12–13. Curtis posits that the more prose-like section of 3:19–20 qualifies it as a later redaction ("Zion-Daughter Oracles," 166–84), but he assumes prosaic, prophetic texts are theologically late and shelves his own evidence (i.e., he traces some "return" terms to the eighth or seventh century B.C.).

[20] Ball, *Rhetorical Study*, 12–13. He more accurately captures the climactic nature of Zephaniah 3:14–17's rhetoric by labeling it an "*outburst* of song" (273, italics ours; cf. Curtis, "Zion-Daughter Oracles," 178).

Many do classify 3:14–15 as a hymn of praise to Yahweh,[21] or even more specifically as an enthronement psalm.[22] They detect such a classification here, since its poetic cline, call to praise (v. 14), reasons or motivations (v. 15), and kingship terminology and activities (3:15–20) are similar to enthronement psalms (e.g., Pss. 47, 95, 96, 97, 98, 100, 149).[23]

Enthronement and praise psalms ostensibly share some structural and thematic parallels with Zephaniah 3, but some observations render either classification unlikely for our text. (1) Unlike most praise hymns (and enthronement psalms), Zephaniah 3 does not signal the motivations for joy with the explicit, logical connector כִּי.[24] (2) Zephaniah 3:14–15 share distinctive vocabulary and features with prophetic texts (e.g., Isa. 12:6; 54:1; Lam. 4:21; Joel

[21] Erhard S. Gerstenberger, *Psalms, Part 1: With an Introduction to Cultic Poetry*, FOTL 14 (Grand Rapids: Eerdmans, 1988), 16–19; Frank Crüsemann, *Studien zur Formgeschichte von Hymnus und Danklied in Israel*, WMANT 32 (Neukirchen-Vluyn: Neukirchener Verlag, 1969), 55–65; Claus Westermann, *Praise and Lament in the Psalms*, trans. Keith R. Crim and Richard N. Soulen (Atlanta: John Knox, 1981), 144–45, who lists Zephaniah 3:14–15 as one of the "eschatological Songs of Praise"; Ben Zvi, *Zephaniah*, 238–39; cf. Ball, *Rhetorical Study*, 262, 270–71. Wendland and Clark comment, "Zephaniah [3:14–17] suddenly breaks into a standard thanksgiving genre of psalmody (with royal overtones)" ("Zephaniah," 32).

[22] Kapelrud, *Zephaniah*, 70–71, 91–96; Boadt, *Jeremiah 26–52*, 228; Rex Mason, *Zephaniah, Habakkuk, Joel*, OTG (Sheffield: JSOT Press, 1994), 25; cf. Ralph L. Smith, *Micah–Malachi*, WBC (Waco, TX: Word, 1984), 143–44. Smith argues, "This pericope is not an enthronement song but it has the structure and vocabulary similar to the enthronement Psalms (47; 95; 97). It is an oracle of salvation probably delivered during the New Year festival, on the enthronement day. The call to singing, the victory over the enemies, the presence of Yahweh as king in their midst are all motifs common to the enthronement festival." See bibliography in Floyd, *Minor Prophets*, 243.

[23] E.g., Kapelrud posits, "The enthronement psalms were used on special occasions, for instance at the great New Year festival when Yahweh visited his people and the expectations were high, as can be seen in the psalms. It was natural for the prophet to use their style and structure when he was speaking of a bright future for his people" (*Zephaniah*, 71).

[24] Ben Zvi, *Zephaniah*, 238.

2:21–24; Hos. 9:1; Zech. 2:14; 9:9) that do not fit the hymn category (e.g., implied *prophecy* of salvation).[25] (3) Hymnic summons to praise usually address the people with MP imperatives (e.g., Ps. 96:1–3), whereas the imperatives in Zephaniah 3:14a–b, d are FS (but see 3:8a, 14b).[26] Zephaniah 3 thus differs from enthronement and praise psalms in important ways.

We conclude that Zephaniah 3:14–15 is *poetic prophecy, a hymn-like summons to rejoice.*[27] The poetic text does include kingship terminology (3:15) and provides reasons (3:15) for rejoicing (3:14), perhaps co-opting enthronement hymn features. But we must not overlook that Zephaniah 3:14–15 ultimately represents Yahweh's prophecy (אָמַר יְהוָה, 3:20).[28] The prophet's word arguably anticipated an imminent and far future fulfillment (1:7, 14; 3:16–20).[29]

[25] Some maintain that Zephaniah links his call to rejoice with future deliverance (3:16–20) rather than only past or present motivations as it is in enthronement psalms (e.g., Ps. 96:4–6; Crüsemann, *Studien*, 55–65; cf. Floyd, *Minor Prophets*, 239–40 and Sweeney, *Zephaniah*, 195, who read 3:16–20 as an elaboration of 3:15). However, grounding the call to rejoice in 3:16–20's future deliverance (1) wrongly presumes a tight logical connection between 14–15 and 16–17, and (2) neglects verse 15's *qatals* (cf. the *yiqtol*), which depict "the judgment and salvation as if already accomplished" (Jason S. DeRouchie, personal comments to author, December 12, 2014).

[26] Floyd, *Minor Prophets*, 244.

[27] Floyd labels 3:14–20 as a "prophetic call to rejoice" that introduces a "prophetic exhortation concerning salvation," (ibid., 244; cf. Sweeney, *Zephaniah*, 195; Crüsemann, *Studien*, 55–65; Nogalski, *Literary Precursors*, 203; Ball, *Rhetorical Study*, 13). Széles argues that the text does not celebrate the ascension of Yahweh to the throne since Zephaniah indicates a routine kingly practice of justice (3:5) and a continual kingly reign (3:15) (*Wrath and Mercy*, 110–11; cf. Ben Zvi, *Zephaniah*, 243). Yahweh is certainly always king (3:5), but in 3:15, Zephaniah views the future celebration of Yahweh's deliverance and presence as so sure, that he employs *qatals*.

[28] The prophet conveys Yahweh's message (Sweeney, *Zephaniah*, 207–8; Floyd, *Minor Prophets*, 244).

[29] Michael Ufok Udoekpo, *Re-thinking the Day of YHWH and Restoration of Fortunes in the Prophet Zephaniah: An Exegetical and Theological Study of 1:14–18; 3:14–20*, ed. Michael Fieger and Sigrid Hodel-Hoenes, DATIM 2 (Bern: Lang, 2010), 37–38; Clendenen, "Textlinguistics and Prophecy," 389n12;

Zephaniah's Discourse Type

Of the seven main discourse types, the book of Zephaniah resembles prophetic hortatory discourse, because directive verbs predominate.[30] According to E. Ray Clendenen, prophetic hortatory discourse includes "three key semantic elements: (1) the situation that needs to be changed [e.g., using verbless clauses]; (2) the change being called for [using directive verbs]; and (3) the arguments or factors used to motivate the change [e.g., using *weqatals*]."[31] Hortatory

---

VanGemeren, *Prophetic Word*, 174–76; Greg A. King, "The Day of the Lord in Zephaniah," *BSac* 152 (1995): 16, 20, 31–32; Stefanos Mihalios, *The Danielic Eschatological Hour in the Johannine Literature*, LNTS 436 (London: T&T Clark, 2011), 21–22; Robert B. Chisholm Jr., *Interpreting the Minor Prophets* (Grand Rapids: Zondervan, 1990), 216–17; Barker and Bailey, *Zephaniah*, 397; contra Sweeney, "Form-Critical Reassessment," 390. VanGemeren argues that Zephaniah's Day of Yahweh (both judgment and blessing) is historical and eschatological (Zeph. 1:3): "Each judgment in history is an intrusion of the eschatological judgment, whether on Israel, Judah, or the nations" (*Prophetic Word*, 175). Yet, Zephaniah seems to envision judgement arriving soon (e.g., 1:7); restoration (3:9–13, 16–20) is more "distant" (i.e., no reference to imminency).

[30] Clendenen, "Textlinguistics and Prophecy," 333–95, contra Floyd (he labels it as "prophetic instruction," *Minor Prophets*, 173). Sweeney labels Zephaniah as "parenesis" (*Zephaniah*, 50–51), but this is a subset of hortatory discourse. For a discussion of the seven discourse types (i.e., historical, predictive, promissory, expository, instructional, hortatory, and interrogative), see Jason S. DeRouchie, *A Call to Covenant Love: Text Grammar and Literary Structure in Deuteronomy 5–11*, GD 30, BS 2 (Piscataway, NJ: Gorgias, 2007), 86–87; cf. Robert E. Longacre, *The Grammar of Discourse*, 2nd ed., TLL (New York: Plenum, 1996), 16–21. Since Zephaniah used directive verbs (i.e., imperatives, cohortatives, and/or jussives), he used hortatory discourse with those verbs at the top band of a cline (Roy L. Heller, *Narrative Structure and Discourse Constellations: An Analysis of Clause Function in Biblical Hebrew Prose*, HSS 55 [Winona Lake, IN: Eisenbrauns, 2004], 468–75; cf. Longacre, *Joseph*, 121; David Allan Dawson, *Text-Linguistics and Biblical Hebrew*, JSOTSup 177 [Sheffield: Sheffield Academic Press, 1994], 116). We employ this textlinguistic cline in our outline of Zephaniah (see § 3.2.1).

[31] Clendenen, "Textlinguistics and Prophecy," 388. He helpfully posits that Hebrew morpho-syntax signals these three dimensions: (1) the indictment usually describes the situation with verbless clauses, "to be" verbs, participles,

discourse beckons the reader to change, employing logical argumentation traceable in the morpho-syntax.

We find those three features in Zephaniah. First, regarding the changes needed, the prophet indicts the oppressive city Jerusalem and her leaders in 3:1–4 and any faithless Jerusalemite in 1:12.[32] Second, Zephaniah motivates his audience with both negative and positive means. To relate the day of Yahweh's wrath, he often employed *yiqtols* and *weqatals* (1:2–6, 8–18; 3:6–7). Zephaniah also leveraged them for positive motivations: e.g., deliverance from Judah's enemies and Yahweh's judgments (2:4–15; 3:9–13, 15–20).[33] Third, charting the main directives, we note that four verses ostensibly contain imperatives (2:1, 3; 3:8, 14) and so supply the basic behavioral intentions and structure for Zephaniah's prophecy.[34]

---

yiqtols, and *qatals*; (2) the instruction calls for change with directives in the imperative, jussive, cohortative or obligatory *yiqtol*, summarizing "why the text was produced"; (3) motivations use predictive discourse with *weqatals*, *yiqtols*, and participles (390–92). See Appendix 3 for Zephaniah's first-position patterns.

[32] Note the הוֹי, three verbless clauses, seven *qatals* and one participle in 3:1–4, and the *yiqtols* in 1:12 (ibid., 394). Her inhabitants were worshipping Baal and the heavens, as well as doing other pagan practices (1:4–6) (Greg A. King, "The Remnant in Zephaniah," *BSac* 151 [1994]: 418). Also, each of Zephaniah's *qatals* in this section (1:7d, 11b–c, 17c) follows a כִּי and so additionally support the negative motivations. Note that some indictments ostensibly do not align with the morpho-syntactical restrictions imposed by Clendenden's system (e.g., 1:8–9 uses *weqatals*, typical of motivations, yet houses information about deceitful, idolatrous leaders). The most sustained indictment section is nevertheless 3:1–4 (see Sweeney, *Zephaniah*, 159).

[33] Clendenen observes that Zephaniah "uses exclusively future orientation in its motivation sections" ("Textlinguistics and Prophecy," 392), interpreting the *qatal* and *wayyiqtol* of 2:10 as "embedded narrative discourse citing Moab/Ammon's past sins" and the *qatals* in 2:11b, 3:15a and c as "prophetic perfects" (e-mail comments to author, October 27, 2017).

[34] See Appendix 1 for a table of Zephaniah's imperatives. On imperatives forming the main-line of hortatory texts, see Dawson, *Text-Linguistics*, 116–17. Below we discuss why we do not include two oft-taken imperatival expressions in our interpretation of Zephaniah's structure (1:7 and 11) but join 3:8 and 14.

Literary Context of Zephaniah 3:14–15

Broader Literary Context of Zephaniah 3:14–15

Few scholars agree on how Zephaniah crafted his argument, but the most common structuring of Zephaniah trades on Westermann's three-part topical outline of prophetic books:

I. Judgment-speeches to the prophet's own nation [Jerusalem and Judah, 1:2–2:3]
II. Judgment-speeches to foreign nations [2:4–15]
III. Salvation-speeches to the prophet's own nation [Jerusalem, Judah, nations, 3:1–20][35]

However, some soundly critique this tripartite outline of the book as lacking sensitivity to Zephaniah's own argument flow, and his syntactical and linguistic features.[36] Despite the unifying Day-of-Yahweh theme, a rigid, tripartite, thematic structure is a superficial analysis.

[35] Claus Westermann, *Basic Forms of Prophetic Speech*, trans. H. C. White (Louisville: Westminster John Knox, 1991), 95. Some propose that Zephaniah has two prophetic collections: judgment (1:2–3:8) and hope (3:9–20) (e.g., Baker, "Zephaniah," 1310). Others dissect the book atomistically, and still others posit a chiastic arrangement of the book. David A. Dorsey reads it as a seven-part chiasm: (A) "*coming judgment upon the wicked of Jerusalem* (1:2–6)"; (B) "*coming judgment of corrupt leaders* (*śārîm*) and rich of Jerusalem (1:7–13)"; (C) "*Yahweh's judgment of all nations*: great and terrible day of Yahweh (1:14–18)"; (D) "*CENTER: call to repentance* (2:1–3)"; (C´) "*Yahweh's judgment of all nations*: oracles against the nations (2:4–15)"; (B´) "*coming judgment of corrupt political leaders* (including *śārîm*) and religious leaders of Jerusalem (3:1–7)"; (A´) "*coming restoration of Jerusalem and its fortunes* (3:8–20)" (*The Literary Structure of the Old Testament: A Commentary on Genesis–Malachi* [Grand Rapids: Baker, 1999], 310–14; we italicize what he presents in bold). He further sees chiastic literary variations within each section. The text may indeed contain chiasms, but they should not counter other natural structures, like those established through discourse analysis (see Craig A. Smith, "Criteria for Biblical Chiasms: Objective Means for Distinguishing Chiasm of Design from Accidental and False Chiasm" [PhD diss., University of Bristol, 2009]).

[36] E.g., Sweeney, *Zephaniah*, 2; cf. Boda, "Zephaniah," 900.

For some measure of objectivity in the enterprise, we employ the textlinguistic model defended by Jason DeRouchie.[37] We accordingly note Zephaniah's hierarchical propositions, formally-signaled textual units, and logical/semantic connections to produce the outline below.

I. Historical Setting of Zephaniah (1:1)
II. Motivation to Seek and Wait in Joy: Day of Yahweh's Judgment on All and Judah (1:2–18)
III. Call for Judah to Wait in Joy, Seeking Yahweh (2:1–3:20)
    A. Seek Yahweh, Motivated by Negative Consequences: Destruction (2:1–3:7)
        1. Call to Seek Yahweh in Repentance (2:1–3)
        2. Motivation for Repentant Seeking: Worldwide Punishment (2:4–3:7)
            a. Judgment Begun: Punishment on Philistia (2:4)
            b. Judgment Continued: Punishment on Nations (2:5–3:7)
                i. Woe to Foreign Nations (2:5–15)
                ii. Woe to Jerusalem and Her Corrupt Leaders (3:1–7)
    B. Wait in Joy for Yahweh, Motivated by Positive Consequences: Restoration (3:8–20)
        1. Call to Wait for Yahweh's Actions (3:8a)
        2. Motivation for Waiting in Joy (3:8b–13)
            a. Initial Motivation for Waiting in Joy: Yahweh's Judgment to Result in Praising Nations (3:8b–10)
                i. Yahweh to Destroy All the Earth (3:8b–c)

[37] DeRouchie, *Covenant Love*, 55–92; DeRouchie, *How to Understand and Apply the Old Testament: Twelve Steps from Exegesis to Theology* (Phillipsburg, NJ: P&R Publishing, 2017); cf. Longacre, *Joseph*, 119–36; Heller, *Narrative Structure*, 468–75.

ii. Yahweh to Transform the Nations into Praisers (3:9–10)

b. Further Motivation for Waiting in Joy (3:11–20)

i. On Yahweh's Future Day, a Humble Remnant (3:11–13)

ii. Parenthetical Call to Joy in Anticipation of Yahweh (3:14–15)

iii. On Yahweh's Future Day, Jerusalem's Salvation Oracle and Promised Deliverance from Yahweh (3:16–20)[38]

To explain how we arrived at the above outline we observe the following. First, since Zephaniah is hortatory discourse, his directive verbs (2:1–3; 3:8, 14) provide the backbone of his argument. We exclude both 1:7 and 1:11 from this macro-structure. (1) Zephaniah 1:7's onomatopoeic "hush" (הַס) occurs six times in the MT (Judg. 3:19; Amos 6:10; 8:3; Hab. 2:20; Zeph. 1:7; Zech. 2:17; cf. Neh. 8:11). Though the LXX reads it as an imperative here (εὐλαβεῖσθε), we agree with Sweeney that verse 7 mainly draws attention to the *announcement* of Yahweh's Day, for the following reasons: "The absence of a syntactic join at v. 7, the appearance of the exclamatory הַס, 'Silence!' at the beginning of the verse [without a vocative addressee named], and the shift in theme from the punishment of apostasy to the Day of YHWH."[39] 1:2–18 likely support the main

[38] Our understanding of Zephaniah's structure is heavily indebted to DeRouchie's analysis (*Zephaniah*). He reads 2:1–3 and 3:8 as Zephaniah's twin peaks of exhortation (see also Chisholm, *Minor Prophets*, 202–15); 3:14–15 as a rhetorical, parenthetical outburst of joy; and בַּיּוֹם הַהוּא as a structural device (3:11–13, 16–20). For our similar interpretation of Zephaniah, see our text hierarchy presentation of 3:8–20 (Appendix 2).

[39] Sweeney, *Zephaniah*, 75. Floyd takes both 1:7 and 11 as commands (*Minor Prophets*, 185) yet subsumed in the announcement of Yahweh's Day (1:2–18; ibid., 165). Chisholm takes only 1:7 as an exhortation but similar to Floyd,

hortatory section that follows. (2) The consonantal form of "wail" (הֵילִילוּ) in 1:11 is either a hiphil *qatal* 3MS (e.g., Jer. 48:39) or Imv MP (see LXX, TJ, Peshitta; cf. Isa. 13:6; 23:1, 6, 14; Jer. 25:34; 48:20, 39; 51:8; Ezek. 30:2; Joel 1:11, 13; Zeph. 1:11; Zech. 11:2), but none of the above occurrences require the imperative form. If read as a *qatal* and considered with 1:10, verse 11 "conveys the general situation of terror among the people of Jerusalem as the threat becomes apparent."[40] Even were 1:11 a grammatical imperative, it likely calls the audience to *sarcastically* "wail"; 1:11 does not rise to 2:1–3's and 3:8's level of hortatory prominence.[41]

Second, in 1:2–18, *weqatals* and *yiqtols* dominate and serve as

---

as part of the "announcement of universal judgment" (*Minor Prophets*, 203); for Chisholm, "two hortatory hinges (2:1–3; 3:8–9)" fundamentally structure Zephaniah (ibid., 201). We agree with Chisholm's analysis about two hortatory hinges, and the *weqatal* and *yiqtol* verb patterns (i.e., negative motivations) indeed predominate in Zephaniah 1 so that 1:2–18 play a supporting/introductory role. Unlike Floyd and Chisholm, however, we do not interpret the expression "silence" (1:7) and the mention of wailing (1:11) as directives (see DeRouchie who argues that 1:7 "is an interjection," and 1:11 is "more likely a *qatal*" [personal comments to author, December 12, 2014; cf. DeRouchie, *Zephaniah*]). Sweeney argued similarly; the section 1:2–18 "contains no overt exhortative or admonitory elements, [yet] it functions as an introduction to the formal parenetic address . . . in that it introduces the Day of YHWH as the time at which YHWH will take action against those who act contrary to the divine expectations" (*Zephaniah*, 51).

[40] Sweeney, *Zephaniah*, 90 (see also 76).

[41] Several observations point to this verb playing a reduced role in the macro-structure of Zephaniah. If an imperative, the verb may call the audience to wail *at their judgment* (cf. 1:7 and 2:1; Clendenen, "Textlinguistics and Prophecy," 391). Furthermore, the identity of the addressee is unclear. יֹשְׁבֵי הַמַּכְתֵּשׁ ("the inhabitants of the Mortar") are unknown but may refer to those located somewhere in Jerusalem's vicinity (see Sweeney, *Zephaniah*, 90–92) and perhaps to a distinct subgroup connected to economic interests, due to the financial terms used in 1:11b–c (כָּל־עַם כְּנַעַן and כָּל־נְטִילֵי כָסֶף). Lastly, since 1:11 seems to intrude into the middle of *weqatals*, this may have "the effect of an interruption inserted into a fairly homogeneous speech (1:8–10, 12–13)" (Wendland and Clark, "Zephaniah," 7). Thus, the addressees and level of prominence do not match 2:1, 3 and 3:8.

mainline, negative motivations. Zephaniah promises the world's and Jerusalem's judgment on the "day of Yahweh," to support his hortatory call to seek Yahweh and wait in joy (2:1–3; 3:8, 14).

Third, we join together the imperatives of 2:1–3 and read them as rhetorically combining to constitute Judah's call "to gather and seek YHWH."[42] They are all 2MP imperatives and have MP address forms (i.e., the *people* of Jerusalem and Judah, 1:4); 2:1 directly addresses the "nation" (MS) as "you" (2MP), and 2:3's audience is the "humble ones" (MP). The addressees seem to overlap, but are not co-extensive; Zephaniah 2:3 addresses "all the humble ones of the land" which suggests the people already obey, but 2:1 addresses the "shameless nation" (ESV) indicating disobedience. Following DeRouchie, we conclude these addressees overlap yet are discrete parties; verse 1 addresses the whole (wicked) nation, and verse 3 addresses a subset in Judah, the faithful contingent.[43]

Fourth, some claim that 2:1–3 ("Seek Yahweh!") constitute the prophet's main hortatory goal,[44] but this would unwarrantedly

[42] Sweeney, *Zephaniah*, 113. Sweeney interprets verses 1 and 3 as addressing Jerusalem/Judah to persuade them to obey; in the prophet's rhetorical strategy "of persuasion, the characterization of the audience plays a crucial role. . . . [Zephaniah] prompt[s] the audience to identify with his message" (ibid., 118). But Sweeney's position is unlikely since prophets of Yahweh did not practice such psychological flattery on their hearers (1 Kings 22:6–8; cf. Isa. 30:9–11; Jer. 6:13–14); they confronted wickedness instead of tickling the ears of the audience (DeRouchie, "Addressees," who suggests that 2:3's addressees overlap with the addressees of 2:1 as a subgroup, and that the "humble" [2:3] refers most pointedly to those in Judah who submit themselves to 2:1's imperative to gather).

[43] DeRouchie, "Addressees." Several scholars share this interpretation (e.g., Robertson, *Zephaniah*, 291–94; James Bruckner, *Jonah, Nahum, Habakkuk, Zephaniah*, NIVAC [Grand Rapids: Zondervan, 2004], 304–6).

[44] Based on the Masoretic pointing and a conjunctive role for the כִּי in 2:4, Sweeney argues that the foremost argument for seeking Yahweh is the Philistine cities' destruction and for 2:1–4 as the book's formal core (*Zephaniah*, 50–51, 111–13). We render 2:4 as 2:1–3's chief ground, but our argument does not depend on the decision. For evidence he also cites 2:1–3's syntactical independence and behavioral import, and 2:4–3:20's supporting logic. But logical

require 3:8a's לָכֵן + imperative ("wait!" חַכּוּ) to support 2:1–3. Rather, using the four verses of imperatives as the backbone for the mainline instructions, his fundamental calls are twofold: (1) gather to humbly seek Yahweh (2:1, 3); and (2) wait in confident joy for Yahweh to act (3:8, 14).[45]

Fifth, the כִּי in 2:4a signals the formal launch of a section that supports the imperatives of 2:1–3.[46] Indeed, *yiqtols* and *weqatals* (typical forms in motivation sections) predominate in 2:3d–9's judgment on the nations, but this mostly negative motivation section continues through to 3:7 despite the shift to historical references

---

conjunctions and imperatives (3:8, 14) prohibit including 3:8–20 as support for 2:1–3.

[45] Several scholars trace Zephaniah's structure according to the imperativals. E. Ray Clendenen outlines Zephaniah as "Exhortation to submit (1:1–18); "Exhortation to Repent" (2:1–3:7); and "Exhortation to Wait" (3:8–20) ("The Minor Prophets," in *Holman Concise Bible Commentary*, ed. David S. Dockery [Nashville: Broadman & Holman, 2010], 377–78; cf. Clendenen, "Textlinguistics and Prophecy," 394, who nuances that final imperative of the outline as "wait confidently" [Zeph. 3:8]). Chisholm rightly structures the book according to two hinges: (1) "Exhortation to seek the Lord in view of the coming judgment" (2:1–3) and (2) "Exhortation to wait on the Lord in view of the coming judgment and salvation" (3:8–9) (*Minor Prophets*, 202–3). Floyd, however, labels 2:1–3:13 as "Exhortation to prepare for the Day of Yahweh" and 3:14–20 as "Exhortation to rejoice in the promise of salvation" (*Minor Prophets*, 165–66). We agree with both Clendenen and Chisholm in labeling 3:8 as the book's terminal exhortation (tacitly coupled together with 3:14), rather than reading 3:14 as the final imperatives in a progression (contra Floyd). First, unique among Zephaniah's imperatives, 3:14a–c changes to feminine imperatives. Second, only in 3:15 does the prophet employ *qatals* (i.e., past time judgments) to ground the imperatives of 3:14, but in Zephaniah judgment was still future (2:1, 3; 3:8). The parallel sections of "on that day" (i.e., 3:11–13 and 3:16–20) "explicate the 'wait' imv [3:8–10]"; thus, "3:14–15 appears to shape a rhetorical, celebrative intrusion" in anticipation of Yahweh's presence and removing judgments (DeRouchie, personal comments to author, December 12, 2014, citing the two arguments above and charting 2:1, 3 and 3:8 as Zephaniah's chief imperatives; see also DeRouchie, *Zephaniah*).

[46] כִּי may play an emphatic role but "never relinquishes its conjunctive or subordinating character" (Sweeney, *Zephaniah*, 112).

(i.e., *wayyiqtols* and *qatals* in 2:8–3:7). The הוֹי-formula occurs at 2:5 and 3:1 and so unifies this section as focusing on judgment.[47]

Sixth, scholars debate the referent to the MP imperative (חַכּוּ) in 3:8, since it departs from the 2FS addressees in 3:1–4 and 7 (i.e., city Jerusalem). Some suggest that it refers to the MP participants in 3:7e (i.e., Jerusalem's wicked leaders) or to the purified remnant of Israel, left inside the city (see 3MP verbs and MP pronouns in 3:12–13).[48] We maintain, however, that 3:8 retains the same primary addressee as in the prior imperatives (2:1–3):[49] the wicked nation of Judah (viewed as a collective whole) and the subgroup of faithful ones in Judah. Several observations suggest this interpretation. (1) Both verse sets (2:1–3; 3:8) are structurally similar (e.g., jarring movement in the prophecy from 3MP to 2MP commands). (2) 3:8

[47] Many observe the parallel "woe" sections. Ball, for example, argues that 2:5–7 and 3:1–20 are woe sections that end with restoration, have eight terms in the same sequence, and detail Judah's blessing and enemy destruction ("Rhetorical Shape," 155–66, who concludes "the punishment is merely the means by which the remnant of Israel will receive restoration and salvation . . . . Therefore, I would understand the ultimate significance of the book as the hope of salvation for the remnant of Israel" [166]). We agree with Ball's conclusion, but his analysis ignores the imperatival links between 2:1, 3; 3:8, and 14. Charting the imperatives provides a stronger representation of Zephaniah's rhetorical discourse (i.e., the woe-sections *support* the imperatives; cf. Floyd, *Minor Prophets*, 169).

[48] Floyd argues for 3:7e (*Minor Prophets*, 234, though he posits that despite all Yahweh's people being addressed here, only some ultimately follow him [3:12b–13]; cf. Vlaardingerbroek, *Zephaniah*, 184). Sweeney holds to the inside-outside distinctions of the city here (*Zephaniah*, 180; note the MP constructions in 3:12–13). We hold, however, that the 3MP's in 3:12–13 refer to the future remnant (i.e., "on that day," 3:11); the remnant denotes those who have followed 2:3 and 3:8a's commands to humbly seek and wait, since the future remnant will be the "humble" who "take refuge" in Yahweh (3:12; see also DeRouchie, "Addressees"; our participant reference chart of 3:8–20 [Appendix 4]; cf. Chisholm, *Minor Prophets*, 210).

[49] Barker and Bailey, *Zephaniah*, 484; DeRouchie, "Addressees"; Roberts, *Zephaniah*, 215, though he holds that Jerusalem's relief would only come after her supposed judgment in 3:8a–b. 3:8, however, does not bring judgment on all Jerusalem.

does not explicitly state an addressee (i.e., no vocative).[50] And (3) the intervening verses between the two sets of imperatives (2:4–3:7) reflect awareness of both wicked Judah (e.g., 3:4b–c [Jerusalem's wicked leaders; cf. 3:3, 6]) and a faithful subgroup cast in MP grammatical forms (2:9 [remnant of Judah, a FS noun standing as the subject for the 3MP verb]). Zephaniah 3:8a calls all in Judah and the faithful subgroup (i.e., Jerusalem's "humble" who would gather to seek Yahweh) to wait.

Though Zephaniah 3:8a likely focuses on Judah, the verse's addressee entails some ambiguity (e.g., no vocative), and Zephaniah may intend to include the "nations" in the call to wait.[51] At several points in Zephaniah, the "past, present and future" experiences of (portions of) the nations are closely interwoven with the experiences of Judah and its faithful contingent (e.g., 1:4b–6, 17).[52] Additionally, Zephaniah 2:1–3:7 contain participant reference candidates for 3:8's imperative that are outside the scope of Judah (e.g., see the 2MP pronominal references to Canaan [2:5b] and Cushites [2:12], and the MP participants of Moab and Ammon [debatable, 2:10]). Floyds interprets the international scale in 2:1–3:7 as suggesting that the "responsive," humble, subgroup in Judah might participate in a "worldwide" response to Yahweh (i.e., "the humble *of the earth*").[53] Given such ambiguity in the immediate literary context of 3:8, the verb plausibly entails a secondary address to the nations.

[50] See our comparison of Zephaniah's vocative addressees (p. 103n83).

[51] Ibid. DeRouchie also argues that Zephaniah intended this same ambiguity of referents in 2:1 and 3 so that he could "raise the possibility in the minds of some from both Judah and other nations that foreigners too could experience protection from the punishing hand of God."

[52] Daniel C. Timmer, *The Non-Israelite Nations in the Book of the Twelve: Thematic Coherence and the Diachronic-Synchronic Relationship in the Minor Prophets*, BIS 135 (Leiden: Brill, 2015), 151; see also DeRouchie, "Addressees."

[53] Floyd, *Minor Prophets*, 216, italics ours. DeRouchie supplies additional evidence (Zephaniah's African ancestry, marked interest in addressing neighboring nations, and vocative address toward Canaan and Cush in 2:5c, 12 ["Addressees"]).

Seventh, in 3:8a Zephaniah's imperatival call to wait follows לָכֵן, a structure in prophetic addresses often introducing judgment (cf. 2:9), as the preceding "woe" on Jerusalem (3:1–7) might lead us to suspect.[54] We interpret the command to wait, nevertheless, in its positive sense for three reasons. (1) The verb חכה ("wait") in the OT consistently carries either a neutral or positive nuance.[55] A negative nuance of the verb is unattested; Yahweh thus likely exhorts the addressees to wait, anticipating what he will do. (2) We argue that 3:8a addresses wicked Judah (collectively), the faithful subgroup in Judah, and perhaps also the nations (i.e., the address is not likely restricted to those deserving punishment). (3) The לָכֵן + "wait" clause in 3:8a finds logical support in Yahweh's judgment on the nations, that is, on the whole earth (3:8; cf. 1:18).[56] Yahweh's wrath

[54] Johannes Vlaardingerbroek concludes that 3:8 is "an announcement of the judging action of God: 'just wait!' and naturally those people are addressed of whom vs. 7 says that all their deeds are corrupt" (*Zephaniah*, HCOT [Leuven: Peeters, 1999], 184).

[55] In the verb's OT occurrences, we find no examples of negative anticipation; sometimes it indicates neutral waiting (2 Kings 7:9; 9:3; Job 32:4; Ps. 106:13; Hab. 2:3; cf. Hos. 6:9), but it often explicitly denotes waiting for something positive (DeRouchie, *Zephaniah*; Ps. 33:20; Isa. 8:17; 30:18 [twice]; cf. Dan. 12:12). Isaiah 30:18 ostensibly denotes positive waiting and shares Zephaniah 3:8's construction: לכן + חכה (cf. Sweeney's survey [*Zephaniah*, 180]). Chisholm reads it as a positive exhortation, a synonym of faith (*Minor Prophets*, 210).

[56] Ben Zvi, *Zephaniah*, 224. לָכֵן does often introduce judgment in the OT (see Westermann, *Prophetic Speech*, 129–209; Daniel Hojoon Ryou, *Zephaniah's Oracles against the Nations: A Synchronic and Diachronic Study of Zephaniah 2:1–3:8*, BIS 13 [Leiden: Brill, 1995], 276–77), but the conjunction can signal deliverance (e.g., Hos. 2:14; cf. Hos. 2:6; Ernst R. Wendland, *The Discourse Analysis of Hebrew Prophetic Literature: Determining the Larger Textual Units of Hosea and Joel*, MBPS 40 [Lewiston: Mellen Biblical Press, 1995], 40). Ryou argues for a literary break after 3:8 and not after 3:7, so that 3:8 provides a sarcastically negative answer to Yahweh's disappointment (3:6–7): Judah is to wait for Yahweh's destruction (*Oracles*, 276–77, 130). But Ryou's reading is unlikely, since (1) 3:8–20 can provide an effective conclusion to the previous unit (2:4–3:7) that bi-laterally supports the conceptually-related imperatives, 2:1–3 and 3:8 (Floyd, *Minor Prophets*, 203). Zephaniah may thus have a

will be "on them" (עֲלֵיהֶם [3:8b]). Some interpret this antecedent to refer only to 3:7e's corrupt Jerusalem leaders, however, that interpretation unwarrantedly ignores the nearest referent in the clause itself: the "nations" (MP) or "kingdoms" (FP [3:8b]).[57] Thus, 3:8 does not introduce judgment restrictively targeting wicked Judah/Jerusalem but calls Judah—the nation as a whole and the faithful subgroup—and the nations (likely) to patiently wait, anticipating his judgment on the earth's wicked (incl. Jerusalem's wicked, 1:2–18; 3:1–5, 7).[58]

Eighth, precise reduplication of the formula בַּיּוֹם הַהוּא in clause-initial position in 3:11 and 16 (cf. בָּעֵת [3:19–20]) serves as major structural justification for unifying 3:8–20.[59] Following the

---

"double-sandwich structure" since motivation flanks both sides of both clusters of imperatives (2:1–3 and 3:8). Daniel J. Brendsel observes, "The motivation section that opens the second half would thus parallel that which opens the first half inasmuch as the 'tyrannical city' could almost be taken as a typological analogue/prototype of the cosmos . . . much like the destruction of the cosmos in ch. 1 is mirrored/typologically foreshadowed in the destruction of Jerusalem/the temple (a micro-cosmos)" (personal comments to author, July 24, 2015). (2) 3:9's כִּי־אָז likely provides further support to 3:8 *and* transitions from punishment to grace (2 Sam. 19:27; e.g., Ball, *Rhetorical Study*, 235–36). (3) The verb חכה ("wait") never carries a negative nuance in the OT.

[57] Roberts argues that 3:8b's judgment targets the corrupt Jerusalem leaders (*Zephaniah*, 215–16; cf. John Goldingay and Pamela J. Scalise, *Minor Prophets II*, NIBCOT [Peabody, MA: Hendrickson, 2009], 124–25), but several rightly prefer the nearer anaphoric referent (i.e., גּוֹיִם in 3:8a; Ben Zvi, *Zephaniah*, 224; Ryou, *Oracles*, 132; Sweeney, *Zephaniah*, 181–82, who defends the MP pronominal suffix's textual integrity).

[58] Since 3:8 refers to *global* judgment (e.g., "all the earth"), the verse seems to suggest that "sinful Jerusalem" "would be severely punished when the Lord poured out His burning anger upon the entire world (v.8b; cf. 1:2–2:3)" (Chisholm, *Minor Prophets*, 210; cf. House, *Zephaniah*, 66–67; Barker and Bailey, *Zephaniah*, 484–85; Floyd, *Minor Prophets*, 202–03, 234–35). Sweeney points to Isaiah 8–9 as evidence that Yahweh will punish both wicked Israel and the nations before installing Jerusalem as the epicenter for the nations (*Zephaniah*, 181–82). Foreseeing the day after judgment, Zephaniah 3:9–20 prophesy a Gentile and Jewish remnant.

[59] Richard D. Patterson, *Nahum, Habakkuk, Zephaniah*, WEC (Chicago: Moody, 1991), 374; DeRouchie, *Zephaniah*. See our text hierarchy (Appendix 2).

call to wait in 3:8, כִּי conjunctions precede several clauses (3:8b–9), and the formula בַּיּוֹם הַהוּא (3:11–13) introduces the sub-unit about the future day of Yahweh's blessings for the humble remnant of Israel. 3:11a's "day" likely recalls 3:8a's "day."[60] Both sub-sections exclusively use *yiqtol* and *weqatal* verbs (3:8b–10, 11–13), so they function as motivation to wait for Yahweh to act.

In 3:16's parallel implementation of the formula, we observe that aside from the textually difficult verse 18,[61] 3:16–20 again employ motivational *yiqtol* and *weqatal* verbs to describe the future blessings. Additionally, temporal markers punctuate the section as future-oriented and thus linked to 3:11 and 16's future day (הִנְנִי ... בָּעֵת הַהִיא [3:19a], בָּעֵת הַהִיא [3:20a], וּבָעֵת [3:20b]). After the future saying to Jerusalem by an unknown speaker (3:16–17), first person verbs and pronouns unify 3:18–20 as a prophetic utterance of Yahweh (3:20; e.g., "I gathered" [אָסַפְתִּי; v. 18]; "I

[60] Wendland and Clark plausibly assert that "in that day" (3:11; cf. 3:16) anaphorically refers to the day Yahweh rises up (3:8a–9); furthermore, they posit that the 2FS pronouns (3:11) imply the addressee is the personified city Jerusalem (and its inhabitants), which is further expanded into the "remnant of Israel" perhaps even including Gentiles (3:13) ("Zephaniah," 31–32).

[61] Zephaniah 3:18 contains numerous challenges for interpretation, but its participle-first phrase and *qatal* verbs (3:18a–b; i.e., Yahweh's deliverance) perhaps function like prophetic perfects (cf. 3:15), setting the stage for the restoration details in 3:16–17, 19–20. Floyd's translation of the MT is reasonable: "Those from the assembly who were sorrowful I have removed from you; they were a burden on her, a reproach" (*Minor Prophets*, 237; cf. Ben Zvi, *Zephaniah*, 252–54; Berlin, *Zephaniah*, 145–47). Most modern commentators consider this one of the most difficult verses to interpret in Zephaniah, and even ancient translations (e.g., Targums, LXX) vary considerably. For a survey of the interpretations and whether to take the first two words of 3:18 with verse 17, see ibid.; Ball, *Rhetorical Study*, 187–88; Sweeney, *Zephaniah*, 203–4. Verse 19 begins with the forward-looking discourse marker הִנְנִי (for this marker, see Duane A. Garrett and Jason S. DeRouchie, *A Modern Grammar for Biblical Hebrew* [Nashville: Broadman & Holman, 2009], 321–22), so we find warrant that 3:16–20 overall sustain a future orientation. For a table charting the verbs in Zephaniah 3:8–20, see our text hierarchy (Appendix 2).

will save" [וְהוֹשַׁעְתִּי; v. 19]),[62] and a lexical parallelism in 3:19–20 further unifies them: "to gather" (קבץ [vv. 19c, 20b]), "for a praise" and "for a name" (לִתְהִלָּה וּלְשֵׁם [vv. 19d, 20c]), and "in all the earth" (בְּכָל הָאָרֶץ [vv. 19d, 20c]).[63] The final section (3:16–20) elaborates on the prophesied restoration (e.g., 3:20 promises בְּשׁוּבִי אֶת־שְׁבוּתֵיכֶם),[64] developed in 3:9–13.

Textual Limits of Zephaniah 3:14–15

We argue that Zephaniah 3:14–15 stand out as a discrete discourse unit. (1) They begin with three sets of asyndetic imperatives (i.e., the fourth imperative links syntactically to the third with a *waw*). Imperatives elsewhere in Zephaniah, especially when grouped, begin a new unit (e.g., 2:1–3; 3:8). (2) Vocatives accompanying these asyndetic imperatives combine to effectively cut the *waw*-conjunctive series found in 3:13e–f. Thus, 3:13 ends by assuring that no one will make the remnant afraid, just before shifting to the four imperatives calling Jerusalem to rejoice (3:14).[65] (3) Almost all early Hebrew

[62] Wendland and Clark, "Zephaniah," 14. Sweeney argues that אָמַר יְהוָה in 3:20d signals Zephaniah's role in reporting Yahweh's speech in 3:18–20 (*Zephaniah*, 196). Lines between speakers are often blurry in Zephaniah.

[63] Wendland and Clark, "Zephaniah," 14; David W. Baker, *Nahum, Habakkuk, and Zephaniah*, TOTC (Downers Grove, IL: InterVarsity Press, 1988), 88. In addition, an *inclusio* may envelope Zephaniah (1:1–6; 3:18–20): e.g., "to gather," "all the earth," "utterance of Yahweh," "hands" (see Ball, *Rhetorical Study*, 281–83; Ben Zvi, *Zephaniah*, 324; Wendland and Clark, "Zephaniah," 14; Kselman, "Zephaniah," 1080).

[64] For a survey of interpretations and a defense of this referring to a general "reversal of fortunes" rather than specifically to a "return from captivity," see Udoekpo, *Re-thinking*, 189–93; cf. Curtis, "Zion-Daughter Oracles," 181 (cf. also Zeph. 2:7; Hos. 6:11; Joel 4:1; Amos 9:14).

[65] This marks verses 14–15 as "syntactically independent from the preceding block of material . . . [and] a new rhetorical stage in the prophet's speech" (Sweeney, *Zephaniah*, 194; cf. Wendland and Clark, "Zephaniah," 13). Lexical cohesion does occur between Zephaniah 3:11–13 and 14–15 (see קרב, סור, עליז/עלז, and ישראל; Ben Zvi, *Zephaniah*, 241), but we interpret this as tying together the rhetoric of 3:11–13 and 3:14–15. Zephaniah 3:11–13 sparks 3:14's joy, because the prophet deems 3:11–13 as "so certain, that it is as if they

manuscripts mark 3:14 as a new unit (i.e., *setumah* or *petuḥah* before 3:14).[66] (4) The speaker shifts from Yahweh (3:8–13) to Zephaniah in 3:14. Yahweh refers to himself with first person pronominal references in 3:6–12, then in 3:15a, c, Zephaniah refers to Yahweh in the third person.[67] After verse 14's imperatives, verse 15 follows with a couple of asyndetic, *qatal* clauses, which naturally "support" the imperatives; so, we posit that the speaker of the support (3:15) and imperatives (3:14) match.[68] 3:14–15 cohere together.

Commentators propose many variations on how to read Zephaniah's structure after verses 14–15, but the most common outlines

---

have already happened (v. 15). . . . Therefore, the joy of the future becomes joy for the present, but it is still a joy (3:14) in the waiting (3:8)," while the remnant awaits deliverance (DeRouchie, personal comments to author, December 12, 2014; see also DeRouchie, *Zephaniah*).

[66] After Zephaniah 3:13, the Murabba'at manuscript has a break, Leningrad Codex placed a *setumah* (i.e., the sections 3:1–13, 14–20), the Aleppo (i.e., divisions 3:1–13, 14–15, and 16–20) and Cairo Codices put a *petuḥah* (i.e., 3:1–13, 14–20), but the Petersburg Codex placed breaks to divide chapter 3 into three parts (3:1–7, 8–15, 16–20). For evidence and discussion, see Berlin, *Zephaniah*, 18; Sweeney, *Zephaniah*, 3–5.

[67] The speaker shift may happen in 3:12b, where Yahweh is referred to in third person. If the speaker remains the same in 3:12b–15 this would provide coherency between 3:11–13 and 14–15. The prophet, incited by his prophetic word preceding 3:14, would have then transitioned to a rhetorical interjection of praise (3:14–15; cf. DeRouchie, *Zephaniah*). Nevertheless, since Yahweh speaks in 3:9a, 10–12a (i.e., the 1cs verbs and pronominal suffixes) and plausibly refers to himself in the third person (בְּשֵׁם יְהוָה [3:9b, 12b]), we hold that 3:8–13 is entirely Yahweh's speech (Wendland and Clark, "Zephaniah," 13).

[68] Wendland and Clark, "Zephaniah," 13; Sweeney, *Zephaniah*, 194–95. For the supporting function of the *qatal*, see Garrett and DeRouchie, *Modern Grammar*, 74. Additional arguments that Zephaniah is the speaker at 3:14 include: (1) In Zephaniah's other imperatives (2:1, 3; cf. 1:11), he uses the vocative (as here), whereas the imperative clearly given by Yahweh does not include a vocative (3:8a). (2) Given that the asyndetic *qatals* of 3:15a–b ground the imperatives of 3:14, this would parallel Zephaniah's normal convention for his 17 כִּי grounding clauses in which there is no clear change of speaker (1:7b, 7c, 11b, 17c [debatable], 18c; 2:4a [debatable], 7d, 10b, 11b, 14e; 3:8b, 8c, 9a, 11b, 13d, 20c; cf. Wendland and Clark, "Zephaniah," 13).

are that the unit ends at 3:15d,[69] 3:17,[70] or 3:20.[71] In 3:14–20, despite speaker changes, we observe features that promote coherence: (1) FS (3:14a, c, 18–19) and MP address forms (3:14b, 20) for the Jerusalem-Israel-remnant; (2) a replicated movement, from Yahweh's deliverance and removal of enemies (3:15, 18) to promised fearlessness and restoration (3:16, 19–20); and (3) the remnant motif.[72]

In favor of sub-dividing 3:14–20 into 3:14–17 (and vv. 18–20), most observe a chiasm of verbal and thematic elements that unifies those verses in some way. Since ten words occur twice in 3:14–17 (ברנה-רני; בת; זיון; ישראל; בשמחה-שמחי; ירושלם; בקרבך; תיראי; אל; עליך), the argument that Zephaniah intended the reader to notice parallel elements is quite strong.[73] Scholars do not agree on the chiasm's central element, but these are the most important features:

A Zion/Israel/Jerusalem [בַּת־צִיּוֹן] is called to "sing" [רָנִּי] and "rejoice" [שִׂמְחִי] (14)
  B Reason: YHWH's forgiveness and protection (15a–b)
    C *King* "YHWH is within you [יְהוָה בְּקִרְבֵּךְ]" [city] (15c)
      D "You will never again fear" [לֹא־תִירְאִי] (15d)

[69] For identifying the units as 3:14–15, 16–20, see Sweeney, *Zephaniah*, 194–97; Wilhelm Rudolph, *Micha, Nahum, Habakuk, Zephanja*, KAT (Gütersloh: Gerd Mohn, 1975), 295, 298–99; Emil G. H. Kraeling, *Commentary on the Prophets* (Camden, NJ: Thomas Nelson, 1966), 2:271.

[70] Udoekpo, *Re-thinking*, 117–18; Floyd, *Minor Prophets*, 239; Nogalski, *Literary Precursors*, 203, who cites the chiasm and prophetic speaker as the reasons for reading 3:14–17 as a unit.

[71] House, *Zephaniah*, 133. See Ball (*Rhetorical Study*, 264–65) for various proposed outlines.

[72] Floyd, *Minor Prophets*, 239–40; Ball, *Rhetorical Study*, 262, 273 (both subdivide it as 3:14–17, 18–20).

[73] Ball, *Rhetorical Study*, 270–71. Dorsey misses the chiasm of 3:14–17 in favoring of seeing a six-part chiasm in 3:8–20 and a macro-chiasm of the whole book of Zephaniah (*Literary Structure*, 310–13).

E Focus again on "that day" (16a)
D′ "Do not fear" Jerusalem/Zion [צִיּוֹן אַל־תִּירָאִי] (16b–c)
C′ *Warrior* "YHWH is within you [יְהוָה אֱלֹהַיִךְ בְּקִרְבֵּךְ]" (17a)
B′ Reason: his salvation and love (17b)
A′ [YHWH] himself will "rejoice" [בְּשִׂמְחָה] and "sing" [בְּרִנָּה] for you [Zion] (17c–e)[74]

Thus, there is a glorious movement from 3:14–15 commanding Zion to rejoice with the assurance of King Yahweh's presence and no fear, to 3:16–17 commanding Zion to not fear, with the assurance of Warrior Yahweh's saving presence and joy over her.

While we do observe the chiasm, we do not consider it sufficient evidence for uniting 3:14–15 and 3:16–17 as one seamless unit in Zephaniah's argument. Rather, the chiastic elements produce coherence between sections 3:14–15 and 16–20. First, verse 16 signals a new unit by fronting the future-oriented marker בַּיּוֹם הַהוּא. This phrase marks a new unit in 3:11,[75] so 3:11–13 and

[74] The chiasm above adapts Wendland and Clark's chiasm but modifies it to our versification system ("Zephaniah," 32). Baker produced one of the more detailed chiasms of these verses, finding 13 lines, also with verse 16a as central: "Jerusalem's future message," (*Zephaniah*, 87). J. Alec Motyer reads this as a seven-part poem similar to Zephaniah 1:14b–18's poem ("Zephaniah" in *The Minor Prophets: An Exegetical and Expository Commentary*, ed. Thomas Edward McComiskey [Grand Rapids: Baker, 1998], 3:956). Nogalski simplifies the chiasm: (A) "Rejoice, Zion, YHWH has withdrawn his judgment (14–15a)"; (B) "King YHWH is in your midst (15ba)"; (C) "Do not fear, Zion (15bb)"; (C′) "Do not fear, will be said of Zion (16)"; (B′) "Warrior YHWH is in your midst (17a)"; (A′) "YHWH will rejoice over you Zion (17b)" (*Literary Precursors*, 203). For an analysis of the literary parallelism, see Ball, *Rhetorical Study*, 262–71. Lastly, Floyd notes that the three commands to rejoice (v. 14) correspond to the three descriptions of Yahweh's rejoicing (v. 17c–e) (*Minor Prophets*, 243). Despite such diverse reconstructions of the chiasm, we retain its basic features above.

[75] Ben Zvi, *Zephaniah*, 238, 245, 322; Barker and Bailey, *Zephaniah*, 490; Patterson, *Zephaniah*, 374. Motyer argues, "Each occurrence of this formula

16–20 emerge as tandem, future-oriented sections. Second, the [x] + *yiqtol* construction commonly ends or closes a hortatory discourse unit.[76] Consistent with this, if verse 16 begins a new sub-division, an x + *yiqtol* ends the previous unit and opens the next (3:15d, 16a). Third, the *yiqtol* of 3:16a introduces direct speech, and the quotative frame extends from 3:16b–17e with its pronouns referring to the addressee in 3:16a; the quotative frame thus stands syntactically independent from the speech content and forms a different rhetorical structure for verses 16–17 than verses 14–15.[77] Fourth, early Hebrew manuscript evidence is somewhat split on the divisions, but no manuscripts break after verse 17. Both the Aleppo and Petersburg Codices contain a break after 3:15, and Leningrad and Cairo Codices join 3:14–20. We thus find warrant for reading a break after 3:15 and drawing 3:14–15 together.

Zephaniah 3:14–15 as Parenthetical, Rhetorical Peak of Joy

Having argued that Zephaniah 3:8a's call to wait functions on the same rhetorical level as 2:1–3 and finds motivation in 3:8b–20, and that 3:14–15 are a discrete unit of prophetic poetry, we now discern how 3:14–15 functions. We posit that skewed discourse

---

refers to the previously described event or period of time . . . . [Here,] it refers to the time when Yahweh will dwell in the midst of his people (3:14–15)" ("Zephaniah," 957). Nogalski argues that this construction does not signal a new independent unit but instead thematically divides the removal of enemies to Yahweh's joy over Zion (3:14–15/16–17; cf. 3:9–10/11–13, *Literary Precursors*, 203n78). But in 3:11, more than simple thematic shifting occurs, since the shift highlights 3:11–20's future-orientation.

[76] See, e.g., Garrett and DeRouchie's patterns for directive discourse (*Modern Grammar*, 331).

[77] Cynthia L. Miller, "Discourse Functions of Quotative Frames in Biblical Hebrew Narrative," in *Discourse Analysis of Biblical Literature: What It Is and What It Offers*, ed. Walter R. Bodine, SBLSS (Atlanta: Scholars Press, 1995), 155–82. From a textlinguistic perspective of "inclusio, [it] is normally not sufficient in itself—considered in isolation—to delimit a larger textual unit," but other factors like speaker and speaker frames must be considered (Wendland, *Hebrew Prophetic Literature*, 63).

elements mark 3:14–15 as Zephaniah's rhetorical peak, but 3:14 does not link to his other exhortations as progression.[78] Longacre identified several features that can mark a "surface structure peak": "Incidence of Particles and Onomatopoeia," "Rhetorical Underlining," "Heightened Vividness," "Concentration of Participants," "Change of Pace," "Change of Vantage Point and/or Orientation."[79] Zephaniah 3:14–15 have all these features.

First, 3:8–13 contain four prose particles, but none are in 3:14–15; 3:14–15 likely constitute an eruptive section.[80] Second, the prophet punctuates his hortatory address with five imperatives in both chapters 2 and 3 (two in 2:1; three in 2:3; one in 3:8; four in 3:14). The prophet uses an increasing number of imperatives, culminating in 3:14 where the stacked imperatives total more than any other one verse in the book (four).[81] Third, unlike the other stacked imperatives (קשׁשׁ [Zeph. 2:1], בקשׁ [Zeph. 2:3]), the imperatives in 3:14 are not the same consonants/roots; they represent four different yet relatively synonymous verbs for loud rejoicing.[82] Fourth, Zephaniah's terms for vocative addressees in the other imperatives

[78] For an exposition of peak described as a "zone of [discourse] turbulence," see Longacre, *Joseph*, 18–19. Zephaniah 3:14–15 represent a parenthetical call to joy in the wait (see DeRouchie, *Zephaniah*).

[79] Longacre, *Grammar of Discourse*, 38–48.

[80] See Longacre on "incidence of particles" and "onomatopoetic expressions" (ibid., 37–48). Also, see Curtis's statistical analysis of Zephaniah's prose particles ("Zion-Daughter Oracles," 176). Many argue that 3:14–17 constitute an "outburst of song," unchained from Zephaniah's logical structure (e.g., Ball, *Rhetorical Study*, 273). But due to the structural marker at 3:16a, we follow DeRouchie (*Zephaniah*), who restricts the outburst to 3:14–15.

[81] For a discussion of "rhetorical underlining" (e.g., "repetition"), see Longacre, *Grammar of Discourse*, 39). Also, see Appendix 1 for a table of Zephaniah's imperatives.

[82] See, e.g., Sweeney, *Zephaniah*, 195, 197–98. Stacking imperatives towards the end of the prophetic address has precedent in the Twelve (Hag. 1:5, 7, 8 [2x]; 2:2, 4 [4x], 11, 18 [2x], 21; Mal. 1:8, 9; 3:7, 10 [2x], 22; cf. Hos. 14:2–3), and the Minor Prophets tend to close their addresses with hope. Longacre argues that the discourse peak may achieve "*heightened vividness* . . . by a shift in the nominal-verbal balance" (*Grammar of Discourse*, 40, italics original).

are Zephanian *hapax legomena*,[83] whereas 3:14's vocative terms are used elsewhere in the book and bring together the book's chief addressees. Addressing Zion, Israel, and Jerusalem in this way draws together principal addressees, crowding "the stage" in a climactic yet unique way.[84] Fifth, 3:14 is the only place where Zephaniah uses FS imperative verbs, and he repeats this grammatical form three times.[85] Sixth, 3:14's imperatives (excl. 3:14d) are asyndetic like 2:1–3 but uniquely do not leverage explicit conjunctions for their motivations (cf. 1:7, 11). See this represented in the table below.

[83] Zephaniah 1:7's interjection implicitly addresses Jerusalem's inhabitants (1:4–6) but without a vocative; Zephaniah 1:11 is to the "inhabitants of Mortar" (יֹשְׁבֵי הַמַּכְתֵּשׁ), using the rare noun מַכְתֵּשׁ (Judg. 15:19; Prov. 27:22); Zephaniah 2:1 is for "the undesirable/unashamed nation " (הַגּוֹי לֹא נִכְסָף), using כסף as a verb for the only time in the book (cf. nominal form in 1:11, 18) and גּוֹי, which is the only other non-3:14 vocative repeated (cf. 2:5, 9, 11, 14; 3:6, 8); Zephaniah 2:3 addresses for the only time the land's "humble" (עַנְוֵי; cf., 3:12, עָנִי) who "do" (פָּעָלוּ) his command; and Zephaniah 3:8 does not include a vocative.

[84] Berlin rightly notes, "All of the main 'characters' – God, Israel, and the nations – who earlier were bringing judgment or suffering destruction are here joined together [Zeph. 3:14–20] .... The creation which was to have been swept away is reaffirmed" (*Zephaniah*, 148; cf. Floyd, *Minor Prophets*, 239–44). "Daughter of Zion" (בַּת־צִיּוֹן) includes terms used elsewhere (צִיּוֹן, [3:16]; בַּת, [3:10]); "Israel" (יִשְׂרָאֵל [MT]; θύγατερ Ιερουσαλημ [LXX]) is mentioned often (Zeph. 2:9; 3:13, 15); and "Daughter of Jerusalem" (בַּת יְרוּשָׁלָם) includes "Jerusalem" (יְרוּשָׁלָם [3:16]; cf. 1:4, 12). Longacre defines "concentration of participants": "One hallmark of peak . . . is the *crowded stage*. . . . Everybody except very subsidiary characters are on stage" (*Grammar of Discourse*, 40, italics original).

[85] A peak can achieve "*heightened vividness . . . by a shift to a more specific person*" (Longacre, *Grammar of Discourse*, 41, italics original).

Table 3: Zephaniah 3:14–15 Compared to the Argument Structures for the Mainline Directives

	2:1 "Gather" (2x)	**2:3 "Seek" (3x)**	**3:8a "Wait" (1x)**	**3:14 "Rejoice/ Shout" (4x)**
Patterns of Verb-First & Support Structure in Zephaniah's Imperatives	Temporal: 2:2a–b, c, d • בְּטֶרֶם + nom. copula (comes) • בְּטֶרֶם + *yiqtol* (comes) • בְּטֶרֶם + *yiqtol* (comes)	Reasons: 2:3d, 4a–d • אוּלַי + *yiqtol* (protected) • כִּי + 3 *yiqtols* (destroyed)	Reasons: 3:8b, c, 9a–10 • כִּי + nom. copula (gather) • כִּי + *yiqtol* (consumed) • כִּי־אָז + *yiqtol* (enable)	Reasons: 3:15a, b, c, d • Ø + *qatal* (removed) • Ø + *qatal* (turned away) • Ø + nom. copula (Yahweh in midst) • Ø + *yiqtol* (not fear)

Zephaniah always provides support (motivation) for his summons, but only at 3:14–15 did he do so without logical connectors (i.e., asyndetic *qatals*, nominal copula, and *yiqtol* verbs).[86]

Seventh, we observe a crescendo in the deliverance motif (3:9–20), further affirming 3:14–15 as peak. The prophet temporally framed the deliverance by agglutinating future-markers in 3:11a, 16a, 19a, 20a, 20b (e.g., "the day," "that time") that elsewhere refer to Yahweh's day of judgement (e.g., 1:7, 14; 2:2). Also, Zephaniah's overall tone significantly shifts from judgment (e.g., "I will destroy everything," 1:2) to deliverance themes and terminology.[87] My adaptation of Wendland and Clark's table below illustrates that from Judah's perspective, the book's negative (i.e., judgment) and neutral (i.e., vindication) tones give way to positives (i.e., deliverance).

[86] Longacre provides evidence that "changing the pace" and "transition[ing] to less conjunction and transition (asyndeton)" can indicate a movement to peak (ibid., 45).

[87] Udoekpo argues that 1:14–18's judgment anticipates and foreshadows 3:14–20's climactic "reversal of fortunes," signaled in part by the terms שׁבות and שׁוב (*Re-thinking*, 27, 165). King posits that 2:1–3 corresponds to Zephaniah's *present* goal "to motivate the people of Israel to engage in wholehearted worship of Yahweh and to carry out righteous ethical practices" (1:4–6; 2:3; 3:1–4, 5, 12–13). 3:14–20 was his *future*, ultimate goal: the joyful day of Yahweh, "the establishment of Yahweh's kingdom on earth" ("Day of the Lord," 30–32; cf. Udoekpo, *Re-thinking*, 39). For a concise overview of Zephaniah's major themes, see Barker and Bailey, *Zephaniah*, 396–403. One feature of peak is a "change of vantage point and/or orientation" (Longacre, *Grammar of Discourse*, 45–47); Zephaniah moves from promising judgment and deliverance to calling for joy in the wait in Zephaniah 3:14–15.

Table 4: Relative Connotative Tone of Sections in Zephaniah (Judah's Perspective)[88]

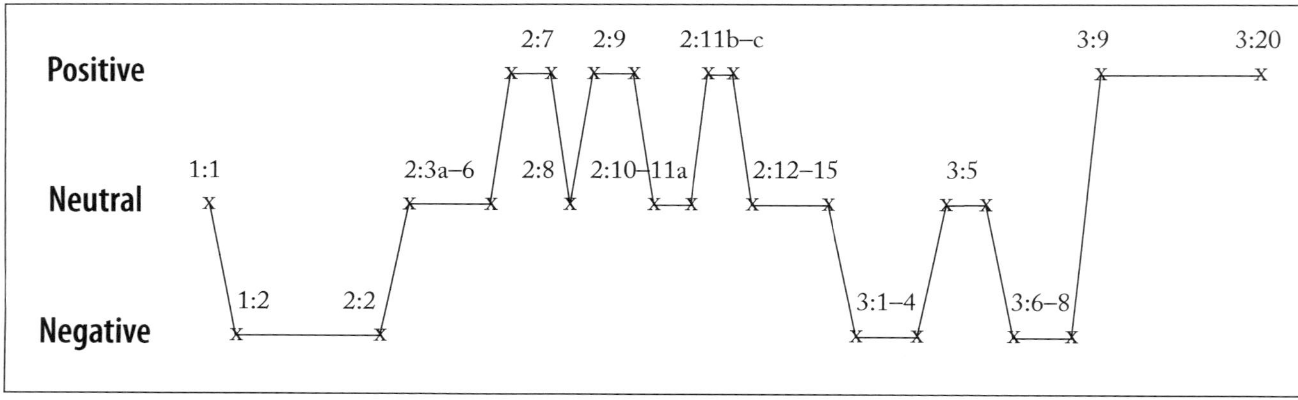

[88] This table is adapted from Wendland and Clark, "Zephaniah," 39. While we have minor discrepancies with their conclusions retained in the chart above (e.g., 2:11 seems neutral), it effectively situates Zephaniah 3:14–15 in the judgment-deliverance movement. About the shift in tone, Elizabeth Achtemeier notes that in 3:14–17, "the Book of Zephaniah ends in almost unimaginable joy" (*Nahum–Malachi*, IBC [Atlanta: John Knox, 1986], 86). Also, Robertson observes, "One of the most awesome descriptions of the wrath of God in judgment found anywhere in Scripture appears in the opening verses of Zephaniah . . . . One of the most moving descriptions of the love of God for his people found anywhere in Scripture appears in the closing verses of Zephaniah" (*Zephaniah*, 334).

Except for brief glimmers of hope (2:3d, 7, 9, 11b–c), Judah receives a sustained word of deliverance only in 3:9–20. Verses 14–15 stand at the center of this bright, future hope.

Eighth, the remnant's deliverance is still future in 2:1, 3 and 3:8 (e.g., "before" [2:2], "perhaps" [2:3d]), and a future day of deliverance textually envelopes 3:14–15 (i.e., 3:11–13, 16–20). Yet, 3:15's supporting *qatal* verbs seem to portray the deliverance as already accomplished. Verses 14–15 appear to call his audience to rejoice as if they were already in the future. An outburst calling for joy in the wait naturally follows the preceding list of promises to the future, humble Jerusalem-remnant (3:12–13; cf. 3:11). What emerges from this evidence is that 3:14–15 stand as the peak of Zephaniah and a rhetorical call to joy while waiting (3:8).[89]

Summarizing Zephaniah 3:14–15's Literary Context

In sum, Zephaniah ministered and likely composed his prophetic book during King Josiah's reign (seventh century B.C.). Zephaniah employs prophetic hortatory discourse to exhort Judah to seek Yahweh (2:1–3) and wait for him in joy (3:8, 14). His rhetorical peak (3:14–15) is parenthetical and poetic-prophetic, calling for anticipatory joy while waiting (3:8a) for Yahweh to accomplish his judgment and nations-transformation (3:8b–10). On that awaited day, He will come to transform, deliver, and return his humble, trusting remnant (11–13, 16–20).

[89] We follow DeRouchie (*Zephaniah*), who argues that 3:14–15 constitute a rhetorical, parenthetical call to joy in the wait. Many see 3:14–20 as rhetorically climactic in some sense (e.g., Coggins and Han, *Six Minor Prophets*, 93; Sweeney, *Zephaniah*, 194, 207; contra House, *Unity of the Twelve*, 209 [3:8–13] and Floyd, *Minor Prophets*, 241, who reads an imperatival progression between Zephaniah 2:1–3; 3:8, 14). But we gain exegetical precision when identifying 3:14–15 as Zephaniah's discourse "peak." According to Longacre, "*Heightened vividness* . . . by a tense shift" may mark a peak (*Grammar of Discourse*, 40, italics original); the move to *qatal* verbs in 3:15 confirms such an analysis.

Select Exegetical Analysis of Zephaniah 3:8–20

We now exegetically focus on expressions important to 3:14–15: רָנִּי בַּת־צִיּוֹן in 3:14, מֶלֶךְ יִשְׂרָאֵל יְהוָה בְּקִרְבֵּךְ in 3:15/17, אַל־תִּירָאִי/לֹא־תִירְאִי in 3:15–16, and גִּבּוֹר יוֹשִׁיעַ in 3:17. We also analyze the immediately preceding (3:8–13) and final sections (3:18–20).

Zephaniah 3:8–13: Wait for Day of Judgment and Remnants!

3:8a calls Judah (and likely the nations) to wait for him to act (see § 3.2.1). This call is grounded in Yahweh's decision of coming universal judgment (3:8b–c) and in the temporally sequential (כִּי־אָז),[90] worshipful activity of many peoples (3:9–10). The future day without shame in 3:11–13 corresponds most directly to 3:8–10, both units including the phrase בְּשֵׁם יְהוָה (3:9, 12).

The first occurrence of the phrase בְּשֵׁם יְהוָה (3:9) refers to promises for the nations. The glorious *yiqtols* in 3:9–10 declare that Yahweh will change the speech and practice of the nations. We observe the following. First, the term "peoples" is grammatically plural in 3:9a–b (עַמִּים . . . כֻּלָּם [MT]; cf. 3:20 and the "scattered ones" in 3:10) and so does not exclusively refer to the "*people* of Judah" who are always grammatically singular (Zeph. 2:8, 9, 10; 3:12; cf. 1:11).[91]

[90] On rendering this expression in 3:9 as "for then" *and* as a climactic reason for 3:8a's exhortation to wait, see Roberts, *Zephaniah*, 216; Sweeney, *Zephaniah*, 183; Ball, *Rhetorical Study*, 235–36; Ryou, *Oracles*, 69.

[91] Contra Roberts, *Zephaniah*, 217, who considers the MT reading is due to "scribal error" and emends the text to a singular "people" (i.e., Jerusalem). This argument lacks manuscript evidence (Ben Zvi, *Zephaniah*, 224) and hinges on reading 3:8–13 as sustaining a Jerusalem focus (e.g., as though 3:8's judgment only addressed Jerusalem's leaders). The pronominal referent to עֲלֵיהֶם in 3:8b is not the sinners in 3:7e but an anaphoric reference to the nearer גּוֹיִם in 3:8a (ibid.; Ryou, *Oracles*, 132), which may entail the wicked "nation" of Judah (as a collective whole [2:1; DeRouchie, "Addressees"]). King correctly argues, "This is probably the clearest statement in Zephaniah of the universal dominion of Yahweh. . . . As a prelude to destroying the earth (ארץ), Yahweh will assemble 'nations' (גוים) and 'kingdoms' (מַמְלָכוֹת, 3:8)" ("Day of the Lord," 21).

The "people of Judah" broadens to "the peoples"; after judging all the peoples/nations, Yahweh blesses them. Second, Yahweh will change the peoples' speech to be "pure" (בְּרוּרָה), rendering it sincere and appropriate enough for worship (Zeph. 3:9b–c; cf. 3:13; Job 33:3).[92] Third, though the Hebrew word שָׂפָה often refers to the physical "lip" of a person, the term can metaphorically denote "speech" or "language" (see Gen. 11:1, 6; Isa. 19:18; 28:11), which fits the action of calling in 3:9b.[93] However, this observation does not constitute an argument for this being a common language. Rather, Zephaniah's parallel purpose clauses draw attention to the transformed speech's goal of *unified worship/reliance* on Yahweh: (1) to call solely on Yahweh's name (לִקְרֹא [3:9b]) and (2) to "serve him with one accord (i.e., one shoulder)" (לְעָבְדוֹ שְׁכֶם אֶחָד [3:9c]).[94] Furthermore, all

---

Zephaniah 3:9 and 13 suggest that Judah and the nations "will undergo the same process (i.e., a purification of their lips so that there might be no deceit in their mouths/on their tongues)" (Daniel J. Brendsel, personal comments to author, July 25, 2015; see also Timmer, *Non-Israelite Nations*, 151, 166).

[92] This participle's root ברר can mean "to separate," "select," or "purify" (Hamp, "בָּרַר bārar," in *TDOT*, 2:308–12), a range of meaning perhaps encapsulated by the idea "special speech" (Sweeney, *Zephaniah*, 184). Yet, sincere, purified speech is an entrance requirement for coming to Yahweh (Ps. 15:2–3; cf. Isa. 6:1–7; see Berlin, *Zephaniah*, 133; Ben Zvi, *Zephaniah*, 225–26, though he denies that the lips would be used for worshipping Yahweh). Furthermore, the purpose of purified speech is to call on Yahweh (Zeph. 3:9b). The focus is thus not on an ethnic language but on the people's *Yahweh-oriented* speech and acts (Széles, *Wrath and Mercy*, 107).

[93] Ball, *Rhetorical Study*, 236; Sweeney, *Zephaniah*, 182–84, though he considers the text to signal a common language shared by the nations (cf. Zeph. 3:9 [LXX]).

[94] The idiom שְׁכֶם אֶחָד is an OT *hapax legomenon* (cf. 1 Kings 22:13; Jer. 32:29). The LXX and Peshitta subtly change the metaphor to read "one yoke," misleading some commentators to posit animal imagery and others to read a burden-bearing metaphor (cf. Gen. 21:14; 24:15; Isa. 22:22; see discussion in Vlaardingerbroek, *Zephaniah*, 197). But the LXX and Peshitta translations are variations on the sense "one accord" (see Sweeney, *Zephaniah*, 184; Ben Zvi, *Zephaniah*, 226; Ball, *Rhetorical Study*, 241–44, who proposes it alludes to unified worship at Shechem). This phrase may imply eschatological, world peace (cf. Isa. 2:4; Széles, *Wrath and Mercy*, 108).

"the lands of the nations" (אִיֵּי הַגּוֹיִם) will worship Yahweh (2:11c), but here Zephaniah promises that with changed speech they will call on Yahweh. Calling, especially on Yahweh's name, often denotes a request that Yahweh deliver (e.g., 1 Kings 18:24; 2 Kings 5:11; Ps. 116:4; Joel 3:5).[95] Thus read, Zephaniah's terms highlight the peoples' united dependence on him. Fourth, as many as seven terms from Zephaniah 3:9 are shared with Genesis 11:1–9 (עמי, שׂנה, קרא, כלם, יהוה, בשם, אחד), to likely indicate that the peoples' calling/depending on the Lord's name reverses the Tower of Babel.[96] A diverse group of ethnic groups including those beyond Cush will verbally worship him (3:9–10; cf. 2:11).[97]

[95] Ben Zvi, *Zephaniah*, 226; Robertson, *Zephaniah*, 328. Many rightly understand the purpose of purified speech to entail praising Yahweh (Berlin, *Zephaniah*, 133; Roberts, *Zephaniah*, 217; John D. Watts, *The Books of Joel, Obadiah, Jonah, Nahum, Habakkuk, and Zephaniah*, CBC [New York: Cambridge University Press,1975], 179), devoid of pride and falsehood (Zeph. 3:11, 13; Ball, *Rhetorical Study*, 237). Such a call for deliverance may approximate "hosanna" (see § 5.1.1)

[96] Ball, *Rhetorical Study*, 236; Watts, *Zephaniah*, 178–79. Sweeney also argues that verse 9 depends on the tower of Babel narrative in Genesis 11:1–9, reversing the judgment rendered there, since all are to call on Yahweh rather than build a tower (*Zephaniah*, 182–84; cf. Isa. 18–19; Chisholm, *Minor Prophets*, 212). Ben Zvi argues against Zephaniah 3:9 reversing Genesis 11:1–9 due to a lack of shared unique or significant words (i.e., only אחת and שׁם), yet even he admits that a loose connection may be possible (*Zephaniah*, 225n736).

[97] Ben Zvi argues that the dispersed daughters refer to the peoples but imply a return of exiled Israel (*Zephaniah*, 227–30; cf. Nogalski, *Literary Precursors*, 202n75). With Sweeney, we find evidence that Zephaniah refers chiefly to Gentile peoples: the verb פוץ commonly refers to Yahweh's defeat of enemies (Num. 10:35; Ps. 68:2), and Zephaniah 3:8b–10 focuses on the nations (*Zephaniah*, 184–86; cf. Robertson, *Zephaniah*, 329–30). Adam Kubiś claims, "The universalistic dimension of Zeph 3:1–20 appears to be rather secondary. In fact, the universal perspective is present only at one point in the oracle (vv. 9–10) and actually serves to underline the complete restoration of the humble, God-fearing remnant of Israel (vv. 11–20) which is the focus of this prophecy" (*The Book of Zechariah in the Gospel of John*, *EBib* 64 [Pendé: Gabalda, 2012], 87). However, though Judah is indeed Zephaniah's primary audience, universal Yahweh-worship figures prominently in Zephaniah. (1) In both 2:11 and 3:9–10 the universal picture immediately follows judgment (King,

The second occurrence of the phrase בְּשֵׁם יְהוָה (3:12) occurs in the paragraph 3:11–13 that focuses on future expectations (i.e., בַּיּוֹם הַהוּא) for the then shame-free, Yahweh-praising remnant of Jerusalem. We observe that Zephaniah weaves the remnant motif throughout this unit. First, in this section Zephaniah's remnant terminology includes שְׁארִית (3:13; cf. 2:7, 9) and הִשְׁאַרְתִּי (3:12) to refer to those spared from Yahweh's judgment.[98] Second, Yahweh likely directs his speech to the FS city Jerusalem in 3:11a–b (cf. 3:7e),[99] but 3:11c remarkably retains the FS participant to refer to a haughty-less Jerusalem. 3:12 then distinguishes between "your (FS) midst" and the people (MS) who take refuge (3CP) in Yahweh. We surmise that Zephaniah's 3MP occurrences constitute a reference to the mixed, future remnant (3:13; cf. 2:7a, 9cd),[100] comprised of both a faithful remnant of Judah and the Gentile nations (cf. § 3.2.1).

"Day of the Lord," 30). (2) Zephaniah closely associates the experiences of Judah and the nations (see § 3.2.1). (3) We posit below that the nations play a role with the future remnant in 3:19–20 and perhaps throughout 3:8–20 (see, e.g., § 3.3.7).

[98] Gerhard F. Hasel, "Remnant," in *ISBE*, 4:130–34; King, "Remnant," 414–15. We follow Lester V. Meyer's baseline definition: "What is left of a community after it undergoes a catastrophe" ("Remnant," *ABD*, 5:669–71).

[99] The antecedent to the FS occurrences in 3:11 is debatable. Immediately following 3:9–10's details about the Yahweh-worshipping remnant peoples that survive the judgment of 3:8b-c, 3:11 may signal that the Gentile remnant joins up with the Jerusalem remnant. This is possible, especially given 3:10's FS and MP referents. However, the referents in 3:7e and 3:11a share the same characteristic (i.e., עֲלִילָה), and both 3:7 and 3:11–12 arguably refer to 2FS participants as third person plurals. 3:7 likely refers to city Jerusalem as the primary referent.

[100] For a defense of this interpretation of the participants, see Sweeney, *Zephaniah*, 186–87. We observe also that in 2:3, Zephaniah refers to his audience as "humble ones" (MP), so perhaps Zephaniah terminologically merges the present and future humble referents in 3:12 to motivate humble Jerusalem to be part of the humble remnant of 3:11–13, 16–20's day. Furthermore, Zephaniah 3 may programmatically expand the remnant. He identifies the remnant as "the house of Judah (2:7a), "my people" (2:9c), and "my nation" (2:9d), but in 3:13 for the first time as "Israel," depicting Israel's future remnant with the same verbs used for Judah's house (2:7).

Third, Yahweh will remove from Jerusalem her exulting prideful ones (עַלִּיזֵי גַּאֲוָתֵךְ [3:11b]). The adjective "exultant" or its verb form (i.e., עלז) does refer to an appropriate posture towards God or even God's own activity (Zeph. 3:14d; cf. Pss. 60:6; 149:5). But in Zephaniah 3:11, it contrasts pious humility and so carries a negative connotation of boastful self-exultation (cf. the "exultant" [הָעַלִּיזָה] city [2:15]).[101] Fourth, Yahweh describes the remnant as "meek and poor" (עָנִי וָדָל [3:12a]). However these debated words are translated, they do not merely denote financial poverty but include attitudinal humility, since the parallel *weqatal* clause indicates they take refuge in Yahweh (cf. 2:3).[102] Verse 13 further prophesies the remnant's *behavior* and non-lying, non-deceitful *speech*.[103] In this way, Yahweh provides a litany of promises about the remnant.

Yahweh motivates Judah and the nations to humbly wait (3:8a). He promises that through his judgment on all, a cadre of Yahweh-dependent peoples will emerge (3:8b–10). For that future day, Yahweh promises a remnant in Jerusalem, purged of wickedness and wicked ones (3:11–13), that is, a humble remnant resting in him.[104]

Zephaniah 3:14: Rejoice, Daughter of Zion!

Zephaniah then summons the remnant to rejoice in 3:14, emphasizing this with four different but relatively synonymous

[101] G. Vanoni, "עָלַז *ʿālaz*," in *TDOT*, 11:119; cf. King, "Remnant," 416.

[102] Ben Zvi, *Zephaniah*, 231–33, who also notes that the antithesis of haughtiness (לְגָבְהָה) occurs in 3:11c (see also J. David Pleins, "Poor, Poverty," *ABD*, 5:408, 411). King posits that since Yahweh's people were already exhorted to be humble (2:3), 3:12 foresees their becoming increasingly submissive to him ("Remnant," 419–20; cf. Széles, *Wrath and Mercy*, 109–10), but we hold that 3:12 depicts the future remnant characterized by humility.

[103] For a defense of the remnant's referential continuity in 3:12–13, see Ben Zvi, *Zephaniah*, 234–38.

[104] For a further examination of the remnant motif in Zephaniah, see VanGemeren, *Prophetic Word*, 177–79, and King, "Remnant," 414–27—especially their arguments that historical and eschatological remnant motifs merge in Zephaniah. The purging here influences how we interpret the satisfied judgments in 3:15.

verbs: רָנִּי, הָרִיעוּ, שִׂמְחִי, וְעָלְזִי.[105] Our analysis below speculates that a prophecy of a unified people (3:13) triggered Zephaniah 3:14–15 to exhort joy from his audience,[106] casting the addressees in terms of a personified, future, re-unified remnant.

First, we focus on the meaning of the first imperative (רָנִּי [qal stem]). It can refer to a shout, whether in lament (e.g., Lam. 2:19) or joy (e.g., Isa. 24:14). But here it means the latter (i.e., "shout of joy") due to the parallel imperatives in the verse, especially the verb שׂמח which always carries the positive sense of articulated "joy."[107] This sense of רנן occurs in the qal form only once in the Psalms (Ps. 35:27) but often in the prophets and Isaiah 40–66 to celebrate Yahweh's kingship and to praise him for his interventions of deliverance.[108] Zephaniah 3:14 thus uses standard prophetic terminology to call Yahweh's people to vocal joy.

[105] G. Vanoni categorizes these four verb roots as basically synonymous "expressions of joy" ("שָׂמַח *śāmaḥ*," in *TDOT*, 14:146). Széles provides their standard definitions in short compass: "*Ranan* means to shout aloud, to exult . . . ; *rua'* means to yell, shout, roar, sound a trumpet; *sameah* means to shout with joy . . . ; *'alaz* is to be glad, delighted, make merry" (*Wrath and Mercy*, 111). Of note in this group, the second imperative רוע (hiphil MP) often refers to praising Yahweh (e.g., Pss. 47:2; 66:1; 100:1) but also can denote a loud battle shout by the victor or defeated (Josh. 6:5; 1 Sam. 17:52; Isa. 42:13). Due to Yahweh defeating enemies in verse 15, the second interpretation is likely (see Vlaardingerbroek, *Zephaniah*, 208; Sweeney, *Zephaniah*, 197).

[106] DeRouchie, *Zephaniah*. The restored people may entail 3:9–10's nations.

[107] Vanoni, "שָׂמַח *śāmaḥ*," 149–50. Many argue that the use here can include the idea of loud articulation (e.g., Motyer, "Zephaniah," 956; R. Ficker, "רנן *rnn* to rejoice," in *TLOT*, 3:1240; J. Hausmann, "רָנַן *rānan*," in *TDOT*, 13:515–22; Vlaardingerbroek, *Zephaniah*, 208).

[108] See Hausmann, "רָנַן *rānan*," 517–18 (e.g., Jer. 31:7; Isa. 12:6; 24:14; 35:6; 42:11; 44:23; 49:13; 54:1; 61:7; Zech. 2:14). Barker and Bailey conclude that this is "a cultic shout of praise" (*Zephaniah*, 493), one legitimate interpretation of the verb. The imperative form of רנן occurs frequently in poetic or prophetic texts (Deut. 32:43; Pss. 32:11; 33:1; 81:2; 98:4; Isa. 12:6; 26:19; 44:23; 49:13; 52:9; 54:1; Jer. 31:7; Lam. 2:19; Zeph. 3:14; and Zech. 2:14). Sweeney explains that this verb was used more often in prophetic literature than the psalms and so represents "prophetic attempts to emulate the hymn rather than of the hymn itself" (*Zephaniah*, 197). His explanation is more reasonable

Second, scholarly hypotheses on the original setting for Zephaniah 3:14–15 subtly impact scholars' interpretations of the passage, and the proposals vary significantly. Some think that the call to rejoice draws from a tradition in the fertility cult to summon female participants to respond with joy at the assurance of fecundity.[109] Others propose that Zephaniah reflects the tradition of victory celebrations established in Israel's history (e.g., Ex. 15:20–21; 1 Sam. 18:6–7; Ps. 149; Isa. 52:7–10), since town heralds apparently exhorted a city to rejoice upon receiving the messengers' news of victory in battle.[110] Still others leverage the similarities that Zephaniah 3:14–15 share with enthronement psalms (e.g., Pss. 47; 95; 97) to propose a background of the annual enthronement festival, perhaps during the New Year.[111] Lastly, several argue for a temple origin, whether as part of the formal temple liturgy or as the location of the prophecy's proclamation.[112] We could multiply further possible proposals—some more plausible than others, but they are all speculative.

---

than concluding its non-Psalm, poetic occurrences reflect exclusive cultic usage (see Ficker, "רנן *rnn*," 1240, contra Vlaardingerbroek, *Zephaniah*, 208). Note that the LXX translates the verb as χαῖρε σφόδρα (see Hans Conzelman, "χαίρω, χαρα, συγχαίρω," in *TDNT*, 9:359–72).

[109] Crüsemann, *Studien*, 55–65. But most scholars deem this background proposal as quite unlikely, since the root רנן and feminine addressee do not occur solely in fertility cults (see, e.g., Ficker, "רנן *rnn*," 1242; Vanoni, "שָׂמַח *śāmaḥ*," 146; Floyd, *Minor Prophets*, 244).

[110] Roberts, *Zephaniah*, 222; Floyd, *Minor Prophets*, 245; Achtemeier, *Nahum–Malachi*, 85; cf. Sweeney, *Zephaniah*, 195, who considers the basic thrust to be celebratory.

[111] John Gray, "The Kingship of God in the Prophets and Psalms," *VT* 11 (1961): 17–19; Smith, *Micah–Malachi*, 144. Paralleling themes in Zephaniah 3:14–20, worshippers sang the enthronement psalms during the New Year's festival with a call for בַּת־צִיּוֹן to rejoice, details of God's glory, references to foreign gods, and use of the trumpet (Boadt, *Jeremiah 26–52*, 228–29). Keller argues, "Cette fête comportait la célébration de la victoire de YHWH sur les forces du chaos et son entrée glorieuse en Sion" ("Sophonie," 213n5). Despite these connections, we do not have any firm evidence that Zephaniah proclaimed his message, in whole or in part, on New Year's Day.

[112] Mason, *Zephaniah*, 25; cf. Sweeney, *Zephaniah*, 197, who finds evidence

Whatever the supposed *sitz im leben* for 3:14–15, the text's fourfold call to rejoice and assertions of King Yahweh's deliverance ostensibly warrant the "celebratory" label.[113]

Third, 3:14a's verb addresses Zion as a personified female (בַּת־צִיּוֹן). The genitive construct is polysemic in Hebrew grammar, so scholars debate the syntactical assignment for בַּת־צִיּוֹן: a genitive of apposition ("Daughter Zion"),[114] possession (i.e., Zion has a daughter),[115] or location (i.e., Daughter in Zion).[116] For example, Stinespring argued that "daughter" can be a term of endearment (see

---

in the OT and from the Second Temple period of prophetic activity in the temple.

[113] On this point, modern commentators broadly agree (e.g., Floyd, *Minor Prophets*, 245–46; Sweeney, *Zephaniah*, 195; Berlin, *Zephaniah*, 148; Széles, *Wrath and Mercy*, 110–11; Vlaardingerbroek, *Zephaniah*, 193–94).

[114] W. F. Stinespring, "No Daughter of Zion: A Study of the Appositional Genitive in Hebrew Grammar," *Encounter* 26 (1965): 133–41; Ball, *Rhetorical Study*, 265; Motyer, "Zephaniah," 956–57; Berlin, *Zephaniah*, 141–42; Donald Leigh Williams, "Zephaniah: A Re-interpretation" (PhD diss., Duke University, 1962), 287; Sweeney, *Zephaniah*, 198; Ronald J. Williams and John C. Beckman, *Williams' Hebrew Syntax*, 3rd ed. (Toronto: University of Toronto Press, 2007), 15; cf. Magnar Kartveit, "Daughter of Zion," *TL* 27 (2004): 25–41; Kartveit, *Rejoice, Dear Zion! Hebrew Construct Phrases with 'Daughter' and 'Virgin' as Nomen Regens*, ed. John Barton, Reinhard G. Kratz, and Markus Witte, BZAW 447 (Berlin: de Gruyter, 2013); and several English translations (e.g., NRSV, NAB, NIV, NET). The recent scholarly literature on בַּת־צִיּוֹן represents a burgeoning interest in discerning the meaning and backgrounds to the expression, especially among feminist circles. See recent bibliography in Michael H. Floyd, "The Daughter of Zion Goes Fishing in Heaven," in *Daughter Zion: Her Portrait, Her Response*, ed. Mark. J. Boda, Carol J. Dempsey, and LeAnn Snow Flesher, AIL 13 (Atlanta: Society of Biblical Literature, 2012), 177–78. The OT sometimes refers to Jerusalem as בַּת־צִיּוֹן (Ps. 9:15; Isa. 1:8; 10:32; 16:1; 62:11; Jer. 4:31; 6:2, 23; Lam. 1:6; 2:1, 4; 4:22; Mic. 1:13; 4:8, 10, 13; Zech. 2:14; 9:9) or as בַּת יְרוּשָׁלִָם (2 Kings 19:21; Isa. 37:22; Lam. 2:13, 15; Mic. 4:8).

[115] Michael H. Floyd, "Welcome Back, Daughter Zion!" *CBQ* 70 (2008): 484–504; Floyd, "Fishing," 177–200.

[116] F. W. Dobbs-Allsopp, "Daughter Zion," in *Thus Says the Lord: Essays on the Former and Latter Prophets in Honor of Robert R. Wilson*, ed. John J. Ahn and Stephen L. Cook, LHBOTS 502 [New York: T&T Clark, 2009], 125–34;

Ruth 2:8) and that our genitive construct is analogous to appositional expressions like "River Euphrates" where the construct noun provides the class of the absolute noun. He thus idiomatically translates the phrase as "Maid Zion."[117] Floyd counters that, semantically-speaking, בַּת primarily denotes the familial term "daughter," and its grammatical combination with a geographical term indicates that this refers to Zion's daughter and thus to a generational situation (i.e., Zion as mother of the future daughter inhabitants).[118]

The main implication of this decision regards the identity of the personification. A few hold that בַּת־צִיּוֹן refers to the city Jerusalem rather than its inhabitants, since the phrase occurs with architectural imagery (e.g., Ps. 9:15; Isa. 1:8; Lam. 2:8). It is possible that early during the time of King David, "Zion" referred solely to the city Jerusalem.[119] But in Zephaniah 3:14 even if the city were the primary focus, the fate of the city can intertwine with

---

Dobbs-Allsopp, "Syntagma of *bat* Followed by a Geographical Name in the Hebrew Bible: A Reconsideration of Its Meaning and Grammar," *CBQ* 57 (1995): 451–70. He finds parallels with Mesopotamian texts that put names of goddesses in construct with geographical locations where they are worshipped; thus, for him, while Hebrew writers maintained a monotheistic worldview, by extrapolating from the evidence, the term "daughter Zion" means that the daughter is located in Zion. He now admits that much of the divine-goddess-epithet explanation is discredited (Dobbs-Allsopp, "Daughter Zion," 132–33; cf. Peggy L. Day, "The Personification of Cities as Female in the Hebrew Bible: The Thesis of Aloysius Fitzgerald, F. S. C.," in *Social Location and Biblical Interpretation in Global Perspective*, vol. 2, *Reading from This Place*, ed. Fernando F. Segovia and Mary Ann Tolbert [Minneapolis: Fortress Press, 1995], 283–302; Adele Berlin, *Lamentations: A Commentary*, OTL [Louisville: Westminster John Knox, 2002], 12; Floyd, "Welcome Back," 499–502). The OT often referred to cities/nations as a woman or bride (e.g., Ps. 45:13; Isa. 23:10; 47:1; Lam. 4:21; Sweeney, *Zephaniah*, 198).

[117] Stinespring, "No Daughter of Zion," 133–41; cf. Berlin, *Zephaniah*, 141–42; Gen. 33:18; Josh. 19:29; Amos 5:2.

[118] Floyd, "Welcome Back," 484–504; Floyd, "Fishing," 177–200.

[119] Jon D. Levenson argues that the term "Zion" carried at least four different meanings in the OT. It first referred to the Jebusite fortress captured and name-changed by David (2 Sam. 5:7, 9), to the Temple Mount, and then by metonymy to Jerusalem, "the entire temple city" (e.g., Lam. 2:6–8). And later,

that of its inhabitants (Isa. 12:6; Mic. 1:13),[120] so the poetic phrase may refer to both Jerusalem and its inhabitants. More problematic for the city Jerusalem-only thesis is that the phrase parallels both Daughter Jerusalem *and* Israel (a corporate entity, not a geographical location).[121] Parallel Hebrew couplets may join complementary, not identical, meanings (cf. Ps. 96:11); so, the addressees may differ in 3:14. Nevertheless, 3:14–15's personal pronouns, constellation of addressees, and content (i.e., call to rejoice) all seem to refer to Yahweh's people and so do not merely envision a physical city.

Fourth, 3:14a's addressee may not simply personify Jerusalem's inhabitants but could entail a generational-remnant distinction. Floyd holds that Jerusalem (i.e., mother) is the present generation, the "oppressing city" (3:1) subject to Yahweh's judgment. The later generation "will form the 'remnant of the *house* of Judah' (i.e., Judah's

---

Zion and Jerusalem referred to the whole people of Israel (e.g., Isa. 51:16; Zech. 2:11) ("Zion Traditions," *ABD*, 6:1098–1102; cf. Udoekpo, *Re-thinking*, 168–69). Though we doubt the usage of the term צִיּוֹן evolved in such a neat, linear fashion, the 26 occurrences of the phrase בַּת־צִיּוֹן all occur in poetic texts and only in reference to an established Jerusalem (i.e., never to the time of Israel's wilderness wanderings or conquest) (Elaine R. Follis, "Zion, Daughter of," *ABD*, 6:1103; see 2 Kings 19:21; Ps. 9:15; Isa. 1:8; 10:32; 16:1; 37:22; 52:2; Jer. 4:31; 6:2, 23; Lam. 2:1, 4, 8, 10, 13, 18; 4:22; Mic. 4:8, 10, 13; Zech. 2:14; 9:9). Follis notes that half of the texts (incl. Zeph. 3:14) link joy to Jerusalem, but the other half occur in times of destruction and mourning. בַּת־צִיּוֹן is thus poetic and may reflect a time of Yahweh-worship centered in Jerusalem.

[120] Vlaardingerbroek (*Zephaniah*, 208) rightly notes the intertwining of city and its inhabitants. Stinespring ("No Daughter of Zion," 137) proposes that the phrase often refers to the whole people (see Isa. 22:4; Jer. 4:11; 6:26; 8:11, 19, 21, 22; 9:1, 7; 14:17; Lam. 2:11; 3:48; 4:3, 6, 10, esp. Jer. 8:19).

[121] For example, see the inconsistency in J. Andrew Dearman, "Daughter Zion and Her Place in God's Household," *HBT* 31 (2009): 149–50: "The parallelism of the three entities in v. 14 includes, but is not limited to, geography, as the stress on returning people in vv. 18–20 confirms." He builds on data presented in Christl M. Maier, *Daughter Zion, Mother Zion: Gender, Space, and the Sacred in Ancient Israel* (Minneapolis: Fortress, 2008). Also, even texts that describe the physical city can figuratively extend the metaphor to the inhabitants (e.g., "the gate of my people," Ruth 3:11; Obad. 13; Mic. 1:9). For a full response, see Floyd, "Fishing," 186.

descendants, 2:7; cf. 2:9b) and be restored as the new Israel (3:13a). Thus, a personification of the younger generation (i.e., the 'daughter') is being urged in 3:14 to rejoice over the possibility that they will someday constitute the new Jerusalem."[122] The prophet could exhort his audience, cast as Judah's future remnant-inhabitants.

Floyd's position is consistent with the evidence. בַּת־צִיּוֹן elsewhere can entail a generational distinction, especially in literary contexts that extensively focus on physical progeny (e.g., Amos 7:18; Mic. 4:8–12; 5:3). If 3:14a–d's addressees utilize generational language, they could conceptually parallel the remnant Yahweh promises to produce in 3:9–13. Furthermore, Zephaniah 3:10 may signal a similar generational destiny as Zion (3:14), the only other place he employed בַּת (בַּת־פּוּצַי). In Floyd's interpretation, Yahweh "scattered" (פּוּץ) one generation—often interpreted as referring to those he propelled from the Tower of Babel (Gen. 11:8–9)—and Zephaniah prophesies that a later, remnant generation (i.e., "daughter") can hope for speech change (3:9).[123] Beyond the remnant-generation meaning of "daughter of Zion," however, Zephaniah does not draw attention to the grammatically feminine בַּת, contrary to many modern, speculative reconstructions. The prophet uses personification to call his waiting audience (3:8) to whole-heartedly rejoice (בְּכָל־לֵב [3:14]; cf. Isa. 10:30; Jer. 6:26; Zech. 2:10; 9:9).[124]

Fifth, Zephaniah 3:14's intentional inclusion of "Israel" as a

[122] Floyd, *Minor Prophets*, 238, 245.

[123] Floyd, "Welcome Back," 503. He concludes, "The destinies of 'the daughter of Zion' and 'the daughter of [Yhwh's] scattered ones' thus converge." Some interpret 3:10 to refer to Israel's or Judah's exiles (e.g., Vlaardingerbroek, *Zephaniah*, 195–96), which is possible (by extension) and presupposes a *later* "generation."

[124] Barker and Bailey, *Zephaniah*, 494. Many speculate about the significance of the female image: (1) marriage between God and his people (Sweeney, *Zephaniah*, 198); (2) simply due to the grammatical gender of עִיר or אֶרֶץ; (3) an allusion to mythological divinity (see Dobbs-Allsopp, "Syntagma," 456–70; Dobbs-Allsopp, "Daughter Zion," 132–33); or (4) representing the paradigmatic Jerusalem woman leading victory celebrations (cf. Ex. 15:20–21; Judg. 11:34; 1 Sam. 18:6–7; Floyd, *Minor Prophets*, 238, 245; Floyd, "Fishing,"

parallel addressee may hint that a restored people-city would widen to include Yahweh's restored rule over all the nation-people Israel (see 2:9; 3:15).[125] Three observations make that conclusion plausible. (1) Aside from foreign nations, only Judah and Jerusalem (not Israel) are named for judgment, but Yahweh extends hopeful promises to the remnant of Israel (3:13). (2) The verbs in 3:13 for remnant Israel's promises (רעה and רבץ) match the verbs Yahweh used in his promises to "the remnant of the house of Judah" (2:7), and in both 2:7 and 3:13 the FS "remnant" (שְׁאֵרִית) functions as the referent for 3MP pronouns and verbs. Yahweh thus may signal in 3:13 that the humble remnant (inhabitants) of Jerusalem would widen to become a new, restored Israel. The imperative in 3:14b ("shout") is accordingly addressed to Israel as MP. (3) The restoration of Judah alone would fall short of the ideal: an undivided kingdom Israel as during King David's day.[126] This suggests that "Israel" entails an expanded remnant.

188–89; Floyd, "Welcome Back," 499–504). Floyd argues that the phrase "Daughter of Zion" refers to a quintessential female inhabitant of Jerusalem yet by extension to all the remnant, implying that Zephaniah reserved restoration for the next (not present) generation (ibid.). Some passages do provide an extended metaphor of Jerusalem as mother and even conflated with Yahweh's role (e.g., Ps. 86:5; Isa. 66:10–12; 54:1–4), providing general warrant for Floyd's position (cf. Zeph. 3:14, 17). And the בַּת + Place Name expressions are often positive pictures of a celebrating daughter (Karla Bohmbach, "Daughter," in *Women in Scripture: A Dictionary of Named and Unnamed Women in the Hebrew Bible, the Apocryphal/Deuterocanonical Books, and the New Testament*, ed. Carol Meyers, Toni Craven and Ross S. Kraemer [Boston: Houghton Mifflin, 2000], 519). But Zephaniah gives no indication that "daughter" envisions a female. We should not press the image further than Zephaniah does, and we do not have satisfactory certainty on the phrase's origin (Dobbs-Allsopp, "Daughter Zion," 133; Berlin, *Lamentations*, 12).

[125] Sweeney posits that Josiah's unification efforts may have stimulated such a perspective: "The ideology of Jerusalem as the site of the temple and the holy center of Israel of course demands such a choice [the address "Israel"], as the restoration of the city is the necessary prerequisite for the restoration of the nation at large" (*Zephaniah*, 198). As we note above, we speculate whether Zephaniah's remnant (3:11–20) includes Gentiles.

[126] Kapelrud, *Zephaniah*, 71.

Zephaniah 3:14 calls his audience to celebratory, verbal joy. He casts his addressees in terms of the future, expanded remnant of God's people (i.e., Daughter of Jerusalem-Israel).

Zephaniah 3:15a–b: Anticipated Deliverance, Joy's Solid Foundation

Zephaniah 3:15 provides the reasons for the summons to rejoice: (1) two asyndetic, *qatal*-first clauses for Yahweh's deliverance (3:15a–b), (2) a verbless clause for Yahweh's continual presence in Jerusalem (3:15c) followed by (3) a לֹא + *yiqtol* clause (result of fearlessness [3:15d]).[127] To support the exuberant call for the personified remnant to rejoice, Zephaniah treats Yahweh's future deliverance as so sure that he casts Yahweh's arrival as already accomplished.

First, Zephaniah provides the initial reason to rejoice as: "Yahweh has removed your judgments" (הֵסִיר יְהוָה מִשְׁפָּטַיִךְ).[128] The term מִשְׁפָּטַיִךְ is the grammatical plural form of מִשְׁפָּט, according to the vowel pointing of the MT (e.g., Codices Leningrad, Aleppo; cf. some Peshitta witnesses), and the plural form of this word in the OT often means "decrees." The singular form of the word more explicitly refers to a legal, courtroom situation (i.e., "judgment"; cf. *iudicium tuum* [Vulg.]; ἀδικήματά [many LXX manuscripts] "wrong deeds").[129] But TJ's translation posits a different term altogether,

[127] See Ben Zvi, *Zephaniah*, 238.

[128] The hiphil of סור means to "remove" someone or something (cf. 3:11; *HALOT*, 2:748). If it more specifically means "to set aside" (Josh. 11:15; Job 27:2; 34:5), Zephaniah appears to affirm "that the legal claims ('judgments') against Zion have been annulled" (Motyer, "Zephaniah," 956).

[129] Most modern commentators detect the LXX interpretively signaling that the Lord would remove Jerusalem's wickedness (see Anthony Gelston, *The Twelve Minor Prophets*, ed. Adrian Schenker et al., *BHQ* 13 [Stuttgart: Deutsche Bibelgesellschaft, 2010], 110. 111; Sweeney, *Zephaniah*, 199; Kevin J. Cathcart and Robert P. Gordon, *The Targum of the Minor Prophets: Translated, with a Critical Introduction, Apparatus, and Notes*, ArBib 14 [Wilmington, DE: Glazier, 1989], 173n33; Gillis Gerleman, *Zephanja: Textkritisch und Literarisch Untersucht* [Lund: Gleerup, 1942], 61, who labels the LXX reading "a pejorative sense").

since it renders the clause as "banished *deceitful judges* from your midst." This evidence, combined with Zephaniah 3:15's parallelism to the personal term "enemy," leads some to posit a revocalized, substantive participle: "your judges" (מְשֹׁפְטַיִךְ).[130]

But we should not amend the plural reading of the MT (מִשְׁפָּטַיִךְ) for several reasons. (1) TJ's reading (i.e., deceitful judges) is best explained as an amplified, interpretive gloss since the Targum is also concerned to correct corrupt judges accepting bribes (e.g., 2 Sam. 14:14b), and in Zephaniah 3:15a it conveniently "manages to provide divine punishment for such evil judges."[131] (2) The proposed emendation is much more rare, while the MT reading occurs often and in the plural with a negative sense, as it is in Zephaniah 3:15 (e.g., Jer. 48:47; Ezek. 5:8; 39:21).[132] (3) The Hebrew plural can indicate a legal sense (i.e., legal "judgments" or "curses"; e.g., 2 Kings 25:6; Jer. 4:12; 12:1; 39:5), which fits the context here.[133] Indeed,

[130] Patterson, *Zephaniah*, 382; Smith, "Zephaniah," 261–62; Crüsemann, *Studien*, 57; L. H. Brockington, *The Hebrew Text of the Old Testament: The Readings Adopted by the Translators of the New English Bible* (Cambridge: Cambridge University Press, 1973), 263; Kapelrud, *Zephaniah*, 90–91; G. Krinetzki, *Zefanjastudien: Motiv- und Traditionskritik + Kompositions- und Redaktionskritik*, RST 7 (Frankfurt: Lang, 1977), 158. A few Peshitta manuscripts may support this reading.

[131] Leivy Smolar and Moses Aberbach, *Studies in Targum Jonathan to the Prophets*, LBS (New York: KTAV; Baltimore: Baltimore Hebrew College, 1983), 89; cf. Sweeney, *Zephaniah*, 199; Gelston, *Twelve Minor Prophets*, 111. TJ's reading (i.e., *deceitful* judges) too conveniently "avoid[s] the suggestion that God is against judges as a class (cf. *Tg.*'s 'false prophets' in v.4)" (Cathcart and Gordon, *Minor Prophets*, 173n33).

[132] Ben Zvi, *Zephaniah*, 242–43. The proposed emended form occurs only in Job 9:15 and Psalm 109:31.

[133] Berlin, *Zephaniah*, 142; DeRouchie, *Zephaniah*, who posits that "curses" adequately translates the term; cf. Ball, *Rhetorical Study*, 180; Motyer, "Zephaniah," 956; Roberts, *Zephaniah*, 222; Sweeney, *Zephaniah*, 199, though he interprets the plural form with a singular meaning. Zephaniah 2:2 and 3:7 record Yahweh's certain judgments-decrees; 3:15 likely denotes Yahweh's future, just (3:5) removal of his promised decrees. Ahuva Ho summarizes the Jewish rabbinical evidence, noting that many read this as a legal term (not a personal enemy): "'afflictions' (Rashi), 'laws' (Radaq), 'punishments and afflictions'

the prophet asserts Jerusalem's certain judgment, particularly for her wicked inhabitants and leaders (1:4–6; 3:1–4). (4) The parallelism need not pair concrete persons (i.e., judges/enemy). 3:15b's asyndeton suggests that the "enemy" explicates "judgments"; Yahweh has your judgments, that is, your enemy.[134] We then interpret the removal of legal judgments here to indicate that Yahweh would satisfy his justice (3:5) in judging remnant Jerusalem's enemy and leaving a remnant (3:11–13; cf. 3:9–10).

Second, we confront another text critical-interpretive decision in Zephaniah 3:15b: Yahweh "removed your enemy" (פִּנָּה אֹיְבֵךְ).[135] Some Hebrew manuscripts read אֹיְבֵךְ as a singular (e.g., Codices Leningrad and Aleppo), but a strong textual tradition reads the noun as a plural (i.e., איביך), including more than 20 Hebrew manuscripts (e.g., MUR88), LXX, VULG., Peshitta, and TJ. Many scholars suggest following the well-attested plural reading, noting that the text does not single out one enemy (whether transcendental or foreign) as opposing Jerusalem.[136] While the plural reading is certainly

(Abrabanel), 'charges' dropped against Judah, 'punishment,' and 'judgments'" (*The Targum of Zephaniah: Manuscripts and Commentary*, SAIS 7 [Leiden: Brill, 2009], 382). These judgments may represent "curses" (cf. 2:2).

[134] Some argue that it refers to an event sequence: first judgments removed, then the enemy(ies) (Ben Zvi, *Zephaniah*, 242–43). He noted a similar sort of parallelism in Isaiah 16:5 and 40:9. To reinforce the event sequence, we would expect a first-position *waw*, but 3:15b is instead asyndetic, suggesting explication (DeRouchie, *Zephaniah*; cf. DeRouchie, *How to Understand and Apply the Old Testament*, 103–7; DeRouchie, *Covenant Love*, 107–32; Garrett and DeRouchie, *Modern Grammar*, 284–85).

[135] The piel of פנה means to "clear away, remove" someone or something (*HALOT*, 3:938). Motyer translates this as "made . . . turn tail" based on Jeremiah 46:21 and 47:3 and concludes that banishing foes signals the "secure tenure of the blessings of their salvation" ("Zephaniah," 956–57). The difference between removing enemies and their fleeing is not great inasmuch as Yahweh acts and the enemies no longer remain.

[136] Smith, "Zephaniah," 261–62; Rudolph, *Zephanja*, 293; Roberts, *Zephaniah*, 220; Cathcart and Gordon, *Minor Prophets*, 173; cf. *BHS*. For a discussion of the potential arguments for positing a plural original, see Ben Zvi, *Zephaniah*, 240–41, who capably defends the grammatical singular reading.

possible, we posit that the original form was singular but interpret it as a collective noun.[137] (1) It is easier to postulate that the original text was singular and later emended to a plural to more readily match any or all of the enemies named in Zephaniah;[138] but supposing a plural-to-singular change is inexplicable in the context. (2) In either its definite or indefinite form, "enemy" is often used collectively, especially in poetic literature like the Psalms (e.g., Ex. 15:6, 9).[139] (3) The literary context of Zephaniah includes forensic judgment and justice (2:3; 3:5, 8, 11) but also foretells judgment on Israel's neighbor-enemies (2:4–15). A collective singular noun could reflect the many named enemy candidates (e.g., Baal, Assyria, God), so identifying only one particular enemy seems an unwarranted interpretation.[140] Yahweh thus would remove any and all of the remnant's enemies.

[137] Cf. *IBHS*, 114–15. Many defend the singular as original and interpret it as a collective (e.g., Ball, *Rhetorical Study*, 181; Ben Zvi, *Zephaniah*, 240–42; Berlin, *Zephaniah*, 143; Barker and Bailey, *Zephaniah*, 494; Goldingay and Scalise, *Minor Prophets*, 130).

[138] Ben Zvi listed the plural reading as a "vulgarization" of the singular (*Zephaniah*, 241). Sweeney prefers reading a singular original as we do but disagrees with the collective interpretation, since he identifies Assyria as *the* dominant enemy of the period (*Zephaniah*, 199). His reading is possible, but we think that the text is purposefully vague enough to include any enemy. For example, Babylon was indeed a real physical threat, yet Yahweh Himself was sufficient cause for Israel to fear (he would carry out refining judgment on her [Zeph. 1:7–18; 3:1–7]).

[139] Berlin, *Zephaniah*, 143; Ball, *Rhetorical Study*, 181. Robertson holds that Yahweh's turning back of Judah's enemies fulfills OT expectations (cf. Gen. 22:17; 49:8; Deut. 28:7; *Zephaniah*, 336–37). However, (1) some of Robertson's references are messianic (unlike Zeph. 3). (2) In analyzing the Jewish literature (chap. 4), we have no evidence that Jewish circles considered Zephaniah's vision fulfilled, even after their "return" from Babylon.

[140] Berlin, *Zephaniah*, 143; Barker and Bailey, *Zephaniah*, 494; *IBHS*, 113–14; Udoekpo, *Re-thinking*, 173. Watts considers evidence for Assyria as the enemy (*Zephaniah*, 182); Liudger Sabottka speculates that the enemy was Baal (*Zephanja: Versuch einer Neuübersetzung mit philogischen Kommentar*, BibOr 25 [Rome: Pontifical Biblical Institute, 1972], 127–28); Ben Zvi argues that the enemy may have been the wicked ones located in the midst of Jerusalem

Third, in the first and foremost reason to rejoice, Zephaniah asserts that Yahweh removed all of the judgments/enemy against Jerusalem, thus satisfying his wrath. However, we do not interpret 3:15's parallel *qatal* forms as actually referring to the past nor even to what had been already inaugurated.[141] Verses 11–13 and 16–20 *anticipate* Yahweh's future deliverance (cf. 2:2, 3d). Furthermore, 3:11–20 function together as positive motivation for the imperative to wait for Yahweh's day of action (3:8a). With most commentators, we conclude that 3:15a–b's verbs are "perfectives of confidence," reflecting the certainty of the events.[142] To encourage his audience to rejoice in the wait, Zephaniah treats as completed what will yet

(Zeph. 3:11–13) (*Zephaniah*, 242); and Patterson noted that the term "enemy" can refer to an adversary at law (Job 9:15; 13:24; 33:10; 1 Kings 21:20) and posited that God Himself was Israel's adversary (*Zephaniah*, 382; cf. Lam. 2:5). Patterson's reading is possible. Yahweh would bring refining judgment on his people (Zeph. 1:7–18; 3:1–7), and Zephaniah seems to explain that his presence should not cause fear for some (Zeph. 3:15, 16–17). By not naming Babylon, the prophet may highlight Yahweh as Jerusalem's real cause for fear (DeRouchie, *Zephaniah*). However, this need not deny that Yahweh would use enemy nation(s) as the means for meting out his judgment (cf. Zeph. 1:14–16). We posit that 3:15 does not single out one enemy.

[141] The *qatal* can present a past event as "the basis for present argumentation (Gen 43:9, 11, 13)" (Robert E. Longacre, "Discourse Perspective on the Hebrew Verb: Affirmation and Restatement," in *Linguistics and Biblical Hebrew*, ed. Walter Bodine [Winona Lake, IN: Eisenbrauns, 1992], 188), and Floyd maintains that 3:15a–b's deliverance "has already begun to happen (v. 15a)" and "completed" before 3:17 can take place (*Minor Prophets*, 243). For an explanation of the ingressive perfective syntactical option, see *IBHS*, 480–95. Floyd's position, however, over-realizes the future deliverance (3:11–13, 16–20) which Zephaniah harnesses to motivate present obedience (3:8a). Alternatively, in Hebrew narrative hortatory discourse the *qatal* can accomplish a "performative utterance" by itself (Heller, *Narrative Structure*, 471–73). The prophet/Yahweh, however, did not thereby perform a speech act of deliverance, so this designation is likewise not appropriate at 3:15.

[142] Barker and Bailey, *Zephaniah*, 494; cf. Williams and Beckman, *Hebrew Syntax*, 68. The perfect of confidence is rare but most often occurs in predictive discourse (Longacre, "Discourse Perspective," 182), which configures with 3:11–13, 16–20. Ben Zvi rightly concludes that these *qatals* do not reflect Yahweh's activity having "actually happened in the past (cf. Isa 43:3; Num 17:27;

happen: Warrior Yahweh will deliver his remnant, executing justice in removing her enemy.[143]

Zephaniah 3:15c (and 17a): Yahweh, King of Israel, in Your Midst

In continuity with the common OT assertion that Yahweh reigns as king (e.g., Ex. 15:18; Num. 23:21; Deut. 33:2–5; Judg. 8:2–3), Zephaniah 3:15c asserts, "Yahweh [is] king of Israel in your midst" (מֶלֶךְ יִשְׂרָאֵל יְהוָה בְּקִרְבֵּךְ). For Zephaniah's argument, this asyndetic, nominal copula clause affirms King Yahweh's presence, providing the reason for his removal of judgments/enemies in 3:15a–b and the second cause for joy.[144] Jerusalem should rejoice because Yahweh's presence as king of Israel would imply security for the remnant.

We discuss four issues. First, some understand that King Yahweh's benevolent presence in 3:15c implies his previous absence during judgment.[145] But we disagree. (1) That position reads eerily

24:17)," but then he states that they are "an expression of praise to YHWH, as well as reassurance to the speaker (cf. Ps 3:8; 55:19)" (*Zephaniah*, 238–39). This amounts to imposing the hymn of praise structure (which itself varies considerable in the Psalms) onto Zephaniah.

[143] 3:15's deliverance seems to entail the satisfaction of God's wrath (Barker and Bailey, *Zephaniah*, 494–95; cf. Sweeney, *Zephaniah*, 199). Motyer similarly argues, "It is one thing to deal with sin within the sinner so that conscience no longer accuses (Zeph. 3:11): this is the guiltiness of sin. It is a different thing to deal with sin as it outrages the holy character of God: this is the offense of sin, and it constitutes a deeper and more necessary work, for there can be no salvation until God is satisfied" ("Zephaniah," 956–57). Lastly, Ben Zvi disagrees with treating Yahweh as a military warrior in 3:15 (*Zephaniah*, 243–44, 247–49), but see Sweeney's response (*Zephaniah*, 202).

[144] Sweeney, *Zephaniah*, 199; Berlin, *Zephaniah*, 143, though she thinks that 3:15c necessarily entails people *acknowledging* Yahweh as king. On the backgrounding function of copulative clauses in hortatory or directive discourse, see Garrett and DeRouchie, *Modern Grammar*, 331; Longacre, *Joseph*, 121–23 (i.e., "Band 4"). Other texts join Yahweh's presence and a summons to joy (e.g., Isa. 12:6; Zech. 2:14–15; cf. Ps. 46:6; Jer. 14:9). Also, Udoekpo finds that Yahweh's kingship implies security and removal of false gods (*Re-thinking*, 174–75).

[145] See, e.g., Sweeney, *Zephaniah*, 199, who argues that Isaiah earlier implied

similar to the condemned in Jerusalem wrongly claiming that Yahweh was absent or powerless (Zeph. 1:12). (2) We do not find exegetical difficulty in asserting both that righteous Yahweh would personally dispense justice on Jerusalem's wicked (בְּקִרְבָּהּ [3:5]) and would be present to deliver her remnant (בְּקִרְבֵּךְ [3:15c]; cf. 3:5, 17; 2 Sam. 7:9; Isa. 44:6).[146]

Second, the nominal copula in 3:15c naturally translates as "Yahweh is king of Israel," but we understand Zephaniah to encourage his audience with a vision of the remnant's *coming* King of Israel, Yahweh.[147] This interpretation aligns with Yahweh's first-person promises to bring about a judgment-surviving remnant in 3:11–13, which likely spurred Zephaniah 3:14–15 to call for joy in the first place. Furthermore, King Yahweh's presence results in future blessing (note the *yiqtol* [3:15d]). And the asyndetic clause arguably supports Yahweh's future-treated-as-past deliverance (3:15a–b); he would come as King of Israel to dispel enemies. Lastly, since the prophet arguably uses "Israel" to represent the expanded extent of Yahweh's

---

Yahweh would hide his face during judgment and that Zephaniah implies the same (Isa. 8:17; Ezek. 8–11; cf. Motyer, "Zephaniah," 957).

[146] James Bruckner, *Jonah, Nahum, Habakkuk, Zephaniah*, NIVAC (Grand Rapids: Zondervan, 2004), 334; Udoekpo, *Re-thinking*, 174–75. Since righteous Yahweh is present in Jerusalem to judge her (3:3, 5) and is then present within her in blessing (3:11, 12, 15, 17), this draws "attention to the ethical change that would take place in the city" (Chisholm, *Minor Prophets*, 214; cf. Berlin, *Zephaniah*, 143, who observes that Yahweh would replace Jerusalem's wicked in her midst).

[147] We agree with Ben Zvi that Yahweh does not hereby *become* king, but *is* king of Israel (*Zephaniah*, 243; Kapelrud, *Zephaniah*, 70, despite his reading the structure as an enthronement Psalm [e.g., Pss. 47; 97, 98]). Baker argues that 3:15 "continues the motif of God's continued presence in Zion, the city of David, as promised in the covenant in 2 Samuel 7 and picked up in Isaiah and some Psalms (e.g., Pss. 2; 89)" (*Zephaniah*, 117–18). This does not deny, however, that like 3:15a–b, Zephaniah treats as reality what will yet happen (note 3:15d's *yiqtol* clause). Thus, Yahweh will arrive in a significant way to dispense justice and expel enemies. Gray labels 3:15 an "epiphany" of King Yahweh and suggests that Yahweh's kingship would extend over people and even over Baal's kingship (Zeph. 1:4) ("Kingship of God," 17–19).

remnant (3:13, 14b), Yahweh coming as "King of *Israel*" suggests that he would reign over the remnant he delivers. Zephaniah 3:15c thus encourages his audience to rejoice with the future-treated-as present: Yahweh would come to deliver as king of the future remnant people.

Third, as part of the chiasm (3:14–17), 3:17b restates Yahweh God's presence for the remnant (בְּקִרְבֵּךְ) but with one major difference: it is a future statement, since a *yiqtol* passive speech verb introduces the oracle set בַּיּוֹם הַהוּא (3:16a; cf. 3:11).[148] We also observe the following. (1) The niphal speech verb in 3:16a implies that the unknown future speaker(s) to Jerusalem in 3:16b–17 is not in focus. (2) We pair this future day (3:16–20) with Yahweh's promised actions on the future day of 3:11–13.[149] Thus the speaker will exhort Zion to not fear, presupposing Yahweh's accomplished judgment on all the wicked (3:8b–c) and continuing the blessings for his delivered remnant people. (3) Jerusalem will receive an oral address (יֵאָמֵר [3:16a]); this perhaps envisions a public event.[150] Though

[148] Floyd, *Minor Prophets*, 243; Cuffey, "Remnant," 206 (cf. Amos 9:11 and Obad. 8); Sweeney, *Zephaniah*, 200–201, though he unwarrantedly restricts the saying to the near future. Scholars posit that the identity of the speaker would be Yahweh (Vlaardingerbroek, *Zephaniah*, 212; Keller, "Sophonie," 214; cf. LXX), the prophet (Sweeney, *Zephaniah*, 200; Ben Zvi, *Zephaniah*, 245–46), Jerusalemites or even enemies (see discussion in Coggins and Han, *Six Minor Prophets*, 122; Ho, *Zephaniah*, 390). But the niphal (here passive) *yiqtol* leaves the future speaker of 3:16b–17 unstated (Ben Zvi, *Zephaniah*, 245), so that the focus is properly on the content of the utterance. On quotative speech framing, see Miller, "Quotative Frames," 155–82. For the argument that Zephaniah's "day of Yahweh" is a day of judgment *and* salvation, see King, "Day of the Lord," 22–31; Udoekpo, *Re-thinking*.

[149] Barker and Bailey, *Zephaniah*, 495. Floyd argues that "this description of things to come [3:16–17] does not just recount what Yahweh will do, but rather quotes something that will be said to Jerusalem because of what he will have done [3:15]" (*Minor Prophets*, 240). House asserts that in 3:16, "All tension built over the threatened judgment is relieved as the foreshadowing changes to fulfilled promise" (*Zephaniah*, 60–61). Floyd and House's comments seem predicated on unchaining 3:11–13 from 3:16–20.

[150] Barker and Bailey, *Zephaniah*, 495.

Zephaniah mentions Yahweh's coming as Israel's King to stimulate joy for his audience-as-personified-remnant (3:14–15), in this future "day," a speaker will orally restate his presence and deeds to remnant Jerusalem (3:16–17).

Fourth, an inconspicuous absence stands out in this passage. Zephaniah 3:16 does not mention the Davidic king, though Zion (i.e., David's city, 2 Sam. 5:7) remains. O. Palmer Robertson argues that Yahweh's kingship was rendered historically visible in the Davidic throne in Jerusalem (2 Sam. 7), and eighth century prophets predicted that after its destruction the Davidic kingdom would be restored (e.g., Isa. 9:5–6; 11:1–5; Hos. 3:5; Amos 9:11–12; Mic. 5:2). He then speculates, "Could it be that Zephaniah simply could not see beyond the utter devastation of the monarchy in Israel? Could he be looking back to the time of Samuel in which Yahweh maintained his lordship over Israel without the intermediary figure of a Davidic king (cf. 1 Sam. 12:12)?"[151] King Josiah of Judah's reforms likely included even Naphtali (2 Chron. 34:6–7), testifying that the hope of a reunified reign over all Palestine could have been fueled in Zephaniah's time.[152] And Zephaniah mentioned Israel twice, both

[151] Robertson, *Zephaniah*, 336–37; see also Barker and Bailey, *Zephaniah*, 494; Kapelrud, *Zephaniah*, 71; James D. Nogalski, *The Book of the Twelve: Micah–Malachi*, SHBC (Macon, GA: Smyth & Helwys, 2011), 748; Paul L. Redditt, "The King in Haggai–Zechariah 1–8 and the Book of the Twelve," in *Tradition in Transition: Haggai and Zechariah 1–8 in the Trajectory of Hebrew Theology*, ed. Mark J. Boda and Michael H. Floyd, LHBOTS 475 (New York: T&T Clark, 2008), 74–76. Edgar W. Conrad further argues that Zephaniah 3:14–15 addresses the community of Judah as king as did the similarly structured text Isaiah 40:9–11 (*Fear Not Warrior: A Study of 'al tîrā' Pericopes in the Hebrew Scriptures*, BJS 75 [Chico, CA: Scholars Press, 1985], 117–18). But Zephaniah 3 only mentions Yahweh's kingship, not human kingship (in judgment or blessing), though Zephaniah 1:8 does condemn the king's sons (Robertson, *Zephaniah*, 337). Judah's king thus does not cleanly escape from association with judgment. Also, Conrad's reading imposes an Isaianic structure (under the guise of "genre") on Zephaniah.

[152] Barker and Bailey, *Zephaniah*, 381. If Zephaniah preached after or even during Josiah's reform (cf. Zeph. 1:1), Zephaniah's prophecy would plausibly reflect this northern expansion.

times positively: to affirm that Yahweh is Israel's God (2:9) and that Israel will have a remnant (3:13). Even if both these references to Israel envision only the ten northern tribes, the composite picture from the dual address "Jerusalem"/"Zion" and "Israel" (Zeph. 3:14–16) suggests a restoration of all God's chosen people under Yahweh's (not a human's) kingship. From Jerusalem's pre-exilic perspective, Yahweh's kingship over all his remnant people would furnish great comfort.

Zephaniah 3:15d (and 16b–c): Do Not Fear

Zephaniah addresses his audience-as-remnant with a third cause for joy. In textlinguistic terms, many read the asyndetic לֹא + *yiqtol* clause as the *result* of King Yahweh's presence: "so that you will no longer fear evil" (3:15d).[153] In form-critical labeling, this clause occurs in a prophetic word of salvation as a formula of (re)assurance, implying promised "deliverance from adversity or future security (e.g., Gen 15:1; 35:17; 1 Sam 22:23; Isa 7:4–9; 37:6–7; 40:9; 41:10; Job 5:21–22)."[154] Indeed, verse 15d's *yiqtol* presupposes the permanent removal of fear's basis—the "evil/disaster" (רָע; cf. Ps. 23:4)—and verses 15a–b listed a legitimate "evil" to fear: judgments, that is, enemy (cf. 3:7, 13).[155] Coupled with Yahweh's presence (cf. Isa. 43:5),

[153] Baker, *Zephaniah*, 118; cf. Longacre's categorization of this construction as a result clause (*Joseph*, 121–23). This clause has textual issues, but we argued that the root is ירא ("to fear"; see § 2.2.2). Alternatively, 3:15d's *yiqtol* may sustain a 3:14-like imperatival force (DeRouchie, *Zephaniah*). Either way, John 12:15 could legitimately derive a directive (μὴ φοβοῦ) from Zephaniah 3:15d's consonants.

[154] Sweeney, *Zephaniah*, 200; see also Barker and Bailey, *Zephaniah*, 495; Vlaardingerbroek, *Zephaniah*, 213; Berlin, *Zephaniah*, 144. Conrad concludes, "The War Oracle in Zephaniah, which immediately follows the Directive, functions in the same way [as Isaiah's War Oracles]: to assure the community in its celebration of the victory of the warrior Yahweh—a royal vocation" (*Fear Not Warrior*, 118).

[155] Motyer correctly argues that "רָע has the sense of trouble or calamity (Isa. 45:7), not moral wrong, since the flow of the context (Zeph. 3:15–19) affirms Yahweh's determination to eliminate threats and dangers from his people"

the promise of no longer needing to fear would greatly encourage and motivate Jerusalem to rejoice in the wait.[156]

We examine now the chiasm's parallel expression in 3:16b. On the day the speaker will declare Yahweh's blessings and deliverance, he calls Jerusalem/Zion[157] to not fear (אַל־תִּירָאִי).[158] We make two comparisons with 3:14–15. First, whereas 3:15d explicitly stated the objective cause of fear, 3:16b's exhortation does not focus on any particular fear source so that it may more broadly encompass the subjective emotion of fear itself.[159] Verse 16c then reinforces this

("Zephaniah," 957; cf. C. Dohmen, "רעע r"," in *TDOT*, 13:578; contra Ben Zvi, who discerns the possible cause for fear as only distress in judgment, and not also military enemies [*Zephaniah*, 248–49]).

[156] Verse 15's future judgment-treated-as-certain was the ground for present joy (DeRouchie, *Zephaniah*). Udoekpo (*Re-thinking*, 176), Kubiś (*Zechariah*, 89–90), and Vlaardingerbroek (*Zephaniah*, 210) argue that Zephaniah 3:16a–c antithetically parallels Zephaniah 3:14a–c, but in our understanding of Zephaniah 3:14–17's textlinguistic discourse, rejoicing and not fearing are not two sides of the same activity. The promise of no fear (3:15d) functions as *motivation/rationale* to rejoice in the wait. Also, 3:14–15 address his contemporary audience as a future remnant, while the prophet sets the exhortation to not fear (3:16b) in the future day (3:16–20).

[157] Scholars debate whether to interpret the lamed prefix on Jerusalem (לִירוּשָׁלַםִ) as a vocative or an indirect object (see discussion and bibliography in Berlin, *Zephaniah*, 144–45), but since "Jerusalem" stands in synonymous parallelism with "Zion" (3:16a–b), this grammatical decision does not greatly impact the interpretive value.

[158] For this clause in salvation oracles, see Willem A. VanGemeren, "Oracles of Salvation," in *Cracking Old Testament Codes*, ed. D. B. Sandy and R. L. Giese Jr. (Nashville: Broadman & Holman, 1995), 139–55.

[159] Mayer I. Gruber, "Fear, Anxiety and Reverence in Akkadian, Biblical Hebrew and Other North-West Semitic Languages," *VT* 40 (1990): 411–22. He notes that though the Hebrew verb *yr'* ("to fear") may refer to "both reverence and fright," Zephaniah 3:16's fear refers to *anxiety*. Esarhaddon's juxtaposition of verbs similar to Zephaniah were used to convey his anxiety, defined as "unjustified fear" (ibid., 417–18, 420). However, limiting the sense *only* to anxiety is unwarranted in Zephaniah 3 given the mention of justifiable fears, judgments and enemy. Motyer ("Zephaniah," 957) mentions that Zephaniah mentioned objective (3:15) and subjective (3:16) aspects of fear, so that Yahweh delivers his people "from both fear and fearfulness." He also rightly interprets

subjective dimension (e.g., anxiety) in its parallel, idiomatic exhortation to not lose courage (i.e., "do not let your hands be slack," 3:16c).[160] Second, both 3:15c and 3:17a connect Yahweh's presence with non-fear. Whereas 3:16–17 refer to an exhortation delivered to Jerusalem on a future day, Zephaniah 3:15d prophetically assures no fear for his contemporary audience-cast-as-future-remnant. In Zephaniah 3:14–15, future joy was to be present joy, a joy during the wait.[161]

Zephaniah 3:17b–e: Yahweh as Saving Warrior and Singer

Aside from the temporal shift between 3:15 and 16–17, a second major difference in the parallel lines of 3:15c and 17a is Yahweh's description. In verse 15 he is a king, and in verse 17 he is a singing, rejoicing warrior. We briefly outline his glorious description in 3:17b–d.

First, Zephaniah described Yahweh with an adjective and *yiqtol* verb in 3:17b (גִּבּוֹר יוֹשִׁיעַ) that Berlin translates as "a warrior who saves."[162] The military/warrior title often designated David, his heroes, various judges and prophets (e.g., Josh. 1:14; Judg. 6:12; 11:1; 1 Sam. 16:18; 2 Sam. 10:7), and even Yahweh himself (e.g., Deut. 10:17; Ps. 24:8; cf. Ex. 15:3). So, Yahweh's warrior function is deeply

---

Zephaniah to distinguish misplaced, banished fear (3:15 and 16) from godly, reverential fear (3:7).

[160] Vlaardingerbroek notes that the imagery of weak hands is used to describe the reaction to a message/event (*Zephaniah*, 213; see 2 Sam. 4:1; 2 Chron. 15:7; Neh. 6:9; Isa. 13:7; Jer. 6:24; 50:43; Ezek. 7:17; 21:12). This is "an idiom that appears periodically throughout the Bible to express the need to take courage and act, whether in the face of adversity or in the face of opportunity" (Sweeney, *Zephaniah*, 201; see also Patterson, *Zephaniah*, 382).

[161] DeRouchie, *Zephaniah*.

[162] Berlin, *Zephaniah*, 145. The adjective גִּבּוֹר most often denotes warrior-like, military activity (e.g., Ps. 24:8; Zeph. 1:14; see H. Kosmala, "גָּבַר gābhar," in *TDOT*, 2:374) but can also mean "hero" or "mighty, powerful" (Ben Zvi, *Zephaniah*, 247–49, who rejects any military influence in Zephaniah's term; cf. Berlin, *Zephaniah*, 145). Yahweh's implied conquest of enemies in 3:15 leads us to favor the warrior sense (see Sweeney, *Zephaniah*, 202).

rooted in his historical actions for his people.[163] Many detect a positive and negative dimension to such Yahweh-Warrior activity. His military-like conquest of enemies (i.e., *negatives* for those judged [3:15a–b]) and his kingship over Israel surely would (3:15d) and should produce no fear (i.e., *positive* peace and tranquility for the remnant [3:16b]).[164]

Second, the next three asyndetic lines of verse 17 depict Yahweh rejoicing over the remnant. Bailey provides a compact translation: "God delights, he quiets [or renews?], bursts into song over you."[165] Due to the lexical recursions found in 3:14 and 17, the text

[163] Sa-Moon Kang, *Divine War in the Old Testament and in the Ancient Near East*, BZAW 177 (Berlin: de Gruyter, 1989), 197–204. Kang plausibly argues that the divine warrior motif did not enter into Israel's history in Isaiah's time, but received concrete expression in Yahweh's military interventions during the conquest and especially the Davidic kingdom (cf. Pss. 47:3–4; 118:7) (ibid., 198, contra Roy A. Rosenberg, "Yahweh Becomes King," *JBL* 85 [1966]: 297–307). The exodus, too, likely played into this (Ex. 15:3; Deut. 10:17). It is of course possible that the Yahweh-as-divine-warrior motif sometimes functions as an anti-Baal polemic, since that Canaanite god is described with similar warrior imagery (Kang, *Divine War*, 199–204; J. P. Hyatt, "Was Yahweh Originally a Creator Deity?" *JBL* 86 [1967]: 377, though they overly credit Canaanite influence on Israel's use of the motif).

[164] For positive and negative dimensions of the Divine-Warrior, see Sweeney, *Zephaniah*, 202; Barker and Bailey, *Zephaniah*, 496. VanGemeren summarizes, "The vision focused on the presence of the great King, the Divine Warrior. He protects, vindicates his remnant, and grants them the benefits of his victory. They need not fear because the great King is with and for his people" (*Prophetic Word*, 178). Also, Patrick D. Miller Jr. studied Canaanite parallels to the divine warrior motif and concluded that Yahweh's victory results in salvation and sometimes also judgment for his people (*The Divine Warrior in Early Israel*, HSM 5 [Cambridge, MA: Harvard University Press, 1973], 173–74). He plausibly asserts, "Whether over the gods or more particularly over Israel, it is the establishment of Yahweh's eternal rule and sovereignty that is the ultimate goal of Yahweh's wars" (174; cf. Ex. 15:18; Deut. 33:5; Num. 23:21; Pss. 24:9; 29:10; 68:25).

[165] Barker and Bailey, *Zephaniah*, 496–97. Commentators debate the meaning of the second verb. For an overview of the six main possible interpretations, see ibid.; cf. Patterson, *Zephaniah*, 383; Ben Zvi, *Zephaniah*, 251; Sweeney, *Zephaniah*, 202. The LXX supplies a plausible rendering (καινιεῖ, "he will renew"),

indicates that the joy demanded in 3:14 is here gloriously expressed over them anthropomorphically, by the Divine Warrior, Yahweh.[166] Yahweh is a singing warrior that delights in his remnant people!

Zephaniah 3:18–20: Yahweh's Restoration, Attractive to Nations

3:16–20 details the future deliverance for the remnant. Due to 3:14–17's chiasm, we examined verses 16 and 17 above, so we turn now to the final portion, Zephaniah 3:18–20.

In first-person speech, Yahweh promises an ingathering of his remnant. Bailey summarizes, "He will deal with Israel's oppressors, save her cripples, and bring her scattered people home. . . . The prophet pictures a day when all the sorrows associated with the people's sin and judgment would be removed."[167] Assuming a pre-exilic composition date, this prophecy would stand in theological tension with Judah's subsequent exile to Babylon (586 B.C.).[168]

---

interpreting Zephaniah to make a new covenant-like promise. The result is that the remnant "will live at peace and in harmony in the new world order. The world of creation is the sphere of redemption (2:7; 3:13, 19–20)" (VanGemeren, *Prophetic Word*, 178–79; cf. Udoekpo, *Re-thinking*, 181; Ben Zvi, *Zephaniah*, 251–52, who sees an implied treaty here, though he makes the unwarranted interpretation that God's love refrains him from any judging activity). Robertson refers to this verse as the OT's John 3:16 (*Zephaniah*, 339–40).

[166] Udoekpo, *Re-thinking*, 180 (cf. Ps. 104[103]:31; Isa. 9:16; 62:5; 65:19; Jer. 32:41).

[167] Barker and Bailey, *Zephaniah*, 497–98; cf. Udoekpo, *Re-thinking*, 181–93.

[168] For a defense of the authenticity of these verses, see Sweeney, *Zephaniah*, 196–97, 205–6. Barker and Bailey argue that the return from 70-year-long exile (Jer. 29:10–14) was the "immediate fulfillment" of Zephaniah 3 (*Zephaniah*, 499; cf. VanGemeren, *Prophetic Word*, 305–9). An assessment of Jewish view(s) on exile exceeds the limits of this monograph. However, (1) we find no evidence that Jewish literature considered Zephaniah 3:14–15 as fulfilled (see chap. 4). (2) Many scholars present evidence that Second Temple Jews considered themselves as remaining in exile after the return (see, e.g., N. T. Wright, *New Testament and the People of God*, vol. 1, *Christian Origins and the Question of God* [Minneapolis, Fortress, 1992], 268–72; A. C. Brunson, *Psalm 118 in the Gospel of John: An Intertextual Study on the New Exodus Pattern in the Theology of John*, WUNT, 2nd ser., 158 [Tübingen: Mohr Siebeck, 2003], 63–69, who additionally traces the "new exodus" motif in John [153–79]).

Yahweh here discusses four groups: "those suffering without feasts, the oppressors of Zion, the lame, and the outcast."[169] We examine the last three. First, in 3:19a, Yahweh uses the הִנְנִי-participle construction, announcing that he would deal with Zion's oppressors (presumably in judgment).[170] Who are these oppressors here? They could be nations mentioned in Zephaniah (2:8, 12, 13), a group(s) internal to the city (e.g., 3:1), or simply unknown. However, the verse's grammar suggests a more universal application since it refers to "*all* (כָּל) your oppressors." Their identity could thus extend to the Assyrians (Nah. 1:12), Babylonians, and/or any other enemies taking advantage of Yahweh's people (cf. Isa. 60:14).[171]

As for the second and third groups, Yahweh promises to "rescue" and "gather" them (Zeph. 3:19b–c). Their identity is linked to Zephaniah 3:19d where the *waw*-series continues with a *weqatal* in verb-first position. The two participles in 3:19b–c are FS in grammatical form ("she that is lame" and "she that is outcast"), but then MP pronominal suffixes in 3:19d refer to the lame and outcast of 3:19b–c. Many scholars understand 3:19 to refer to the FS, future Jerusalem (3:16–17; cf. 3:11), since the shift from 2FS to 3MP occurs both in 3:12–13 ("a humble people," the "remnant of Israel") and in 3:14b ("Israel"). The participles would then ultimately represent inclusive "metaphors for all [remnant] Israel" (cf. Mic. 4:6–8).[172] However, an alternative analysis is possible.

[169] Nogalski, *Literary Precursors*, 204.

[170] On this meaning of this הִנְנִי construction, see Barker and Bailey, *Zephaniah*, 498; Nogalski, *Literary Precursors*, 211. Sweeney analyzes the textual issues of the participle עֹשֶׂה concluding that it refers to "YHWH's efforts to bring punishment upon Jerusalem's oppressors" (*Zephaniah*, 206).

[171] Barker and Bailey, *Zephaniah*, 498–99. Nogalski concludes that Zephaniah 3:19a draws on Isaiah 60:14 and that Zephaniah 3:18–19 quotes Micah 4:6–7 (*Literary Precursors*, 205–8; cf. Ben Zvi, *Zephaniah*, 256–58). Sweeney takes the unlikely position that Micah 4:6–7 is later and depends on Zephaniah 3:19 (*Zephaniah*, 206–7).

[172] Sweeney, *Zephaniah*, 206–7. Based on Micah 4:6–8, Nogalski sees a subtle distinction in Yahweh's people here: "to the inhabitants of a devastated

Zephaniah 3:19–20 may merge the remnant of Judah and the nations, based on the chapter's participant references. (1) Zephaniah 3:9–10 highlighted the peoples worshipping Yahweh, referring to them with a FS noun + MP Ptc construction ("daughter of the dispersed") and with 3MP verbs and pronouns. This would suggest that 3:19 picks up on 3:9–10's promised global restoration, alongside remnant Judah (3:12–13, 14b). (2) Then in 3:20 Yahweh shifts to another group that likely refers primarily to remnant Judah (i.e., "you [2MP] . . . among all the peoples").[173] Even still, only two 2MP verbs occur in Zephaniah 3 (3:8a, 14b), and at least the first may entail a secondary application to the nations (see § 3.2.1). So, Yahweh's gathering in verses 19–20 may blend the remnant of the nations with remnant Judah (i.e., all who waited for Yahweh [3:8a]).

In both interpretations, Yahweh brings back *his remnant people*. These are glorious promises: no personal or physical hindrance

---

Jerusalem [lame] and the diaspora Jews who had been deported or fled from Jerusalem as a result of its destruction [outcast]" (*Literary Precursors*, 208). Others interpret those in 3:19 as the same as 3:20, so that both the lame and outcast refer to exiles returning to Jerusalem (see Barker and Bailey, *Zephaniah*, 499; Motyer, "Zephaniah," 961). Zephaniah nevertheless distinguishes between two remnants. Second person pronouns in 3:20 likely refer primarily to remnant Judah; third person pronouns in 3:19 may signal the inclusion of the Gentiles (3:9–10).

[173] Jason S. DeRouchie ponders this shift and possible interpretation (personal comments to author, February 9, 2015, who also observed that 3:19 would then return "to the theme of global restoration marked in 3:9–10, mixing the remnant from the nations with the remnant from Judah as a single people for the praise of God"). In further correspondence, he notes that including the nations in 3:19's lame and outcast is possible, but the Jerusalem-remnant view has good evidence: "The fact that the promise to deal with Jerusalem's oppressors ('your,' 2fs) is directly followed by a description of the lame and outcast may suggest that the latter were part of those oppressed (i.e., Judeans in Jerusalem). The comparison with 3:7, 14 suggests the possibility that the 3mpl of 3:19 could actually refer to the same group addressed by 2mpl in 3:20" (DeRouchie, e-mail comments to author, February 17, 2015).

to prevent their return; instead, Yahweh will gather them, honoring and providing for them (Zeph. 3:19d, 20c–d; cf. Isa. 42:16; Jer. 31:7–9)![174]

Yahweh promises to set this rescued and gathered remnant in all the earth "a praise and a name" (לִתְהִלָּה וּלְשֵׁם [3:19d]) and then chiastically promises to give "you" (remnant Judah) among all the earth's peoples "a name and a praise" (לְשֵׁם וְלִתְהִלָּה [3:20c]). The OT does affirm that Yahweh's holy people would mediate his glory to the nations (Ex. 19:5–6) and grant a new, great name (e.g., Gen. 12:2; Isa. 65:15; 66:2). But DeRouchie plausibly argues that in 3:20, Yahweh chiefly promises to put his remnant among the nations for "*Yahweh's worth and honor* . . . . It is God's name, God's fame that is to be exalted in the lives of his saints."[175]

Two observations render that conclusion plausible. First, in both 3:19 and 20 Yahweh attaches the lamed preposition to both nouns, which may signal their function as a *dativus commodi* (i.e., *for* a name and *for* a praise).[176] Second, outside of Zephaniah 3 the OT juxtaposes the two terms תְּהִלָּה and שֵׁם twice, but of this set Jeremiah (perhaps Zephaniah's contemporary) provides the closest parallels.[177]

[174] Motyer, "Zephaniah," 961; Barker and Bailey, *Zephaniah*, 499. Nogalski (*Literary Precursors*, 49–51) observes that the end of Zephaniah (3:18–20) and the beginning of Haggai (1:1–4) contain catchwords (e.g., "the time," "to bring" "people") to provide evidence of intentional linkage between books in the Book of the Twelve (cf. also Hab. 3:1–19 and Zeph. 1:1–18; ibid., 45–49). Zephaniah 3:18–20 may introduce Haggai, a (post-)exilic book.

[175] Jason S. DeRouchie, "Made for Praise: A Meditation on Zephaniah 3:20," in *Devotions on the Hebrew Bible*, ed. Milton Eng and Lee M. Fields (Grand Rapids: Zondervan, 2015), 109, italics original.

[176] Ibid., 109–10; Sweeney, *Zephaniah*, 208. For the *dativus commodi*, or lamed of advantage, see Williams and Beckman, *Hebrew Syntax*, 107. Berlin seems to interpret 3:19's construction as a *lamed* of product (*Zephaniah*, 147), but this ignores the parallels with Jeremiah we document below.

[177] DeRouchie, "Made for Praise," 109. Deuteronomy 26:19 and Jeremiah 13:11 (cf. Jer. 33[40]:9) both juxtapose the terms and have the lamed prefix. Some hold that Zephaniah and Jeremiah referenced Deuteronomy (Robertson, *Zephaniah*, 345; cf. Larry L. Walker, "Zephaniah," in *Daniel–Malachi*, ed. Tremper Longman III and David E. Garland, REBC [Grand

Jeremiah 13:11 declares that Yahweh would set his people "for me [לִי]" לְשֵׁם וְלִתְהִלָּה that is, his people would be for *Yahweh's own namesake* (see also Jer. 33:9; cf. Ezek. 36:22–23, 26–27).[178] In light of the parallels, Zephaniah's Yahweh exalts himself in his remnant, for an attractive name and praise before the earth's peoples (3:19–20, 9–10).

Summarizing the Exegetical Analysis of Zephaniah 3:8–20

In Zephaniah 3:8–20, the prophet calls Judah (and the nations, arguably) to wait in joy, since after he judges all (3:8b–c) he promises to grant the peoples Yahweh-glorifying speech and deeds (3:9–10). The prophet provides further motivation by envisioning the future day of restoration for Yahweh's faithful remnant, when he will free them to non-fearing and reverent word and deed (3:11–13; cf. 16–20). Verses 14–15 call the would-be-remnant to rejoice during the wait. "Daughter of Zion"—the personified, faithful, remnant generation—should exult, because Yahweh's promised deliverance and presence as a warrior-king are sure and because he guarantees the removal of fear ahead of the wicked's judgment. Verses 16–20

Rapids: Zondervan, 2008], 694, who rightly notes that Zephaniah 3:20c "includes a *worldwide recognition* of their glory that exceeds the original localities of the exile," italics ours). Others invoke Jeremiah 13:11 and 33:9 to interpret Deuteronomy 26:19 as Israel's becoming Yahweh's glory (e.g., Gerhard von Rad, *Deuteronomy: A Commentary*, trans. Dorothea Barton, OTL [Philadelphia: Westminster, 1966], 162). Deuteronomy refers to his people's elevation above the הַגּוֹיִם and indeed matches the order of Zephaniah 3:19d's two terms. However, the case is stronger for Zephaniah paralleling Jeremiah. Jeremiah refers to Yahweh's people as a praise among all the גּוֹיֵי הָאָרֶץ (33:9; cf. Zeph. 2:11; 3:19d, 20c), as לְעָם (13:11; cf. Zeph. 3:20c), and in the same order as Zephaniah 3:20c's two lamed-prefixed terms. Furthermore, other OT verses include both terms (1 Chron. 16:35; Pss. 48:11; 66:2; 100:4; 102:22; 106:47; Isa. 48:9; Jer. 33:9) but not juxtaposed as they are in Jeremiah.

[178] DeRouchie, "Made for Praise," 109–10. By virtue of Ezekiel 36, he associates the remnant's praise with the new creation and concludes, "The ultimate end of new covenant transformation is worship. All things are from God, through God, and *to God* (Rom 11:36)" (ibid., 109, italics original).

envision Yahweh's joyful day when Singing Warrior Yahweh lovingly returns his people from exile and his own name-praise expresses itself in his remnant, entailing remnant peoples (3:9–10; cf. 3:19–20) and remnant Judah (3:11–13, 16–20).

4

The Use of Zephaniah 3:14–15 in Early Jewish Literature

In this chapter, we survey how early Jewish literature employed Zephaniah 3:14–15. We aim to avoid parallelomania yet "(1) collect the references in Judaism [to the OT text] . . . , (2) note any trends or patterns of similar or antithetical employments of the OT reference within the Jewish literature itself, (3) compare these Jewish uses to the manner in which the NT authors use the OT text."[1] Most scholars consider the most important specimens of Jewish literature to include the LXX (see §§ 2.2.2; 2.5), OT Apocrypha, OT Pseudepigrapha, Judean Desert scrolls, Philo, Josephus, Targums, and rabbinic literature (i.e., Mishnah, Talmuds, midrashim).[2] Aside from

[1] G. K. Beale, *Handbook on the New Testament Use of the Old Testament: Exegesis and Interpretation* (Grand Rapids: Baker, 2012), 103. G. K. Beale and D. A. Carson provide five reasons to study Jewish sources of the OT passage: (1) identify potential examples of interpretation contemporary to the NT, (2) display interpretative differences, (3) discover interpretive "foil[s]" to the NT, (4) find similar, proximate language despite no direct, textual dependency, and (5) discern the NT's "direct dependence" on the Jewish source ("Introduction," in *Commentary on the New Testament Use of the Old Testament*, ed. G. K. Beale and D. A. Carson [Grand Rapids: Baker, 2007], xxiv). As noted in our criteria (§ 1.3.1), we identify markers in John 12 that allude to Zephaniah 3. For the admonition to avoid parallelomania, see Samuel Sandmel, "Parallelomania," *JBL* 81 (1962): 1–13.

[2] Beale, *Handbook*, 108. We follow Craig A. Evans's dating of Jewish rabbinic texts (*Ancient Texts for NT Studies: A Guide to the Background Literature*

Philo and Josephus, they all include at least some arguable reference or use of Zephaniah 3, but the most explicit data is in the rabbinic literature.

Zephaniah 3:14–15 in OT Apocrypha

Though the OT Apocrypha does not clearly quote Zephaniah 3:14–15, two books may allude to them (Bar. 4:21–22 and Tob. 13:10b–13).[3] Zephaniah 3 and Baruch 4 share the rare phrase "from the hand of enemies" and the similar summons to Israel not to fear (θαρσεῖτε [Bar. 4:5, 21]; cf. Zeph. 3:16 [LXX]).[4] And similar to Zephaniah 3:14–15's calls for joy based on Yahweh's sure deliverance, Baruch joyfully hopes for his deliverance. If Baruch alludes to Zephaniah 3, he seems to use the prophecy as a means of encouragement. Second, Tobit 13:10–13 shares terms similar to Zephaniah 3:9, 14–16 and 20, the nations coming "in the Lord's name," and the Lord's love for his distressed people. Tobit's

---

[Peabody, MA: Hendrickson, 2005], 217; cf. David Instone-Brewer, *Techniques and Assumptions in Jewish Exegesis before 70 CE*, TSAJ 30 [Tübingen: Mohr Siebeck, 1992]).

[3] To our knowledge, no scholars trace either Baruch's or Tobit's expressions to Zephaniah. We tenuously propose this as an allusion based on a computer search of Zephaniah 3's terms in the LXX. Baruch 4:21–22 reads: "Take courage, my children, cry to God, and he will deliver you from the power and hand of the enemy. For I have put my hope in the Everlasting to save you, and joy has come to me from the Holy One, because of the mercy which soon will come to you from your everlasting Savior" (RSV). Tobit 13:10b–13 reads: "May he cheer those within you who are captives, and love those within you who are distressed, to all generations for ever. Many nations will come from afar to the name of the Lord God, bearing gifts in their hands, gifts for the King of heaven. Generations of generations will give you joyful praise. Cursed are all who hate you; blessed for ever will be all who love you. Rejoice and be glad for the sons of the righteous; for they will be gathered together, and will praise the Lord of the righteous" (RSV). Evans dates Baruch to 100 B.C. and Tobit to the second century B.C. (*Ancient Texts*, 12–13, 17).

[4] The LXX rarely employs the phrase ἐκ χειρὸς ἐχθρῶν (Judg. 2:18; 1 Sam. 4:3; 10:1; 12:10, 11; Ps. 30:16; Zeph. 3:15; Mic. 4:10; Bar. 4:18, 21).

prayer, like Zephaniah 3, rejoices *in hope* of a future return from captivity, but unlike Zephaniah its distant nations bring *physical* (e.g., "in their hands") *gifts* to the King (cf. John 12's crowd with branches).

Zephaniah 3:14–15 in OT Pseudepigrapha

The most significant connection to Zephaniah 3 in the OT Pseudepigrapha is 3 Enoch 26:6's apocryphal, physical description of a prince, using a potential allusion to Zephaniah 3:5 (i.e., Yahweh's justice; cf. Zeph. 3:15).[5] But even if 3 Enoch "apocalyptically" alludes to Zephaniah 3:5, we have no Jewish apocalyptic readings of Zephaniah 3:15's acts of Yahweh.[6]

Zephaniah 3:14–15 in Judean Desert Scrolls and Qumran

We have few traces of Zephaniah 3 in the Judean desert. The Murabba'at Scroll's section on Zephaniah 3:14–15 is legible

[5] P. Alexander translates 3 Enoch 26:6: "From his ankles to his knees they resemble stars of lightning; . . . and from his neck to his forehead, 'unfading light'" ("3 [Hebrew Apocalypse of] Enoch: A New Translation and Introduction," in *The Old Testament Pseudepigrapha*, ed., James H. Charlesworth [Garden City, NY: Doubleday, 1983], 1:280). He dates the work to the fifth–sixth century A.D. and connects the text to Zephaniah 3:5. Whereas Zephaniah 3:5 refers to Yahweh's *justice* as לָאוֹר לֹא נֶעְדָּר ("every new day he does not fail" [ESV]), 3 Enoch's "unfading light" describes Prince Śerapi'el's (seraphim leader [3 En. 26:8]) *physical brilliance*. Evans posits that the work depends on traditions antedating the second century A.D. (*Ancient Texts*, 31).

[6] Ehud Ben Zvi cites the Apocalypse of Zephaniah as evidence that the book of Zephaniah was interpreted in apocalyptic terms (*A Historical-Critical Study of the Book of Zephaniah*, BZAW 198 [Berlin: de Gruyter, 1991], 26). However, (1) that pseudepigraphal book contains few clear quotations or allusions to Zephaniah, and (2) the strongest connection to the OT book Zephaniah is its association with the prophet's name. There is little evidence to support the claim of apocalyptic usage of Zephaniah in Jewish literature.

but does not have any major textual differences from the MT at that point.[7] The Naḥal Ḥever Scroll of the Twelve Prophets (8ḤevXII gr) does not have any extant fragments of Zephaniah 3 except for verses 6–7 (and even those do not have significant textual differences with the MT).[8] Also, of the Zephaniah fragments found in Qumran, none include 3:14–15. But the Qumran community may have (eschatologically?) applied the book to their contemporary situation, since the word *pesher* is on two Zephaniah fragments.[9]

[7] Marvin A. Sweeney, *Zephaniah: A Commentary*, ed. Paul D. Hanson, Hermeneia (Minneapolis: Fortress, 2003), 25. The differences include its division marker (3:14) and plural "enemies" (3:15; see chap. 3).

[8] 8ḤevXII gr (8Ḥev 1) reads 3:7 as πηγὴ αὐτῆς ("her spring"), and the MT reads מְעוֹנָהּ ("her dwelling"). This difference might only represent orthographic confusion and not a different *Vorlage* (Sweeney, *Zephaniah*, 27).

[9] 4QpZeph (4Q170) includes 1:12–13 and ends with פשרו; 1QpZeph (1Q15) includes 1:18–2:2 with some words introduced by פשר (see analysis in Maurya P. Horgan, *Pesharim: Qumran Interpretation of Biblical Books*, CBQMS 8 [Washington, DC: Catholic Biblical Association, 1979], 63–65, 191–92; Ben Zvi, *Zephaniah*, 22, 26; Sweeney, *Zephaniah*, 28–29). Other fragments of Zephaniah are outside our passage (e.g., 4QXIIb [4Q77] with Zeph. 1:1–2; 2:13–15; 3:19–20; 4QXIIg [4Q82] with Zeph. 3:3–5; 4Q464 with Zeph. 3:9; 1QS 5:1 with Zeph. 1:6; cf. Michael Owen Wise, Martin G. Abegg, and Edward M. Cook, *The Dead Sea Scrolls: A New Translation* [San Francisco: Harper San Francisco, 1996], 132, 402; Hanne von Weissenberg, "'Aligned' or 'Non-Aligned'? The Textual Status of the Qumran Cave 4 Manuscripts of the Minor Prophets," in *Perspectives on the Formation of the Book of the Twelve: Methodological Foundations, Redactional Processes, Historical Insights*, ed. Rainer Albertz, James D. Nogalski, and Jakob Wöhrle, BZAW 433 [Berlin; Boston: de Gruyter, 2012], 383–87). For a well-reasoned defense that a text designated as "Qumran *pesher*" marries form and content that includes contemporizing OT passage(s) for the eschatological Qumran community, see Stephen E. Witmer, "Approaches to Scripture in the Fourth Gospel and the Qumran *Pesharim*," *NovT* 48 (2006): 313–19. Zephaniah's *pesher* fragments are unfortunately too fragmentary for us to confidently interpret them.

Zephaniah 3:14–15 in Rabbinic Literature (Targums, Talmuds and Midrashim)

Targum Jonathan[10]

> *Give praise*, O *congregation* of Zion, shout for joy, O Israel; rejoice and exult with all (your) heart, O *congregation* of Jerusalem. 15. The Lord has banished *the deceitful judges from your midst*; he has removed your enem*ies*; the King of Israel, the Lord, *has promised to make his Shekinah dwell* in your midst; no longer be afraid of evil. 16. At that *time* it shall be said to Jerusalem, "Do not be afraid, O Zion; do not let your hands be slack." 17. The Lord your God *has promised to make his Shekinah dwell* in your midst; the mighty *deliverer* will rejoice over you with joy, *he will subdue your sins* by his love, he will exult over you with exultation.[11]

Due to Zephaniah's chiasm, we include verses 16–17 above. Like Zephaniah 3 (MT) and John 12, the Targum directs Zion to rejoice

[10] Ahuva Ho summarizes his position on the Targum's date: "Whether TJ is pre- or post-70, the finding of fragments of Tg Leviticus and Job in Qumran among the Dead Sea scrolls have definitively shown that the former is correct. Most scholars agree that even if the bulk of TJ is attributed to the Common Era, its roots are to be found earlier. It is also commonly agreed that its roots are Palestinian with later revisions made in Babylonia" (*The Targum of Zephaniah: Manuscripts and Commentary*, SAIS 7 [Leiden: Brill, 2009], 25; cf. Robert P. Gordon, *Studies in the Targum to the Twelve Prophets: From Nahum to Malachi*, VTSup 51 [Leiden: Brill, 1994], 5–34). Michael Owen Wise explains that Aramaic early influenced the people of Judah whether as part of a diglossia situation from Hasmonean times or as a *lingua franca* after the Persian empire ("Accidents and Accidence," in *Studies in Qumran Aramaic*, ed. T. Muraoka, AbrNSup 3 [Louvain: Peeters, 1992], 131–41).

[11] Kevin J. Cathcart and Robert P. Gordon, *The Targum of the Minor Prophets: Translated, with a Critical Introduction, Apparatus, and Notes*, ArBib 14 (Wilmington, DE: Glazier, 1989), 173, italics original. Ho's translation of the end of verse 15 departs significantly from Cathcart and Gordon's version

and not fear. But in Zephaniah 3:14–15 the Targum is unique at several important points and so mostly functions as an antithetical comparison to our OT and NT passages. First, in 3:14 instead of the phrase "Daughter" Zion/Jerusalem, TJ rendered the word as "congregation" (אתשנכ), a term of endearment that also historically referred to the synagogue (post-Temple).[12] The Targum likewise reads "congregation" instead of "daughter" in Zechariah 2:14 and 9:9, verses quite similar to our text.[13] Second, instead of Yahweh removing "judgments," TJ singles out and holds a negative view of evil "judges," as those provoking Yahweh to exile his people.[14] Third, there is textual disagreement among the Targums at 3:15. A few Targums place "judges" in parallelism with "enemies" (perhaps

---

(cf. 3:17a): Yahweh "*has decided to let His Shekinah dwell* in your midst; do not fear *from before* misfortune any more" (*Zephaniah*, 381, italics original).

[12] Ho, *Zephaniah*, 378. Ho notes that since the "synagogue" refers to the gathered assembly and occurs here in 3:14 with rejoicing vocabulary, TJ emphasizes corporate prayer. Also, this likely reflects the targumist's idiosyncratic viewpoint rather than a different *Vorlage* (ibid.; cf. Sweeney, *Zephaniah*, 32).

[13] Cathcart and Gordon, *Minor Prophets*, 173n32; Ho, *Zephaniah*, 380. The phrase כנישתא דישראל describes Israel instead of "daughter" or "virgin" in other passages in the Targums (e.g., Jer. 4:31; 31:4, 13; Amos 8:13; ibid., 378n773). TJ often renders "daughter" as "congregation" (Isa. 37:22), as "the people of" (Isa. 23:12) and even as a reference to a foreign (non-Israel) nation (e.g., Isa. 47:1; Jer. 48:18; 50:42), perhaps reflecting a pre-70 A.D. translation (ibid., 381). Pierre Grelot argues that TJ's Zechariah 2:14 is based on a Tosefta passage and both find their source in an Aramaic version of Zephaniah 3 ("Une Tosephta Targoumique sur Zacharie, II, 14–15," *RB* 73 [1966]: 197–211), but see modifications to this position by both Ho (*Zephaniah*, 389) and Gordon (*Studies*, 101).

[14] Ho plausibly argues, "The removal of negative elements from within the Israelite society is interpreted as sending them to exile, according to the admonition in Deut 28:64, 29:27 (same interpretation in Zeph 3:11,18), rather than endorsing death as it does elsewhere (e.g., Deut 28:61–63) . . . . The exile was a divine decree for those who did not observe the law and for those who failed to respect the sanctity of the Temple and Jerusalem" (*Zephaniah*, 382–83). He also furnishes evidence of a rabbinical program to condemn false teaching and practices (384–85). Sweeney similarly notes the targumist's interest in condemning idolatry and false prophets (Zeph. 1:5; 3:2, 4, 15; *Zephaniah*, 32–33).

equating the two) and state that the *king of Israel [is] Yahweh*. But other targumic manuscripts place an athnach under "Israel" rather than under "your enemies," pluralize "kings," and thus seem to imply that *the kings of Israel were enemies*. If a targumist followed this latter interpretation, he (1) "views the removal of the kings from Israelite society (vs. 14) as a blessing and a cause for rejoicing,"[15] and (2) pessimistically, does not mention the kingship of Yahweh at all.

Lastly, instead of declaring Yahweh is simply "in your midst," additional elements focus on the intention or certainty of Yahweh's *Shekinah*. Ho plausibly argues that TJ's term *Shekinah* is likely derived from the Hebrew clause וְשָׁכַנְתִּי בְּתוֹךְ (cf. Ex. 25:8; 29:45; Num. 5:3; 1 Kings 6:13; Ezek. 43:9; Zech. 2:14), an idea further "developed in the Second Temple period and [that] is inherently the Divine Presence" in conjunction with select "attributes" (e.g., merciful, holy).[16] Also, scholars are divided as to how to interpret TJ's verb אֲמַר ("to say"). In Zephaniah 3:5, 15, and 17, the targumist may have indicated that Yahweh's presence had indeed departed Israel (perhaps after the temple's destruction in A.D. 70) and *possibly promises* his return.[17] But at least one scholar interprets the targumist's verb in 3:15 and 17 to signal that Yahweh *never abrogated his decision* to remain in the Jerusalem temple with his people (cf.

Other scholars note that the Targums do not condemn judges *per se*, but only wicked ones (e.g., Cathcart and Gordon, *Minor Prophets*, 173n33; Leivy Smolar and Moses Aberbach, *Studies in Targum Jonathan to the Prophets*, LBS [New York: KTAV; Baltimore: Baltimore Hebrew College, 1983], 88–89).

[15] Ho, *Zephaniah*, 387 (see textual evidence in ibid., 386–88; cf. 2 Kings 17:8, 21; 21:9–16; 23:26–27; Jer. 19:4). Ho also argues, "TJ adds Kings in general to the list of wicked leaders. Looking at the text from a post 70 CE perspective, kings like Herod and his descendants, who caused misery and severe social and economic malaise, are well within the parameters of such an accusation. Human kingship contradicts God's plans for Israel" (ibid., 387). Ho prefers TJ's second manuscript tradition above; Cathcart and Gordon follow the first one (*Minor Prophets*, 173).

[16] Ho, *Zephaniah*, 326–27. For his overview of this term in rabbinic literature, see 326–32.

[17] Smolar and Aberbach think the targumist theologically doubts Yahweh's

Isa. 17:11; 56:5; Zeph. 3:7; Zech. 9:1), providing them security and peace.[18] In either interpretation, the presence of Yahweh (continued or promised), albeit in the mediated form of his *Shekinah*, encourages the targumist and God's people.

The Talmuds

The Mishnah[19] and Tosefta do not directly reference Zephaniah 3:14–15, but the Tosefta (t. Ber. 6:2) and some Talmudic passages do refer to 3:9. T. Berakot 6:2 applies Zephaniah 3:9 to the conversion of Gentiles located outside of Israel,[20] an interpretation consistent with the plural עַמִּים in many of Zephaniah's MT manuscripts. The Jerusalem Talmud likewise referenced 3:9, indicating it entailed the Gentiles's (i.e., sons of Noah) pure speech but interpreted their conversion as temporary (y. 'Abod. Zar. 2a).[21] And b. 'Abod. Zar. 24a records a rabbinical dispute about whether Zephaniah 3:9 pertains to the Gentile proselytes' turning away from

---

presence but considers possible his return in the "mystical future" (*Targum Jonathan*, 222–23; cf. Cathcart and Gordon, *Minor Prophets*, 173, who render the verb as "promised" but certain, cf. 2 Sam. 23:16; Isa. 12:6; Jonah 1:16). Gordon, however, concludes that the targumist views Yahweh's absence in historical terms: an absence beginning shortly after A.D. 70 but only temporary (*Studies*, 134). But see Bruce G. Chilton (*The Glory of Israel: The Theology and Provenience of the Isaiah Targum*, JSOTSup 23 [Sheffield: JSOT Press, 1983], 69–71), who argues that some of Isaiah's *Shekinah* passages antedate A.D. 70 (e.g., Isa. 8:18; 17:11; 26:21), a possibility also for Zephaniah (see Ho, *Zephaniah*, 17).

[18] Ho, *Zephaniah*, 329–30, 388. Ho challenges those who date TJ as post-70 A.D.

[19] The Mishnah contains no reference to Zephaniah (Ben Zvi, *Zephaniah*, 26; cf. *The Mishnah: A New Translation*, trans. Jacob Neusner [New Haven: Yale University Press, 1988], 1158–62; Alexander Samely, *Rabbinic Interpretation of Scripture in the Mishnah* [New York: Oxford University Press, 2002], 459–62).

[20] Some date the Tosefta to the early third century (see Evans, *Ancient Texts*, 224–27).

[21] Heinrich W. Guggenheimer, ed., trans., *Fourth Order: Neziqin. Tractates Ševi'it and 'Avodah Zarah*, vol. 13, *The Jerusalem Talmud*, SJ 61 (Berlin, New York: de Gruyter, 2011), 287, who interprets the Talmud as "implying that the Gentiles will accept the Jewish style of worship" (cf. b. Ber. 57b). The Jerusalem

idolatry *or also* to their turning to the Lord.[22] None of the authorities in this Talmud interpret 3:9 as referring to a universal language,[23] but they discuss the unity of the Gentiles's worship.

Regarding direct references to Zephaniah 3:14–15, the Babylonian Talmud strongly condemns judges based on 3:15 (b. Sanh. 98a; b. Šabb. 139a). B. Sanhedrin 98a is significant:

> R. Papa said: . . . "When the haughty cease to exist [in Israel], the magi shall also cease [among the Persians]," as it is written, *And I will purely purge away thy haughty ones and take away all thy tin.* "When the judges cease to exist [in Israel], the *chiliarchi* shall cease likewise," as it is written, *The Lord hath taken away thy judgments, he hath cast out thine enemy* [Zeph. 3:15].[24]

This rabbinical teaching thus applied Zephaniah's judicial term "judgments" to judges (cf. TJ) and indicated that removing evil judges in the future is the prerequisite for the removal of Israel's particular (Persian?) enemies.[25] Ho comments, "The redemption of

Talmud was completed ca. A.D. 300–425 (Evans, *Ancient Texts*, 228).

[22] The Babylonian Talmud may have been compiled A.D. 500–550 (Evans, *Ancient Texts*, 228–29).

[23] Other rabbinic teaching does interpret Zephaniah 3:9 as "referring to the restoration of primordial conditions, when all people spoke Hebrew and all worshiped the one God of Israel. It is used as an eschatological source for states or events that will take place in the days of the Messiah" (Ho, *Zephaniah*, 358–59, who presents evidence from rabbinic literature).

[24] I. Epstein, ed., trans., *The Babylonian Talmud* (London: Soncino, 1935–52), 6:663, italics original; however he neglected to note that "purge" likely draws from Zephaniah 3:11. B. Šabbat 139a and b. Sanhedrin 98a contain nearly identical content.

[25] According to Epstein, the rabbi's term *magi* refers to the "Guebres, who caused the Jews much suffering under the Sassanians," and the term *chiliarchi* refers to "the name of a class of oppressive Persian officers" (ibid., 2:701; cf. Ho, *Zephaniah*, 385). Ho argues that the Targums followed rabbinic teaching with their rendering "judges," that rabbis frequently condemned judges to blame them as the source of any catastrophe, and that Yahweh's Shekinah will

Israel is dependent on the integrity of their judges, but reality is too dystopian."[26] The MT text of Zephaniah, by contrast, does not isolate one enemy, and the original term was most likely a collective singular, accommodating any of Yahweh's people's enemies (see § 3.3.3).

B. Sanhedrin 98a is set in a larger discussion about the timing of the Son of David's coming and refers to Zephaniah 3 again as providing some prerequisites for that time:

> Ze'iri said in R. Ḥanina's name: The son of David will not come until there are no conceited men in Israel, as it is written, *For then I will take away out of the midst of the them that rejoice in thy pride*: which is followed by, *I will also leave in the midst of thee an afflicted and poor people, and they shall take refuge in the name of the Lord* [Zeph. 3:11–12].[27]

The Babylonian Talmud sustains a long discussion about the timing of the "coming of the Messiah," "the son of David" (b. Sanh. 96b–98a). And according to b. Sanhedrin 98a, Zephaniah's prerequisite is: no wicked man in Israel. A few lines later in the same discussion, the Talmud furthermore quotes R. Joshua as saying, "If they are meritorious, [the Messiah will come] *with the clouds of heaven* [Dan. 7:13]; if not, *lowly and riding upon an ass* [Zech. 9:7]."[28]

This rabbinical discussion is therefore highly significant to the Zephaniah Proposal. It (1) links the son of David with the

---

not dwell with Israel until wicked ones are removed (e.g., b. Šabb. 139a; ibid., 383–385).

[26] Ho, *Zephaniah*, 385.

[27] Epstein, *Babylonian Talmud*, 6:662, italics original. Ben Zvi unfortunately narrows the importance of this passage to the "enemy(ies)" textual issue (*Zephaniah*, 242n803). Richard J. Coggins and Jin H. Han notice the messianic interpretation and date the work to the fourth century (*Six Minor Prophets through the Centuries: Nahum, Habakkuk, Zephaniah, Haggai, Zechariah, and Malachi*, BBC [Malden, MA: Wiley-Blackwell, 2011], 122).

[28] Epstein, *Babylonian Talmud*, 6:664, italics original, but the citation ostensibly referred to Zechariah 9:9 (not verse 7).

Messiah, (2) lists Zephaniah 3 as having conditions for the Messiah's coming,[29] (3) implies there is a righteousness prerequisite(s) for his arrival,[30] and (4) includes Zechariah 9:9 to depict this future coming, though his humbly riding an ass may signal that Israel did not merit righteousness. Contrastively, Zephaniah 3 focuses neither on a messianic nor on a human king but instead stresses Yahweh's kingship (3:5, 15). Yet this rabbinic testimony furnishes evidence of a messianic hope rooted in Zephaniah and Zechariah, so we should not be surprised if John linked Zechariah 9 and Zephaniah 3 to Messiah King Jesus's entry.

Midrashim

At least three midrashim use Zephaniah 3:14–15. First, Midrash Psalms 95.1 identifies Zephaniah 3:15's removal of the wicked (judges?) as rationale for 3:14's call to rejoice/gloat.

> *Come let us sing joyously to the Lord; let us shout for joy to the Rock of our salvation* (Ps. 95:1). Elsewhere, this is what Scripture says: *Sing, O daughter of Zion, shout, O Israel; be glad and rejoice with all thy heart, O daughter of Jerusalem* (Zeph. 3:14). Why? Because *The Lord hath taken away thy judgments, He hath cast out thine enemy* (*ibid.* 3:15). At the fall of the wicked, every one shouts for joy.[31]

[29] A Jewish Talmudic tradition lists (prophet?) Zephaniah as one of eight human princes (Mic. 5:4) who are the first to enter the messianic era (b. Sukkah 52b; see Saadia Gaon, *The Book of Beliefs and Opinions*, trans. Samuel Rosenblatt, YJS 1 [New Haven: Yale University Press, 1948], 276, 429; Ben Zvi, *Zephaniah*, 22; B. J. Bamberger, "The Changing Image of the Prophet in Jewish Thought," in *Interpreting the Prophetic Tradition: The Goldenson Lectures 1955–1966*, LOBS [Cincinnati: HUC Press; New York: KTAV, 1969], 306–7).

[30] Also, the Babylonian Talmud referenced Zephaniah 3:13 ("The remnant of Israel shall not do iniquity, nor speak lies") sometimes to indicate the people of Israel's above-reproach comportment (b. Qidd. 45b; b. B. Meṣ. 106b) and other times their meritorious standing (b. Pesaḥ. 91a).

[31] *The Midrash on Psalms*, trans. W. G. Braude, YJS 9 (New Haven: Yale

Second, Midrash Psalms 147.2 broadens the group of praise-singers to "all" (incl. Gentiles).

> When the Holy One, blessed be He, reigns, everything will sing praises unto Him . . . When the Holy One, blessed be He, is King, it will be proper to praise Him. Why? Because everything will belong to the kingdom of the Holy One, blessed be He. Then all will sing, all will shout praises, all will laud Him because all will see Him reigning [Isa. 52:7–9] . . . So Scripture says again: *Sing, O daughter of Zion, shout, O Israel; be glad, and rejoice with all thy heart, O daughter of Jerusalem* (Zeph. 3:14). At what event? When *The Lord hath taken away thy judgments . . . The King of Israel, even the Lord, is in the midst of thee* (ibid. 3:15). So when the Holy One, blessed be He, reigns, in that hour ye are to sing praises unto Him.[32]

Both midrashim's quotations of Zephaniah basically follow the MT's text and assume that Zephaniah 3:15 awaits fulfillment, but the interpretational approaches differ. The first midrash licenses *gloating over the wicked enemy's fall*, whenever that may be. By contrast, Zephaniah's firm confidence for the call to joy was *Yahweh*: his anticipated removal of the punishments-enemy (3:15). The second midrash seems to explicate the inclusion of the nations and to add "eschatological" details to Zephaniah 3:14–15: *in the moment* when the Lord

University Press, 1959), 2:136, italics original; cf. Ho, *Zephaniah*, 384. This midrash (Midr. Pss.) was compiled around A.D. 750–800 (Evans, *Ancient Texts*, 242–43). Similar to Midrash Psalms 95.1, a rabbinic text (Lev. Rab. 31.9) quotes Zephaniah 3:5 as an anti-idolatry polemic. It highlights Yahweh's unceasing justice on the shameless unrighteous, interpreted as those shamelessly bowing down to the sun and moon (see translation and commentary in Jacob Neusner, *Judaism and Scripture: The Evidence of Leviticus Rabbah*, CSHJ [Chicago: University of Chicago Press, 1986], 532).

[32] Braude, *Midrash on Psalms*, 2:372, italics original; see also Ho, *Zephaniah*, 384.

visibly reigns and subjugates all things to his kingdom, *everyone* (*incl. Gentiles*) should sing his praises; and the attending circumstance to the singing will be Yahweh's removal of Zion's "judges" or "decrees" (i.e., מִשְׁפָּטַיִךְ).[33] Similar to this midrash's interpretation of Zephaniah 3, in the FG King Jesus's entry (1) was publicly witnessed, (2) included praises at the event, (3) portrayed an inclusive group of worshippers (e.g., "the world," "the Greeks"), and (4) claimed the Lord's presence as king. John's narrative is strikingly similar to Midrash Psalms 147.2.

A third midrash (S. Eli. Rab. 18) places Zephaniah 3:14–15 between two passages from Zechariah (Zech. 2:14 and 2:3; cf. 9:9) and associates Zephaniah with messianic hopes.

> *Sing and rejoice, O daughter of Zion* (Zech. 2:14). Sing all kinds of song and rejoice in all sorts of gladness. Why? Because *I come, and I dwell in the midst of thee, saith the Lord* (*ibid.*). And sing because in time *The Lord will take away thy judgments, will cast out thine enemy* (Zeph. 3:15). Indeed, *The Lord showed me four craftsmen* [*who will restore your glory*] (Zech. 2:3): Messiah the son of David, Messiah the son of Joseph, Elijah, and the Righteous Priest.[34]

This midrash provides evidence that some Jewish traditions associated Zechariah 2:14 (cf. Zech. 9:9) and Zephaniah 3:14–15 apparently due to their similar (1) calls for the daughter of Zion to rejoice and (2) rationales for that call, Yahweh's presence and deliverance. Also, the midrash ostensibly views Yahweh's deliverance as

[33] Ho, *Zephaniah*, 384. Ho argues that TJ drew from these rabbinic teachings and that Midrash Psalms 138.2 connects the "time" with the era of the rebuilt Temple (ibid., 389–90).

[34] *Tanna debe Eliyyahu: The Lore of the School of Elijah*, trans. W. G. Braude and I. J. Kapstein (Philadelphia: Jewish Publication Society of America, 1981), 214, italics original. This work's compilation dates to A.D. 300 or A.D. 850 (Evans, *Ancient Texts*, 239–40).

yet-to-be-accomplished (Zeph. 3:15). But unlike Zephaniah 3, the midrash links the deliverance with messianic personage(s) (cf. b. Sanh. 98a).[35]

One more Jewish reading of Zephaniah 3:14–15 does not fit any of the preceding categories: *sedarim* with *hafṭarot* targumic readings in Palestinian synagogues. The synagogue read Torah portions with the Prophets during the week/sabbath or festival, followed by a homily. Since they selectively paired the readings, this evidence may provide interpretational insights.[36]

Jacob Mann identified two sedarim that included our passage: Seder 9 and Seder 104.[37] Seder 9 read Genesis 11:1 with Zephaniah 3:9–17 and 20, which contain verbal links to the nations in their initial verses. Ben Zion Wacholder observes, "The account of

[35] Jewish interpreters debate the identity of these craftsmen/messiahs (see, e.g., Braude's and Kapstein's discussion, *Tanna debe Eliyyahu*, 214n52), but this rabbinical teaching does reflect a specific, messianic expectation and hoped-for deliverance from exile (i.e., treating Zephaniah 3:15 as a future prophecy).

[36] Dating the origin of these reading pairs is complicated by their connection to the debated dating of the written Targums (see Sweeney, *Zephaniah*, 30–31). Additionally, scholars debate the frequency of the readings as a triennial (e.g., Jacob Mann, *The Palestinian Triennial Cycle: Genesis and Exodus*, vol. 1, *The Bible As Read and Preached in the Old Synagogue*, repr. with new matter, LOBS [New York: KTAV, 1971], 3–11) or an annual cycle (e.g., Isaiah Sonne, preface to *The Palestinian Triennial Cycle: Leviticus and Numbers to Seder 106*, by Jacob Mann and Isaiah Sonne, vol. 2, *The Bible As Read and Preached in the Old Synagogue* [Cincinnati: Mann-Sonne Publication Committee, Hebrew Union College, 1966], xxi–xxxii); therefore, we remain nondogmatic on when (i.e., days of the week/festivals) the synagogue read Zephaniah. Great variety was always possible (cf. Charles Perrot, "The Reading of the Bible in the Ancient Synagogue," in *Mikra: Text, Translation, Reading and Interpretation of the Hebrew Bible in Ancient Judaism and Early Christianity*, ed. Martin Jan Mulder, CRINT 2.1 [Assen/Maastricht: Van Gorcum; Philadelphia: Fortress, 1988], 141, who argues that Zephaniah 3:20 was read at Pentecost—a significant connection if Acts 2 contains an echo of Zephaniah 3:9).

[37] For textual support for these sedarim, see Mann, *Genesis and Exodus*, 91–92; Mann and Sonne, *Leviticus and Numbers*, 201; Perrot, "Reading of the Bible," 141, 143. The passages for "Seder 9" are well-documented. "Seder 104" is derived from triangulated data and so is less certain.

the tower of Babel, introduced in Seder 9 by 'All the earth had the same *language* (*safah*)' (11:1) was concluded with Zeph. 3:9: 'For then (in the day of judgment) will I restore to the peoples a clear *language* (*sáfah*) that they may all call in the name of the Lord.'"[38] For Seder 104, Numbers 4:17–18 explains how not to "cut off" the Kohathites, and Zephaniah 3:7–15 includes Numbers's verbs (כרת and לקח). Jewish homilies exploited further connections: e.g., physical and spiritual service (עבודה [Num. 4:19]; cf. Zeph. 3:9) of all nations, and the remnant of Israel and their promised name among the nations (Zeph. 3:13, 20).[39]

Although Zephaniah 3:7 and 3:9 seem to play a more central role in these homilies than did Zephaniah 3:14–15, these sedarim readings afforded Jewish rabbis ample fodder for forging textual connections between Zephaniah and the rest of the OT. Zephaniah 3:14–15 was regularly and publicly read and thus played an important role in Jewish worship and/or festivals.

Summarizing the Use of Zephaniah 3:14–15 in Early Jewish Literature

We note two consistent threads in the Jewish literature: (1) "king of Israel" refers to Yahweh (excluding TJ's pluralization, "kings"), and (2) Yahweh's deliverance was still future. None of the Jewish literature on Zephaniah 3:15 considered the deliverance accomplished.

[38] Ben Zion Wacholder, "Prolegomenon," in *The Palestinian Triennial Cycle: Genesis and Exodus*, by Jacob Mann, vol. 1, *The Bible As Read and Preached in the Old Synagogue*, repr. with new matter, LOBS [New York: KTAV, 1971], xxxi; cf. Mann and Sonne, *Leviticus and Numbers*, 91, though they take the unlikely position that the initial catchwords were the only reason these texts were read together (see the critique by Isaiah Sonne, "Preface," xxi–xxxii; cf. Ben Zvi, *Zephaniah*, 24–25). Genesis 11 and Zephaniah 3 also have the phrase "the name."

[39] Mann and Sonne (*Leviticus and Numbers*, 201–8) document such interpretive "Seder 104" homilies.

The literature, nevertheless, also represents a diverse interpretive milieu, similar and dissimilar to Zephaniah 3:14–15 and John 12. If the Apocrypha and pseudepigrapha (i.e., Tob., Bar., 3 En.) alluded to Zephaniah 3, Yahweh's future deliverance provided the basis for joy and encouragement during trials. MUR88's text confirms the MT, and we find Zephaniah *pesher* fragments in the limited evidence from Judean Desert scrolls. TJ condemns evil judges (and perhaps Israel's kings), comforts the "congregation," and portrays a relational distance with Yahweh (i.e., *Shekinah*). A few passages in the Babylonian Talmud and Midrashim read Zephaniah 3 in a messianic context: Zephaniah 3:11–15 contain prerequisites for the Daniel 7:13/Zechariah 9:9-like coming of the Messiah, son of David (S. Eli. Rab. 18; cf. b. Sanh. 98a). And some midrashim conclude that all will rejoice, whether to gloat over the wicked's fall or to praise Yahweh. Lastly, cyclical (festival/sabbath), sedarim readings included Zephaniah. Given this evidence, John 12 may have easily associated Zephaniah 3:14–15's king with festival time (i.e., Passover), the timed arrival of a "messiah," Gentile-inclusion, and similar OT texts (e.g., Zech. 9:9).

5

Hermeneutical and Theological Use of Zephaniah 3 in John 12

In this chapter, we conduct an exegetical overview of John 12:12–15 to better situate the Zephaniah Proposal in the Entry Narrative. We then examine the hermeneutical possibilities for the proposal and consider its chief theological implications for John 12.

Detailing John 12:12–15's Correction and Affirmation

Some scholars, including Zephaniah Proposal proponent A. C. Brunson, challenge the "majority" view by arguing that Jesus's entry in John 12 does not correct nationalistic, messianic ambitions of the crowd but rather affirms the crowd's true (but incomplete) faith.[1]

[1] A. C. Brunson, *Psalm 118 in the Gospel of John: An Intertextual Study on the New Exodus Pattern in the Theology of John*, WUNT, 2nd ser., 158 (Tübingen: Mohr Siebeck, 2003), 266–83; cf. Wayne A. Meeks, *The Prophet-King: Moses Traditions and the Johannine Christology*, NovTSup 14 (Leiden: Brill, 1967), 87; Herman Ridderbos, *The Gospel according to John: A Theological Commentary*, trans. John Vriend (Grand Rapids: Eerdmans, 1997), 424; Marie de Mérode, "L'accueil triomphal de Jésus selon Jean, 11–12," *RTL* 13 (1982): 51–52. J. F. Coakley ("Jesus' Messianic Entry into Jerusalem [John 12:12–19 par]," *JTS* 46 [1995]: 461–82) surveys and refutes the three main scholarly interpretations of Jesus's intentions (i.e., correction, political challenge, or a moot question) before he posits a fourth possibility: Jesus was

However, we find evidence that that Passover crowd misunderstood some of Jesus's kingly identity and nature, and the FG's Entry Narrative (with Zeph. 3) informs *and corrects* it.[2]

The Crowd's Conceptions of Jesus's Kingship

We make the following observations regarding the nature of the crowd's understanding of Jesus. First, the entry crowd took up palm branches (τὰ βαΐα τῶν φοινίκων [12:12]). The OT prescribed them for the Feast of Tabernacles (Lev. 23:40) but not Passover.[3] Palm branches could symbolize many different things (e.g., righteousness [Ps. 92:12], fruitfulness [Song 7:8–9]), but there is

---

passive and forced to ride the donkey by over-zealous followers. In the final analysis, we find his proposal unlikely given that the Synoptics show Jesus orchestrating details of this event (see Matt. 21:1–9; Mark 11:1–10; Luke 19:28–40).

[2] Most modern commentators advocate the position that Jesus and the FG affirm yet correct the crowd's welcome of Jesus (e.g., Mavis M. Leung, *The Kingship-Cross Interplay in the Gospel of John: Jesus' Death as Corroboration of His Royal Messiahship* [Eugene, OR: Wipf & Stock, 2011], 166; Adam Kubiś, *The Book of Zechariah in the Gospel of John*, *EBib* 64 [Pendé: Gabalda, 2012], 101–14; Daniel J. Brendsel, *"Isaiah Saw His Glory": The Use of Isaiah 52–53 in John 12*, BZNW 28 [Berlin: de Gruyter, 2014], 161–70; M. J. J. Menken, *Old Testament Quotations in the Fourth Gospel: Studies in Textual Form*, CBET 15 [Kampen: Kok Pharos, 1996], 86–87; Bruce G. Schuchard, *Scripture within Scripture: The Interrelationship of Form and Function in the Explicit Old Testament Citations in the Gospel of John*, SBLDS 133 [Atlanta: Scholars Press, 1992], 76–80).

[3] Brunson argues that the crowd's palm branches draw from Psalm 118's Tabernacles *lulab* liturgy (m. Sukkah 3.9; the crowd may have had Tabernacles *lulabs* in their Jerusalem homes) and its royal context. So, for him, they (1) signal John's crowd welcomed a noteworthy person and (2) symbolize Jesus's triumph over Lazarus's death (*Psalm 118*, 222; cf. C. K. Barrett, *The Gospel according to St. John*, 2nd ed. [Philadelphia: Westminster, 1978], 417; John Spencer Hill, "τὰ βαΐα τῶν φοινίκων (John 12:13): Pleonasm or Prolepsis," *JBL* 101 [1982]: 133–35, though he implausibly connects the phoenix and Jesus's death-resurrection victory). Some Jews referred to Tabernacles *lulabs* as "hosannas" (b. Sukkah 37b; cf. D. A. Carson, *The Gospel according to John*, PiNTC [Grand Rapids: Eerdmans, 1991], 432).

evidence that palm branches achieved the status of a national Jewish symbol by the first century A.D. They were used in (royal) triumphant Maccabean entries: the temple rededication (1 Macc. 4:52–59) and purification (2 Macc. 10:1–8) in 164 B.C., and Simon's victorious procession (1 Macc. 13:51–52) in 141 B.C.[4] Both Rome (to celebrate victory over Judea) and Jewish insurrectionists (during their first and second century wars against Rome) minted coins with the image of the palm.[5] And Jewish literature often linked Jewish, end-time victory with palms (e.g., T. Naph. 5:4; Lev. Rab. 30; Rev. 7:9).[6] The palm branches may reflect the crowd's national, political, and even militaristic hopes for Jesus.

Second, the crowd went to meet (εἰς ὑπάντησιν [John 12:13, cf. 12:18]) Jesus. Many note that such terms (i.e., παρουσία, ἀπαντάω and ὑπαντάω) commonly describe the welcome into the city

[4] W. R. Farmer, "The Palm Branches in John 12,13," *JTS* 3 (1952): 62–66; Raymond E. Brown, *The Gospel according to John*, AB (Garden City, NY: Doubleday, 1966–70), 1:461–62; Carson, *John*, 432; Brendsel, *Isaiah*, 165–66; Andreas J. Köstenberger, *John*, BECNT (Grand Rapids: Baker, 2004), 367–69; Leung, *Kingship-Cross Interplay*, 155–56; cf. Barrett, *John*, 417. W. R. Farmer argues that the Maccabeans continued to be revered into the first century A.D. (*Maccabees, Zealots, and Josephus: An Enquiry into Jewish Nationalism in the Greco-Roman Period* [New York: Columbia University Press, 1956], 125–58; cf. Brent Kinman, "Jesus' Royal Entry into Jerusalem," *BBR* 15 [2005]: 245).

[5] H. J. Hart, "Judaea and Rome: The Official Commentary," *JTS* 3 (1952): 172–98; cf. F. F. Bruce, *The Gospel of John: Introduction, Exposition and Notes* (Grand Rapids: Eerdmans, 1983), 176n8; Köstenberger, *John*, 369; Craig S. Keener, *The Gospel of John: A Commentary* (Peabody, MA: Hendrickson, 2003), 2:869; Ben Witherington III, *John's Wisdom: A Commentary on the Fourth Gospel* (Louisville: Westminster John Knox, 1995), 221; Carson, *John*, 432; contra Brunson, *Psalm 118*, 215–23, who thinks these are more likely associated with Psalm 118 Tabernacles *lulabs*.

[6] For references to the palms as a Jewish symbol in Josephus, see Köstenberger, *John*, 369 (cf. 2 Macc. 10:7). Coakley ("Messianic Entry," 472) and Meeks (*Prophet-King*, 86; cf. Brian A. Mastin, "The Date of the Triumphal Entry," *NTS* 16 [1969]: 76–82) note that they may simply symbolize "victory," but we posit that the evidence from non-Tabernacles palms could nevertheless favor the view that their use in John 12 portrays *national* victory.

that Hellenistic kings or military officials received; sometimes, the leader was subversive or even controversial.[7] Thus, the crowd perhaps "met" Jesus as a national, political deliverer.[8]

Third, the crowd cries, "Hosanna," originally a transliteration of the imperative הוֹשִׁיעָה נָּא (Ps. 118:25).[9] In Jesus's day in Palestine, Jews may have recited Psalm 118 as many as 18 days per year (Feast of Booths, Hanukkah, and the first day of Passover and of Weeks), it was part of the Hallel festival songs in the temple (Pss. 113–18),[10]

[7] Coakley provides a list of Greco-Roman examples of (military) leaders welcomed in these terms ("Entry," 470–72). Many note a possible connection with this term and the Hellenistic greeting of political rulers (e.g., Kinman, "Entry," 231–32; Leon Morris, *The Gospel according to John*, NICNT, rev. ed. [Grand Rapids: Eerdmans, 1995], 518; Brown, *John*, 1:460–62; Brendsel, *Isaiah*, 166; Ridderbos, *John*, 422). David R. Catchpole examines examples of Jewish and Hellenistic welcomings of leaders ("The 'Triumphal' Entry," in *Jesus and the Politics of His Day*, ed. Ernst Bammel and C. F. D. Moule [Cambridge: Cambridge University Press, 1984], 319–22). The term ὑπάντησιν is rare in the NT (Matt. 8:34; 25:1; cf. Judg. 11:34). Various backgrounds are possible, but the term often referred to royal or political welcomings in extra-biblical texts (Leung, *Kingship-Cross Interplay*, 156–57; contra Brunson, *Psalm 118*, 157, and Mastin, "Triumphal Entry," 81).

[8] Kinman asks, "Why, if the Entry was such a politically charged event, did the Romans not arrest Jesus as he made his royal procession?" He posits that the Roman troops concentrated on the temple (cf. *J.W.* 5.243–45) and that perhaps the entry crowd was rather small. The result is that "the Entry, unique among Jesus' actions (excluding, possibly, the so-called Temple cleansing), provided Jesus' opponents a way of exploiting a Roman governor's concern with sedition to achieve their own aims because of the political associations that were often attached to such events. The Entry left Jesus open to a charge of sedition, even if such a charge was a distortion of what really happened or what Jesus really intended" ("Entry," 251–52, 235; cf. Keener, *John*, 2:867).

[9] Scholars debate whether John's term derives from Hebrew or Aramaic (for discussion, see Brunson, *Psalm 118*, 203–14; Joseph A. Fitzmyer, "Aramaic Evidence Affecting the Interpretation of Hosanna in the New Testament" in *Tradition and Interpretation in the New Testament: Essays in Honor of E. Earle Ellis for His 60th Birthday*, ed. E. Earle Ellis, Gerald F. Hawthorne, and Otto Betz [Grand Rapids: Eerdmans, 1987], 110–18; Eric Werner, "'Hosanna' in the Gospels," *JBL* 65 [1946]: 97–122).

[10] See m. Pesaḥ. 5.5–7; 9.3; 10.6–7 (Passover); b. Pesaḥ. 117a, 118a, 119a;

and when *hosanna* was sung at festival (m. Sukkah 3.9; 4.5) all were to wave a *lulab* with palm branches (b. Sukkah 37b). The FG's crowd may easily have recalled the Psalm in its OT context a few days before Passover.[11]

In Psalm 118:25 (MT), *hosanna* most likely entails a plea to Yahweh for deliverance (note the synonymous parallelism at Ps. 118:25b).[12] Psalm 118 also thanks Yahweh for his *past* deliverance (118:1, 5, 13–14, 15–18, 21, 29), so Psalm 118:25 seems to signal that a full deliverance had not yet been accomplished.[13] And then later, some pre-Christian, Jewish literature used the term *hosanna* liturgically, sometimes to denote a messianic hope.[14]

The cry in John is less clear, however. Scholars debate whether it functions as a plea (e.g., σῶσον δή [LXX] "give salvation now"), praise (e.g., ὡσαννά [Did. 10:6] "hail!"), or both.[15] But even if the

---

b. Sukkah 45a; b. 'Arak. 10a; James A. Sanders, "A New Testament Hermeneutic Fabric: Psalm 119 in the Entrance Narrative," in *Early Jewish and Christian Exegesis: Studies in Memory of William Hugh Brownlee*, ed. Craig A. Evans and William F. Stinespring, SPHS 10 (Atlanta: Scholars Press, 1987), 179–80; Eduard Lohse, "ὡσαννά," in *TDNT*, 9:682; cf. Köstenberger, *John*, 369–70; Brunson, *Psalm 118*, 82–94.

[11] Brunson documents Psalm 118's prescribed and frequent use for the Feast of Booths (*Psalm 118*, 45–62).

[12] In the OT, the hiphil imperative הוֹשִׁיעָה often represents a petition for deliverance (Josh. 10:6; 2 Sam. 14:4; 2 Kings 6:26; Pss. 12:2; 20:10; 28:9; 60:7; 86:16; 108:7). For further evidence of the petitionary sense here, see Werner, "'Hosanna,'" 97–122. Brunson argues that Psalm 118 MT's term is a petition for deliverance, functioning to praise-confess Yahweh's sovereignty (*Psalm 118*, 204–14).

[13] John Goldingay, *Psalms*, ed. Tremper Longman III, BCOTWP (Grand Rapids: Baker, 2006–2008), 3:362. Brunson finds this past-future tension resolved in that *hosanna* "request[s] that Yahweh in mercy confirm and preserve through the upcoming year the salvation he has already effected," (*Psalm 118*, 205).

[14] Eduard Lohse, "Hosianna," *NovT* 6 (1963): 113–19; cf. Rudolf Schnackenburg, *The Gospel according to St John*, trans. K. Smyth et al., HTKNT (New York: Crossroad, 1980–82), 2:525.

[15] The literature discussing these positions is abundant (see, e.g., Werner, "'Hosanna,'" 97–122; Wilhelmus J. C. Weren, "Jesus' Entry into Jerusalem:

crowd did not intend the MT's supplication nuance, they may still have implicitly retained the original address to Yahweh in their cry to Jesus. Jews of the time were familiar with Psalm 118:25 (i.e., its Yahweh-address).[16] And John's crowd does not specify an address for *hosanna* with a dative (cf. Matt. 21:9, 15), leaving open the question whether they addressed their cry to Psalm 118:25's Yahweh,[17] though the crowd did not clearly identify Jesus as Yahweh. Given the Psalm's literary context, the crowd's *hosanna* may have expected some form of Yahweh-action *on their behalf*, perhaps relief from Rome's domination (e.g., John 11:48).

Fourth, the FG crowd's cry continues with Psalm 118:26:

Mt 21, 1–17 in the Light of the Hebrew Bible and the Septuagint," in *The Scriptures in the Gospels*, BETL 131 [Louvain: Leuven University Press; Peeters, 1997], 134; Leung, *Kingship-Cross Interplay*, 158; Brunson, *Psalm 118*, 203–14; Coakley, "Entry," 474, who indicates that either plea or praise fits the FG here). In Matthew 21:9, 15 and Didache 10.6 datives follow the *hosanna* which may signal that it became a praise-greeting at some point in history (Fitzmyer, "Aramaic Evidence," 111; Lohse, "ὡσαννά," 682). Without such an accompanying dative, the FG's *hosanna* does not unambiguously reflect or post-date such a supposed semantic shift from the OT petition (Brunson, *Psalm 118*, 206).

[16] See the preceding paragraphs and Brunson, *Psalm 118*, 211–12. Due to the routine festival usage of *hosanna*, "every Jew knew of its [*hosanna*'s] occurrence in Psalm 118:25" (Carson, *John*, 432; George R. Beasley-Murray, *John*, 2nd ed., WBC [Nashville: Thomas Nelson, 1999], 210, though neither of these scholars note a connection with Yahweh and Jesus here).

[17] Brunson argues that the crowd's *hosanna* was in some way "identifying Jesus' kingship with Yahweh's rule" (*Psalm 118*, 213). He notes that in the OT, the *hosanna*-plea for deliverance is uttered more often to Yahweh (Pss. 12:2; 20:10; 28:9; 60:7; 108:7) than to a human king (2 Sam. 14:4; 2 Kings 6:26; see ibid., 205). Also, its transliteration may reflect ingrained, Jewish, liturgical usage with an awareness of the original context, so translating the term (cf. σῶσον δή [LXX]) was unnecessary (ibid., 211–14; contra Leung, *Kingship-Cross Interplay*, 159; cf. Greek renderings of Semitic terms in John 1:41; 4:25; 9:7). Brunson concludes, "The supplication does not explicitly ask Yahweh to save King Jesus. Although this may implicitly be in view, the Johannine focus is not on Yahweh establishing the reign of Jesus, but on identifying Jesus' ministry with Yahweh" (*Psalm 118*, 213).

εὐλογημένος ὁ ἐρχόμενος ἐν ὀνόματι κυρίου. Although it is not explicit, Psalm 118's original blessing may have been for a *human* (Davidic?) *king*. The activity in Psalm 118:10–15 envisions a political king-like leader (note the singular pronouns, cf. 118:17–19, 21) who militarily defeats enemies in Yahweh's name and by his help. Psalm 118:26a then blesses a singular individual who comes in Yahweh's name (i.e., הַבָּא); the blessing thus seems intended for a militarily-successful, human king.[18]

Rabbinical texts interpreted Psalm 118 messianically (e.g., Ps. 118:24 with Isa. 12:5–6; cf. Midr. Pss. 118.22), but in the FG itself, the phrase ὁ ἐρχόμενος is particularly charged with messianic connotations. John often connects the terms "Messiah" or "Christ" with the "coming (one)" verb (e.g., 4:25; 7:27, 31, 41, 42; 11:27), and identifying Jesus as Messiah is the FG's aim (20:31). Also, "'he who comes' can have messianic overtones, especially when the coming is 'in the

[18] Brunson finds sufficient evidence for Psalm 118 as a royal psalm based on some of the internal considerations cited above (*Psalm 118*, 34–37; cf. Sigmund Mowinckel, *The Psalms in Israel's Worship* [Oxford: Blackwell, 1962], 1:180–81; Carson, *John*, 432 [possibly Davidic]). We note that the parallel blessing in verse 26b addresses a plural pronoun. We thus tenuously posit that Psalm 118:26a–b blesses the king (first himself, then him as the people's representative) but acknowledge that the verse may be antiphonal: first blessing the king, then the people. Either way, Psalm 118:10–15 describes a human, kingly leader who is then blessed in Psalm 118:26a. A. E. Harvey argues that Psalm 118 was sung at festivals as "a way of welcoming a pilgrim as he drew near to the temple" (*Jesus and the Constraints of History* [Philadelphia: Westminster, 1982], 127; cf. Mowinckel, *Israel's Worship*, 1:180–81). But this is unlikely. Rabbinic literature did not utilize the psalm for approaching pilgrims (Coakley, "Entry," 473; Solomon Zeitlin, "The Hallel: A Historical Study of the Canonization of the Hebrew Liturgy," *JQR* 53 [1962]: 22–29), although they did use it in liturgical temple dialogue (b. Pesaḥ. 119a; Midr. Pss. 118.22; cf. Sanders, "Hermeneutic Fabric," 181). Brunson lists more than two dozen *Sitz im Leben* proposals (*Psalm 118*, 23–45), so we are not dogmatic on its supposed "original" use. For post-exilic readings of Psalm 118 as a messianic-royal psalm, see ibid., 37–45; cf. Margaret Daly-Denton, *David in the Fourth Gospel: The Johannine Reception of the Psalms*, AGJU 47 (Leiden: Brill, 2000), 181–82.

name of the Lord' (see 5:43; 17:6),"[19] in Yahweh's Name. Furthermore, the entry crowd included some Lazarus-sign folks (John 12:12, 18), and in the Lazarus pericope, Martha confessed Jesus as *the Christ, the coming one* (John 11:27).[20] Popular perception and even John's Gospel linked "the coming one" with some form of messianic hope.

Lastly, the title "king of Israel," a key part to the Zephaniah Proposal, ensures that the Entry Narrative's focal point is Jesus's kingship (12:13; cf. 12:15b). In the crowd's view, the title perhaps carried a messianic sense. The Jewish pseudepigraphal Psalms of Solomon 17–18 refer to the "king of Israel" as a messianic personage, so popular-level, Jewish notions of a messianic king of Israel may have been current.[21] Furthermore, the crowd's title juxtaposes their

[19] Brendsel, *Isaiah*, 167–68. That John connects "the coming one" (ὁ ἐρχόμενος) to messianic ideas is well-documented and need not be fully repeated here (see, e.g., Köstenberger, *John*, 370). John often uses ὁ ἐρχόμενος absolutely, that is, without specifying the origination or destination of Jesus's coming (e.g., 1:15, 27, 30; 4:25; 6:14; 7:27, 31, 41, 42; 11:27). Also, the grammar of Psalm 118 may lead us to suppose that "blessed *in the Lord* is the coming one" due to analogous passages (e.g., Deut. 10:8; 21:5; 1 Chron. 16:2; Ps. 129:8; Coakley, "Entry," 475), but since the FG's parallel identification is "the king of Israel," the intended meaning is likely "blessed [is] the coming-in-the-name-of-the-Lord-one" (see Carson, *John*, 432; Ridderbos, *John*, 423; Morris, *John*, 520). Reading the prepositional phrase with "to come" is confirmed by the other time this construction (ἔρχομαι + ἐν + ὄνομα of x) occurs in John (5:43; i.e., Jesus comes in the Father's name).

[20] Kinman, "Entry," 247.

[21] Leung, *Kingship-Cross Interplay*, 64; Richard A. Horsley and John S. Hanson, *Bandits, Prophets, and Messiahs: Popular Movements in the Time of Jesus* (Harrisburg, PA: Trinity Press, 1999), 102–117 (see Pss. Sol. 17:4, 21, 32, 42; cf. Sib. Or. 5:108). R. B. Wright dates the composition of Psalms of Solomon to the first century B.C. and no later than A.D. 70 ("Psalms of Solomon: A New Translation and Introduction," in *The Old Testament Pseudepigrapha*, ed. James H. Charlesworth [Garden City, NY: Doubleday, 1985], 2:639–41). Even still, (1) Pss. Sol. 17 stresses Yahweh's ultimate kingship: "It is God who rules—the psalms [of Solomon] are clear on that—but his agent is the Lord Messiah" (ibid., 2:646). (2) In the OT, the full title "king of Israel" never designates a messiah but does refer to Yahweh (see § 2.4.1). Meeks notes that Philo applies the expression "king of the seeing nation, of Israel" (βασιλέως τοῦ ὁρῶντος,

messianic Psalm 118 quote. Yet this does not necessarily deny that John, in eliciting the title's *OT* usage, found added significance for the title (i.e., a Zephanian allusion to Jesus's divinity).

For the crowd, the royal-messianic title likely carried hints of *national* hopes. (1) The phrase refers to Jesus as *Israel*'s (i.e., God's people's) king.[22] And (2) Nathanael confesses this title to Jesus (John 1:49), juxtaposed to the messianic title ὁ υἱὸς τοῦ θεου ("the Son of God").[23]

To further argue John 12 affirms the crowd's view of Jesus's kingship, Brunson (and Meeks) maintains that Nathanael displays his true but incomplete belief as a disciple of Jesus: "the true Israelite [1:47] who believes in Jesus and acclaims him as the true

---

Ἰσραήλ [*Somn.* 2.44]) to Judah, which may reflect a Davidic-Messianic tradition (*Prophet-King*, 79n1). But Philo's expression does not match John 12:13, and if Philo sees the phrase as carrying messianic import, he does not explicate that sense. Based on the Zephaniah Proposal and the title's OT usage, we argue that John alludes to King Jesus's *divinity* (for the crowd-narrator distinction, see § 5.2.3.1).

[22] W. Gutbrod argues that outside of its occurrences in this title, the proper name "Israel" in John always refers to God's people collectively and is thus nearly a "supratemporal entity," stretching back to the OT but including the present (1:31; 3:10) ("Ἰσραήλ, Ἰουδαῖος, Ἑβραῖος," in *TDNT*, 3:385–86, who asserts that rabbinic literature may have employed the term in this way).

[23] Nathanael likely had messianic hopes attached to "Son of God" and the title "king of Israel" when read together; messianic texts link "king" with "son (of God)" (e.g., 2 Sam. 7:14; Ps. 2:7). For evidence of this connection in the Dead Sea scrolls, especially in connection with Zechariah 3:8, see Craig R. Koester, "Messianic Exegesis and the Call of Nathanael (John 1.45–51)," *JSNT* 39 (1990): 27–34, though note that none of the examples contain the full title "king of Israel." The title does not only carry a messianic sense in John, however. Similar to our analysis below on John 12, Koester proposes two-levels of understanding of the terms in John 1: "The evangelist could assume that readers knew that 'Son of God' was more than a royal title, since Jesus was of divine origin, God's 'only begotten Son' (1.1, 14, 18). Later the Gospel will affirm that Jesus is also a king, but whose power comes from above, not from the world (18.36). Jesus pointed more directly to this second level of meaning in 1.51, by stating that Nathanael and others like him would see God made manifest in himself as the Son of man" (ibid., 27).

king of Israel [1:49]."[24] There are several problems with this view. First, John always uses ἀληθῶς ("truly") as an adverb, so in 1:47 it is probably not an adjective (i.e., "true").[25] Second, Palestinian Jews often referred to each other as "Israelite," so Nathanael's designation might not denote him as "true/new Israel," as developed in Romans 2:28–29; 9:6.[26] Third, Jesus noted that Nathanael's belief responded to miraculous foreknowledge (1:50–51). Carson argues, "Such a foundation can be insecure (4:48; 14:11; *cf.* Mt. 7:21–23), though certainly better than nothing (10:25, 38)."[27]

Given these considerations, Nathanael's confession "king of Israel" (1:49) likely entails a national (Jewish) view of Jesus's kingship.[28] Now, if the large, Passover crowd was largely comprised of

[24] Brunson, *Psalm 118*, 269; cf. Meeks, *Prophet-King*, 82–83, 87.

[25] Carson, *John*, 160 (see John 4:42; 6:14, 55; 7:26, 40; 8:31; 17:8); cf. Ridderbos, *John*, 89. This results in reading the statement as, "Behold, truly an Israelite." Brunson, however, seems to assume an adjectival sense (see *Psalm 118*, 269).

[26] For evidence of this, see K. G. Kuhn, "Ἰσραήλ, Ἰουδαῖος, Ἑβραῖος," in *TDNT*, 3:359; cf. Carson, *John*, 160. Furthermore, Gutbrod concluded his survey of "Israel[ite]" terms in John: "We do not detect in John any extension of the name to the new people of God. The true Israelite is the man who is bound to the Law, and therewith to God" ("Ἰσραήλ, Ἰουδαῖος, Ἑβραῖος," 386). Koester argues that Zechariah 3:8 and 10 (with Gen. 27:35; 28:12; 32:28) play a role in John 1:45–51; Jesus's terms for Nathanael had been fitting for Jacob or "Israel" ("Messianic Exegesis," 23–34). Meeks, however, argues that in the FG context, Nathanael represents "the 'true Israelite,' the countertype to 'the Jews' who deny the King *of the Jews* . . . . [He is] the prototype of the Christian believer" (*Prophet-King*, 82–83, italics original). But his position is unlikely for two reasons: (1) John 1:50–51 seems to constitute Jesus's correction/mild rebuke of Nathanael. (2) Ridderbos speculates that Nathanael might represent true Israel but correctly notes that Jesus nevertheless focuses on Nathanael's uniqueness *in Israel*, on his being a certain kind of Israelite (i.e., without guile; *John*, 89–90). In 1:49 "King of Israel" thus seems to reflect a national view of Jesus (though we posit that at the narrative-level, *John* develops the title ironically, clarifying in John 12 and 18 the nature of Jesus's kingship).

[27] Carson, *John*, 162.

[28] Köstenberger summarizes, "Since Nathanael is himself an Israelite, he is affirming Jesus as his own king as well as that of his nation" (*John*, 84; cf.

Jews (12:9, 13, 18), their using the same title as in John 1:49 could imply a similar national sense. The entry crowd likely acclaimed Jesus as their (i.e., God's people's) king.

These strands of evidence together (i.e., 6:14–15, branches, "meeting," *hosanna*, Psalm 118, and Israel's king) signal that the Jewish crowd likely had narrow, national (even militaristic) hopes for Messiah-King Jesus. They may have expected Jesus (and perhaps even Yahweh) to act politically for the people of Israel, though they did not likely explicitly connect Jesus to Yahweh.

Affirming and Correcting the Crowd's View of Jesus's Kingship

In keeping with the above interpretation of John 12:12–13, we expect the postpositive δέ (John 12:14)[29] to grammatically mark Jesus's finding and sitting on a donkey as a response to the crowd's misguided hopes. In this way, John gives his readers the correct understanding of the event.[30] We find further evidence that John

---

Morris, *John*, 146–47; Francis J. Moloney, "'The Jews' in the Fourth Gospel: Another Perspective," *Pacifica* 15 [2002]: 28, 31, as noted by Ruth Sheridan, *Retelling Scripture: 'The Jews' and the Scriptural Citations in John 1:19–12:15*, BIS 110 [Leiden: Brill, 2012], 227).

[29] Some read this conjunction as functioning syntactically as an adversative (e.g., Brown, *John*, 1:462; J. A. T. Robinson, *The Priority of John* [London: SCM, 1985], 232; Brendsel, *Isaiah*, 169) or as a transitional element (e.g., "on his part," Ridderbos, *John*, 424; cf. Köstenberger, *John*, 370–71). The latter interpretation might align better with how δέ often linguistically functions in John, as a "development marker" (e.g., John 4:51). So here, the development would reflect "changes in initiative" (cf. John 1:36–38a) since the narrative "develop[s] through the actions of a different participant" (Stephen H. Levinsohn, *Discourse Features of New Testament Greek: A Coursebook on the Information Structure of New Testament Greek*, 2nd ed. [Dallas: SIL International, 2000], 82, who defines this function as introducing "information that represents a significant development, as far as the author's purpose is concerned"). John's narrative, though terse, transitions to Jesus's response, which we understand as both correction and affirmation.

[30] Ridderbos, *John*, 423; Barrett, *John*, 418; Köstenberger, *John*, 370–71. Since Mark and the Synoptics (Mark 11:1–10; Matt. 21:1–9; Luke 19:28–40) have Jesus get the donkey before the crowd calls—assuming Markan priority and

12's crowd was misguided in their welcoming of Jesus. First, in John 6:14–15, Jesus's kingship was misunderstood by the 5,000 Galileans; they tried to *make* Jesus king, but he fled. Since people came to Jerusalem from all over for the Passover (John 12:12–13; cf. 11:55–56), it is plausible that some of the attendees were Galileans and present at Jesus's entry.[31] Second, John 12:17–18 provide the main motivation for the crowd's meeting Jesus: his Lazarus-sign.[32] Leung rightly summarizes, "In John's Gospel, this kind of 'sign-based' faith is deemed as valid but inadequate to lead one to salvation (cf. John 2:23–24; 3:2–3; 6:30)."[33] Third, Jesus's disciples lacked understanding about his entry (ταῦτα, John 12:16) until Jesus was glorified. If the disciples did not immediately realize the implications of Jesus's entry, neither did the large entry crowd.[34]

John's awareness of it—the FG's restructuring of the event may reinforce the corrective force (Brendsel, *Isaiah*, 169; Andrew T. Lincoln, *The Gospel according to Saint John*, BNTC [Peabody, MA: Hendrickson, 2005], 343–44; Barrett, *John*, 415–16; Urban C. von Wahlde, *The Gospel and Letters of John: Commentary on the Gospel of John*, ECC [Grand Rapids: Eerdmans, 2010], 2:530).

[31] See Brendsel, *Isaiah*, 165; Köstenberger, *John*, 368; Carson, *John*, 431; Keener, *John*, 2:868; Morris, *John*, 518, all of whom reference Josephus's Jerusalem population figures for Passover as evidence; cf. Kinman, "Entry," 251. Coakley plausibly suggests that Jesus's previous ministry in Jerusalem (John 2:3; 7:12; 8:31; 10:21) may have produced a following eager to hail him as king, especially given the backdrop of Lazarus's healing ("Messianic Entry," 468–70; for the Lazarus-*inclusio*, see § 2.1). Brunson admits the parallels to John 6:14–15's feeding miracle yet argues that Jesus's responses differ: he does not flee in John 12 (*Psalm 118*, 268; cf. Meeks, *Prophet-King*, 88–89). But Jesus's responses need not be identical for John 12 to function as a corrective.

[32] Carson observes two crowds in verses 17–18: those present at Lazarus's tomb and those who came to Jesus because of that miracle (i.e., "Lazarus-sign" crowd; *John*, 435; cf. John 12:9, 11). Due to the shared term "meeting" (ὑπάντησις), the 12:18 crowd was likely the 12:13 entry crowd (John A. Dennis, *Jesus' Death and the Gathering of True Israel: The Johannine Appropriation of Restoration Theology in the Light of John 11.47–52*, WUNT 217 [Tübingen: Mohr Siebeck, 2006], 42).

[33] Leung, *Kingship-Cross Interplay*, 166.

[34] Köstenberger, *John*, 372; Barrett, *John*, 419; Leung, *Kingship-Cross Interplay*, 166. E. C. Hoskyns observes misunderstandings in John 12:1–8, 16, and

In 12:14–15 the narrative "action" stops with Jesus sitting on the donkey, and the FG asserts that it fulfils Zechariah 9:9's coming donkey-riding king. Most scholars rightly hold that Jesus's donkey-riding indicated he was a messianic figure: "There was apparently some expectation that the Messiah, as the successor of David, would ride on a donkey when he arrived (cf. 1 Kgs 1:38)."[35] Additionally,

---

29–34 (*The Fourth Gospel*, ed. F. N. Davey, 2nd ed. [London: Faber & Faber, 1956], 422). Brendsel additionally argues: (1) "Later in John 12, 'the crowd' is clearly depicted as lacking perception (12:29) and misunderstanding the necessity of Christ's death (12:34)"; and (2) John 12:13's κραυγάζω may have a "fanatical" "unfavourable sense" (cf. John 18:40; 19:6, 12, 15; but note 11:43) (*Isaiah*, 165, following R. H. Lightfoot, *St. John's Gospel*, ed. C. F. Evans [Oxford: Clarendon, 1956; repr., London: Oxford University Press, 1963], 249). Brunson surveys the main interpretations of "these things" in John 12:16 and argues that the disciples misunderstood Jesus's identity (*Psalm 118*, 279–83, though he is not convinced that the crowd had national, political hopes for Jesus). For support, D. A. Carson's assessment of 64 misunderstandings in the FG finds that many are misunderstandings of "Jesus' person, teaching and purposes" ("Understanding Misunderstandings in the Fourth Gospel," *TynBul* 33 [1982]: 79, 91). The verb μιμνῄσκομαι ("to remember") occurs three times in the FG (2:17, 22; 12:16), and 2:22 states that the disciples' remembrance occurred after Jesus's resurrection. It is plausible that the disciples more fully realized Jesus's identity post-resurrection; however, the evidence above suggests that John *also corrects* the crowd's view of King Jesus.

35 Craig R. Koester, *Symbolism in the Fourth Gospel: Meaning, Mystery, Community*, 2nd ed. (Minneapolis: Fortress, 2003), 125. We briefly present the plausibility that John 12:15's donkey ride affirms that Jesus fulfills *messianic* prophecy. First, Zechariah 9:9 was interpreted messianically in late Jewish literature (e.g., Gen. Rab. 56:2; 75:6; 98:9; b. Sanh. 98a; cf. Eccl. Rab. 1:9), though we have no clear evidence of that interpretation before A.D. 100 (Kim Huat Tan, *The Zion Traditions and the Aims of Jesus*, SNTSMS 91 [New York: Cambridge University Press, 1997], 139; cf. Andreas J. Köstenberger, "John," in *Commentary on the New Testament Use of the Old Testament*, ed. G. K. Beale and D. A. Carson [Grand Rapids: Baker, 2007], 473, who notes a possible reference to Zechariah 9 at Qumran and rabbinic, messianic readings). Leung plausibly speculates that such a late messianic association with Zechariah partially "explain[s] the disciples' failure to call to mind the royal prophecy of Zech 9:9 at Jesus' arrival in Jerusalem" (*Kingship-Cross Interplay*, 168). Second, Zechariah 9:9's donkey may refer to Genesis 49:10–11, due to their two major verbal agreements: (1) "coming" and (2) the "donkey." Genesis 49 was interpreted

John's abbreviated quotation skips over the king's OT description "righteous, having salvation/saved, humble,"[36] and King Jesus sits on a donkey rather than Zechariah 9:10's war horse (cf. Gen. 49:10–11; 1 Kings 4:26; Isa. 31:1–3).[37] These combined observations likely imply that Jesus's entry, correctly understood, was: (1) kingly and messianic but peaceful (Zech. 9:10; cf. Isa. 2:4; Mic. 4:3);[38] that is, "in more humble terms than those of the prevailing nationalism of the day."[39] Furthermore, (2) Jesus's kingship extends beyond the

---

messianically around the time of Jesus (e.g., at Qumran; see Menken, *Quotations*, 88–89, 94–95; Kubiś, *Zechariah*, 51–54).

[36] For a recent, thoughtful treatment of Zechariah 9:9's description of the king (עָנִי, וְנוֹשָׁע, צַדִּיק) including its messianic significance and connections to Isaiah 52–53's Servant, see Brendsel, *Isaiah*, 174–77.

[37] Thomas Edward McComiskey argues that the donkey "stands out in this text as a deliberate rejection of this symbol of arrogant trust in human might, expressing subservience to the sovereignty of God"; the donkey is not an animal for warfare ("Zechariah" in *The Minor Prophets: An Exegetical and Expository Commentary*, ed. Thomas Edward McComiskey [Grand Rapids: Baker, 1998], 3:1166). If so, Jesus's donkey ride itself functioned to correct the crowd's political-national hopes.

[38] Carson argued that John 12 quotes Zechariah 9:9 to depict King Jesus as gentle, coming in peace, and secondly that Zechariah 9:9–10's further promises must be noted in John 12. He summarizes Zechariah's added import for Jesus's entry: the Gentle King's arrival is connected to (1) "the cessation of war," (2) "the proclamation of peace to the nations" (Zech. 9:10; Ps. 72:8), and (3) "the blood of God's covenant that spells release for prisoners" (cf. John 1:29, 34; 3:5; 6:35–58; 8:31–34) (*John*, 433–34). In this book, we explore the first two.

[39] Köstenberger, *John*, 371; cf. Barnabas Lindars, *The Gospel of John*, NCB (Grand Rapids: Eerdmans, 1972), *John*, 424; Schuchard, *Scripture*, 71–84. Some scholars note that John does not explicitly highlight the humility of King Jesus, but Zechariah's value to John is simply that this king sits on a donkey (e.g., Brown, *John*, 1:462; Francis J. Moloney, *The Gospel of John*, SP [Collegeville, MN: Liturgical, 1998], 358–59). However, (1) John abbreviates the narrative and plausibly intends for Zephaniah's and Zechariah's context to color our understanding of King Jesus. (2) We do not hold that Jesus's donkey sitting exclusively signified humility, though the donkey was a lowly animal (cf. Prov. 26:3; Sir. 33:24; Köstenberger, *John*, 371). It may also signify *peace* rather than war (cf. Zech. 9:10; Judg. 5:10; 2 Sam. 16:2; Menken, *Quotations*,

people of Israel (Zech. 9:10; Zeph. 3:9–10, see below). The disciples and the FG thus later connect Jesus's entry with Zechariah 9:9's king to interpret the event.

Adding to this the evidence we have forwarded for the Zephaniah Proposal (see § 2.4), we hold that the disciples'/John's later understanding *also* permitted the connection of a Zephanian βασιλεὺς τοῦ Ἰσραήλ with μὴ φοβοῦ. This allusion connects Jesus to Zephaniah's King Yahweh. Zephaniah thus functions to further inform and correct the crowd's view of the nature of Jesus's kingship; it is messianic and divine but not national(istic) or Rome-engaging.

Hermeneutical Use of Zephaniah in the Entry Narrative

Hermeneutical Options

We now examine John 12's hermeneutical use of Zephaniah 3. Beale distinguishes the main (hermeneutical) methods for the NT authors' use of the OT as follows: to indicate (1) "direct fulfillment" of OT prophecy, (2) "indirect fulfillment" of OT typological prophecy, (3) the certain future fulfillment of OT prophecy, (4) an "analogical or illustrative use" (for universal principle) of the OT, (5) the "symbolic use" of the OT, (6) an "abiding authority" carried over from the OT, (7) a "proverbial use" of the OT, (8) a "rhetorical use" of the OT, (9) the OT "segment as a blueprint" for a NT segment,

---

87n29; Schuchard, *Scripture*, 79), and yet the donkey was indeed a fitting kingly mount (cf. Gen. 49:10–11; 1 Kings 1; 2 Sam. 18:9; Brunson, *Psalm 118*, 275–77, though he argues that it chiefly signals Jesus's kingly authority). We conclude that in the FG, Jesus's donkey ride implies King Jesus's humility and peace to partially correct the crowd's national-military expectations (cf. Mark 11:9, which explicates humility). Below, we explore the other dimension to the crowd's misunderstanding of Jesus's kingship; he enters peacefully but to battle against Satan (12:31; cf. Koester, *Symbolism*, 125–26). Similar to our analysis below, Koester outlines the FG's three main corrections to the crowd's view of Jesus's kingship: (1) universal reign, not a national Messiah, (2) death displaying divine love, not simply crowd-received glory, and (3) war against Satan, not Rome.

(10) an "alternate textual use" of the OT, (11) an "assimilated use" of the OT, or (12) an "ironic or inverted" use of the OT.[40] To this list, we add (13) Jewish (rabbinic) reading strategies,[41] as some posit for the Zephaniah Proposal.

De-Limiting the Hermeneutical Options

We briefly mention and quickly dispatch a few options listed above. First, in the Entry Narrative, "king of Israel" refers specifically to Jesus, and the command "do not fear" is tied to that event. So, John does not primarily use Zephaniah to signal (3) un-fulfilled prophecy, (4) gnomic principles, or (6) abiding authorities.[42] Second, "do not fear" is an imperative and so does not qualify as a symbol (5), and Zephaniah's concrete divine king does not match the more

[40] For support, definitions, and examples, see G. K. Beale, *Handbook on the New Testament Use of the Old Testament: Exegesis and Interpretation* (Grand Rapids: Baker, 2012), 55–93. For John's hermeneutical and theological presuppositions, we refer the reader to Beale's work (ibid., 95–102).

[41] These include midrashic, *pesher*, *gezerah shawah*, and *qal wahomer* practices (see Craig A. Evans, "The Old Testament in the New," in *The Face of New Testament Studies: A Survey of Recent Research*, ed. Scot McKnight and Grant R. Osborne [Grand Rapids: Baker Academic, 2004], 130–33; cf. E. Earle Ellis, "How the New Testament Uses the Old," in *New Testament Interpretation: Essays on Principles and Methods*, ed. I. Howard Marshall [Grand Rapids: Eerdmans, 1977], 199–208; M. P. Miller, "Targum, Midrash, and the Use of the Old Testament in the New Testament" *JSJ* [1971]: 29–82; Andrew David Naselli, *From Typology to Doxology: Paul's Use of Isaiah and Job in Romans 11:34–35* [Eugene, OR: Pickwick, 2012], 119–20). Such Jewish practices are not hermeneutical strategies but are "rhetorical devices"—at least in Paul's writings (Richard B. Hays, *Echoes of Scripture in the Letters of Paul* (New Haven: Yale University Press, 1989), 13)—but we include these practices as a separate category since some scholars propose them as a separate use.

[42] Beale writes, "Sometimes the introductory formula 'as it is written' indicates that an OT passage is being adduced as an abiding authority that continues into the present situation of the NT writer" (*Handbook*, 72). John 12:15 does introduce Zephaniah and Zechariah with this formula but explicitly connects those passages to Jesus's actions, so that the primary reference point of "do not fear" is the entry. This, however, does not necessarily deny that the exhortation can provide abiding encouragement for John's readers (see § 5.2.3.1.).

abstract symbolism intended by this category (e.g., Dan. 7:3–8; Rev. 13:2).[43] More precise usage of the OT better explains John's use of Zephaniah here. Third, since John plausibly drew his terms from either Zephaniah's MT or LXX textual tradition,[44] John does not seem to exploit the differences in the versions to make a theological point (10). Fourth, John uses these terms *not only to persuade* his readers to receive his message (8) but to *enhance their understanding* of Jesus's entry (e.g., John 12:14–15), helping his reader to not misunderstand as the disciples originally had done (John 12:16). Fifth, due to the brevity and frequency of these expressions, John may have assimilated general (i.e., alluding non-consciously to OT terms [11]) or oft-repeated terms (i.e., retaining the common meaning of their repeated OT application [7]).[45] But in chapter 2 we argue that Zephaniah 3:14–15 and its context plausibly stand as an OT candidate for John's two above expressions. The preceding options do not best explain John's use of Zephaniah.

Some scholars maintain that the FG here practices *gezerah shawah*, a Jewish reading strategy (13) that combines two passages based on verbal connections. Frédéric Manns observes two connections

[43] For examples of this usage of the OT, see ibid., 71–72. Brunson does argue that John's narrative evokes the ancient tradition of kingship at one level but also that John's text mainly focuses on Jesus as a divine king (see his summary in *Psalm 118*, 238–39). We agree with Brunson that John affirms the crowd's messianic hopes and connects Jesus with Zephaniah's divine king, but we also hold that the crowd had political ambitions for King Jesus that the FG corrects (i.e., Zephaniah functions as a corrective). The FG thus did not use Zephaniah symbolically.

[44] See § 2.5. We find John's expression βασιλεὺς τοῦ Ἰσραήλ in Zephaniah 3:15 (LXX; cf. MT), though some LXX manuscripts render "king" a verb. John's μὴ φοβοῦ matches Zephaniah 3:15 or 16 in the MT (לֹא־תִירְאִי; אַל־תִּירָאִי) but not the LXX (οὐκ ὄψῃ; θάρσει), although John may have retrofitted θάρσει (LXX) into a negative.

[45] Some argue that "do not fear" does not allude to the OT but is simply a stereotypical expression (see, e.g., Douglas J. Moo, *The Old Testament in the Gospel Passion Narratives* [Sheffield: Almond, 1983], 180; cf. Morris, *John*, 521n48).

between Psalm 118 and Zechariah 9: the verb *to come* and the title *king of Israel* (John 12:15), "une glose" added to Psalm 118 that links to Zechariah 9:9's coming king.[46] In a similar fashion, Daly-Denton reads "king of Israel" as the bridge between the two OT quotes:

> Jesus enacts Zech 9:9 in order to correct their [crowd's] understanding, that is, in order to make Zech 9:9 colour their reception of Ps 117:26 . . . . John amplifies the Ps 117 quotation with the gloss, ὁ βασιλεὺς τοῦ Ἰσραήλ in order to show that ὁ ἐρχόμενος is to be understood as the king described in Zech 9:9. The gloss, ὁ βασιλεὺς τοῦ Ἰσραήλ reinforces the *gezerah shawah*.[47]

On the literary level, John perhaps used Zephaniah's "king of Israel" (and/or "do not fear") to facilitate expounding on Jesus as Psalm 118's "coming one" and Zechariah 9:9's coming "king." But Manns and Daly-Denton's *gezerah shawah* exegesis permits only a surface-level, textual interaction with the OT and NT.[48] Indeed, Naselli rightly argues, "The value of this hermeneutical warrant [Jewish reading strategies] is limited because it lacks the explanatory power at the most significant levels. . . . [It] does not answer whether the meaning that these techniques discover is really in the OT. It does not explain how Jewish Christians and non-Christians can arrive at contradictory conclusions by using the same exegetical methods."[49]

[46] Frédéric Manns, "Exégèse rabbinique et exégèse johannique," *RB* 92 (1985): 533; cf. Daly-Denton, *David*, 178–79.

[47] Daly-Denton, *David*, 178–79. Both Daly-Denton and Manns ("Exégèse rabbinique," 533) interpret "the king of Israel" as John's interpretive gloss (i.e., not the crowd's words at the entry). Some similarly refer to John 12:15's μὴ φοβοῦ as a literary bridge between "King of Israel" (12:13) and Zechariah's king (12:15) (e.g., Schuchard, *Scripture*, 78; Brunson, *Psalm 118*, 238–39).

[48] Positing this Jewish method here would be further challenged if Zechariah 9:9 has less in common with Psalm 118 than it does with Zephaniah 3, Isaiah 40 and Genesis 49 (cf. Menken, *Quotations*, 89).

[49] Naselli, *Typology to Doxology*, 119. Keener speculates whether Zephaniah

Here, its exegetical payoff is minimal. The method does not engage the OT nor explain the Christian hermeneutic.

Zephaniah 3 in John 12: Irony, Fulfillment of OT Prophecy, Blueprint

The preceding nine options do not adequately describe John's use of Zephaniah. We now discuss the remaining options: (12) irony, (1, 2) fulfillment of prophecy, and (9) blueprint.

Zephaniah 3 as Johannine Irony

First, John 12:15's "king of Israel" may be an ironic expression.[50] The disciples (and John) later reflect on Jesus's entry (12:16),

---

and Zechariah are midrashically connected (*John*, 2:870n22), and Barnabas Lindars holds that John 12 is a "*pesher* . . . commentary" on colt-riding (*New Testament Apologetic: The Doctrinal Significance of the Old Testament Quotations* [Philadelphia: Westminster, 1961], 114; cf. Lindars, *John*, 423–24). But Naselli's broad critiques apply to those positions. Also, Stephen E. Witmer posits that John 6:31–58 may qualify as "one of the most *pesher*-like passages in the Fourth Gospel" ("Approaches to Scripture in the Fourth Gospel and the Qumran *Pesharim*," *NovT* 48 [2006]: 326) but that sufficient hermeneutical, thematic, and exegetical differences exist between *pesher* texts and the FG to discourage labeling the whole FG as "*pesher* exegesis" (326–28). For differences between rabbinical approaches (including *pesher* and midrash) and NT hermeneutics, see Ellis, "New Testament," 206; cf. Dan G. McCartney, "The New Testament's Use of the Old Testament," in *Inerrancy and Hermeneutic: A Tradition, A Challenge, A Debate*, ed. Harvie M. Conn [Grand Rapids: Baker, 1988], 107–16).

[50] Much hinges on a definition of "irony." If the term refers to "an apparent subversion of the OT text in the NT (e.g., Hos 13:14)" (Daniel J. Brendsel, personal comments to author, July 25, 2015) and/or ridicule/mocking, then John 12 does not qualify (for additional examples of this dimension of irony, see Beale, *Handbook*, 92–93). However, formal irony is broader than that. For our purposes, we follow Paul D. Duke's definition of irony: "a double-leveled literary phenomenon in which two tiers of meaning stand in some opposition to each other and in which some degree of unawareness is expressed or implied" (*Irony in the Fourth Gospel* [Atlanta: John Knox, 1985], 17; cf. D. C. Muecke, *The Compass of Irony* [London: Methuen, 1969], 35). However we interpret μὴ φοβοῦ (even if it implies "rejoice"), John ostensibly does not use it to mean

so John could intend for "the king of Israel" to reflect both the *crowd's view* and *his editorial pen*.[51] In John, the title immediately follows the crowd's Psalm 118 quote but *precedes* Jesus's actions and later memory; John likely intends the title to reflect something of the crowd's view. Yet, John supplies the correct implications for the title, returning to it in 12:15. The FG expression thus entails two perspectives: (1) The crowd who went to Jesus as their national, messianic king; and (2) the FG writer who presents the correct, post-glorification-discovered implications for Israel's King Jesus.[52]

In the FG proper, implications for Jesus as King of Israel clash with the crowd's national(istic), even military expectations. John hints that his (kingly) anointing was for his death (e.g., 12:1–8).[53] Furthermore, in accordance with Zephaniah 3, John signals that Jesus's kingship has a divine hue, extends to all peoples (12:19–21), and is *otherworldly* in origin, affirmed by Jesus at his trial (18:36–37; cf. 19:19).[54] John employs Zephaniah to fill out his

---

the opposite, to strike fear in his audience. The crowd had joyfully cried to him (12:12–13), and Jesus's following increased (12:18–19). We posit that the Zephanian reality behind this command, however, is ironic: the arrival of a divine King Jesus (i.e., associated with Yahweh), not just a human, national king.

[51] Coakley ("Entry," 475) takes this as the crowd's cry; for Barrett, John wrote it (*John*, 418).

[52] Brunson posits three levels of understanding: (1) the crowd's and disciples' at the entry event, (2) disciples' after Jesus's glorification (John 12:16), and (3) the FG narrative/reader (*Psalm 118*, 282). But surely the second and third levels are in fundamental harmony. We distance ourselves, however, from a reader-response hermeneutic and do not hold John's entire Gospel to be a "two-level drama" (D. Moody Smith, *The Fourth Gospel in Four Dimensions: Judaism and Jesus, the Gospels and Scripture* [Columbia, SC: University of South Carolina Press, 2008]). For a critique of this latter viewpoint, see Andreas J. Köstenberger, *A Theology of John's Gospel and Letters: Biblical Theology of the New Testament*, BTNT (Grand Rapids: Zondervan, 2009), 159–61.

[53] For further development of this theme, see Koester, *Symbolism*, 127–30; Brendsel, *Isaiah*, 187–211.

[54] For a defense of these three Zephanian implications for Jesus's entry, see § 5.3. King Jesus, for example, does not battle Rome but enemy Satan (12:31). Also, many see a linguistic connection and subtle contrast in the terms used for

narrative irony; Jesus is king but not one aligning with the crowd's hopes.[55]

This situation accords with Duke's category of dramatic, not verbal, irony: "While in verbal irony the real meaning may be momentarily or indefinitely hidden from a 'victimized' audience, the audience [e.g., reader] of dramatic irony sees the irony clearly, and the real meaning is hidden from the victimized speaker[s] or actant[s]."[56]

King Jesus. Köstenberger's view represents many: "'King of Israel' is the designation used by Palestinian Jews (1:49; 12:13; cf. Matt. 27:42; Mark 15:32); 'king of the Jews' is the term employed by Gentiles and Diaspora Jews (John 18:33, 39; 19:3, 19; cf. Luke 23:37–39)" (*John*, 84n109; cf. Schnackenburg, *John*, 1:318; P. J. Tomson, "'Jews' in the Gospel of John as Compared with the Palestinian Talmud, the Synoptics, and Some New Testament Apocrypha," in *Anti-Judaism and the Fourth Gospel*, ed. Reimund Bieringer, Didier Pollefeyt, and Frederique Vandecasteele-Vanneuville [Louisville: Westminster John Knox, 2001], 176–212). Furthermore, John plausibly intends for Jesus's designations of kingship (e.g., "king of the Jews") to be ironic at his trial and execution (18:28–19:16, 19–22). Despite Pilate's and the Jews's rejection of "king" Jesus, Jesus was indeed king (for the irony in King Jesus's trial and crucifixion, see Duke, *Irony*, 126–37; cf. Severino Pancaro, "'People of God' in St John's Gospel," *NTS* 16 [1970]: 123–25). Given a connection between Jesus's two kingship titles ("king of Israel/Jews") in John and the ironic usage of the title in Jesus's trial/crucifixion, Schuchard posits, "Jesus' arrival in Jerusalem both anticipated and illustrated the paradoxical irony of Jesus' ultimate crucifixion as the King of the Jews" (*Scripture*, 79; cf. Mérode, "L'accueil triomphal," 61–62). Some exceed the evidence, however, when they argue that the term "*Israel* is always used in a deeper theological sense [irony] than may appear on the surface (cf. 1:31, 49; 12:13)—that, in fact, some readers of the Gospel know Israel to mean 'the true Israel,' God's new people through Jesus Christ" (Duke, *Irony*, 46, italics original; cf. Pancaro, "'People of God,'" 123–25). We posit, however, that John does not clarify that the title (1:49) is ironic until John 12 and 18.

[55] R. Alan Culpepper notes that in general, the FG's ironies are "corrective; one perspective contradicts, exposes, and invalidates the other" (*Anatomy of the Fourth Gospel: A Study in Literary Design*, FFNT [Philadelphia: Fortress, 1983], 168). Robinson summarizes John's purposes for emphasizing Jesus's kingship: "King of Israel—yes (cf. 1.49); but not that sort of king [i.e., not political] (cf. 18.36f.)" (*Priority*, 232).

[56] Duke, *Irony*, 23. He outlines several types of irony (ibid., 18–27; cf. Culpepper's analysis of irony and lists of dramatic irony in the FG [*Anatomy*,

To advance John's view of Jesus's kingship, the crowd's "cry" takes on corrected meanings that the crowd had not realized.

Zephaniah 3 as Johannine Fulfillment of OT Prophecy

Second, since Zephaniah 3:14–15 is a prophetic text, we must discern whether John's usage reflects direct or indirect fulfillment of OT prophecy. Beale makes a clear distinction between these two options: "The direct fulfills what was explicitly predicted by the words of a prophet, while the indirect fulfills what was implicitly foreshadowed by historical events, which have been narrated."[57] Direct fulfillments optionally employ fulfillment formulas.

In chapters 3–4, we argue that Zephaniah 3:14–15 does not refer to an inaugurated event that occurred in Zephaniah's past, but Zephaniah referred to King Yahweh's sure, future, beneficent presence and deliverance to encourage God's people to rejoice in the wait. And Jewish literature consistently regarded these verses as an unfulfilled prophecy of the future.

The FG provides two signals that Jesus's entry is *direct fulfillment* of Zephaniah: (1) John 12:14 introduces the Zephaniah 3 allusion and Zechariah 9:9 quotation with a fulfillment formula (καθώς ἐστιν γεγραμμένον).[58] (2) A logical inference follows the preceding

---

165–80, esp. 176–77]). Menken comments on John 12:12–13, 14–16: "The evangelist often has people make statements about Jesus which are, from John's point of view, insufficient in what the speakers themselves mean, but true at a higher level, see, e.g., 6:14–15; 11:49–52; 19:14; it is not necessary that the insufficiency of the statement is explicitly indicated" (*Quotations*, 87n29).

[57] Beale, *Handbook*, 58. Indirect fulfillment of OT typological prophecy includes "(1) analogical correspondence, (2) historicity, (3) a pointing-forwardness, (4) escalation, and (5) retrospection" (ibid., 57).

[58] Beale labels "it is written" as a fulfillment formula (ibid., 56; John 6:31 and 12:14 quote the OT [Menken, *Quotations*, 81]). Craig A. Evans argues that John's first half introduces OT quotes with "written," linking Jesus's ministry and "scriptural expectation"; his latter half uses fulfillment formulas, because "it is in Jesus' rejection and crucifixion that the Scriptures find their ultimate fulfilment" ("New Testament Use of the Old Testament," in *NDBT*, 78). John 12:15a may seem to meet the criteria for quotations (see § 1.3.1), but we argue

argument. If a Zephanian μὴ φοβοῦ finds fulfillment in King Jesus's sitting on a donkey,[59] this may logically imply that important Zephanian reason(s) for "no fear" (e.g., Yahweh's presence) are likewise directly fulfilled in John 12.[60] Indeed, Jesus's disciples later remember what happened to him at his entry and recall the OT correspondences (cf. plural ταῦτα's [12:16]), which plausibly include both Zephaniah allusions (12:13 and 15).[61] Furthermore, we trace below important Zephanian themes in John 12 that correspond to the prophetic expectation envisioned in Zephaniah 3:14–15.

---

it is an allusion (see § 2.4.4).

[59] We hold that John's imperative μὴ φοβοῦ ultimately targets *his reader(s)* (see Wahlde, *John*, 2:530; 3:307; Brendsel, *Isaiah*, 185n121; Sheridan, *Retelling*, 228; contra Menken, *Quotations*, 86, who holds that it assuaged the terror-struck [due to the Lazarus-sign] *crowd*). For Schuchard, μὴ φοβοῦ replaced "rejoice," since the disciples "do not 'rejoice' until after Jesus' glorification" (Schuchard, *Scripture*, 76n29; see John 12:20; cf. 14:28; 16:22).

[60] John 12:15's μὴ φοβοῦ is an imperative but is "fulfilled" since John 12 meets the conditions for giving the command. We attempt to represent our argument in a logical syllogism. (1) John's Zephanian imperative "no fear" is a result (cf. the fulfillment formula) of Jesus's arrival. (2) Zephaniah 3's "no fear" is the result of Yahweh's presence/arrival. (3) So, John's imperative is the result of Yahweh's presence/arrival.

[61] We leave open the exact meaning of the third ταῦτα–expression in 12:16, since the verb ἐποίησαν ambiguously refers to either the disciples' or crowd's actions (see Ridderbos, *John*, 424; Leung, *Kingship-Cross Interplay*, 168; Morris takes the former view [*John*, 521], and Menken argues for the latter [*Quotations*, 86]). At the very least, the combined meaning of John 12:16's ταῦτα–expressions is that both the OT and entry actions were later understood. Nicolas Farelly's comment represents our view: "What the disciples did not understand was both that this particular event was a fulfillment of prophecy, and that the meaning and significance of this event lay in Jesus riding a young donkey. The nature of Jesus' kingship is the focal point of this narratival aside: Jesus' kingship was both real and representative of God's kingship, but also carried out by the weakness of the cross" (*The Disciples in the Fourth Gospel: A Narrative Analysis of Their Faith and Understanding*, WUNT, 2nd ser., 290 [Tübingen: Mohr Siebeck, 2010], 60–61; cf. Lincoln, *John*, 344–45). Also, in John 2:22, the disciples' remembrance occurs after Jesus's resurrection and follows the first time John mentions Jesus's "hour" (2:4).

Zephaniah 3 as a Limited Johannine Blueprint

Third, we speculate whether John also used Zephaniah as a blueprint for part of the Entry Narrative. Beale indicates that such a blueprint normally involves a large portion of the OT and includes (a) a thematic sequence or outline, unique to one OT context, and/or (b) the clustering of quotations or allusions from the same OT portion.[62] Some plausibly argue that John 12 largely follows the textual progression and themes of Isaiah 52's Servant.[63] We posit, however, that Zephaniah played some role in structuring John's entry, even if complementing his use of Isaiah. The table below displays our proposal on the right-hand side and directly quotes Brendsel's Isaianic progression on the left-hand side.[64]

[62] Beale, *Handbook*, 80.

[63] Brendsel, *Isaiah*, 180–84; cf. Craig A. Evans, "Obduracy and the Lord's Servant: Some Observations on the Use of the Old Testament in the Fourth Gospel," in *Early Jewish and Christian Exegesis: Studies in Memory of William Hugh Brownlee*, ed. Craig A. Evans and William F. Stinespring, SPHS 10 (Atlanta: Scholars Press, 1987), 235–36; Catrin H. Williams, "The Testimony of Isaiah and Johannine Christology," in *"As Those Who Are Taught": The Interpretation of Isaiah from the LXX to the SBL*, ed. C. Mathews McGinnis and P. K. Tull, SBLSymS 27 (Atlanta: Society of Biblical Literature, 2006), 107–24; James Hamilton, "The Influence of Isaiah on the Gospel of John," *Perichoresis* 7 (2007): 139–62; Carson, *John*, 450; Carson, "John and the Johannine Epistles," in *It Is Written: Scripture Citing Scripture: Essays in Honor of Barnabas Lindars*, ed. D. A. Carson and H. G. M. Williamson (Cambridge: Cambridge University Press, 1988), 249. John names Isaiah in John 12:38, 39, 41.

[64] The left-hand side of Table 5 adapts Brendsel's Isaianic textual progression for John 12:9–19 (*Isaiah*, 181). He argues that John 12 reads Isaiah 52–53 contextually so that John 12:15a derives from Isaiah 40:9 (ibid., 185–86), rendering "do not fear" "a meaningful part of the Isaianic influence and structuring" in John 12 (ibid.; Brendsel, personal comments to author, July 25, 2015). We are in basic agreement with him that Isaiah 52–53 influences John 12's structure. However, (1) Brendsel reads essential components for a textual progression in John 12:12–19 in Isaiah 52 and does not include Isaiah 40 in his proposed base progression. Therefore, we compare the proposed blueprints of Zephaniah 3 and Isaiah 52 rather than expand the *progression* to include the "influence" of Isaiah 40. (2) We argue for the plausibility that "do not fear"

Table 5: Proposed Blueprints for John 12:9–19: Isaiah 52:7–12 and Zephaniah 3:14–15

Isaiah 52:7–12 Progression	Zephaniah 3:14–20 Progression
1. The return of Yahweh as king to Jerusalem (Isa 52:8); The return of Jesus as king to Jerusalem (John 12:12)	1. Exhortation to joyful shouts to Jerusalem (Zeph. 3:14); Joyful shouts by Jerusalem (John 12:13)
2. The arrival elicits shouts of joy and the exhortation to rejoice (Isa 52:8–9); The arrival elicits shouts of joy (John 12:13)	2. Rationale of the shouts: Yahweh is King of Israel (Zeph. 3:15c); Rationale of the shouts: Jesus is King of Israel (John 12:13c)
	3. Encouragement/exhortation: do not fear, daughter of Zion (Zeph. 3:15d, 16a); Encouragement/exhortation: do not fear, daughter of Zion (John 12:15a)
3. "All the nations/ends of the earth" see the salvation of God (Isa 52:10); The "world" goes after Jesus (John 12:19)	4. Yahweh's name and praise in them (i.e., his remnant "peoples" [Zeph. 3:9–10]) "in all the earth" (Zeph. 3:19), the restoration would be "before your eyes" (Zeph. 3:19–20); The "world" goes after Jesus (John 12:19)

alludes to Zephaniah 3:15, though we also considered a potential textual fusion of Isaiah 40:9 and Zephaniah 3:15 (see § 2.4.1). And (3) we posit that Zephaniah 3's phrase "king of Israel" makes a particular contribution to the textual progression in John 12. Brendsel claims that "only 'the king of Israel' remains as a unique potential connection to Zeph 3" (personal comments to author, July 25, 2015). But additional, shared verbal parallels and themes in Zephaniah 3 and John 12 (incl. "Do not fear, daughter of Zion") enhance the probability that Zephaniah 3 contributes to the blueprint, supplying John 12 with the very vocabulary that Isaiah 52 lacks.

John may have modeled some of his Entry Narrative on Zephaniah 3, which perhaps supplied details to a larger Isaianic progression in John 12. First, Zephaniah 3 contains all the basic features noted in Brendsel's posited Isaianic textual progression. Zephaniah 3:14 commanded anticipatory joy due to Yahweh, King of Israel's coming; John 12 narrates exuberant (albeit nationalistic) joy at Jesus King of Israel's coming. Also, Zephaniah 3:19's "lame" and "crippled" can refer to a global restoration of the "peoples" (3:9–10) for God's name and praise "in all the earth,"[65] a thematic parallel to the "world" and "Greeks" going to King Jesus (John 12:19–21). Second, John 12 clusters Zephaniah 3:14–15's vocabulary that is missing in Isaiah 52 (i.e., "king of Israel," "daughter of Zion," "do not fear") and contains other Zephanian themes.[66]

We do note contrasting emphases with a Zephanian and Isaianic Progression. Zephaniah 3 demands shouts of joy from Zion/Jerusalem then details the reasons (i.e., King Yahweh's arrival) and outcome (i.e., no fear). In John 12:12–13 the crowd joyfully shouts near Jerusalem; then 12:13c, 15a provide the rationale of their exuberant approach (i.e., the King's arrives) and the rhetorical outcome it should provoke (i.e., no fear). By contrast, an Isaianic Progression observes Isaiah and John introducing the king first, *then* detailing the shouts. In our judgment, Zephaniah's and Isaiah's progressions contain emphases compatible to John's narrative.

[65] We chart Zephaniah 3's participants and conclude that 3:19 may refer to 3:9–10's "peoples." 3:20's "you" likely refers initially to remnant Judah and by extension to the remnant from the world, so that 3:19–20 may include both Jewish and Gentile remnants (see § 3.3.7; Appendix 4; cf. Jason S. DeRouchie, *Zephaniah*, ZECOT [Grand Rapids: Zondervan, forthcoming). Zephaniah 3 thus records a tension between the promised ingathered nations (3:9–10; cf. 3:19) and Yahweh's promised praise among them (3:20), a tension perhaps relieved by a divine Messiah Jesus entering to reconstitute a new people—Jew and Gentile—in himself (cf. John 11:50–52; 12:19–20).

[66] See § 2.4 and the discussion in § 5.3 for evidence. We argue that "king of Israel" alludes to Zephaniah 3:15c making a particular contribution to John 12; "daughter of Zion" comes from Zechariah 9:9, but Zephaniah 3:14a shares this addressee; and "do not fear" alludes to Zephaniah 3:15d (perhaps with

Zephaniah's progression is nevertheless more limited than that proposed for Isaiah 52. Zephaniah's most explicit lexical marks occur in John 12:13–15 and not the rest of John 12. If Zephaniah 3 functions as a blueprint, it plays a limited role perhaps to complement or supplement a larger Isaianic pattern in the chapter.

Concluding Zephaniah 3's Hermeneutical Use in the Entry Narrative

John may have employed Zephaniah 3 as a bridge, perhaps something like the Jewish method *gezerah shawah*, but other hermeneutical options better explain John's rationale for using Zephaniah. John seems to employ Zephaniah to support his narrative irony and direct fulfillment in the Entry Narrative, and perhaps as supplementation for an Isaianic blueprint.

Theological Use of Zephaniah 3 in John 12

We now trace four important implications for John 12's allusions to Zephaniah 3:14–15. First, the FG's fulfillment of Zephaniah strengthens allusions to King Jesus and Yahweh. Second and third, Zephaniah 3's Gentile ingathering and Warrior-King themes correspond to John 12. Fourth, John's last "hour" language stresses that Zephaniah's eschatological "day" has dawned.

King Jesus as Zephaniah's King Yahweh

At the rhetorical peak of Zephaniah (3:14–15), *Yahweh*, King of Israel's presence (and removed judgments/enemies) would be cause for Jerusalem to rejoice, with the reassuring result: "no fear." With FG allusions to Zephaniah 3, Jesus approaches Daughter Jerusalem in association with *Yahweh* King of Israel, thereby addressing all Jerusalem's *fears*. Jesus's entry thus would entail and in some way, represent the public, exile-ending arrival of *Yahweh*.[67]

Isa. 40:9, in textual fusion).

[67] Some Zephaniah Proposal proponents posit some level of reference to Jesus's divinity here (see, e.g., P. C. Mateos, "Uso e interpretación de Zacarías

We have argued that the entry *crowd* had messianic and misguided national hopes for King Jesus (§ 5.1), but aided by Zephaniah the *FG narrative also* alludes to Jesus's Yahweh-connection.[68] The crowd correctly identifies Jesus as king but did not recognize "that Jesus shared in the identity of Yahweh."[69]

An allusion to Jesus's association with Yahweh in the entry is possible. First, the only other occurrence of μὴ φοβέω in the FG arguably alludes to Jesus's divinity (as part of a theophany). In John 6:20, Jesus said to his disciples, ἐγώ εἰμι· μὴ φοβεῖσθε. This construction compares with the OT divine epiphany (reassurance) "formula: Do

---

9,9–10 en el Nuevo Testamento," *EstAg* 7 (1972): 478; 8 (1973): 2–3; Brunson, *Psalm 118*, 236–39; Brown, *John*, 1:462–63; O. Palmer Robertson, *The Books of Nahum, Habakkuk, and Zephaniah*, NICOT [Grand Rapids: Eerdmans, 1990], 338). Schuchard finds Jesus's divinity implied from John's supposed usage of Isaiah 44 (*Scripture*, 78), and Brendsel posits some form of divine association here based on Zechariah 9 and Isaiah 52 (*Isaiah*, 178). Sheridan thematically connects Zephaniah 3:15, 17's King Yahweh in the *midst* of the people and Messiah-King Jesus's coming into the people's *midst*. She concludes, "Jesus' messianic status is properly understood not only with reference to his 'kingly identity' but to his identity as 'Lord'" (*Retelling*, 228; cf. Brunson, *Psalm 118*, 232–34). Robertson similarly asserts, "When Jesus finally was known to be Lord, equivalent to God himself, then his disciples understood the significance of these words (John 12:16)" (*Zephaniah*, 338).

[68] Brendsel considers that Zephaniah 3 may help affirm Jesus's Yahweh-connection in John 12 but subsumed under John's larger point: "Zephaniah is perhaps helpful to assert/underline Yahweh's arrival as one of John'c concerns in John 12 . . . His full concern seems to me to be that at the entry the king-identified-with-Yahweh arrives at Jerusalem, and that is what Isaiah/Zechariah (not Zephaniah) prophesy" (personal comments to author, July 25, 2015). Although John 12 does not focus solely on Jesus's divine identity, John's allusions to Zephaniah help clarify that Jesus's association with Yahweh is an important feature of the Entry Narrative.

[69] Andreas J. Köstenberger and Scott R. Swain, *Father, Son and Spirit: The Trinity and John's Gospel*, NSBT 24 (Downers Grove, IL: InterVarsity Press, 2008), 38. They argue, "Coupled with the emphatic presentation of Jesus as sharing the identity of Yahweh, the one and only true God, the compelling message of John's Gospel is that there is no other god besides the One who is 'the way and the truth and the life'" (ibid., 157).

not be afraid; I am the God of your ancestors."[70] Furthermore, even in OT occurrences of μὴ φοβοῦ outside of Zephaniah, the clause regularly occurs with "une manifestation divine."[71] John 12:15's μὴ φοβοῦ may counter fears induced by realizing Jesus's divine agency or function as re-assurance of Yahweh's salvation (Zeph. 3); read either way, the clause implies that Jesus is associated with Yahweh.[72]

[70] Brown, *John*, 1:533; cf. Kubiś, *Zechariah*, 87 (possible); Sheridan, *Retelling*, 227. John has only two occurrences of μη + φοβέω (6:20; 12:15; cf. φοβέω [John 6:19; 9:22; 19:8]). It may be argued that Jesus does not employ the divine name (Ex. 3:14) at 6:20 but uses ἐγώ εἰμι to simply say "I who you know am here." However, the FG uses ἐγώ εἰμι absolutely—without a predicate—seven times (see 4:26; 6:20; 8:24, 28, 58; 13:19; 18:5, 6, 8), and in John 8:58, at least the Jews immediately understood that claim to be a blasphemous assertion to divinity (cf. 8:59; Jarl E. Fossum, *The Image of the Invisible God: Essays on the Influence of Jewish Mysticism on Early Christology*, NTOA 30 [Freiburg, Schweiz: Universitätsverlag, 1995], 127; Shirley Lucass, *The Concept of the Messiah in the Scriptures of Judaism and Christianity*, LSTS 78 [London: T&T Clark, 2011], 165). Richard Bauckham similarly argues for interpreting "all seven occurrences as a set, while understanding those where an ordinary meaning is possible as instances of double entendre" (*The Testimony of the Beloved Disciple: Narrative, History, and Theology in the Gospel of John* [Grand Rapids: Baker, 2007], 245).

[71] Marie-Joseph Lagrange, *Évangile selon Saint Jean*, 5th ed., *EBib* (Paris: Gabalda, 1936), 325; cf. Anthony T. Hanson, *The Prophetic Gospel: A Study of John and the Old Testament* (Edinburgh: T&T Clark, 1991), 164; Kubiś, *Zechariah*, 86; e.g., Gen. 15:1; 21:17; 26:24; 28:13 (LXX); Judg. 6:23; Isa. 41:10; 44:2; Lam. 3:57; Luke 1:13, 30; Rev. 1:17. In that case, the imperative would function to counter the fear-inducing encounter with God (G. Wanke, "φοβέω," in *TDNT*, 9:203), but note that the clause does not refer exclusively to theophanies (e.g., Judg. 4:18; Ruth 3:11; 1 Sam. 4:20; 22:23; 2 Kings 6:16).

[72] We acknowledge that the *rationale* for John's μὴ φοβοῦ is hotly contested, but in keeping with the Zephaniah Proposal, we focus on Zephaniah's contributions to John. Zephaniah 3:15 used it as re-assurance/word of divine salvation, and some scholars see that meaning intended in John 12:15 (Sheridan, *Retelling*, 228; Kubiś, *Zechariah*, 91–92). Those proposals not fully accounting for an allusion to Zephaniah (and so not treated here) include the following: (1) It emphasizes Jesus's peaceful nature as a non-war-horse-sitting king (Lagrange, *Jean*, 325; cf. Kubiś's observation that the FG often stresses Jesus's peaceful mission, John 14:27; 16:33; 20:19, 21, 26; [*Zechariah*, 86]). (2) The reassuring μὴ φοβοῦ better fits the context of Jesus's looming Passion

Second, John 12:13's βασιλεὺς τοῦ Ἰσραήλ probably reflected the Jewish crowd's political-messianic expectations given its juxtaposition with ὁ ἐρχόμενος. But based on our evidence for the Zephaniah Proposal, *John* alludes to Jesus's connection with Zephaniah's divine "king of Israel" (12:13, 15). Even if John draws the title from another OT occurrence, none designate a messianic king, but it does often refer to Yahweh/God.[73] An allusion to Zephaniah's divine "King of Israel" would then parallel the common OT expectation of Yahweh, King of Israel's arrival, frequent in the Psalms and Prophets.[74] Additionally, Second Temple, Qumran, and rabbinical literature likewise emphasized Yahweh's kingship.[75] A sustained

than Zechariah 9:9's "rejoice!" (see discussion in ibid., 88). (3) King Jesus's Lazarus sign (11:1–44) struck fear in the crowd that needed to be addressed (Menken, *Quotations*, 85–88; Menken, "The Quotations from Zech 9,9 in Mt 21,5 and in John 12,15," in *John and the Synoptics*, ed. A. Denaux, BETL 101 [Leuven: Leuven University Press, 1992], 574; Menken, "The Minor Prophets in John's Gospel," in *The Minor Prophets in the New Testament*, ed. M. J. J. Menken and Steve Moyise, LNTS 377 [London: T&T Clark, 2009], 83–84). This proposal is quite unlikely, since John 12:15 does not address the crowd and because the entry crowd was joyful (for a more extensive critique, see Kubiś, *Zechariah*, 89–91; Sheridan, *Retelling*, 228; Brunson, *Psalm 118*, 237; cf. Schuchard, *Scripture*, 76). (4) John may comfort his audience experiencing persecution, which was the promised consequence to following Martyred King Jesus; "fear not" marks the inauguration of Isaiah 40's new exodus (John 16:2; Brendsel, *Isaiah*, 185). Brendsel's argument is plausible (and not incompatible with the Zephaniah Proposal): "If the king himself faces rejection [John 12:9–11, 17–19] and ultimately death, what might this imply for his people (note, e.g., John 15:18–16:4)? Such a question would surely have weighed heavily on John's readers, many of whom were likely experiencing the fulfillment of Jesus' words in John 16:2" (ibid.). For a survey and assessment of the main options, see Kubiś, *Zechariah*, 86–92.

[73] For evidence see §§ 2.4.1; 5.1.1.

[74] See, e.g., Ex. 15:18; Pss. 5:2; 21:28; 24:7–10; 47; 93; 96–97; 99; 146:10; Isa. 6:5 (Brunson, *Psalm 118*, 236–37; § 2.4.1).

[75] Second Temple literature testifies "to the ultimate kingship of Yahweh" (Brunson, *Psalm 118*, 237; cf. Tob. 13:6–7, 10–11, 15; Jth. 9:12; Sir. 51:1; 2 Macc. 1:24 "Lord God . . . the only and kind king"; 7:9; 13:4; 3 Macc. 2:2; 5:35; 1 Esd. 4:46; Pss. Sol. 5:19; 17:1, 46). At Qumran, "only God is regularly called 'King'" (Meeks, *Prophet-King*, 165). And rabbinical texts hope in "God

hope for Yahweh's kingship (e.g., Zeph. 3:15) resonates with a significant strand of OT and Jewish hope.

We detect further evidence that the FG plausibly intends to connect King Jesus with Yahweh in some way. (1) Leading up to John 12, Jews charge Jesus four times with death-deserving blasphemy, as they rightly understood him to claim equality with God (5:17–18; 8:58; 10:30–33, 38–39).[76] Jewish leaders then diabolically plot Jesus's death, compelled by his miraculous Lazarus-sign (11:47–48; 12:10–11), and their menacing presence and the Lazarus-sign form an *inclusio* to the Entry Narrative.[77] John 11's portrait of Jesus impacts Jesus's entry.

Many scholars argue that the Lazarus-sign narrative itself (John 11; cf. 10:37–38) presents Jesus as human but also as suprahuman (divine). For example, Jesus has foreknowledge that he will raise

---

primarily as the King of Israel" (K. G. Kuhn, "מלכות שמים in Rabbinic Literature," in *TDOT*, 1:574). Brunson (*Psalm 118*, 237) perhaps overstates his case by arguing that Yahweh as king "dominates" the Jewish literature. Many have traced the evidence for Qumran having some sort of hope for a Davidic messiah-king (e.g., 4QMMT [4Q394] 95; see Craig A. Evans, "The Messiah in the Dead Sea Scrolls," in *Israel's Messiah in the Bible and the Dead Sea Scrolls*, ed. Richard S. Hess and M. Daniel Carroll [Grand Rapids: Baker, 2003], 97; Travis D. Trost, *Who Should Be King in Israel?: A Study on Roman Imperial Politics, the Dead Sea Scrolls, and the Fourth Gospel*, SBL 139 [New York: Lang, 2010], 29–76). Nevertheless, (1) in extra-biblical, Jewish literature "king of Israel" rarely designated a messianic personage (Psalms of Solomon 17 is the lone exception we have found), (2) the OT's "king of Israel" never designated a messianic personage but is often a title for Yahweh (see § 2.4.1), (3) a *significant expectation* of Yahweh's kingship does exist in Jewish literature, and (4) in Jewish literature Zephaniah 3 consistently retained the title's reference to Yahweh (see chap. 4).

[76] Brunson, *Psalm 118*, 249. Lucass argues these Jewish reactions meant that they understood Jesus to have invoked the Divine Name (*Concept of the Messiah*, 165; cf. Fossum, *Image*, 128).

[77] For evidence of the *inclusio* and the Entry Narrative structured as 12:9–19, see § 2.1.2. The Jews plotted to kill Jesus for many reasons (e.g., fear of Roman military response, 11:48; 18:3, 12), but they also reacted to what they perceived as divine claims (John 5, 8, 10) and as demonstrations of God's glory (e.g., the Lazarus-sign).

Lazarus (11:4) and prays only so that the crowd better understands the nature of his unique and divine agency (11:41–42); Jesus's great concern is God's and his own glory (11:4, 40); and Jesus's claim "*I am* the resurrection and the life" (11:25) resembles a "formula of divine self-identification."[78] Jesus is human (e.g., 11:35) yet has a unique relationship with the Father.

(2) The well-known Psalm 118's *hosanna* was originally directed to Yahweh. Its occurrence in the Entry Narrative could have stimulated John, upon reflecting on the event (12:16), to exploit a Yahweh-Jesus connection (John 12:13; see § 5.1.1).

(3) John's Entry Narrative portrays Jesus as "the coming one" but does not explicitly connect Jesus to David (cf. Matt. 21:9, 15; Mark 11:10). One possible explanation for this, Leung posits, is "John's overall emphasis on Jesus' provenance from above [see 1:9; 3:31; 5:42, 43; cf. 3:16, 34; 7:29; 8:23; 12:45; 13:16] . . . . John 12:13

[78] Andrew T. Lincoln, "The Lazarus Story: A Literary Perspective," in *The Gospel of John and Christian Theology*, ed. Richard Bauckham and Carl Mosser (Grand Rapids: Eerdmans, 2008), 218, italics ours (see also ibid., 217–24). Menken notices a general pattern further linking the Lazarus miracle and other NT miracles: "The Lazarus miracle as told by John is an extraordinary demonstration of Jesus' divine power, of God's glory in him [11:4, 40–42]. . . . It is precisely Jesus' divine power to work miracles which arouses, according to NT miracle narratives, fear [φοβέω] in the audience who do not understand him or only partly understand him" (*Quotations*, 85; e.g., Matt. 17:6–7; 28:4–5; Mark 4:41; 5:15; 6:49–50; Luke 5:9–10; 7:16). John 12:15's imperative μὴ φοβοῦ does not address the crowd, but in the NT, "fear" or "do not fear!" does often occur in the presence of divine power. In favor of Jesus's divinity here, the FG often recorded or implied Jesus's oneness with God (e.g., 10:16, 30; 11:52), a unity manifested even in Jesus's crucifixion (13:31; see, e.g., Koester, *Symbolism*, 235–39, 250). Many studies agree that John documents Jesus's divinity (e.g., Bauckham, *Beloved Disciple*, 239–52; David M. Ball, *"I Am" in John's Gospel: Literary Function, Background and Theological Implications*, JSNTSup 124 [Sheffield: Sheffield Academic Press, 1996], esp. 276–83; Andrew T. Lincoln, *Truth on Trial: The Lawsuit Motif in the Fourth Gospel* [Peabody, MA: Hendrickson, 2000], esp. 182–93, 419–31; Catrin H. Williams, *I Am He: The Interpretation of 'Anî Hû' in Jewish and Early Christian Literature*, WUNT, 2nd ser., 113 [Tübingen: Mohr Siebeck, 2000]).

[i.e., "coming in the name of the Lord"] is tantamount to asserting that he comes from God. Since Jesus' heavenly provenance is implied in this quotation, it is unsurprising that the evangelist does not explicitly bring forth the Davidic hope in the entry story."[79] Indeed, Jesus comes from God/above/heaven (e.g., 3:31; 6:38; 8:42; 16:28; 17:8), and the destination is almost always to the/this world, though John 1:11 notes that Jesus "came to his own."[80] Similarly in John's sending motif, Jesus is sent from the Father (e.g., 13:16) yet equal to the Sender, a point reinforced following Jesus's entry (e.g., 12:44–45).[81]

(4) Zechariah 9, in juxtaposition with Zephaniah 3 in John 12, seems to anticipate Yahweh's arrival. First, in Zechariah 9:1–8, Yahweh progresses from north to south in judging the nations, until he reaches the culminating point of encouraging Jerusalem (Zech. 9:8). Brendsel writes, "*Yahweh* will 'camp around my house,' with the result that 'no oppressor will pass over them anymore' (v. 8). Verses 1–8 lead us to expect Yahweh's return to Jerusalem bringing judgment and salvation, but in Zech 9:9 we are told of a coming *human* king."[82] Second, Zechariah 9:10 returns to Yahweh declaring in first-person his military (king-like) activities, which reinforces Yahweh's promised kingly action.

[79] Leung, *Kingship-Cross Interplay*, 160–61; cf. Daly-Denton, *David*, 183–84; Schuchard, *Scripture*, 54, 82; Köstenberger and Swain, *Father, Son and Spirit*, 111–27, who discuss the theme of Jesus's divine identity in the FG.

[80] John most frequently mentions Jesus's coming destined for the "world" (1:9; 3:19; 6:14; 9:39; 11:27; 12:46; 16:28; 18:37; see Menken, *Quotations*, 90). Brunson surveys John's "coming one" motif, highlighting the divine origination assumed in the clause (*Psalm 118*, 240–64).

[81] Leung, *Kingship-Cross Interplay*, 160–61 (cf. John 3:16, 34; 7:29; 8:23; 12:45; 13:16).

[82] Brendsel, *Isaiah*, 178, italics original; cf. Terry Collins, "The Literary Contexts of Zechariah 9:9," in *The Book of Zechariah and Its Influence*, ed. C. Tuckett (Burlington, VT: Ashgate, 2003), 30, 34–37; David L. Petersen, *Zechariah 9–14 and Malachi: A Commentary*, OTL [Louisville: Westminster John Knox, 1995], 57–58. For a thorough survey and assessment of the proposals regarding the king's identity, see Kubiś, *Zechariah*, 27–74.

Additionally, Collins observes that structural and linguistic elements unify much of Isaiah 30:27; 35:4; 40:9–11; 62:11; Zephaniah 3:14–17; and Zechariah 9:9, leading him to classify these texts as a literary form called "the proclamation of the coming of the *Lord*."[83] These texts name God/Yahweh as the principal actor; he plays a decisive role in the coming.

At least one way of interpreting this evidence is that "in Zech 9:9 the appearing of the humble king is somehow *the manifestation* of the arrival of Yahweh in judgment and salvation."[84] The ambiguity over Zechariah 9's king and Yahweh's kingly activities may have led the FG to allude to Jesus's association with Yahweh.[85]

In Psalm 118's address, the coming one motif, John 12's immediate literary context, and Zechariah 9's literary context, the FG makes suggestive connections between Jesus and Yahweh. By alluding to Zephaniah 3's Yahweh, King of Israel, John would reinforce or perhaps clarify that Jesus's messianic entry to Jerusalem does in some way represent the coming of Yahweh.

[83] Collins, "Zechariah 9:9," 30–35 (e.g., "Daughter Zion," "shout" in Zech. 2:10; Zeph. 3:14; see § 2.4.2). We noted that some read John's "king of Israel" as depending on Isaiah 52:7, and that text also highlights the arrival of *God* (Evans, "Obduracy," 235–36; Williams, "Testimony," 119; cf. Brendsel, *Isaiah*, 178).

[84] Brendsel, *Isaiah*, 178, italics original.

[85] Kubiś argues that this conclusion is possible but not explicit; he notes that the parallels with divine comings lead some scholars to argue that Zechariah 9:9 "also depicts God's coming, and that the king must be identified as God himself" (*Zechariah*, 42; cf. Joachim Becker, *Messianic Expectation in the Old Testament* [Philadelphia: Fortress Press, 1980], 72–73; Carroll Stuhlmueller, *Rebuilding with Hope: A Commentary on the Books of Haggai and Zechariah*, ITC [Grand Rapids: Eerdmans; Edinburgh: Handsel Press, 1988], 121–25; and Paul D. Hanson, *The Dawn of the Apocalyptic: The Historical and Sociological Roots of Jewish Apocalyptic Eschatology*, rev. ed. [Philadelphia: Fortress, 1979], 292–324). Petersen tightly associates Zechariah 9:9 and Zephaniah 3:14–15: "By connotation through allusion [to Zeph. 3:14–15], the author [of Zech. 9:9] indicated that the arrival of this king should be celebrated in much the same way that Yahweh's presence as king deserves accolade" (*Zechariah 9–14*, 58).

The World and Greeks as Zephaniah 3's Promised Nations and Remnant

The FG's entry plausibly intends to signal that Jesus comes as King for all, not a national king as the crowd expected. John 12 may develop this second Zephanian theme at three points.

(1) John 12:15 "omitted" Zechariah 9:9's detail about the king coming "to you" (לָךְ/σοι; cf. Matt. 21:5), which may signal that King Jesus's coming was not narrowly destined for Jerusalem (Jews). At least two observations support that possibility. First, Jesus's "coming 'to his own' (1:11) belongs to his coming into the world, but at the stage of the gospel where we meet the Entry Narrative, many of his people have already rejected Jesus (cf. only the concluding remarks on unbelief in 12:37–43)."[86] In John 12, Jewish misunderstanding (e.g., sign-faith) and rejection of Jesus stand in tension with Gentile faith (12:20–21). Second, Zechariah 9:10 foresees the king's worldwide, peaceful rule (cf. Gen. 49:10). Since John does not narrowly stipulate the destination for Jesus's coming, John effectively avoids an ethnic limitation on Jesus's kingship.[87]

(2) The Pharisees comment that "the [whole] world" (κόσμος [12:19]) was going after Jesus. We make the following exegetical points. First, the Pharisees's comment responds to Jesus's growing popularity, which likely entails his acclaim by the entry crowd. John 12:19 logically connects to the 12:18 entry crowd's meeting Jesus (see the οὖν). Second, the phrase to go "after" (ὀπίσω) frequently denotes discipleship in the Gospels (e.g., Matt. 16:24; Mark 1:17, 20; 8:34; Luke 9:23; cf. John 6:66), and if that meaning carries here, the Pharisees claimed that those going to Jesus were devoted to

[86] Menken, *Quotations*, 91.

[87] Mateos, "Zacarías 9,9–10," 5; Menken, *Quotations*, 90–91. Thus read, John 12:15 retains the second person singular pronoun "your" (σου) to affirm that Jesus is indeed Israel's king, but based on Zechariah 9:10 and John 12:19–20, Jesus *also* comes as king of all (ibid., 91; cf. John 18:36–37, which emphasize Jesus's otherworldly [in origin], universal kingship). John's reading of Zechariah 9 may parallel his contextual reading of Zephaniah (3:9–10).

him.[88] Third, the "[whole] world" (κόσμος)[89] is likely a hyperbolic statement (cf. John 3:26; 21:25; Acts 17:16; 19:35; Col. 1:6). "Large" crowds of predominantly Jewish people in the region were indeed following Jesus (e.g., 12:9, 12), so the Pharisees lament (12:19a) and exaggerate the numbers. Most commentators, however, read this statement as also reflecting Johannine irony; Pharisees lament that "everyone" in Judea was going to Jesus, and John ironically presents the world as people without ethnic distinction.[90]

Κόσμος carries different senses in John. But the term does denote sinful humanity in many literary contexts: "people everywhere without racial distinction but who are lost and in rebellion against God," people that Jesus came to deliver (e.g., John 3:16–17; 12:46–47).[91] Though John 12:19 alone would not necessitate irony,

[88] Keener, *John*, 2:871; J. Ramsey Michaels, *The Gospel of John*, NICNT (Grand Rapids: Eerdmans, 2010), 682n92; but note John 1:15, 27 and 30.

[89] The word ὅλος is textually debatable. Important Greek witnesses do not include it (e.g., 𝔓[66] B 579), and the earliest Greek witnesses that do support reading ὅλος are late (i.e., D L Q) or are testified in daughter translations (e.g., Latin, Peshitta and Coptic; see Kurt Aland and Barbara Aland, *The Text of the New Testament: An Introduction to the Critical Editions and to the Theory and Practice of Modern Textual Criticism*, trans. Erroll F. Rhodes, rev. and enl. ed. [Grand Rapids: Eerdmans; Leiden: Brill, 1989], 335–37). When John uses the word κόσμος, he rarely adds an adjective and never combines it with ὅλος (that combination only occurs four times in the NT: Matt. 16:26; Mark 8:36; Luke 9:25; 1 John 5:19). Even without the adjective, the Pharisees's statement is likely hyperbolic and exaggerated (Carson, *John*, 435; Michaels, *John*, 682).

[90] Carson also sees "irony within irony" due to the unbelief in 12:37–40; thus, "the Evangelist does not accord a very high place to the [Jewish] crowd's positive response to Jesus" (*John*, 435; cf. John 2:23–25; 6:60; 8:30; Köstenberger, *John*, 373).

[91] Carson, *John*, 435. Κόσμος in John can sometimes refer to the neutral universe (e.g., John 17:5, 24; 21:25; cf. BDAG, s.v. κόσμος) or refer to Jesus's or his disciples' opponent(s), carrying a strongly negative sense (e.g., 15:18, 23, 24–25; 16:7–8, 20, 33; 17:14; see Wayne A. Meeks, "The Man from Heaven in Johannine Sectarianism," *JBL* 91 [1972]: 44–72; Judith L. Kovacs, "'Now Shall the Ruler of This World Be Driven Out': Jesus' Death as Cosmic Battle in John 12.20–36," *JBL* 114 [1995]: 234–35). Neither of those two meanings is likely here given that John 12:19 refers to *people following King Jesus*. Κόσμος

the Pharisees's complaint prefaces the Greeks's going to see Jesus (12:20–21) and so unwittingly introduces their arrival (cf. 11:50–52).[92] John thus implies that Jesus's kingship, acclaimed in his entry, is not restricted to Jews.

(3) In John 12:20, Greeks seek Jesus. John 12:20–36 immediately follows the entry pericope and has the same Passover setting.[93] It further connects to Jesus's entry by referring to his Passion glorification (δοξάζω [12:16, 23]). Also, the Pharisees's hyperbole—the "world" goes to Jesus—closes the Entry Narrative (12:19) yet juxtaposes to the Greeks coming (12:20). An ingathering theme has been building in the narrative (cf. John 10:15–16; 11:50–52; 12:11, 19, 32),[94] but for the first time, just after Jesus's entry, worshipping Greeks seek Jesus.

---

occurs 105 times in Johannine literature. For a survey, with most referring to "'humanity,' describing all people without ethnic distinctions" (i.e., not simply "the Jews"), see Lars Kierspel, *The Jews and the World in the Fourth Gospel: Parallelism, Function, and Context*, WUNT, 2nd ser., 220 (Tübingen: Mohr Siebeck, 2006), 157–60, 177; cf. H. Sasse, "κοσμέω, κόσμος, κόσμιος, κοσμικός," in *TDNT*, 3:868–898.

[92] Several scholars consider the Pharisees's comment an unwitting prophecy that John further develops in 12:20–21 (e.g., Köstenberger, *John*, 373–75; Sheridan, *Retelling*, 222; Brown, *John*, 1:463). Culpepper includes John 12:19 in a list of FG passages where "the characters naively make statements which convey meanings they do not suspect [i.e., dramatic irony]" (*Anatomy*, 176–77; cf. John 5:7; 7:4; 11:50; 19:14). Zephaniah 3:19's lame and outcast may entail Zephaniah 3:9–10's "peoples" (see § 3.3.7) and so may parallel John's meaning of "world" (12:19).

[93] For the defense of John 12:20–36 as a coherent textual unit, see C. H. Dodd, *Historical Tradition in the Fourth Gospel* (Cambridge: Cambridge University Press, 1963), 366–69. We follow Moloney's structure of the passage (*John*, 352; cf. Stefanos Mihalios, *The Danielic Eschatological Hour in the Johannine Literature*, LNTS 436 [London: T&T Clark, 2011], 124–26).

[94] Francis J. Moloney, *Signs and Shadows: Reading John 5–12* (Minneapolis: Fortress, 1996), 188. Some Zephaniah Proposals add John 12:32 in relation to Zephaniah's ingathering: "Jesus relates this [John 12:20's Greeks] to his being lifted up so that he can draw all men to himself [12:32]" (Brown, *John*, 1:463; cf. Sheridan, *Retelling*, 227). Given that John 12:33 refers to Jesus's death on the cross, 12:32 would reinforce the necessary means of Jesus's cross for Gentile inclusion (and Jewish ingathering). Craig R. Koester argues that already

Most agree that the term Ἕλληνές (12:20) refers not to Jews in the diaspora but to Gentiles.[95] In the NT, it may be an umbrella term referring "to Gentiles from any part of the Greek-speaking world, including Greek cities in the Decapolis" who came to worship Israel's God at festival time (cf. Luke 7:2–5; John 7:35; Acts 10).[96] So, the Gentile Greeks correspond broadly to the Yahweh-worshipping *Gentile peoples* (עַמִּים/λαοὺς) prophesied in Zephaniah 3:9–10 (and possibly 3:19–20),[97] though a prophesied Gentile inclusion is not unique to Zephaniah.

---

in John 4:42 the Samaritans's declaring Jesus to be the "Savior of the world" anticipates Jesus's rule extending to all peoples ("'The Savior of the World' [John 4:42]," *JBL* 109 [1990]: 665–80).

[95] See Köstenberger, *John*, 377. "Greek(s)" can refer to non-Jews in the NT (cf. Acts 16:1; 21:28; Rom. 1:16). For an extended defense that these are Gentiles (not Diaspora Jews), see W. E. Moore, "Sir, We Wish to See Jesus—Was This an Occasion of Temptation?" *SJT* 20 (1967): 78; Johannes Beutler, "Greeks Come to See Jesus (John 12:20f)," *Bib* 71 (1990): 342–43; Carson, *John*, 435. J. L. Martyn argues that these were atypical Gentiles as evidenced by the Greek construction Ἦσαν ἀναβαινόντων: they "*regularly* come to Jerusalem to worship at Passover" so "they worship the God of Israel by observing Passover" ("A Gentile Mission that Replaces an Earlier Jewish Mission?" in *Exploring the Gospel of John: In Honor of D. Moody Smith*, ed. R. A. Culpepper and C. Clifton Black [Louisville: John Knox, 1996], 131–32, italics original). Even though 12:19–21 may not reflect a "change" in Jesus's mission, it nevertheless surely hints that Jesus's reign extends to Gentiles.

[96] Köstenberger, *John*, 377; cf. Witherington, *John's Wisdom*, 223. For evidence that the "Greeks" could represent the Gentile world (i.e., part of "the nations"), see Willis Hedley Salier, *The Rhetorical Impact of the Sēmeia in the Gospel of John*, WUNT, 2nd ser., 186 (Tübingen: Mohr Siebeck, 2004), 122; H. B. Kossen, "Who Were the Greeks of John xii 20?" in *Studies in John: Presented to Professor Dr. J. N. Sevenster on the Occasion of his Seventieth Birthday*, NovTSup 24 (Leiden: Brill, 1970), 97–110; cf. Jörg Frey, "Heiden-Griechen-Gotteskinder: Zu Gestalt und Funktion der Rede von den Heiden im 4 Evangelium," in *Die Heiden: Juden, Christen und das Problem des Fremden*, WUNT, 1st ser., 70 (Tübingen: Mohr Siebeck, 1994), 249–68. Josephus documented Gentiles coming to worship in Jerusalem for Passover (*J. W.* 6.427; 7.45; cf. *Ant.* 18.63–64; Matt. 8:5–13; 15:21–28; Mark 7:24–30; Luke 7:1–10), so Gentiles coming to Jerusalem during John 12's Passover was not in itself remarkable.

[97] Brown, *John*, 1:462–63 (cf. John 11:50, 52; 12:32). Zephaniah shares this

Furthermore, John 12:20–21's Greeks/peoples came to "worship" (προσκυνήσωσιν) then "to see" (ἰδεῖν) Jesus, a term often denoting spiritual sight not just curiosity.[98] Their actions thus thematically approximate Zephaniah 3:9–10's prophecy of the peoples' worship: they would call (לִקְרֹא/ἐπικαλεῖσθαι) on Yahweh's Name (cf. John 12:13d) and serve (לְעָבְדוֹ/δουλεύειν) Him.[99]

We add some OT precision to this connection. Zephaniah

motif with several texts, including Zechariah 9:10 (Brown, *John*, 1:463). Also, Beutler plausibly argues that Isaiah 52:15 has influenced John 12:20 ("Greeks Come to See Jesus," 333–47; cf. Brendsel, *Isaiah*, 151–60), and Köstenberger agrees that the Greeks here "may invoke the Isaianic notion of Gentiles flocking to God in the end times (Isa. 42:4; 49:6)" (*John*, 377; cf. Evans, "Obduracy," 232–36; Williams, "Testimony," 120). If this is correct, as is probable based on the many lexical connections with Isaiah 52–53 here, Zephaniah could *thematically parallel* the Isaianic eschatological vision (contra Kubiś, *Zechariah*, 87, who discounts the Zephanian Gentiles connection in John because he unwarrantedly judges it too minor a theme in Zephaniah 3).

[98] The verb "to see" (ὁράω) in John may simply refer to physical sight, but it often refers to accepting/refusing Jesus "as the revealer" (1:18, 33, 34, 39, 50, 51; 3:3, 11, 32, 36; 4:45; 5:37; 6:2, 36, 46; 8:38, 57; 9:37; 11:32, 40; Moloney, *John*, 352; Moloney, *Signs and Shadows*, 187; cf. Beutler, "Greeks Come to See Jesus," 342–45, who links the request to Isaiah 52:15 [LXX]). This "seeing" likely reflects the Greeks's desire to believe, furthermore, because the Greeks come to Philip and Andrew (12:22) whom John named together as Jesus's followers (1:40, 43) (Mihalios, *Danielic Eschatological Hour*, 136).

[99] The LXX sometimes rendered the MT verb עבד as προσκυνέω (e.g., Josh. 23:7; Ps. 97[96]:7); and the LXX's προσκυνέω sometimes stands in synonymous parallelism with δουλεύω (e.g., 1 Kings 22:53; 2 Kings 21:3, 21). The "worship" term in John 12:20 is associated with the "serving" term in Zephaniah 3:9; Zephaniah 3:9 prophesies that the Gentiles would worship Yahweh (i.e., serve and call on him), and John 12 narrates that as the Greeks's purpose in coming to Jerusalem. Additionally, DeRouchie speculates whether Psalm 118's "'hosanna' constitutes [Zephaniah's] 'calling on Yahweh's name,'" since Joel 3:5 connects "hosanna," "calling on Yahweh's name," and salvation (personal comments to author, February 9, 2015). In John 12:13, a Jewish, national-political cry for deliverance (Psalm 118's *hosanna*) could approximate a call on Yahweh's name. If so, this Jewish *hosanna* (John 12:13) subtly contrasts the Greeks's assumed *hosanna*-like worship (John 12:20–21; Zeph. 3:9). John does not narrate the Greeks's actual worship, but we assume that they did make it the temple for Passover and actually met with Jesus (Brendsel, personal

3:14–15 (i.e., King Yahweh's arrival) called for joy in anticipation of an eschatological time of deliverance, Gentile inclusion, and remnant gathering. That is, Zephaniah 3:8–20 calls Judah to wait in joy (1) because all the earth will be judged and (2) because then *Gentile peoples* (עַמִּים/λαούς) will unite in worshipping Yahweh's Name with right speech (3:9–10; cf. 3:19–20) while (בַּיּוֹם הַהוּא) *Yahweh's remnant* will take refuge in and return to him (3:11–13, 16–20). A joyful entry of a Zephanian King Yahweh thus expects a time of ingathering Gentiles. If John 12:12–19's joyful entry alludes to Zephaniah's King Yahweh, we are not surprised that his arrival incorporates Greek Gentiles.[100]

The entry crowd may have missed the global implications of

---

comments to author, July 25, 2015).

[100] Sheridan, *Retelling*, 227. She posits that the Zephaniah-Zechariah incorporation in John 12:15 "signif[ies] in part that all those addressed by Jesus in chapter 12 (Jews, Pharisees, Greeks) are 'Israel' in this sense [a positive nuance for those receiving Jesus as divine]—at least potentially." The entry crowd was largely Jewish, but Jewish leaders were seeking to kill Jesus (11:53; 12:10) and so were ostensibly not part of a supposed "true" Israel. In Sheridan's favor, however, John 12 ends "with an implicit call to hardened opponents," perhaps indicating that the opponents were "potentially" "Israel" (Brendsel, personal comments to author, July 25, 2015). See also Brown (*John*, 1:462–63; cf. John 11:50, 52; 12:32), who argues that due to the Zephaniah Proposal in John 12, the FG corrects the crowd's narrow nationalistic appropriation of the Lazarus-sign. They should have understood it as having "universal" implications as evident in Zephaniah 3:19's saving the lame and gathering the outcast (e.g., Lazarus). Now, we agree that 3:19 can entail Gentile ingathering (i.e., the king's "universal" reign; cf. 3:9–10). However, Zephaniah's connection to the Lazarus-sign requires some precision. (1) Zephaniah 3:19 thematically parallels John 12 in terms of restoration/healing but does not provide verbal parallels with Lazarus's physical condition (e.g., Lazarus was "sick" and "dead" [e.g., 11:4, 14; 12:9], not simply "lame" [Zeph. 3:19]). (2) Zephaniah's thematic parallels with the Lazarus-sign reinforce King Jesus's association with divinity. Yet, we do not dismiss the possibility that Zephaniah 3:17's Yahweh-warrior motif also played a role; the Lazarus miracle perhaps made the crowd think that Jesus was a "warrior-king who would liberate them from the Romans" (Schuchard, *Scripture*, 78, drawing on Isa. 44). By alluding to Zephaniah 3 the FG corrected this misunderstanding about Jesus (i.e., political revolutionary)

King Jesus's coming, but the FG's Zephaniah allusions reinforce King Jesus's global and divinely-associated rule, with a caveat. We have hints that Jesus's entry ushers in only a partial fulfillment of the promised Gentile ingathering. Only "some" (τινες [12:20]) Greeks come, and the narrative does not even report that they actually saw Jesus. Jesus must first go to the cross in order to draw "all" kinds of people (πάντας [12:32]) to himself.[101] And the focus of Jesus's mission does not shift from Israel to actively engaging Gentiles,[102] but John 12:20's Greek Gentiles seem to come as a foretaste (already) of what would come as a result of Jesus's Passion (12:24, 32).

---

and described him as the king-identified-with-Warrior-Yahweh nearing Jerusalem (see § 5.3.3.1).

[101] Andreas J. Köstenberger, *Encountering John: The Gospel in Historical, Literary, and Theological Perspective*, EBS (Grand Rapids: Baker, 1999), 194; Ridderbos, *John*, 439–40. That Gentiles sought out Jesus foreshadows the effects of the cross (cf. John 12:32; Eph. 1:9–10; 2:14–22; Col. 1:20–23). For an elaboration of Jesus's death as the prerequisite for this Gentile mission (John 10:14–16; 11:51–52; 12:20), and how Isaiah 52–53 might help explain such a requirement for the Servant, see Brendsel, *Isaiah*, 154–57. Also, John 12:32 is not universalism, as though all people without exception would come to Jesus. (1) John 12:31's judgment theme asserts that some will lose their life and others will have eternal life (Carson, *John*, 444). (2) Already in John 1:9–12, John introduces the theme that all (i.e., not only Jews but even non-Jews) may believe in Jesus (cf. 1:12–13; 3:16; 10:16; 12:32). Again, this salvation is not for every person (1:10–11; 3:19–21): "John [1:9] does not speak of *internal* illumination in the sense of general revelation . . . . but of *external* illumination in the sense of objective revelation requiring a response . . . . As the remainder of the Gospel illustrates, not all did in fact *receive* the light, though it was *available* to all through Jesus' presence and teaching" (Köstenberger, *John*, 35–36, italics original).

[102] According to Dennis, "The Gentiles will benefit salvifically on the heels of Israel's restoration, but Israel's restoration remains the focus and priority" (*Gathering of True Israel*, 306; see John 10:16; 11:52; 12:20–21; cf. Martyn, "Gentile Mission," 131–32). This ought not deny, however, that John signals the dawn of Gentile-ingathering (see Köstenberger's title for John 12:20–36 [*John*, 375]).

King Jesus as Zephaniah's Warrior-Deliverer

Jesus's Entry and Zephaniah's Divine Warrior-Deliverer

Zephaniah 3 envisions the day when Yahweh is present as a warrior who delivers (גִּבּוֹר יוֹשִׁיעַ/δυνατὸς σώσει [3:17]),[103] a sure deliverance for his people from judgments/enemies (3:15a–b). If John alludes to Jesus as Zephaniah's King Yahweh, does John 12 also allude to him as Warrior and Deliverer? How would that correct the crowd's hope of political deliverance?

Due in part to his adherence to the Zephaniah Proposal, Brunson holds that John depicts Jesus as Warrior King. Note the following arguments. (1) The crowd's *hosanna* entails a cry for deliverance, and Psalm 118 blesses a victorious warrior-king.[104] (2) John 12:15 quotes Zechariah 9:9 in whose literary context hostilities do not end with Zion's coming king; Yahweh extends his worldwide rule through force and conquest (Zech. 9:11–17; cf. 9:1–8). And in Zechariah 9:10, the roles of the king and Yahweh are somewhat blurry.[105] (3) Zechariah 9:9 (LXX) describes the king by the participle σῴζων (i.e., "bringing deliverance"; see TJ, VULG., but niphal

[103] Robertson, *Zephaniah*, 338. He argues that Zephaniah 3:17 is a messianic echo of Isaiah 9:5 based on their shared terms: "The coming son of David . . . [is] 'God the Mighty Hero' (*'ēl gibbôr*—Isa. 9:5 [Eng. 6]). The emerging picture of a virgin-born son of David's house called God-with-us (7:14) who also is Father-of-eternity (9:5 [Eng. 6]) gives expression to the reality by which all human needs and the promises of God may be synchronized. Only a God-man who rules in fulfillment of the promises to the fathers can be King of Israel ruling in Zion as fulfillment of the promises given to David" (cf. Kenneth L. Barker and D. Waylon Bailey, *Micah, Nahum, Habakkuk, Zephaniah*, NAC [Nashville: Broadman & Holman, 1998], 496). Zephaniah 3, however, does not explicitly forge a *divine-messianic* connection nor necessarily depend on Isaiah here, yet Robertson rightly observes that the NT does suggest Jesus is a divine-Davidic Messiah (e.g., Rom. 1:4). The FG's use of Zephaniah would highlight Jesus's connection to Yahweh; the FG (not Zeph.) draws together the Messiah and Yahweh (see also Isa. 52–53 and Zech. 9).

[104] See § 5.1.1; Brunson, *Psalm 118*, 278.

[105] Ibid., 274.

passive in the MT[106]). If John accessed the LXX, as is possible,[107] it may have provided a "suggestive link between Jesus and Yahweh [and his saving role]."[108] (4) King Jesus may come in peace *and* as a warrior. Peace and war are theologically compatible in Revelation for example: "Jesus is to his own a gentle king, but to his enemies the Lamb who is a Lion, the fearsome warrior King of kings who implacably and utterly destroys all his foes (Rev. 5.5; 19:11–21)."[109]

There are two main challenges to concluding that John *alludes in the Entry Narrative* to Jesus as a warrior-deliverer. First, John's entry does not explicitly feature warrior-deliverer terms, but only

[106] The MT's niphal נוֹשָׁע is likely passive and is probably the preferred, original reading (see evidence in Brendsel, *Isaiah*, 175n80; contra Petersen, *Zechariah 9–14*, 55, who argues for a "medio-passive" in harmony with the LXX's active participle). (1) The other occurrence of this niphal participle has the passive sense (Ps. 33:16; cf. Deut. 33:29), and (2) in Zechariah 9 (MT), Yahweh, not the human king, is clearly the definitive deliverer. Kubiś posits that the passive sense would have clashed with the FG's portrait of the Savior (43:17; 4:42; 5:34; 10:9; 12:47; *Zechariah*, 81), but an alternative explanation is possible. It may be that Zechariah 9:9's "king himself is a beneficiary of God's saving act, and as a result, mediates that same deliverance to the people" (Brendsel, *Isaiah*, 175, who focuses on the connections between the *niphal* passive and the Isaianic Servant). Anthony R. Petterson further notes that whether taken as a passive or active, the verbal action entails deliverance for the people: "The salvation of the king means the salvation of his people, and in this sense the king 'has salvation' or 'brings salvation' and so the difference between the passive and the reflexive is not that great when it comes to the final meaning" (*Behold Your King: The Hope for the House of David in the Book of Zechariah*, LHBOTS 513 [London: T&T Clark, 2009], 139; cf. Collins, "Zechariah 9:9," 29–40).

[107] Menken argues that John's quote of Zechariah 9:9 could depend on either the MT or LXX (*Quotations*, 82–83), and we argue the same for his allusions to Zephaniah 3 (see § 2.5).

[108] Brunson, *Psalm 118*, 273. He also explains, "The original context of Zech 9 shows that the coming of Zion's king, as gentle/humble as he may be, is that of a warrior whose kingdom will be extended by conquest and force" (ibid., 272; cf. Weren, "Entry," 128).

[109] Brunson, *Psalm 118*, 274, contra Leung, *Kingship-Cross Interplay*, 165. For more arguments tracing this theme *in the entry*, see Brunson, *Psalm 118*, 271–77.

the literary contexts of John's OT texts contain them (e.g., Ps. 118, Zeph. 3; Zech. 9).[110] Second, there is indeed no fundamental theological contradiction between Jesus bringing peace and war, but the peaceful element in Jesus's entry predominates; Jesus's peaceful donkey-riding corrected the crowd's national-military expectations.[111] We therefore posit that the FG's entry does not include explicit markers for this Zephanian theme (but an echo is possible).

Immediately following Jesus's entry, however, his passion hour-day arrives, and there the FG does detail Jesus defeating and delivering (12:31, 47).[112] Perhaps, then, the Entry Narrative's echo served to *identify* Jesus as a warrior-deliver, and John *later developed* the theme to clarify that King Jesus entered, not to engage Rome, but the spiritual power(s) at his cross.

[110] Our method has been to examine whether John's entry contains warrior theme "markers" (i.e., an allusion; see § 1.3.1). It seems that Brunson's warrior king theme may very well function as an echo in the entry: "John first introduces Jesus as the warrior king of Ps 118 who has returned triumphant from battle, and then as Zion's king, whose mission of peace is extended by war. Jesus thus enters Jerusalem as a warrior king whose victory is *proleptically celebrated* by his people. Paradoxically the way to triumph and glory passes through death and apparent defeat, but the blood Jesus will shed is that of the new covenant which secures release for the prisoners (cf. Zech 9.11), and gains the decisive and final victory" (Brunson, *Psalm 118*, 275, italics ours). As we argued above, the crowd's militant expectations of Jesus render it unlikely that *the crowd* had an appropriate understanding of warrior-Jesus. John, however, makes clear that Jesus's victory would be accomplished through his cross and resurrection (e.g., 12:20–36). The entry therefore *triggers* pericopes that stipulate the nature of Jesus's battle in the Passion (e.g., 12:31), but the entry itself does not depict him in battle regalia.

[111] See Leung, *Kingship-Cross Interplay*, 165–66; Köstenberger, "John," 472–74; Witherington, *John's Wisdom*, 222–23; contra Brunson, *Psalm 118*, 271–77.

[112] Leung, *Kingship-Cross Interplay*, 166; Koester, *Symbolism*, 126; Schuchard, *Scripture*, 79; Kubiś, *Zechariah*, 112. Also, the FG reports that Jesus "delivers" his people (σῴζω [John 3:17; 5:34; 10:9; 12:47]). In John 12:47 Jesus states the purpose for his entry-like "coming" (ἦλθον; cf. 12:13): to "deliver" (σώσω) the world.

John 12:31's Ruler as Zephaniah's Enemy

We turn, then, to briefly note the defeat mentioned in John 12:31. Paralleling King Jesus's first revelation in response to the Greeks (12:23–28a) following his entry, he makes a second revelation (12:31–32)[113] about a spiritual enemy: "Now is the judgment of this world; now the ruler of this world (ὁ ἄρχων τοῦ κόσμου τούτου) will be driven out" (12:31).

We observe several, suggestive connections. First, John likely identifies this "ruler" with Satan. Jewish literature associates "ruler of the world" with an evil one, and John casts the ruler's activity as oppositional, even diabolical (14:30; 16:11; cf. 17:15).[114] Also, John records satanic opposition to Jesus (e.g., 6:70; 8:44) and reports Satan's role in Jesus's betrayal (13:2, 27). John thus presents Satan as one of Jesus's enemies, though he never employs the term ἐχθρός.[115]

[113] For this view of the unit John 12:20–36, see Mihalios, *Danielic Eschatological Hour*, 124–26; Moloney, *John*, 352; Ignace de la Potterie, "L'exaltation du Fils de l'homme (Jn 12:31–36)," *Greg* 49 (1968): 461–62.

[114] Kovacs, "Cosmic Battle," 227–47, esp. 229–31. In Jewish (though not rabbinical) literature, "ruler of the world" sometimes referred to an evil, spiritual being (see Mart. Isa. 1:3; 10:29; A. F. Segal, "Ruler of This World: Attitudes about Mediator Figures and the Importance of Sociology for Self-Definition," in *Aspects of Judaism, in the Greco-Roman Period*, ed. E. P. Sanders, A. I. Baumgartner, and Alan Mendelson, vol. 2, *Jewish and Christian Self-Definition*, ed. E. P. Sanders et al. [Philadelphia: Fortress, 1981], 245–68, 403–13; Köstenberger, *John*, 383–84, who notes similar terms in 2 Cor. 4:4; 6:15; Eph. 2:2; 6:12). Qumran may have distinguished "the now of a time of war and the then of a time of salvation" (Schnackenburg, *John*, 2:391; cf. Ridderbos, *John*, 438n194).

[115] John reports that Jesus's threat(s) were and would be threats for his disciples (e.g., John 15:18, 20, 24, 25). Furthermore, though we examine King Jesus engaging enemy Satan in John 12:31 as an important implication of the entry, we do not deny that John records many other "enemies" (e.g., sin, death, and human threats). Indeed, "the Jews," chief priests and/or Pharisees were the main human threats to Jesus (e.g., John 11:51–53) and even Lazarus (12:10–11, 19); yet, the FG sometimes made distinguishing between human and demonic threats difficult (e.g., John 8:44; Keener, *John*, 2:880, who connects Israel's "put out" rulers in 12:42 with the ruler of 12:31). Also, Köstenberger

The connection to Zephaniah 3 would be purely thematic. Zephaniah 3:15b anticipates Yahweh's removal of remnant Judah's enemy (אֹיְבֵךְ [MT]; ἐχθρῶν [LXX]), which could include any and all of her enemies. Furthermore, in Zephaniah 3:15d King Yahweh's arrival ensures that his people no longer fear "evil/disaster" (רָע [MT]; κακὰ [LXX]; cf. 3:16b). The cause of fear is sufficiently general to include any and all enemies: attacking nations wreaking physical disaster or even spiritual enemies (e.g., Satan or even God; see § 3.3.3). John 12:31's ruler-enemy Satan may represent a particularization (i.e., thematic parallel) of Zephaniah 3:15's prophecy.[116]

Second, John 12:31b states that Satan "will be thrown out" (ἐκβληθήσεται), a term frequently denoting violent expulsion in John (2:15; 6:37; 9:34, 35; cf. 10:4), but 12:31a–b stand as parallel clauses (note the double "now" [νῦν]). Satan's expulsion-defeat thus further explains the judicial judgment of John 12:31a (κρίσις).[117] Similarly, in our analysis of Zephaniah 3:15a–b, we argued that the verbs סור and פנה describe the defeat of Yahweh's people's enemy(ies) in judicial terms, suggesting that Yahweh's defeating the enemy(ies) would be a form of judgment. Furthermore, Zephaniah 3:15a–b's asyndetic parallel clauses likely explicated the removed "judgments" (מִשְׁפָּטַיִךְ) as the removed "enemy," (see § 3.3.3); we

---

summarizes Satan's role in Johannine literature: "The cosmic conflict between the world of light and the world of darkness is, first and foremost, a struggle between God and his Messiah on the one hand and Satan on the other. . . . In both John's gospel and 1 John, Satan is shown to be at the root of all sin, hatred, and murder, and is the true spiritual father of those who reject Jesus as the Messiah (John 8:31–47; 1 John 3:8–15), deny their sinfulness (1 John 1:8, 10), and have no room for his atoning sacrifice (2:2; 4:10)" (*Theology*, 281; cf. Wendy E. Sproston, "Satan in the Fourth Gospel," in *Studia Biblica 1978*, vol. 2, *Papers on the Gospels*, ed. E. A. Livingstone, JSNTSup 2 [Sheffield: JSOT Press, 1980], 307–11).

[116] "Ruler" may allude to apocalyptic-cosmic warfare (Kovacs, "Cosmic Battle," 227–47) or echo Daniel's king (7:8, 11; 11:36–45; cf. Isa. 16:4–5; Ezek. 7:27; 38:2–3; 39:1; Mihalios, *Danielic Eschatological Hour*, 130).

[117] Mihalios refers to this verse as "the defeat by judgment of the 'ruler of this world'" (*Danielic Eschatological Hour*, 130).

observe a similar order in John 12:31a–b: arrived judgment, enemy-ruler removal.[118]

Third, the timing of his judgment and defeat was "now" (νῦν [12:31]), including the time of Jesus's cross-hour (12:32–33);[119] Jesus's Zephanian entry and the Greeks's coming decisively inaugurated that hour (12:23, 27, 32; 13:1). Due to that Passion time frame and Satan's judgment juxtaposed with Jesus's cross-death (12:31–33), Mihalios plausibly asserts, "John presents Satan as God's final adversary, who will be judged and defeated on the cross (cf. 12.33)."[120]

[118] Ridderbos argues that in John 12:31a Jesus asserts he would judge the wicked world: "However much, in the coming and work of Jesus, 'this world' is the object of God's love (3:16) and the Son of man is therefore the great bringer of salvation (1:51; 6:27) who gives his life for the life of the world (6:51, 53; cf. 3:17; 12:47), this does not alter the fact that his coming also entails great crisis for the world. Because he has come as the light of the world, he brings out the sin of this world in its aversion and estrangement from God. His coming means judgment for those who love darkness rather than light (cf. 3:19ff.)" (*John*, 438). If a Zephanian King Jesus has entered and one of his Zephanian roles is to judge *enemies*, we are not surprised if he judges wicked ones (i.e., the world) in John 12:31a.

[119] Carson comments on John 12:31's adverb "now": "The judgment of the world, the destruction of Satan, the exaltation of the Son of Man, the drawing of men and women from the ends of the earth—these might all be reserved for the end times. But the end times have begun already. It is not that there is nothing reserved for the consummation; rather, it is that the decisive step is about to be taken in the death/exaltation of Jesus" (Carson, *John*, 444–45; cf. Brown, *John*, 477). John provides evidence that the now-hour reflects both present (14:30; 16:32; cf. 3:18; 13:12, 27) and future reality (e.g., Jesus's cross-death, 12:31–33; cf. 8:28; 6:62; 19:37); the judgment is not purely anticipatory, but the (Passion) hour has already begun (Ridderbos, *John*, 438–39). See § 5.3.4.2 for possible connections with Zephaniah's eschatological day and the already but not-yet eschatological hour.

[120] Mihalios, *Danielic Eschatological Hour*, 130, who holds that the "ruler" echoes Daniel 7 and 11. If Jesus deposes the world ruler, this would entail Jesus having entered as a sort of "warrior king" whose "kingship has both transcendent and universal dimensions. The power Jesus wielded was not that of a militia seeking to do battle with Rome but the power of God preparing for conflict with Satan" (Koester, *Symbolism*, 111).

Summarizing King Jesus as Zephaniah's Warrior-Deliverer

We do not posit that John alludes to Zephaniah in the reference to Satan's defeat at Jesus's cross. However, a certain thematic congruency with Zephaniah 3 and John 12:31 is logical given the allusions to Zephaniah 3 in Jesus's entry (see § 2.4). (1) Were Zephaniah 3:15 fulfilled in some sense in King Jesus's entry, we might expect him to defeat fear-provoking enemies (2) in judicial terms (Zeph. 3:15a–b, 17); in the paragraph following the Entry Narrative (12:20–36), John declares that Jesus judges and defeats enemy Satan in his arrived Passion-hour (John 12:31). (3) In Zephaniah, King Yahweh's arrival assures the no-fear result (3:15d), known to Jerusalem "in that time" (3:16b). In King Jesus's entry manifesting Yahweh's presence, Jesus arrived to dispel fear (John 12:12–15); then in John 12:31b, Jesus "now" engages a formidable enemy. Contrary to the entry crowd's expectations, this enemy was not national-political but spiritual (i.e., Satan). Following Jesus's Zephanian entry, his day of cross-glorification would entail Satan's defeat,[121] a possible particularization of Zephaniah's prophesied "warrior-deliverance" motif.

King Jesus's Arrival as Inducing Zephaniah's Day of Yahweh

Jesus's Day of Death and Hour of Glorification

Immediately preceding the Entry Narrative, Jesus connects Mary's anointing him and the "day" of his burial/death (ἡμέραν τοῦ

[121] Jesus's cross thus represents a cosmic irony: Satan thought it was Jesus's demise, but it was in fact the moment of his great triumph over him. Köstenberger writes, "Paradoxically, at the cross the world and its ruler are judged, while Jesus is glorified and salvation is procured for all" (*John*, 385; cf. Schnackenburg, *John*, 2:398–410). If we are justified in locating the entry as part of the trigger to Jesus's Passion hour, the entry connects to what Jesus "came" to do. For example, Schuchard observes, "Jesus' purpose is to drive out 'the ruler of this world' (12.31). Jesus comes, then, to dispel darkness (cf. 8.12), to liberate from sin (cf. 8.31–36) and death (cf. 5.24). He comes to save, not to destroy (cf. 3.16–17)" (*Scripture*, 79). This deliverance motif as developed in the FG would thematically correspond to Zephaniah 3:15's prophecy.

ἐνταφιασμοῦ [12:7]).[122] Jesus thereby predicts his own death with an ambiguous time reference, a foreshadowing of things to come, before his entry.

Then, triggered by Jesus's entry, Greeks come and Jesus "responds" by saying ἐλήλυθεν ἡ ὥρα ἵνα δοξασθῇ ὁ υἱὸς τοῦ ἀνθρώπου (John 12:23). Udo Schnelle rightly argued that John's term "hour" (ὥρα), along with the glorification terminology (12:16, 23, 27–28) and dead-grain-producing-fruit imagery (12:24), situates "Jesus' entire public ministry in the perspective of a theology of the cross and of the resurrection."[123] Jesus's glorification hour thus likely denotes his Passion death and resurrection (and perhaps also exaltation/ascension to the Father).[124]

John 12:23 marks a significant shift in John's use of "hour,"

[122] John's "day" (ἡμέρα) can refer to a 24-hour (approximate) period of time (e.g., 1:39; 2:1, 12, 19, 20; 4:40, 43; 5:9; 9:14; 11:6, 17, 53; 12:1; 19:31; 20:19, 26), but it also occurs in expressions referring to "the last day" (ἐσχάτῃ ἡμέρᾳ [6:39, 40, 44, 54; 7:37; 12:48]), Jesus's life (8:56), daylight (9:4; 11:9), or a future time after Jesus's departure (14:20; 16:23, 26). Some interpret the term for burial (ἐνταφιασμοῦ) as referring to corpse preparation for burial (Köstenberger, *John*, 364; cf. 19:40). In even that case, the term hints that Jesus would die.

[123] Udo Schnelle, "Cross and Resurrection in the Gospel of John," in *The Resurrection of Jesus in the Gospel of John*, ed. Craig R. Koester and Reimund Bieringer, trans. Roy A. Harrisville and Reimund Bieringer, WUNT 222 (Tübingen: Mohr Siebeck, 2008), 145. John 12:23 ostensibly regards the Son of Man's glorification.

[124] Jesus's "hour" (12:23, 27) arrived "now" (12:31) and included the "lifting up" of the Son of Man to die (12:32–34; cf. 3:14–15; 8:28). So, most commentators agree that Jesus's hour refers to his "passion, death, and resurrection," though his exaltation/ascension may also be in view (see, e.g., Brown, *John*, 1:146; Carson, *John*, 439). Koester argues that in the FG, Jesus's "crucifixion, resurrection, and ascension are aspects of a single event"; even after Jesus's exaltation to the Father, he retained marks from the crucifixion (20:17, 19–23, 27–28), and the Holy Spirit glorifies Jesus post-ascension (2:22; 7:39; 12:16; 14:26; 16:14; *Symbolism*, 238–39). Also, many conclude that John 12:23 alludes to Isaiah 52:13 due to the strong verbal parallels (e.g., "will be raised and lifted up and highly exalted [δοξασθήσεται]," Carson, *John*, 437–38; cf. Brendsel, *Isaiah*, 151–53).

a term likely alluding to Daniel 12:1.[125] Until this point in John, Jesus's Danielic hour had "not yet" come (οὔπω; e.g., 2:4; 7:30) or was promised to come (4:21, 23; 5:25, 28; cf. 16:25), but "now" it arrived.[126] *Before* Jesus's entry, he forecasted his day of death; *immediately after* his entry, his death-hour arrives.

Jesus's Arrived Passion Hour as Zephaniah's Day

We speculate whether Zephaniah's vision partially explains why the Entry Narrative transitions to the arrival of Jesus's Passion-death-resurrection.[127] First, based on our analysis above,

[125] See a recent, cogent defense for this in Mihalios, *Danielic Eschatological Hour*, 124–39, especially since the expression "Son of man" also occurs in Daniel 7; cf. G. K. Beale, "The Old Testament Background of the 'Last Hour' in 1 John 2,18," *Bib* 92 (2011): 231–54.

[126] Mihalios, *Danielic Eschatological Hour*, 125–26. In John 12:23 Jesus said that his hour "has come" (ἐλήλυθεν; for the consummative perfect, see Daniel B. Wallace, *Greek Grammar beyond the Basics: An Exegetical Syntax of the New Testament* [Grand Rapids: Eerdmans, 1996], 577), an hour that is "now" (νῦν [12:27, 31]). Mihalios also argues that John 12:23, 32–34 combine allusions to Isaiah 52:13 and Daniel's hour (7:13–14; 12:1–3; *Danielic Eschatological Hour*, 126–39; cf. Brendsel's treatment of Isaiah 52's contributions, *Isaiah*, 151–60). Again, we are not claiming that John alludes to Zephaniah here, but given Zephaniah's presence in the entry, we observe congruencies between Zephaniah's eschatological program and the motif of eschatological arrival in John's narrative.

[127] Some observe a shift introduced by the entry (e.g., Meeks, *Prophet-King*, 83) and derived, for example, from Zechariah's eschatology. We do not posit that Zephaniah alone provokes John 12's movement, since Zechariah, for example, corresponds well with the FG: "John may conceive of Jesus' visitation of the Holy City in terms of Zechariah's 'day of the Lord,' when 'living water will flow out from Jerusalem,' the 'LORD will be king over the whole earth' (Zech. 14:8–9; cf. 13:1), and a great Feast of Tabernacles will be celebrated by all the nations (Zech. 14:16)" (Köstenberger, "John," 473–74; cf. Daly-Denton, *David*, 127). Daniel J. Brendsel summarizes his critique of our argument for the relevant parallels with Zephaniah (e.g., "day," "now," and "no longer"): the "evidence . . . is slight, uncertain, and only very loosely related" to John 12's entry (personal comments to author, July 27, 2015). However, (1) a shift occurs beginning in John 12:20 that links to the Entry Narrative (12:19; see § 5.3.2). And (2) we do not posit Zephaniah's exclusive influence in John here but how

Zephaniah's terms and themes intersect with the arrived hour in John's narrative flow: (1) John's entry alludes to King Jesus manifesting the presence of Zephaniah's King Yahweh, whose arrival dispels fear (John 12:13–15; Zeph. 3:14–15). (2) As evidence of Jesus's global kingship, Zephaniah-like Greek Gentiles seek him (John 12:19–22; Zeph. 3:9–10, 19). They definitively "trigger" the irrevocable arrival of Jesus's Danielic Passion *hour*.[128] (3) King Jesus's "now-hour" entails his Zephaniah-like defeat-judgment of enemy Satan at the cross (John 12:31; Zeph. 3:15).

Second, Zephaniah placed his call for a proleptic celebration of King Yahweh's arrival (3:14–15) in the middle of eschatological terms (e.g., לְיוֹם/εἰς ἡμέραν [3:8]; בַּיּוֹם הַהוּא/ἐν τῇ ἡμέρᾳ ἐκείνῃ [3:11]; בַּיּוֹם הַהוּא/ἐν τῷ καιρῷ [3:16]; בָּעֵת הַהִיא/ἐν τῷ καιρῷ ἐκείνῳ [3:19, 20]) and expectations. Zephaniah ostensibly shares close verbal parallels with Danielic "hour" terminology (e.g., בָּעֵת הַהִיא/κατὰ τὴν ὥραν ἐκείνην; ἐν ἐκείνῃ τῇ ἡμέρᾳ [Dan. 12:1]). Since Zephaniah used eschatological terms to prophesy points two and three above, a Zephaniah-like logic seems to parallel the arrival of Jesus's hour in the FG. (1) Referring to the eschatological time of Yahweh-worshipping Gentile nations, Zephaniah uses the term "day" (בַּיּוֹם/ἡμέρᾳ [Zeph. 3:11; cf. 3:16]) and so shares a verbal link with John 12:7, Jesus's predicted death-day (ἡμέραν). For John 12:19–23, the arrival of Greek Gentiles become the definitive signal that Jesus's Passion day/hour arrived. (2) The timing of Satan's

---

Zephaniah's eschatological day *thematically parallels* and may *help explain* the shift in John 12 to Jesus's arrived cross-hour.

[128] Moloney writes, "The advent of the Greeks is the event that triggers Jesus' explanation of the hour of his glorification (vv. 23–36)" (*Signs and Shadows*, 187; cf. Carson, *John*, 435). Mihalios plausibly posits that the Johannine rationale for entering the Greeks immediately before recording that Jesus's hour had arrived is that "this hour has been defined as the moment at which the worship of God will be reshaped, delocalized, even universalized (Jn 4.21, 23). Furthermore, we have the use of hour in Jn 5.25, 28. This hour concerns the eschatological time when judgment and resurrection will take place" (*Danielic Eschatological Hour*, 137).

judgment and defeat was "now" (νῦν, two times [12:31]) which recalls Jesus's Passion "hour" in 12:23 (cf. John 12:32–33, ostensibly referring to Jesus's death).[129] The "now-hour" time frame for Satan's demise (Zeph. 3:15a–b) could thematically correspond with Zephaniah's expectation that fearing enemies would occur "no longer" (עוֹד/οὐκέτι [3:15d]) and/or that there should not be fear "on that day" (בַּיּוֹם הַהוּא/ἐν τῷ καιρῷ [3:16a]) of Yahweh's arrival (which entails the defeat of enemies) to Jerusalem. The shift in terms used for Jesus's Passion hour (John 12:23–36) thus thematically parallels Zephaniah's prophetic-eschatological expectations and terms for King Yahweh's entry.

But this temporal shift partially accords with Zephaniah 3's prophetic expectation. Zephaniah 3's King Yahweh does not *suffer to death*, so that element of Jesus's hour-day does not readily correspond with the prophecy.[130] Indeed, Zephaniah 3 does not even envision a

[129] Köstenberger, *John*, 384. John 12:23 likely alludes to Daniel 12:1's "hour" (Mihalios, *Danielic Eschatological Hour*, 124–39), and Zephaniah 3:8, 11, 16, 19–20 share verbal parallels with his phraseology.

[130] It may be argued, however, that Zephaniah 1 provides the framework of death and sacrifice as part of satisfying Yahweh's judgment (Zeph. 1:7–8): "To speak of the day of the Lord as a day of sacrifice (1:7–8) places it within the long biblical tradition that where there is sin there must also be death—and this because Yahweh is the Holy One" (J. Alec Motyer, "Zephaniah" in *The Minor Prophets: An Exegetical and Expository Commentary*, ed. Thomas Edward McComiskey [Grand Rapids: Baker, 1998], 3:917; cf. Barker and Bailey, *Zephaniah*, 427–28). Many commentators identify those to be sacrificed in Zephaniah 1:7–8 as the wicked in Judah: "The Judeans would not eat the sacrificial meal Yahweh was preparing, however, for the implication of Zephaniah's words is that Judah would be the sacrifice (cf. Isa. 34:6–7; Jer. 46:10)! Yahweh's guests, consecrated by him to eat the sacrifice (see 1 Sam. 16:5 for this practice) would not be the Judeans, but either the foreign armies he would bring against Judah (Isa. 13:3–5) or the birds and beasts of prey who would feed on the corpses of the dead (Ezek. 19:17–20)" (Roberts, *Nahum, Habakkuk, and Zephaniah*, 177–78). Might this ultimately point to Jesus who suffers and dies as the quintessential Zephanian "sacrifice," absorbing the wrath of God, thus providing a Zephanian connection to Jesus's suffering in the Passion?

human, messianic figure. Late Jewish tradition did associate Zephaniah 3 with the coming of the Son of Man (cf. John 1:49, 51), but even those texts did not include an expectation of his "suffering."[131]

John 12's allusions to Zephaniah instead chiefly reinforce Jesus's divine connection. Many find evidence that the FG hints at Jesus's divine identity in his Passion hour. To provide two examples, Jesus died because he said he was God ("Son of God" amounted to blasphemy [John 19:7; cf. Matt. 26:65]). And after Jesus's resurrection, Thomas confesses him as "my Lord and my God" (20:28; cf. 1:1), "perhaps the most overt instance of worship of Jesus as God in any of the Gospels."[132] Zephaniah 3 may underline such divine features in Jesus's redemptive "hour."

Conclusion

In this chapter, we first conducted an exegetical overview of the Entry Narrative, concluding that King Jesus's entry affirms yet corrects the crowd's understanding of Jesus's kingship. His kingship is messianic but not national(istic) or Rome-engaging. We then examined John's hermeneutical use of Zephaniah, arguing that he used it as irony and fulfilled prophecy (and perhaps as a limited blueprint). Finally, we explored Zephaniah's theological implications for John 12. With allusions to Zephaniah, John more clearly alludes to King Jesus in connection with Yahweh (not just as Messiah). Zephaniah 3 also accords with implications for Jesus's entry, to correct the crowd's view of Jesus's kingship: (1) global, not

[131] See, e.g., b. Sanh. 98a and § 4.4. Other OT passages like Isaiah 52:7–12 do incorporate both a Suffering Servant figure and Yahweh's kingship (see Brendsel, *Isaiah*, for Isaiah 52's role in John 12).

[132] Köstenberger, *Theology*, 431; see also ibid., 356–60; Koester, *Symbolism*, 235–39. Koester argues that in Jesus's crucifixion, he "conformed so completely to the divine will that his death revealed the depth of his unity with the Father and became the visible sign of Jesus' return to God who had sent him. . . . Some, by faith, recognized the divine dignity of the crucified Jesus and are thereby delivered from sin and brought to life" (ibid., 236).

national, kingship, and (2) defeating a spiritual (i.e., Satan), not political enemy (i.e., Rome). We also posited that those Zephanian "corrections" to Jesus's kingship gain logical traction if Jesus "enters" into his inaugurated cross-hour (that entails manifesting his divinity) in accordance with a Zephaniah-like eschatological shift: the Zephanian entry and Gentiles signal that Jesus's Zephaniah-like hour had arrived for his Zephaniah-like warfare on Satan. Zephaniah 3 thus plays an important role in John 12.

6

Conclusion

In this book, we have examined John 12's use of Zephaniah 3 in the Entry Narrative. After surveying in chapter 1 the chief contributions forwarded by Zephaniah Proposal proponents, we analyzed in chapter 2 the literary context of John 12. John's entry (12:9–19) quotes the OT twice to affirm Jesus's kingship in his donkey ride (Ps. 118[117]:25–26; Zech. 9:9). Sandwiched between these two OT quotations, John 12 plausibly alludes to Zephaniah 3:14–15 with βασιλεὺς τοῦ Ἰσραήλ (associated with κύριος) and μὴ φοβοῦ (addressed to θυγάτηρ Σιών), based on Zephaniah's volume, thematic congruency, and available sources. In addition, John 1 may allude to Zephaniah 3 (twice), perhaps forming an *inclusio* with the Entry Narrative that strengthens the Zephaniah Proposal. John 12 may textually fuse Zephaniah with another OT text(s) (e.g., Isa. 40, 44, 52). But when textually compared, John 12 and Zephaniah 3 highlight their uniquely shared expressions and do not contain insurmountable textual issues restricting the FG's appropriation of Zephaniah 3:14–15 or 16 (MT or LXX).

In chapter 3, we demonstrated that Zephaniah presents itself as prophetic-poetry and hortatory discourse. We accordingly traced the textlinguistic argument of Zephaniah, concluding that the prophet calls the humble to seek Yahweh (2:1–3) and wait (3:8a). 3:14–15 constitute the prophecy's peak and is a poetic outburst read with 3:8a: rejoice while waiting for Yahweh to act. In Zephaniah

3:8–20, the prophet calls the humble would-be remnant to wait in joy for deliverance, since after judgment on all the wicked (3:8b–c), Yahweh will grant remnant peoples Yahweh-glorifying speech and deeds (3:9–10). Furthermore, that future day entails restoration for Yahweh's humble remnant freeing them to non-fearing and reverent word and deed (3:11–13; cf. 16–20). 3:14–15 calls his faithful people (as a personified, future remnant daughter) to rejoice in anticipation of Yahweh's sure deliverance and kingly presence; this reassures them to not fear, ahead of the wicked's judgment. Also on Yahweh's day (3:16–20), Rejoicing Warrior Yahweh returns his people from exile and exalts himself in his remnant, in both remnant peoples (3:9–10; cf. 3:19–20 [possible]) and remnant Judah (3:11–13, 16–20).

In chapter 4, Jewish literature's use of Zephaniah 3:14–15 demonstrates two points. First, "king of Israel" referred only to Yahweh. Second, Zephaniah's deliverance awaited future fulfillment. Despite obscure or limited use of Zephaniah in the Apocrypha, pseudepigrapha, and the Judean Desert witnesses, other Jewish literature developed the prophecy. TJ condemns evil judges, comforts the "congregation," and describes a relational distance with Yahweh. Some entries in the Babylonian Talmud and a few midrashim read Zephaniah 3 in a messianic context. Zephaniah 3:11–15 contain prerequisites for the Daniel 7:13/Zechariah 9:9-like coming of the Messiah, son of David (S. Eli. Rab. 18; cf. b. Sanh. 98a). And midrashim conclude that all will rejoice, whether to gloat over the wicked's fall or to praise Yahweh. Lastly, the synagogue's cyclical sedarim readings linked Zephaniah 3:14–15 to Genesis 11 and Numbers 4.

In chapter 5, we conducted an exegetical overview of John 12's Entry Narrative, concluding that it affirms yet corrects the crowd's understanding of Jesus's kingship. His kingship is messianic but not national(istic) nor Rome-engaging. In examining John's hermeneutical use of Zephaniah 3, we argued that he used it as irony, fulfilled prophecy, and perhaps a limited blueprint (adapting Beale's categories in his *Handbook*). As for Zephaniah's theological implications for Jesus's entry, John's allusion to Zephaniah 3 clarifies that he intends a close connection between King Jesus and Yahweh (i.e., not just as the Messiah). Zephaniah 3 also aligns with the Entry Narrative's implications, to correct the crowd's view of Jesus's kingship: (1) global, not national, kingship (i.e., including the world and Greek Gentiles [12:19–21; Zeph. 3:9–10, 19]), and (2) defeat of a spiritual (i.e., Satan [12:31]; cf. Zeph. 3:15, 17), not political, enemy (i.e., Rome). Additionally, King Jesus's entry and seeing Gentiles trigger the arrival of his cross-day-hour (12:7, 23; i.e., his hour manifests Yahweh's presence and engages enemy Satan), shifting to a Zephaniah-like time anticipated for Zephaniah's King's arrival (cf. Yahweh's "day" [Zeph. 3:8, 11–13, 16–20]).

This book connects to scholarship on John's supposed "new exodus" program.[1] Our scope was limited, but further study could explore Zephaniah 3's appropriation of the Pentateuch (esp. Deuteronomy) to examine his theological development of the exodus.[2] Zephaniah 1:4's judgment on Judah, for example, uses imagery that described Yahweh's deliverance of Israel from Egypt (cf. Ex. 3:19–20; Deut. 4:34).[3] In the deliverance envisioned for Yahweh's humble

[1] For two recent studies proposing a "new exodus" in John, see A. C. Brunson, *Psalm 118 in the Gospel of John: An Intertextual Study on the New Exodus Pattern in the Theology of John*, WUNT, 2nd ser., 158 (Tübingen: Mohr Siebeck, 2003); Daniel J. Brendsel, *"Isaiah Saw His Glory": The Use of Isaiah 52–53 in John 12*, BZNW 28 (Berlin: de Gruyter, 2014).

[2] Scholars often discuss shared terms between Zephaniah and Deuteronomy but subsume the issue into questions about Zephaniah's date and/or supposed editorial process (e.g., O. Palmer Robertson, *The Books of Nahum, Habakkuk, and Zephaniah*, NICOT [Grand Rapids: Eerdmans, 1990], 32–34, 253–57; James Nogalski, *Literary Precursors to the Book of the Twelve*, BZAW 217 [Berlin: de Gruyter, 1993], 176–78). But does Zephaniah 3's remnant and return language represent a development on the "new exodus" motif and not just broadly signify a "reversal of fortunes" (cf. Michael Ufok Udoekpo, *Rethinking the Day of YHWH and Restoration of Fortunes in the Prophet Zephaniah: An Exegetical and Theological Study of 1:14–18; 3:14–20*, ed. Michael Fieger and Sigrid Hodel-Hoenes, DATIM 2 [Bern: Lang, 2010], 189–93)?

[3] Kenneth L. Barker and D. Waylon Bailey, *Micah, Nahum, Habakkuk, Zephaniah*, NAC (Nashville: Broadman & Holman, 1998), 417–20.

remnant surviving the judgment (Zeph. 3:11–20; cf. 2:3), Zephaniah 3 itself may represent a "new exodus," especially if it shares terms unique to the exodus.

In conclusion, Zephaniah 3 plays a more important role in John 12 than most scholars observe. Given Zephaniah 3:14–15's function as peak, consistently being regarded in Jewish literature as "unfulfilled," and significant similarities with Zechariah 9:9, we are not surprised that John would capitalize on Zephaniah's pre-exilic prophecy to associate Jesus, King of Israel, with Yahweh and to encourage his audience to not fear. Additional markers imply that Jesus's entry parallels Zephaniah's eschatological expectations (i.e., Gentile ingathering, enemy defeat, "day" arrival). So, John 12 does not seem to neglect the short prophetic book of Zephaniah. Instead, Zephaniah affects the Entry Narrative's presentation of King Jesus and configures remarkably well with John 12.

In John 12, perhaps manifesting Yahweh's presence, Jesus had come to Jerusalem to die as the Messiah, King of Israel *for Jew and Gentile*. And the death of this king would entail a mighty defeat of a spiritual enemy Satan. So even today, the call extends to all his people, "Do not fear, remnant daughter of Jerusalem! Our King is mighty to deliver!"

Appendix 1

Table: Distribution of Imperatives in Zephaniah

	(1:11[1])	2:1[2]	2:3	3:8	3:14
Number of Imperatives	1	2	3	1	4
MT and LXX	(1) Wail הֵילִ֫ילוּ θρηνήσατε	(1) Gather הִתְקוֹשְׁשׁוּ συνάχθητε (2) and gather וָקוֹשּׁוּ καὶ συνδέθητε	(1) Seek (Yahweh) בַּקְּשׁוּ ζητήσατε (2) Seek (righteousness) בַּקְּשׁוּ־ ζητήσατε (3) Seek (humility) בַּקְּשׁוּ ἀποκρίνεσθε	(1) Wait חַכּוּ ὑπόμεινόν	(1) Cry out רָנִּי χαῖρε σφόδρα (2) Shout הָרִיעוּ κήρυσσε (3) Rejoice שִׂמְחִי εὐφραίνου (4) and exult וְעָלְזִי καὶ κατατέρπου

[1,2] See footnotes 1 and 2 on next page.

[1] We place this occurrence in parenthesis, since we doubt the verb is truly an imperative. The consonantal form of this verb is either hiphil *qatal* 3MS or hiphil Imv MP (cf. Isa. 13:6; 23:1, 6, 14; Jer. 25:34; 48:20, 39; 51:8; Ezek. 30:2; Joel 1:11, 13; Zech. 11:2), but none of the above occurrences demand the imperative form. Even if the verb is a grammatical imperative in Zephaniah 1:11, it does not rise to the same level of hortatory prominence as 2:1–3 and 3:8. Additionally, Zephaniah 1:7's "hush" (הַס) is an interjection in the MT, so we do not include it in the table above (but note the LXX's imperative εὐλαβεῖσθε). The *weqatal* and *yiqtol* verb patterns (i.e., motivations) predominate in Zephaniah 1, and the expression "silence" (1:7) and the mention of wailing (1:11) function to support the backbone imperatives (i.e., 2:1, 3; 3:8).

[2] The LXX renders these as two different stems: συνάχθητε καὶ συνδέθητε. Scholars entertain debate on the second verb, since it would be unusual for Hebrew imperatives to parallel the same verb root with different conjugations (e.g., hithpolel and qal) (see Ehud Ben Zvi, *A Historical-Critical Study of the Book of Zephaniah*, BZAW 198 [Berlin: de Gruyter, 1991], 137–39; Marvin A. Sweeney, *Zephaniah: A Commentary*, ed. Paul D. Hanson, Hermeneia [Minneapolis: Fortress, 2003], 114–15). But note that Isaiah 29:9 may juxtapose שׁעע as two imperatives in different conjugations (see Daniel Hojoon Ryou, *Zephaniah's Oracles against the Nations: A Synchronic and Diachronic Study of Zephaniah 2:1–3:8*, BIS 13 [Leiden: Brill, 1995], 90).

Appendix 2

Table: Text Hierarchy of Zephaniah 3:8–20[1]

Text Hierarchy of *BHQ*		Select Notes
		[Speaker: Yahweh]
לָכֵן חַכּוּ־לִי נְאֻם־יְהוָה לְיוֹם קוּמִי לְעַד	3:8	Ø: Inference + main Imv
← כִּי מִשְׁפָּטִי לֶאֱסֹף גּוֹיִם לְקָבְצִי מַמְלָכוֹת לִשְׁפֹּךְ עֲלֵיהֶם זַעְמִי כֹּל חֲרוֹן אַפִּי	b	כִּי ground series (8b–9a) of 8a
←← כִּי בְּאֵשׁ קִנְאָתִי תֵּאָכֵל כָּל־הָאָרֶץ׃	c	כִּי (ground continues)
← כִּי־אָז אֶהְפֹּךְ אֶל־עַמִּים שָׂפָה בְרוּרָה	3:9	כִּי־אָז + *yiqtol*
←← לִקְרֹא כֻלָּם בְּשֵׁם יְהוָה	b	Ø: Inf to 9a
←← לְעָבְדוֹ שְׁכֶם אֶחָד׃	c	Ø: Inf to 9a
←← מֵעֵבֶר לְנַהֲרֵי־כוּשׁ עֲתָרַי בַּת־פּוּצַי יוֹבִלוּן מִנְחָתִי׃	3:10	Ø: Explain 9a–c; long x pre-verb
← בַּיּוֹם הַהוּא לֹא תֵבוֹשִׁי מִכֹּל עֲלִילֹתַיִךְ אֲשֶׁר פָּשַׁעַתְּ בִּי	3:11	בַּיּוֹם temporal marker to 9a
←← כִּי־אָז אָסִיר מִקִּרְבֵּךְ עַלִּיזֵי גַּאֲוָתֵךְ	b	כִּי־אָז ground (11b–13f) to 11a
←←← וְלֹא־תוֹסִפִי לְגָבְהָה עוֹד בְּהַר קָדְשִׁי׃	c	*Waw* + לֹא + *yiqtol*, result of 11b
←← וְהִשְׁאַרְתִּי בְקִרְבֵּךְ עַם עָנִי וָדָל	3:12	*Weqatal*, link to 11b
←←← וְחָסוּ בְּשֵׁם יְהוָה׃	b	*Weqatal*, result of 12a
←←← שְׁאֵרִית יִשְׂרָאֵל לֹא־יַעֲשׂוּ עַוְלָה	3:13	Ø: 13a–c series explain 11b, 12a
←←← וְלֹא־יְדַבְּרוּ כָזָב	b	*Waw* + לֹא + *yiqtol*
←←← וְלֹא־יִמָּצֵא בְּפִיהֶם לְשׁוֹן תַּרְמִית	c	*Waw* + לֹא + *yiqtol*
←←←← כִּי־הֵמָּה יִרְעוּ	d	כִּי 13d–f series grounds 13a–c
←←←← וְרָבְצוּ	e	*Weqatal*
←←←← וְאֵין מַחֲרִיד׃ ס	f	*Waw* + copula

[1] The chart below follows the system of notation and discourse set forth in Jason S. DeRouchie, *A Call to Covenant Love: Text Grammar and Literary Structure in Deuteronomy 5–11*, GD 30, BS 2 (Piscataway, NJ: Gorgias, 2007); DeRouchie, *How to*

Text Hierarchy of *BHQ*		Select Notes
		[Speaker: Zephaniah, outburst]
רָנִּי בַּת־צִיּוֹן	3:14	Ø: Imv's 14a–d (cf. 3:8)
הָרִיעוּ יִשְׂרָאֵל	b	Ø
שִׂמְחִי	c	Ø
וְעָלְזִי בְּכָל־לֵב בַּת יְרוּשָׁלִָם׃	d	Ø
הֵסִיר יְהוָה מִשְׁפָּטַיִךְ ←	3:15	Ø: *Qatal* grounds 14; series 15a–d
פִּנָּה אֹיְבֵךְ ←←	b	Ø: *Qatal*
מֶלֶךְ יִשְׂרָאֵל יְהוָה בְּקִרְבֵּךְ ←←	c	Ø: Nominal copula
לֹא־תִירְאִי רָע עוֹד ←←←	d	Ø: לֹא + *yiqtol*
		[Speaker: Zephaniah, continued]
בַּיּוֹם הַהוּא יֵאָמֵר לִירוּשָׁלִַם ←	3:16	בַּיּוֹם + *yiqtol* link with 3:11a
		[Speaker: Person(s) to Jerusalem]
אַל־תִּירָאִי צִיּוֹן	b	Ø: אַל + *yiqtol*
אַל־יִרְפּוּ יָדָיִךְ׃	c	Ø: אַל + *yiqtol*
יְהוָה אֱלֹהַיִךְ בְּקִרְבֵּךְ ←	3:17	Ø: Nominal copula grounds 16b–c
גִּבּוֹר יוֹשִׁיעַ ←←	b	Ø: Adj + *yiqtol* ground 17a
יָשִׂישׂ עָלַיִךְ בְּשִׂמְחָה ←←	c	Ø: *Yiqtol*
יַחֲרִישׁ בְּאַהֲבָתוֹ ←←	d	Ø: *Yiqtol*
יָגִיל עָלַיִךְ בְּרִנָּה ←←	e	Ø: *Yiqtol*

Understand and Apply the Old Testament: Twelve Steps from Exegesis to Theology (Phillipsburg, NJ: P&R Publishing, 2017).

Text Hierarchy of *BHQ*	Select Notes
	[Speaker: Yahweh]
נוּגֵי מִמּוֹעֵד אָסַפְתִּי מִמֵּךְ ←← 3:18	Ø: Ptc + *qatal* info for 19a–20
הָיוּ מַשְׂאֵת עָלֶיהָ חֶרְפָּה׃ ←←← b	Ø: *Qatal* explains 18a
הִנְנִי עֹשֶׂה אֶת־כָּל־מְעַנַּיִךְ בָּעֵת הַהִיא ← 3:19	הִנְנִי + Ptc introduce 19, link to16a
וְהוֹשַׁעְתִּי אֶת־הַצֹּלֵעָה ← b	*Weqatal* series links to 19a–d
וְהַנִּדָּחָה אֲקַבֵּץ ← c	*Waw* + noun + *yiqtol*
וְשַׂמְתִּים לִתְהִלָּה וּלְשֵׁם בְּכָל־הָאָרֶץ בָּשְׁתָּם׃ ← d	*Weqatal*
בָּעֵת הַהִיא אָבִיא אֶתְכֶם ←← 3:20	Ø: Protasis 20a–b for 20c, cf. 19a
וּבָעֵת קַבְּצִי אֶתְכֶם ←← b	*Waw* + בָּעֵת
כִּי־אֶתֵּן אֶתְכֶם לְשֵׁם וְלִתְהִלָּה בְּכֹל עַמֵּי הָאָרֶץ ← c	כִּי begins apodosis
בְּשׁוּבִי אֶת־שְׁבוּתֵיכֶם לְעֵינֵיכֶם אָמַר יְהוָה ←←← d	Ø: Temporal protasis for 3:20a–c

*Double underline indicates Imv; single underline, *qatal*; thick underline, *yiqtol*; dotted underline, Ptc; and wave underline, *weqatal*. The column on the right documents the speaker, first-position patterns, and various notations.

Appendix 3

Table: Patterns of First-Positions in Zephaniah (156 clauses, in order of appearance)

First-Position Patterns	Chapter 1	Chapter 2	Chapter 3
Ø + x + [Prep] + [x] (=copula)	1:1 1:10b 1:15–16	2:5b 2:14d	3:3a 3:3b 3:15c 3:17a
Ø + x + *yiqtol*	1:2	2:4c 2:7b 2:7c 2:9c 2:14c 2:15d	3:5c 3:7b 3:10 3:16a 3:17b 3:20a
Ø + *yiqtol*	1:3a 1:3b 1:12b	2:15e	3:7c 3:17c 3:17d 3:17e
weqatal	1:3c 1:4a 1:4b–6 1:8a 1:8b 1:9 1:10a 1:12a 1:12c 1:13a 1:13b 1:13d 1:17a 1:17b 1:17d	2:5c 2:6 2:7a 2:7e	3:12a 3:12b 3:13e 3:19b 3:19d
Interj + x (=copula)	1:7a הַס + Prep	2:5a הוֹי + Ptc	3:1 הוֹי + Ptc 3:19a הִנְנִי + Ptc

First-Position Patterns	Chapter 1	Chapter 2	Chapter 3
כִּי + Adj + x (=copula)	1:7b 1:7c		
Ø + *qatal*	1:7d 1:11c	2:8 2:15c	3:4c 3:6a 3:6b 3:6c 3:6d 3:7 3:15a 3:15b 3:18b
Ø + Imv	1:11a	2:1a 2:3a 2:3b 2:3c	3:14a 3:14b 3:14c
כִּי + *qatal*	1:11b	2:10b 2:11b	
Ø + לֹא + *yiqtol*	1:12d 1:12e 1:13c 1:13e		3:5b 3:7d 3:11c 3:15d
Ø + Adj + x (=copula)	1:14a		
Ø + x + Adj (=copula)	1:14b		3:5a
כִּי + x + *qatal*	1:17c	2:14e	
גַּם + x + [לֹא +] *yiqtol*]	1:18a	2:12 2:14b	
waw + x + *yiqtol*	1:18b	2:4d 2:9d	3:19c
כִּי + x + *yiqtol*	1:18c	2:4a	3:8c 3:13d
waw + Imv + x		2:1b	3:14d
בְּטֶרֶם + Inf + x		2:2a	

First-Position Patterns	Chapter 1	Chapter 2	Chapter 3
בְּטֶרֶם + לֹא + *yiqtol*		2:2c 2:2d	
כְּ + x + *qatal*		2:2b	
אוּלַי + *yiqtol*		2:3d	
waw + x + Prep + x (= copula)		2:4b	
כִּי + *yiqtol*		2:7d	3:20c
לָכֵן + x + *yiqtol*		2:9a	
waw + x + כְּ (=copula)		2:9b	
Ø + Pro + [Prep] + [Pro] x (=copula)		2:10a 2:15a	
wayyiqtol		2:10c 2:11c 2:13a 2:13b 2:13c 2:14a	
Ø + Ptc + x (=copula)		2:11a	3:18a
waw + x + Adv + Interj (=copula)		2:15b	
Ø + לֹא + *qatal*			3:2a 3:2b 3:3c
Ø + x + לֹא + *qatal*			3:2c 3:2d 3:5d
Ø + x + Ptc (=copula)			3:4a
Ø + x + *qatal*			3:4b

First-Position Patterns	Chapter 1	Chapter 2	Chapter 3
waw + לֹא + Ptc (=copula)			3:5e
אָכֵן + *qatal*			3:7e
לָכֵן + Imv			3:8a
כִּי + x + Inf			3:8b
כִּי־אָז + *yiqtol* + x			3:9a 3:11b
Ø + x + Inf			3:9b 3:9c 3:20d
Ø + x + לֹא + *yiqtol*			3:11a 3:13a
waw + לֹא + *yiqtol*			3:13b 3:13c
waw + copula + x			3:13f
Ø + אַל + *yiqtol*			3:16b 3:16c
waw + x + Inf			3:20b

Appendix 4

Table: Tracking Participant References in Zephaniah 3:8–20

Participants in *BHQ*	Participants in ESV
8 לָכֵן חַכּוּ־לִי נְאֻם־יְהוָה לְיוֹם קוּמִי לְעַד כִּי מִשְׁפָּטִי לֶאֱסֹף גּוֹיִם לְקָבְצִי מַמְלָכוֹת לִשְׁפֹּךְ עֲלֵיהֶם זַעְמִי כֹּל חֲרוֹן אַפִּי כִּי בְּאֵשׁ קִנְאָתִי תֵּאָכֵל כָּל־הָאָרֶץ	[Yahweh:] 8 "Therefore wait for me," declares the LORD, "for the day when I rise up to seize the prey. For my decision is to gather nations [MP], to assemble kingdoms [FP], to pour out upon them my indignation, all my burning anger; for in the fire of my jealousy all the earth shall be consumed.
9 כִּי־אָז אֶהְפֹּךְ אֶל־עַמִּים שָׂפָה בְרוּרָה לִקְרֹא כֻלָּם בְּשֵׁם יְהוָה לְעָבְדוֹ שְׁכֶם אֶחָד	9 For at that time I will change the speech of the peoples [MP] to a pure speech, that all of them may call upon the name of the LORD and serve him with one accord.
10 מֵעֵבֶר לְנַהֲרֵי־כוּשׁ עֲתָרַי בַּת־פּוּצַי יוֹבִלוּן מִנְחָתִי	10 From beyond the rivers of Cush my worshipers [MP], the daughter [FS] of my dispersed ones [MP], shall bring my offering.
11 בַּיּוֹם הַהוּא לֹא תֵבוֹשִׁי מִכֹּל עֲלִילֹתַיִךְ אֲשֶׁר פָּשַׁעַתְּ בִּי כִּי־ אָז אָסִיר מִקִּרְבֵּךְ עַלִּיזֵי גַּאֲוָתֵךְ וְלֹא־תוֹסִפִי לְגָבְהָה עוֹד בְּהַר קָדְשִׁי	11 On that day you shall not be put to shame because of the [lit. your] deeds by which you have rebelled against me; for then I will remove from your midst your proudly exultant ones, and you shall no longer be haughty in my holy mountain.
12 וְהִשְׁאַרְתִּי בְקִרְבֵּךְ עַם עָנִי וָדָל וְחָסוּ בְּשֵׁם יְהוָה	12 But I will leave in your midst a people [MS] humble and lowly. They shall seek refuge in the name of the LORD,
13 שְׁאֵרִית יִשְׂרָאֵל לֹא־יַעֲשׂוּ עַוְלָה וְלֹא־יְדַבְּרוּ כָזָב וְלֹא־ יִמָּצֵא בְּפִיהֶם לְשׁוֹן תַּרְמִית כִּי־ הֵמָּה יִרְעוּ וְרָבְצוּ וְאֵין מַחֲרִיד ס	13 those who are left [FS] in Israel; they shall do no injustice and speak no lies, nor shall there be found in their mouth a deceitful tongue. For they shall graze and lie down, and none shall make them afraid."

Participants in *BHQ*	Participants in ESV
14 רָנִּי בַּת־צִיּוֹן הָרִיעוּ יִשְׂרָאֵל שִׂמְחִי וְעָלְזִי בְּכָל־לֵב בַּת יְרוּשָׁלָ͏ִם 15 הֵסִיר יְהוָה מִשְׁפָּטַיִךְ פִּנָּה אֹיְבֵךְ מֶלֶךְ יִשְׂרָאֵל יְהוָה בְּקִרְבֵּךְ לֹא־תִירְאִי רָע עוֹד	[Zephaniah:] 14 Sing aloud, O daughter of Zion; shout, O Israel! Rejoice and exult with all your heart, O daughter of Jerusalem! 15 The Lord has taken away the judgments against you; he has cleared away your enemies. The King of Israel, the Lord, is in your midst; you shall never again fear evil.
16 בַּיּוֹם הַהוּא יֵאָמֵר לִירוּשָׁלַ͏ִם	[Zephaniah, cont.:] 16 On that day it shall be said to Jerusalem:
אַל־תִּירָאִי צִיּוֹן אַל־יִרְפּוּ יָדָיִךְ 17 יְהוָה אֱלֹהַיִךְ בְּקִרְבֵּךְ גִּבּוֹר יוֹשִׁיעַ יָשִׂישׂ עָלַיִךְ בְּשִׂמְחָה יַחֲרִישׁ בְּאַהֲבָתוֹ יָגִיל עָלַיִךְ בְּרִנָּה	[Person(s) to Jerusalem:] "Fear not, O Zion; let not your hands grow weak. 17 The Lord your God is in your midst, a mighty one who will save; he will rejoice over you with gladness; he will quiet you by his love; he will exult over you with loud singing.
18 נוּגֵי מִמּוֹעֵד אָסַפְתִּי מִמֵּךְ הָיוּ מַשְׂאֵת עָלֶיהָ חֶרְפָּה 19 הִנְנִי עֹשֶׂה אֶת־כָּל־מְעַנַּיִךְ בָּעֵת הַהִיא וְהוֹשַׁעְתִּי אֶת־הַצֹּלֵעָה וְהַנִּדָּחָה אֲקַבֵּץ וְשַׂמְתִּים לִתְהִלָּה וּלְשֵׁם בְּכָל־הָאָרֶץ בָּשְׁתָּם 20 בָּעֵת הַהִיא אָבִיא אֶתְכֶם וּבָעֵת קַבְּצִי אֶתְכֶם כִּי־אֶתֵּן אֶתְכֶם לְשֵׁם וְלִתְהִלָּה בְּכֹל עַמֵּי הָאָרֶץ בְּשׁוּבִי אֶת־שְׁבוּתֵיכֶם לְעֵינֵיכֶם אָמַר יְהוָה	[Yahweh:] 18 I will gather those of you who mourn for the festival, so that you will no longer suffer reproach [lit. they were a tribute on her a reproach]. 19 Behold, at that time I will deal with all your oppressors. And I will save the lame [fs] and gather the outcast [fs], and I will change their shame into praise and renown in all the earth. 20 At that time I will bring you in, at the time when I gather you together; for I will make you renowned and praised among all the peoples of the earth, when I restore your fortunes before your eyes," says the Lord.

*Double underline indicates 1cs/3ms (Yahweh); single underline, 2fs/3fs; thick underline, 2mp; dotted underline, 3cp; and wave underline, 3mp. Select grammatical parsings (right column) refer to the respective term in *BHQ*.

Bibliography

Achtemeier, Elizabeth. *Nahum–Malachi*. Interpretation: A Bible Commentary for Teaching and Preaching. Atlanta: John Knox, 1986.

Aland, Kurt, and Barbara Aland. *The Text of the New Testament: An Introduction to the Critical Editions and to the Theory and Practice of Modern Textual Criticism*. Translated by Erroll F. Rhodes. Rev. and enl. ed. Grand Rapids: Eerdmans; Leiden: Brill, 1989.

Alexander, P. "3 (Hebrew Apocalypse of) Enoch: A New Translation and Introduction." In *The Old Testament Pseudepigrapha*, edited by James H. Charlesworth, 1:223–315. Garden City, NY: Doubleday, 1983.

Andersen, Francis I., and A. Dean Forbes. "'Prose Particle' Counts of the Hebrew Bible." In *The Word of the Lord Shall Go Forth: Essays in Honor of David Noel Freedman*, edited by Carol L. Meyers and M. O'Connor, 165–83. American Schools of Oriental Research 1. Winona Lake, IN: Eisenbrauns, 1983.

Andersen, Francis I., and David Noel Freedman. *Hosea*. Anchor Bible 24. Garden City, NY: Doubleday, 1980.

Archer, Gleason L., and Gregory Chirichingo. *Old Testament Quotations in the New Testament: A Complete Survey*. Chicago: Moody, 1983.

Baker, David W. *Nahum, Habakkuk, and Zephaniah*. Tyndale Old Testament Commentaries. Downers Grove, IL: InterVarsity Press, 1988.

———. "Zephaniah: Theology of." In *New International Dictionary of Old Testament Theology and Exegesis*, edited by Willem A. VanGemeren, 4:1309–12. Grand Rapids: Zondervan, 1997.

Ball, David M. *"I Am" in John's Gospel: Literary Function, Background and Theological Implications*. Journal for the Study of the New Testament Supplement Series 124. Sheffield: Sheffield Academic Press, 1996.

Ball, Ivan J., Jr. "The Rhetorical Shape of Zephaniah." In *Perspectives on Language and Text: Essays and Poems in Honor of Francis I. Andersen's Sixtieth Birthday, July 28, 1985*, edited by Francis I. Andersen, Edgar W. Conrad, and Edward G. Newing, 155–65. Winona Lake, IN: Eisenbrauns, 1987.

———. *A Rhetorical Study of Zephaniah*. Berkeley, CA: Bibal Press, 1988.

Bamberger, B. J. "The Changing Image of the Prophet in Jewish Thought." In *Interpreting the Prophetic Tradition: The Goldenson Lectures 1955–1966*, 303–23. Library of Biblical Studies. Cincinnati: HUC Press; New York: KTAV, 1969.

Barker, Kenneth L., and D. Waylon Bailey. *Micah, Nahum, Habakkuk, Zephaniah*. New American Commentary 20. Nashville: Broadman & Holman, 1998.

Barrett, C. K. *The Gospel according to St. John*. 2nd ed. Philadelphia: Westminster, 1978.

———. "The Old Testament in the Fourth Gospel." *Journal of Theological Studies* 48 (1947): 155–69.

Bauckham, Richard. "Messianism according to the Gospel of John." In *Challenging Perspectives on the Gospel of John*, edited by John Lierman, 34–68. Wissenschaftliche Untersuchungen zum Neuen Testament, 2nd ser., 219. Tübingen: Mohr Siebeck, 2006.

———. *The Testimony of the Beloved Disciple: Narrative, History, and Theology in the Gospel of John*. Grand Rapids: Baker, 2007.

Beale, G. K. *Handbook on the New Testament Use of the Old Testament: Exegesis and Interpretation*. Grand Rapids: Baker, 2012.

———. "The Old Testament Background of the 'Last Hour' in 1 John 2,18." *Biblica* 92 (2011): 231–54.

———. "Revelation." In *It Is Written: Scripture Citing Scripture: Essays in Honor of Barnabas Lindars*, edited by D. A. Carson and H. G. M. Williamson, 318–36. Cambridge: Cambridge University Press, 1988.

Beale, G. K., and D. A. Carson. "Introduction." In *Commentary on the New Testament Use of the Old Testament*, edited by G. K. Beale and D. A. Carson, xxiii–xxviii. Grand Rapids: Baker, 2007.

Beasley-Murray, George R. *John*. 2nd ed. Word Biblical Commentary 36. Nashville: Thomas Nelson, 1999.

Becker, Joachim. *Messianic Expectation in the Old Testament*. Philadelphia: Fortress Press, 1980.

Becker, Jürgen. *Das Evangelium nach Johannes*. 2 vols. Ökumenischer Taschenbuchkommentar zum Neuen Testament 4. Güttersloh: Mohn, 1979–81.

Beetham, Christopher A. *Echoes of Scripture in the Letter of Paul to the Colossians*. Biblical Interpretation Series 96. Leiden: Brill, 2008.

Bennett, Robert A. "The Book of Zephaniah: Introduction, Commentary, and Reflections." In *The New Interpreter's Bible*, edited by L. E. Keck, 7:657–704. Nashville: Abingdon, 1996.

Ben-Porat, Ziva. "The Poetics of Literary Allusion." *PTL: A Journal for Descriptive Poetics and Theory of Literature* 1 (1976): 105–28.

Ben Zvi, Ehud. *A Historical-Critical Study of the Book of Zephaniah*. Beihefte zur Zeitschrift für die alttestamentliche Wissenschaft 198. Berlin: de Gruyter, 1991.

———. "Twelve Prophetic Books or 'The Twelve': A Few Preliminary Considerations." In *Forming Prophetic Literature: Essays on Isaiah and the Twelve in Honor of John D. W. Watts*, edited by James W. Watts and Paul R. House, 125–56. Journal for the Study of the Old Testament Supplement Series 235. Sheffield: Sheffield Academic Press, 1996.

Berlin, Adele. *Lamentations: A Commentary*. Old Testament Library. Louisville: Westminster John Knox, 2002.

———. *Zephaniah*. Anchor Bible 25A. New York: Doubleday, 1994.

Beutler, Johannes. "Greeks Come to See Jesus (John 12:20f)." *Biblica* 71 (1990): 333–47.

Biblia Hebraica Stuttgartensia. Edited by Karl Elliger and Wilhelm Rudolph. Stuttgart: Deutsche Bibelgesellschaft, 1983.

Biblia Hebraica Quinta. Edited by Adrian Schenker et al. Stuttgart: Deutsche Bibelgesellschaft, 2004–.

Boadt, Lawrence. *Jeremiah 26–52, Habakkuk, Zephaniah, Nahum*. Old Testament Message 10. Wilmington, DE: Glazier, 1982.

Boda, Mark J. "Zephaniah, Book of." In *Dictionary of the Old Testament Prophets*, edited by Mark J. Boda and J. Gordon McConville, 899–907. Downers Grove, IL: InterVarsity Press, 2012.

Bohmbach, Karla. "Daughter." In *Women in Scripture: A Dictionary of*

Named and Unnamed Women in the Hebrew Bible, the Apocryphal/ Deuterocanonical Books, and the New Testament, edited by Carol Meyers, Toni Craven and Ross S. Kraemer, 517–19. Boston: Houghton Mifflin, 2000.

Boismard, M.-É., and A. Lamouille. *Synopse des quatre évangiles en français, avec parallèles des apocryphes et des Pères*. 3 vols. Paris: Cerf, 1977.

Botterweck, G. J., H. Ringgren, and H.-J. Fabry, eds. *Theological Dictionary of the Old Testament*. Translated by J. T. Willis, G. W. Bromiley, D. W. Stott, and D. E. Green. 15 vols. Grand Rapids: Eerdmans, 1974–2006.

Bowman, John. *The Fourth Gospel and the Jews: A Study in R. Akiba, Esther, and the Gospel of John*. Pittsburgh Theological Monograph Series 8. Pittsburgh: Pickwick, 1975.

Bratcher, Robert G., ed. *Old Testament Quotations in the New Testament*. Helps for Translators 3. London: United Bible Societies, 1967.

Braun, F.-M. *Jean le théologien: Les grandes traditions d'Israël et l'accord des Écritures, selon le Quatrième Évangile*. 3 vols. *Etudes bibliques*. Paris: Gabalda, 1964.

Brawley, Robert L. *Text to Text Pours Forth Speech: Voices of Scripture in Luke-Acts*. Indiana Studies in Biblical Literature. Bloomington, IN: Indiana University Press, 1995.

Brendsel, Daniel J. *"Isaiah Saw His Glory": The Use of Isaiah 52–53 in John 12*. Beihefte zur Zeitschrift für die neutestamentliche Wissenschaft 208. Berlin: de Gruyter, 2014.

———. Personal comments to author. June 12, 2015; July 24, 25, 27, 2015.

Brockington, L. H. *The Hebrew Text of the Old Testament: The Readings Adopted by the Translators of the New English Bible*. Cambridge: Cambridge University Press, 1973.

Brown, Raymond E. *The Gospel according to John*. 2 vols. Anchor Bible 29–29A. Garden City, NY: Doubleday, 1966–70.

Bruce, F. F. *The Gospel of John: Introduction, Exposition and Notes*. Grand Rapids: Eerdmans, 1983.

———. *The New Testament Development of Old Testament Themes*. Grand Rapids: Eerdmans, 1968.

Bruckner, James. *Jonah, Nahum, Habakkuk, Zephaniah*. NIV Application Commentary. Grand Rapids: Zondervan, 2004.

Brunson, A. C. *Psalm 118 in the Gospel of John: An Intertextual Study on the New Exodus Pattern in the Theology of John*. Wissenschaftliche Untersuchungen zum Neuen Testament, 2nd ser., 158. Tübingen: Mohr Siebeck, 2003.

Bultmann, Rudolf. *The Gospel of John*. Edited by R. W. N. Hoare and J. K. Riches. Translated by G. R. Beasley-Murray. Philadelphia: Westminster, 1971.

Burge, Gary M. *John*. NIV Application Commentary. Grand Rapids: Zondervan, 2000.

Burney, C. F. *The Aramaic Origin of the Fourth Gospel*. Oxford: Clarendon, 1922.

Carson, D. A. *The Gospel according to John*. Pillar New Testament Commentary. Grand Rapids: Eerdmans, 1991.

———. "John and the Johannine Epistles." In *It Is Written: Scripture Citing Scripture: Essays in Honor of Barnabas Lindars*, edited by D. A. Carson and H. G. M. Williamson, 245–64. Cambridge: Cambridge University Press, 1988.

———. "The Purpose of the Fourth Gospel: John 20:31 Reconsidered." *Journal of Biblical Literature* 106 (1987): 639–51.

———. "Understanding Misunderstandings in the Fourth Gospel." *Tyndale Bulletin* 33 (1982): 59–91.

Carson, D. A., Douglas J. Moo, and Leon Morris. *An Introduction to the New Testament*. 2nd ed. Grand Rapids: Zondervan, 2005.

Catchpole, David R. "The 'Triumphal' Entry." In *Jesus and the Politics of His Day*, edited by Ernst Bammel and C. F. D. Moule, 319–34. Cambridge: Cambridge University Press, 1984.

Cathcart, Kevin J., and Robert P. Gordon. *The Targum of the Minor Prophets: Translated, with a Critical Introduction, Apparatus, and Notes*. The Aramaic Bible 14. Wilmington, DE: Glazier, 1989.

Chilton, Bruce G. *The Glory of Israel: The Theology and Provenience of the Isaiah Targum*. Journal for the Study of the Old Testament Supplement Series 23. Sheffield: JSOT Press, 1983.

Chisholm, Robert B., Jr. *Interpreting the Minor Prophets*. Grand Rapids: Zondervan, 1990.

Christensen, Duane L. "Zephaniah 2:4–15: A Theological Basis for Josiah's Program of Political Expansion." *Catholic Biblical Quarterly* 46 (1984): 669–82.

Clendenen, E. Ray. "The Minor Prophets." In *Holman Concise Bible Commentary*, edited by David S. Dockery, 340–96. Nashville: Broadman & Holman, 2010.

———. "Textlinguistics and Prophecy in the Book of the Twelve." *Journal of the Evangelical Theological Society* 46 (2003): 395–99.

Clowney, Edmund. *Preaching and Biblical Theology*. Grand Rapids: Eerdmans, 1961.

Coakley, J. F. "Jesus' Messianic Entry into Jerusalem (John 12:12–19 par)." *Journal of Theological Studies* 46 (1995): 461–82.

Coggins, Richard J. "The Minor Prophets: One Book or Twelve?" In *Crossing the Boundaries: Essays in Biblical Interpretation in Honour of Michael D. Goulder*, edited by M. D. Goulder, S. E. Porter, P. M. Joyce and D. E. Orton, 57–68. Biblical Interpretation Series 8. Leiden: Brill, 1994.

Coggins, Richard J., and Jin H. Han. *Six Minor Prophets through the Centuries: Nahum, Habakkuk, Zephaniah, Haggai, Zechariah, and Malachi*. Blackwell Bible Commentaries. Malden, MA: Wiley-Blackwell, 2011.

Collins, Terry. "The Literary Contexts of Zechariah 9:9." In *The Book of Zechariah and Its Influence*, edited by C. Tuckett, 29–40. Burlington, VT: Ashgate, 2003.

Conrad, Edgar W. *Fear Not Warrior: A Study of 'al tîrā' Pericopes in the Hebrew Scriptures*. Brown Judaic Studies 75. Chico, CA: Scholars, 1985.

Crüsemann, Frank. *Studien zur Formgeschichte von Hymnus und Danklied in Israel*. Wissenschafliche Monographien zum Alten und Neuen Testament 32. Neukirchener-Vluyn: Neukirchener Verlag, 1969.

Cuffey, Kenneth H. "Remnant, Redactor, and Biblical Theologian: A Comparative Study of Coherence in Micah and the Twelve." In *Reading and Hearing the Book of the Twelve*. Edited by James D. Nogalski and Marvin A. Sweeney, 185–208. Society of Biblical Literature Symposium Series 15. Atlanta: Society of Biblical Literature, 2000.

Culpepper, R. Alan. *Anatomy of the Fourth Gospel: A Study in Literary Design*. Foundations and Facets: New Testament. Philadelphia: Fortress, 1983.

———. *The Gospel and Letters of John*. Nashville: Abingdon, 1998.

Curtis, Byron G. "The Zion-Daughter Oracles: Evidence on the Identity and Ideology of the Late Redactors of the Book of the Twelve." In *Reading and Hearing the Book of the Twelve*, edited by James D. Nogalski and Marvin A. Sweeney, 166–84. Society of Biblical Literature Symposium Series 15. Atlanta: Society of Biblical Literature, 2000.

Daly-Denton, Margaret. *David in the Fourth Gospel: The Johannine Reception of the Psalms*. Arbeiten zur Geschichte des antiken Judentums und des Urchristentums 47. Leiden: Brill, 2000.

Danker, Frederick W., Walter Bauer, William F. Arndt, and F. Wilbur Gingrich. *Greek-English Lexicon of the New Testament and Other Early Christian Literature*. 3rd ed. Chicago: University of Chicago Press, 2000.

Dawson, David Allan. *Text-Linguistics and Biblical Hebrew*. Journal for the Study of the Old Testament Supplement Series 177. Sheffield: Sheffield Academic Press, 1994.

Day, Peggy L. "The Personification of Cities as Female in the Hebrew Bible: The Thesis of Aloysius Fitzgerald, F. S. C." In *Social Location and Biblical Interpretation in Global Perspective*, vol. 2, *Reading from This Place*, edited by Fernando F. Segovia and Mary Ann Tolbert, 283–302. Minneapolis: Fortress Press, 1995.

Dearman, J. Andrew. "Daughter Zion and Her Place in God's Household." *Horizons in Biblical Theology* 31 (2009): 144–59.

Dennis, John A. *Jesus' Death and the Gathering of True Israel: The Johannine Appropriation of Restoration Theology in the Light of John 11.47–52*. Wissenschaftliche Untersuchungen zum Neuen Testament 217. Tübingen: Mohr Siebeck, 2006.

DeRouchie, Jason S. *A Call to Covenant Love: Text Grammar and Literary Structure in Deuteronomy 5–11*. Gorgias Dissertations 30. Biblical Studies 2. Piscataway, NJ: Gorgias, 2007.

———. *How to Understand and Apply the Old Testament: Twelve Steps from Exegesis to Theology*. Phillipsburg, NJ: P&R Publishing, 2017.

———. "Made for Praise: A Meditation on Zephaniah 3:20." In *Devotions on the Hebrew Bible*, edited by Milton Eng and Lee M. Fields, 108–10. Grand Rapids: Zondervan, 2015.

———. Personal comments to author. December 12, 2014; February 9, 2015.

———. "Who Should Seek the Lord Together? Identifying the Addressees in Zephaniah 2:1, 3." Forthcoming.

———. *Zephaniah*. Zondervan Exegetical Commentary on the Old Testament. Grand Rapids: Zondervan, forthcoming.

Devillers, Luc. *La fête de l'envoyé: La section johannique de la fête des tentes (Jean 7,1–10,21) et la christologie. Etudes bibliques* 49. Paris: Gabalda, 2002.

Dietzfelbinger, Christian. *Das Evangelium nach Johannes*. 2 vols. Zürcher Bibelkommentare 4. Zürich: Theologischer Verlag, 2001.

Dobbs-Allsopp, F. W. "Daughter Zion." In *Thus Says the Lord: Essays on the Former and Latter Prophets in Honor of Robert R. Wilson*, edited by John J. Ahn and Stephen L. Cook, 125–34. Library of Hebrew Bible/Old Testament Studies 502. New York: T&T Clark, 2009.

———. "Syntagma of *bat* Followed by a Geographical Name in the Hebrew Bible: A Reconsideration of Its Meaning and Grammar." *Catholic Biblical Quarterly* 57 (1995): 451–70.

Dodd, C. H. *Historical Tradition in the Fourth Gospel*. Cambridge: Cambridge University Press, 1963.

———. *The Interpretation of the Fourth Gospel*. Cambridge: Cambridge University Press, 1953.

Dorsey, David A. *The Literary Structure of the Old Testament: A Commentary on Genesis–Malachi*. Grand Rapids: Baker, 1999.

Duke, Paul D. *Irony in the Fourth Gospel*. Atlanta: John Knox, 1985.

Ellis, E. Earle. "How the New Testament Uses the Old." In *New Testament Interpretation: Essays on Principles and Methods*, edited by I. Howard Marshall, 199–219. Grand Rapids: Eerdmans, 1977.

Ensor, Peter W. *Jesus and His 'Works': The Johannine Sayings in Historical Perspective*. Untersuchungen zum Neuen Testament, 2nd ser., 85. Tübingen: Mohr Siebeck, 1996.

Epp, Eldon Jay. *Perspectives on New Testament Textual Criticism: Collected*

Essays, 1962–2004. Supplements to Novum Testamentum 116. Leiden: Brill, 2005.

Epstein, I., ed., trans. *The Babylonian Talmud*. 35 vols. London: Soncino, 1935–52.

Evans, Craig A. *Ancient Texts for NT Studies: A Guide to the Background Literature*. Peabody, MA: Hendrickson, 2005.

———. "The Messiah in the Dead Sea Scrolls." In *Israel's Messiah in the Bible and the Dead Sea Scrolls*, edited by Richard S. Hess and M. Daniel Carroll, 85–101. Grand Rapids: Baker, 2003.

———. "New Testament Use of the Old Testament." In *New Dictionary of Biblical Theology*, edited by T. D. Alexander and B. S. Rosner, 72–80. Downers Grove, IL: InterVarsity Press, 2000.

———. "Obduracy and the Lord's Servant: Some Observations on the Use of the Old Testament in the Fourth Gospel." In *Early Jewish and Christian Exegesis: Studies in Memory of William Hugh Brownlee*, edited by Craig A. Evans and William F. Stinespring, 221–36. Homage Series 10. Atlanta: Scholars Press, 1987.

———. "The Old Testament in the New." In *The Face of New Testament Studies: A Survey of Recent Research*, edited by Scot McKnight and Grant R. Osborne, 130–45. Grand Rapids: Baker Academic, 2004.

Farelly, Nicolas. *The Disciples in the Fourth Gospel: A Narrative Analysis of Their Faith and Understanding*. Wissenschaftliche Untersuchungen zum Neuen Testament, 2nd ser., 290. Tübingen: Mohr Siebeck, 2010.

Farmer, W. R. *Maccabees, Zealots, and Josephus: An Enquiry into Jewish Nationalism in the Greco-Roman Period*. New York: Columbia University Press, 1956.

———. "The Palm Branches in John 12,13." *Journal of Theological Studies* 3 (1952): 62–66.

Fee, Gordon D. *Papyrus Bodmer II (P66): Its Textual Relationships and Scribal Characteristics*. Studies and Documents 34. Salt Lake City: University of Utah Press, 1968.

Finegan, Jack. *Handbook of Biblical Chronology: Principles of Time Reckoning in the Ancient World and Problems of Chronology in the Bible*. Rev. ed. Peabody, MA: Hendrickson, 1998.

Fitzmyer, Joseph A. "Aramaic Evidence Affecting the Interpretation of Hosanna in the New Testament." In *Tradition and Interpretation in the New Testament: Essays in Honor of E. Earle Ellis for His 60th Birthday*, edited by E. Earle Ellis, Gerald F. Hawthorne, and Otto Betz, 110–18. Grand Rapids: Eerdmans, 1987.

Follis, Elaine R. "Zion, Daughter of." In *The Anchor Bible Dictionary*, edited by David Noel Freedman, 6:1103. New York: Doubleday, 1992.

Floyd, Michael H. "The Daughter of Zion Goes Fishing in Heaven." In *Daughter Zion: Her Portrait, Her Response*, edited by Mark. J. Boda, Carol J. Dempsey, and LeAnn Snow Flesher, 177–200. Ancient Israel and Its Literature 13. Atlanta: Society of Biblical Literature, 2012.

———. *Minor Prophets: Part 2*. Forms of the Old Testament Literature 22. Grand Rapids: Eerdmans, 2000.

———. "Welcome Back, Daughter Zion!" *Catholic Biblical Quarterly* 70 (2008): 484–504.

Fossum, Jarl E. *The Image of the Invisible God: Essays on the Influence of Jewish Mysticism on Early Christology*. Novum Testamentum et Orbis Antiquus 30. Freiburg, Schweiz: Universitätsverlag, 1995.

Fowler, William G. "The Influence of Ezekiel in the Fourth Gospel: Intertextuality and Interpretation." PhD diss., Golden Gate Baptist Theological Seminary, 1995.

Freed, Edwin D. "The Entry into Jerusalem in the Gospel of John." *Journal of Biblical Literature* 80 (1961): 329–38.

———. *Old Testament Quotations in the Gospel of John*. Supplements to Novum Testamentum 11. Leiden: Brill, 1965.

Freedman, David N. "Another Look at Biblical Hebrew Poetry." In *Poetry and Orthography*, vol. 2, *Divine Commitment and Human Obligation: Selected Writings of David Noel Freedman*, edited by John R. Huddleston, 213–26. Grand Rapids: Eerdmans, 1997.

Frey, Jörg. "Heiden-Griechen-Gotteskinder: Zu Gestalt und Funktion der Rede von den Heiden im 4 Evangelium." In *Die Heiden: Juden, Christen und das Problem des Fremden*, edited by R. Feldmeier and U. Heckel, 228–68. Wissenschaftliche Untersuchungen zum Neuen Testament, 1st ser., 70. Tübingen: Mohr Siebeck, 1994.

Fuller, Russell. "The Form and Formation of the Book of the Twelve." In *Forming Prophetic Literature: Essays on Isaiah and the Twelve in Honor of John D. W. Watts*, edited by James W. Watts and Paul R. House, 86–101. Journal for the Study of the Old Testament Supplement Series 235. Sheffield: Sheffield Academic Press, 1996.

Gaon, Saadia. *The Book of Beliefs and Opinions*. Translated by Samuel Rosenblatt. Yale Judaica Series 1. New Haven: Yale University Press, 1948.

Garrett, Duane A., and Jason S. DeRouchie. *A Modern Grammar for Biblical Hebrew*. Nashville: Broadman & Holman, 2009.

Gelston, Anthony. *The Twelve Minor Prophets*. Edited by Adrian Schenker et al. *Biblia Hebraica Quinta* 13. Stuttgart: Deutsche Bibelgesellschaft, 2010.

Gerleman, Gillis. *Zephanja: Textkritisch und Literarisch Untersucht*. Lund: Gleerup, 1942.

Gerstenberger, Erhard S. *Psalms, Part 1: With an Introduction to Cultic Poetry*. Forms of Old Testament Literature 14. Grand Rapids: Eerdmans, 1988.

Goldingay, John. *Psalms*. Edited by Tremper Longman III. 3 vols. Baker Commentary on the Old Testament Wisdom and Psalms. Grand Rapids: Baker Academic, 2006–2008.

Goldingay, John, and Pamela J. Scalise. *Minor Prophets II*. New International Biblical Commentary on the Old Testament 18. Peabody, MA: Hendrickson, 2009.

Goodwin, Charles. "How Did John Treat His Sources?" *Journal of Biblical Literature* 73 (1954): 61–75.

Gordon, Robert P. *Studies in the Targum to the Twelve Prophets: From Nahum to Malachi*. Supplements to Vetus Testamentum 51. Leiden: Brill, 1994.

Gottwald, Norman K. "Poetry, Hebrew." In *Interpreter's Dictionary of the Bible*, edited by G. A. Buttrick, 3:829–38. Nashville: Abingdon, 1962.

Gray, John. "The Kingship of God in the Prophets and Psalms." *Vetus Testamentum* 11 (1961): 1–29.

Greenspoon, L. "The Use and Abuse of the Term 'LXX' and Related Terminology in Recent Scholarship." *Bulletin of the International Organization for Septuagint and Cognate Studies* 20 (1987): 21–29.

Grelot, Pierre. "Une Tosephta Targoumique sur Zacharie, II, 14–15." *Revue biblique* 73 (1966): 197–211.

Grol, H. W. M. van. "Classical Hebrew Metrics and Zephaniah 2–3." In *The Structural Analysis of Biblical and Canaanite Poetry*, edited by W. van der Meer and J. C. de Moor, 186–206. Journal for the Study of the Old Testament Supplement Series 74. Sheffield: JSOT Press, 1988.

Gruber, Mayer I. "Fear, Anxiety and Reverence in Akkadian, Biblical Hebrew and Other North-West Semitic Languages." *Vetus Testamentum* 40 (1990): 411–22.

Guggenheimer, Heinrich W., ed., trans. *Fourth Order: Neziqin. Tractates Ševi'it and 'Avodah Zarah*, vol. 13, *The Jerusalem Talmud*. Studia Judaica 61. Berlin, New York: de Gruyter, 2011.

Haenchen, Ernst. *John*. Edited by R. W. Funk and U. Busse. Translated by R. W. Funk. 2 vols. Hermeneia: A Critical and Historical Commentary on the Bible. Philadelphia: Fortress Press, 1984.

Ham, Clay Alan. "The Minor Prophets in Matthew's Gospel." In *The Minor Prophets in the New Testament*, edited by Maarten J. J. Menken and Steve Moyise, 39–56. Library of New Testament Studies 377. London: T & T Clark, 2009.

Hamilton, James. "The Influence of Isaiah on the Gospel of John." *Perichoresis* 5 (2007): 139–62.

Hanson, Anthony T. *The New Testament Interpretation of Scripture*. London: SPCK, 1980.

———. "The Old Testament Background to the Raising of Lazarus." In *Studia Evangelica*, edited by E. A. Livingstone, 6:252–55. Texte und Untersuchungen zur Geschichte der altchristlichen Literatur 112. Berlin: Akademie-Verlag, 1973.

———. *The Prophetic Gospel: A Study of John and the Old Testament*. Edinburgh: T&T Clark, 1991.

Hanson, Paul D. *The Dawn of the Apocalyptic: The Historical and Sociological Roots of Jewish Apocalyptic Eschatology*. Rev. ed. Philadelphia: Fortress, 1979.

Hart, H. J. "Judaea and Rome: The Official Commentary." *Journal of Theological Studies* 3 (1952): 172–198.

Harvey, A. E. *Jesus and the Constraints of History*. Philadelphia: Westminster, 1982.

Hasel, Gerhard F. "Remnant." In *The International Standard Bible Encyclopedia*, edited by G. W. Bromiley, 4:130–34. Grand Rapids: Eerdmans, 1988.

Hays, Richard B. *Echoes of Scripture in the Gospels*. Waco, TX: Baylor University Press, 2016.

———. *Echoes of Scripture in the Letters of Paul*. New Haven: Yale University Press, 1989.

Heller, Roy L. *Narrative Structure and Discourse Constellations: An Analysis of Clause Function in Biblical Hebrew Prose*. Harvard Semitic Studies 55. Winona Lake, IN: Eisenbrauns, 2004.

Hengel, Martin. "The Old Testament in the Fourth Gospel." In *The Gospels and the Scriptures of Israel*, edited by C. A. Evans and W. R. Stegner, 380–95. Journal for the Study of the New Testament Supplement Series 104. Studies in Scripture in Early Judaism and Christianity 3. Sheffield: Sheffield Academic Press, 1994.

Hill, Andrew E. *Malachi*. Anchor Bible 25D. Garden City, NY: Doubleday, 1998.

Hill, John Spencer. "τὰ βαΐα τῶν φοινίκων (John 12:13): Pleonasm or Prolepsis." *Journal of Biblical Literature* 101 (1982): 133–35.

Ho, Ahuva. *The Targum of Zephaniah: Manuscripts and Commentary*. Studies in the Aramaic Interpretation of Scripture 7. Leiden: Brill, 2009.

Hollander, John. *The Figure of Echo: A Mode of Allusion in Milton and After*. Berkeley: University of California Press, 1981.

Horgan, Maurya P. *Pesharim: Qumran Interpretation of Biblical Books*. Catholic Biblical Quarterly Monograph Series 8. Washington, DC: Catholic Biblical Association, 1979.

Horsley, Richard A., and John S. Hanson. *Bandits, Prophets, and Messiahs: Popular Movements in the Time of Jesus*. Harrisburg, PA: Trinity Press, 1999.

Hoskyns, E. C. *The Fourth Gospel*. Edited by F. N. Davey. 2nd ed. London: Faber & Faber, 1956.

House, Paul R. *The Unity of the Twelve*. Journal for the Study of the Old Testament Supplement Series 97. Bible and Literature Series 27. Sheffield: Sheffield Academic Press, 1990.

———. *Zephaniah: A Prophetic Drama*. Journal for the Study of the Old

Testament Supplement Series 69. Bible and Literature Series 16. Sheffield: Almond, 1988.

Hübner, Hans. *Vetus Testamentum in Novo*, vol. 1.2, *Evangelium secundum Iohannem*. Göttingen: Vandenhoek & Ruprecht, 2003.

Hyatt, J. P. "Was Yahweh Originally a Creator Deity?" *Journal of Biblical Literature* 86 (1967): 369–77.

Instone-Brewer, David. *Techniques and Assumptions in Jewish Exegesis before 70 CE*. Texte und Studien zum antiken Judentum 30. Tübingen: Mohr Siebeck, 1992.

Irsigler, Hubert. *Gottesgericht und Jahwetag: Die Komposition Zef 1,1–2, 3, untersucht auf der Grudlage der Literarkritik des Zefanjabuches*. Arbeiten zu Text und Sprache im Alten Testament 3. Sankt Ottilien: EOS-Verlag, 1977.

Jenni, Ernst, with the assistance of Claus Westermann, eds. *Theological Lexicon of the Old Testament*. Translated by Mark E. Biddle. 3 vols. Peabody, MA: Hendrickson, 1997.

Jones, Barry A. "Zephaniah, Book of." In *The New Interpreter's Dictionary of the Bible*, edited by Katharine D. Sakenfeld, 5:977. Nashville: Abingdon, 2009.

Kaiser, Walter C., Jr. *The Uses of the Old Testament in the New*. Chicago: Moody, 1985.

Kang, Sa-Moon. *Divine War in the Old Testament and in the Ancient Near East*. Beihefte zur Zeitschrift für die alttestamentliche Wissenschaft 177. Berlin: de Gruyter, 1989.

Kapelrud, Arvid S. *The Message of the Prophet Zephaniah: Morphology and Ideas*. Oslo: Universitetsforlaget, 1975.

Kartveit, Magnar. "Daughter of Zion." *Theology and Life* 27 (2004): 25–41.

———. *Rejoice, Dear Zion! Hebrew Construct Phrases with 'Daughter' and 'Virgin' as Nomen Regens*. Edited by John Barton, Reinhard G. Kratz, and Markus Witte. Beihefte zur Zeitschrift für die alttestamentliche Wissenschaft 447. Berlin: de Gruyter, 2013.

Keener, Craig S. *The Gospel of John: A Commentary*. 2 vols. Peabody, MA: Hendrickson, 2003.

Keller, Carl-A. "Sophonie." In *Michée, Nahoum, Habacuc, Sophonie*, 177–222. Commentaire de l'Ancien Testament 11b. Neuchâtel: Delachaux & Niestlé, 1971.

Kierspel, Lars. *The Jews and the World in the Fourth Gospel: Parallelism, Function, and Context*. Wissenschaftliche Untersuchungen zum Neuen Testament, 2nd ser., 220. Tübingen: Mohr Siebeck, 2006.

King, Greg A. "The Day of the Lord in Zephaniah." *Bibliotheca Sacra* 152 (1995): 16–32.

———. "The Remnant in Zephaniah." *Bibliotheca Sacra* 151 (1994): 414–27.

Kinman, Brent. "Jesus' Royal Entry into Jerusalem." *Bulletin for Biblical Research* 15 (2005): 223–60.

Kittel, G., and G. Friedrich, eds. *Theological Dictionary of the New Testament*. Translated by G. W. Bromiley. 10 vols. Grand Rapids: Eerdmans, 1964–76.

Koehler, L., W. Baumgartner, and J. J. Stamm. *The Hebrew and Aramaic Lexicon of the Old Testament*. Translated and edited under the supervision of M. E. J. Richarson. 5 vols. Leiden: Brill, 1994–2000.

Koester, Craig R. "Messianic Exegesis and the Call of Nathanael (John 1:45–51)." *Journal for the Study of the New Testament* 39 (1990): 23–34.

———. "'The Savior of the World' (John 4:42)." *Journal of Biblical Literature* 109 (1990): 665–80.

———. *Symbolism in the Fourth Gospel: Meaning, Mystery, Community*. 2nd ed. Minneapolis: Fortress, 2003.

Kossen, H. B. "Who Were the Greeks of John xii 20?" In *Studies in John: Presented to Professor Dr. J.N. Sevenster on the Occasion of his Seventieth Birthday*, 97–110. Novum Testament Supplements 24. Leiden: Brill, 1970.

Köstenberger, Andreas J. *Encountering John: The Gospel in Historical, Literary, and Theological Perspective*. Encountering Biblical Studies. Grand Rapids: Baker, 1999.

———. *John*. Baker Exegetical Commentary on the New Testament. Grand Rapids: Baker, 2004.

———. "John." In *Commentary on the New Testament Use of the Old Testament*, edited by G. K. Beale and D. A. Carson, 415–512. Grand Rapids: Baker, 2007.

———. *A Theology of John's Gospel and Letters*. Biblical Theology of the New Testament. Grand Rapids: Zondervan, 2009.

Köstenberger, Andreas J., and Scott R. Swain. *Father, Son and Spirit: The Trinity and John's Gospel.* New Studies in Biblical Theology 24. Downers Grove, IL: InterVarsity Press, 2008.

Kovacs, Judith L. "'Now Shall the Ruler of This World Be Driven Out': Jesus' Death as Cosmic Battle in John 12.20–36." *Journal of Biblical Literature* 114 (1995): 227–47.

Kraeling, Emil G. H. *Commentary on the Prophets.* 2 vols. Camden, NJ: Thomas Nelson, 1966.

Krinetzki, G. *Zefanjastudien: Motiv- und Traditionskritik + Kompositions- und Redaktionskritik.* Regensburger Studien zur Theologie 7. Frankfurt: Lang, 1977.

Kselman, John S. "Zephaniah: Book of." In *The Anchor Bible Dictionary*, edited by David Noel Freedman, 6:1077–80. New York: Doubleday, 1992.

Kubiś, Adam. *The Book of Zechariah in the Gospel of John. Etudes bibliques* 64. Pendé: Gabalda, 2012.

Lagrange, Marie-Joseph. *Évangile selon Saint Jean.* 5th ed. *Etudes bibliques.* Paris: Gabalda, 1936.

LeCureux, Jason T. *The Thematic Unity of the Book of the Twelve.* Hebrew Bible Monographs 41. Sheffield: Sheffield Phoenix Press, 2012.

Leung, Mavis M. *The Kingship-Cross Interplay in the Gospel of John: Jesus' Death as Corroboration of His Royal Messiahship.* Eugene, OR: Wipf & Stock, 2011.

Levenson, Jon D. "Zion Traditions." In *The Anchor Bible Dictionary*, edited by David Noel Freedman, 6:1098–1102. New York: Doubleday, 1992.

Levinsohn, Stephen H. *Discourse Features of New Testament Greek: A Coursebook on the Information Structure of New Testament Greek.* 2nd ed. Dallas: SIL International, 2000.

Lieu, Judith M. "Narrative Analysis and Scripture in John." In *The Old Testament in the New Testament: Essays in Honour of J. L. North*, edited by Steve Moyise, 144–63. Journal for the Study of the New Testament Supplement Series 189. Sheffield: Sheffield Academic Press, 2000.

Lightfoot, R. H. *St. John's Gospel.* Edited by C. F. Evans. Oxford: Clarendon, 1956. Reprint, London: Oxford University Press, 1963.

Lincoln, Andrew T. *The Gospel according to Saint John*. Black's New Testament Commentaries. Peabody, MA: Hendrickson, 2005.

———. "The Lazarus Story: A Literary Perspective." In *The Gospel of John and Christian Theology*, edited by Richard Bauckham and Carl Mosser, 211–32. Grand Rapids: Eerdmans, 2008.

———. *Truth on Trial: The Lawsuit Motif in the Fourth Gospel*. Peabody, MA: Hendrickson, 2000.

Lindars, Barnabas. *The Gospel of John*. New Century Bible. Grand Rapids: Eerdmans, 1972.

———. *New Testament Apologetic: The Doctrinal Significance of the Old Testament Quotations*. Philadelphia: Westminster, 1961.

Lints, Richard. *The Fabric of Theology: A Prolegomenon to Evangelical Theology*. Grand Rapids: Eerdmans, 1993.

Lioy, Dan. *The Search for Ultimate Reality: Intertextuality between the Genesis and Johannine Prologues*. New York: Lang, 2005.

Litwak, Kenneth D. *Echoes of Scripture in Luke–Acts: Telling the History of God's People Intertextually*. Journal for the Study of the New Testament Supplement Series 282. London: T&T Clark, 2005.

Lohse, Eduard. "Hosianna." *Novum Testamentum* 6 (1963): 113–19.

Longacre, Robert E. "Discourse Perspective on the Hebrew Verb: Affirmation and Restatement." In *Linguistics and Biblical Hebrew*, edited by Walter Bodine, 177–89. Winona Lake, IN: Eisenbrauns, 1992.

———. *The Grammar of Discourse*. 2nd ed. Topics in Language and Linguistics. New York: Plenum, 1996.

———. *Joseph, A Story of Divine Providence: A Text Theoretical and Textlinguistic Analysis of Genesis 37 and 39–48*. Winona Lake, IN: Eisenbrauns, 1989.

Longenecker, R. N. *Biblical Exegesis in the Apostolic Period*. 2nd ed. Grand Rapids: Eerdmans; Vancouver: Regent College Publishing, 1999.

Losie, L. A. "Triumphal Entry." In *Dictionary of Jesus and the Gospels*, edited by Joel B. Green and Scot McKnight, 854–59. Downers Grove, IL: InterVarsity Press, 1992.

Lucass, Shirley. *The Concept of the Messiah in the Scriptures of Judaism and Christianity*. Library of Second Temple Studies 78. London: T&T Clark, 2011.

Lunde, Jonathan. "An Introduction to Central Questions in the New Testament Use of the Old Testament." In *Three Views on the New Testament Use of the Old Testament*, edited by Kenneth Berding and Jonathan Lunde, 7–39. Grand Rapids: Zondervan, 2008.

Maier, Christl M. *Daughter Zion, Mother Zion: Gender, Space, and the Sacred in Ancient Israel.* Minneapolis: Fortress, 2008.

Mann, Jacob. *The Palestinian Triennial Cycle: Genesis and Exodus.* Vol. 1 of *The Bible As Read and Preached in the Old Synagogue.* Library of Biblical Studies. Repr. with new matter, New York: KTAV, 1971.

Mann, Jacob, and Isaiah Sonne. *The Palestinian Triennial Cycle: Leviticus and Numbers to Seder 106.* Vol. 2 of *The Bible As Read and Preached in the Old Synagogue.* Cincinnati: Mann-Sonne Publication Committee, Hebrew Union College, 1966.

Manning, G. T. *Echoes of a Prophet: The Use of Ezekiel in the Gospel of John and in Literature of the Second Temple Period.* Journal for the Study of the New Testament Supplement Series 270. London: T&T Clark, 2004.

Manns, Frédéric. *L'évangile de Jean et la sagesse.* Analecta (Studium Biblicum Franciscanum) 62. Jerusalem: Franciscan Printing Press, 2003.

———. "Exégèse rabbinique et exégèse johannique." *Revue biblique* 92 (1985): 525–38.

Martin, Albert William, Jr. *Interpretation of the Triumphal Entry in the Early Church.* Ann Arbor, MI: University Microfilms, 1971.

Martyn, J. L. "A Gentile Mission that Replaces an Earlier Jewish Mission?" In *Exploring the Gospel of John: In Honor of D. Moody Smith*, edited by R. A. Culpepper and C. Clifton Black, 124–44. Louisville: John Knox, 1996.

März, Claus-Peter. *"Siehe, dein König kommt zu dir . . . ": Eine traditionsgeschichtliche Untersuchung zur Einzugsperikope.* Erfurter theologische Studien 43. Leipzig: St. Benno-Verlag, 1980.

Mason, Rex. "The Use of Earlier Biblical Material in Zechariah 9–14: A Study in Inner Biblical Exegesis." In *Bringing Out the Treasure: Inner Biblical Allusion in Zechariah 9–14*, edited by Mark J. Boda and Michael H. Floyd, 1–208. Journal for the Study of the Old Testament Supplement Series 370. Sheffield: Sheffield Academic Press, 2003.

———. *Zephaniah, Habakkuk, Joel*. Old Testament Guides. Sheffield: JSOT Press, 1994.

Mastin, Brian A. "The Date of the Triumphal Entry." *New Testament Studies* 16 (1969): 76–82.

Mateos, P. C. "Uso e interpretación de Zacarías 9,9–10 en el Nuevo Testamento." *Estudio Agustiniano* 7 (1972): 471–93; 8 (1973): 1–27.

McCartney, Dan G. "The New Testament's Use of the Old Testament." In *Inerrancy and Hermeneutic: A Tradition, A Challenge, A Debate*, edited by Harvie M. Conn, 101–16. Grand Rapids: Baker, 1988.

McComiskey, Thomas Edward. "Zechariah." In *The Minor Prophets: An Exegetical and Expository Commentary*, edited by Thomas Edward McComiskey, 3:1003–244. Grand Rapids: Baker, 1998.

Meeks, Wayne A. "The Man from Heaven in Johannine Sectarianism." *Journal of Biblical Literature* 91 (1972): 44–72.

———. *The Prophet-King: Moses Traditions and the Johannine Christology*. Supplements to Novum Testamentum 14. Leiden: Brill, 1967.

Menken, M. J. J. *Old Testament Quotations in the Fourth Gospel: Studies in Textual Form*. Contributions to Biblical Exegesis and Theology 15. Kampen: Kok Pharos, 1996.

———. "The Minor Prophets in John's Gospel." In *The Minor Prophets in the New Testament*, edited by M. J. J. Menken and Steve Moyise, 79–96. Library of New Testament Studies 377. London: T&T Clark, 2009.

———. "The Quotations from Zech 9,9 in Mt 21,5 and in John 12,15." In *John and the Synoptics*, edited by A. Denaux, 571–78. Bibliotheca Ephemeridum Theologicarum Lovaniensium 101. Leuven: Leuven University Press, 1992.

Mérode, Marie de. "L'accueil triomphal de Jésus selon *Jean*, 11–12." *Revue théologique de Louvain* 13 (1982): 49–62.

Meyer, Lester V. "Remnant." In *The Anchor Bible Dictionary*, edited by David Noel Freedman, 5:669–71. New York: Doubleday, 1992.

Meyers, Carol L., and Eric M. Meyers. *Haggai, Zechariah 1–8*. Anchor Bible 25B. Garden City, NY: Doubleday, 1987.

Michaels, J. Ramsey. *The Gospel of John*. New International Commentary on the New Testament. Grand Rapids: Eerdmans, 2010.

Mihalios, Stefanos. *The Danielic Eschatological Hour in the Johannine*

Literature. Library of New Testament Studies 436. London: T&T Clark, 2011.

The Midrash on Psalms. Translated by W. G. Braude. 2 vols. Yale Judaica Series 9. New Haven: Yale University Press, 1959.

Miller, Cynthia L. "Discourse Functions of Quotative Frames in Biblical Hebrew Narrative." In *Discourse Analysis of Biblical Literature: What It Is and What It Offers*, edited by Walter R. Bodine, 155–82. Society of Biblical Literature Semeia Studies. Atlanta: Scholars Press, 1995.

Miller, M. P. "Targum, Midrash, and the Use of the Old Testament in the New Testament." *Journal for the Study of Judaism in the Persian, Hellenistic, and Roman Periods* 2 (1971): 29–82.

Miller, Patrick D., Jr. *The Divine Warrior in Early Israel*. Harvard Semitic Monographs 5. Cambridge, MA: Harvard University Press, 1973.

The Mishnah: A New Translation. Translated by Jacob Neusner. New Haven: Yale University Press, 1988.

Mlakuzhyil, George. *The Christocentric Literary Structure of the Fourth Gospel*. Analecta Biblica 117. Rome: Pontifical Biblical Institute, 1987.

Moloney, Francis J. *The Gospel of John*. Sacra Pagina 4. Collegeville, MN: Liturgical, 1998.

———. "'The Jews' in the Fourth Gospel: Another Perspective." *Pacifica* 15 (2002): 16–36.

———. *Signs and Shadows: Reading John 5–12*. Minneapolis: Fortress, 1996.

Moo, Douglas J. *The Old Testament in the Gospel Passion Narratives*. Sheffield: Almond, 1983.

Moore, W. E. "Sir, We Wish to See Jesus—Was This an Occasion of Temptation?" *Scottish Journal of Theology* 20 (1967): 75–93.

Morris, Leon. *The Gospel according to John*. New International Commentary on the New Testament. Rev. ed. Grand Rapids: Eerdmans, 1995.

Motyer, J. Alec. "Zephaniah." In *The Minor Prophets: An Exegetical and Expository Commentary*, edited by Thomas Edward McComiskey, 3:897–962. Grand Rapids: Baker, 1998.

Mowinckel, Sigmund. *The Psalms in Israel's Worship*. 2 vols. New York: Abingdon, 1962.

Muecke, D. C. *The Compass of Irony*. London: Methuen, 1969.

Naselli, Andrew David. *From Typology to Doxology: Paul's Use of Isaiah and Job in Romans 11:34–35*. Eugene, OR: Pickwick, 2012.

———. *How to Understand and Apply the New Testament: Twelve Steps from Exegesis to Theology*. Phillipsburg, NJ: P&R Publishing, 2017.

Neusner, Jacob. *Judaism and Scripture: The Evidence of Leviticus Rabbah*. Chicago Studies in the History of Judaism. Chicago: University of Chicago Press, 1986.

Nicole, Roger. "The New Testament Use of the Old Testament." In *The Right Doctrine from the Wrong Texts? Essays on the Use of the Old Testament in the New*, edited by G. K. Beale, 13–28. Grand Rapids: Baker, 1994.

Nogalski, James D. *The Book of the Twelve: Micah–Malachi*. Smyth & Helwys Bible Commentary. Macon, GA: Smyth & Helwys, 2011.

———. *Literary Precursors to the Book of the Twelve*. Beihefte zur Zeitschrift für die alttestamentliche Wissenschaft 217. Berlin: de Gruyter, 1993.

North, Wendy Sproston. "Jesus' Prayer in John 11." In *The Old Testament in the New Testament: Essays in Honour of J. L. North*, edited by Steve Moyise, 164–80. Journal for the Study of the New Testament Supplement Series 189. Sheffield: Sheffield Academic Press, 2000.

Nurmela, Risto. *Prophets in Dialogue: Inner-Biblical Allusions in Zechariah 1–9 and 9–14*. Åbo: Åbo Akademi University Press, 1996.

Obermann, Andreas. *Die christologische Erfüllung der Schrift im Johannesevangelium: Eine Untersuchung zur johanneischen Hermeneutik anhand der Schriftzitate*. Wissenschaftliche Untersuchungen zum Neuen Testament, 2nd ser., 83. Tübingen: Mohr Siebeck, 1996.

O'Connor, M. *Hebrew Verse Structure*. Winona Lake, IN: Eisenbrauns, 1997.

Painter, John. "The Quotation of Scripture and Unbelief in John 12:36b–43." In *The Gospels and the Scriptures of Israel*, edited by C. A. Evans and W. R. Stegner, 429–58. Journal for the Study of the New Testament Supplement Series 104. Studies in Scripture in Early Judaism and Christianity 3. Sheffield: Sheffield Academic Press, 1994.

Pancaro, Severino. *The Law in the Fourth Gospel: The Torah and the Gospel, Moses and Jesus, Judaism and Christianity according to John*. Supplements to Novum Testamentum 42. Leiden: Brill, 1975.

———. "'People of God' in St John's Gospel." *New Testament Studies* 16 (1970): 114–29.

Parker, D. C. *Codex Bezae: An Early Christian Manuscript and Its Text*. Cambridge: Cambridge University Press, 1992.

Patterson, Richard D. *Nahum, Habakkuk, Zephaniah*. Wycliffe Exegetical Commentary. Chicago: Moody, 1991.

Perri, Carmela. "On Alluding." *Poetics* 7 (1978): 289–307.

Perrot, Charles. "The Reading of the Bible in the Ancient Synagogue." In *Mikra: Text, Translation, Reading and Interpretation of the Hebrew Bible in Ancient Judaism and Early Christianity*, edited by Martin Jan Mulder, 137–60. Compendia Rerum Iudaicarum ad Novum Testamentum 2.1. Assen: Van Gorcum; Philadelphia: Fortress, 1988.

Petersen, David L. *Zechariah 9–14 and Malachi: A Commentary*. Old Testament Library. Louisville: Westminster John Knox, 1995.

Petterson, Anthony R. *Behold Your King: The Hope for the House of David in the Book of Zechariah*. Library of Hebrew Bible/Old Testament Studies 513. London: T&T Clark, 2009.

Pleins, J. David. "Poor, Poverty." In *The Anchor Bible Dictionary*, edited by David Noel Freedman, 5:402–14. New York: Doubleday, 1992.

Porter, Stanley. "Allusions and Echoes." In *As It Is Written: Studying Paul's Use of Scripture*, edited by S. E. Porter and C. D. Stanley, 29–40. Society of Biblical Literature Symposium Series 50. Atlanta: Society of Biblical Literature, 2008.

Potterie, Ignace de la. "L'exaltation du Fils de l'homme (Jn 12:31–36)." *Gregorianum* 49 (1968): 460–78.

Rad, Gerhard von. *Deuteronomy: A Commentary*. Translated by Dorothea Barton. Old Testament Library. Philadelphia: Westminster, 1966.

Rahlfs, Alfred, and Robert Hanhart, eds. *Septuaginta: Id est Vetus Testamentum graece iuxta LXX interpretes*. Rev. ed. Stuttgart: Deutsche Bibelgesellschaft, 2006.

Redditt, Paul L. "The King in Haggai–Zechariah 1–8 and the Book of the Twelve." In *Tradition in Transition: Haggai and Zechariah*

1–8 in the Trajectory of Hebrew Theology, edited by Mark J. Boda and Michael H. Floyd, 56–82. The Library of Hebrew Bible/Old Testament Studies 475. New York: T&T Clark, 2008.

Reim, G. *Studien zum alttestamentlichen Hintergrund des Johannesevangeliums*. Society for New Testament Studies Monograph Series 22. Cambridge: Cambridge University Press, 1974.

Rice, Gene. "The African Roots of the Prophet Zephaniah." *Journal of Religious Thought* 36 (1979): 21–31.

Ridderbos, Herman. *The Gospel according to John: A Theological Commentary*. Translated by John Vriend. Grand Rapids: Eerdmans, 1997.

Roberts, J. J. M. *Nahum, Habakkuk, and Zephaniah: A Commentary*. Old Testament Library. Louisville: Westminster John Knox, 1991.

Robertson, O. Palmer. *The Books of Nahum, Habakkuk, and Zephaniah*. New International Commentary on the Old Testament. Grand Rapids: Eerdmans, 1990.

Robinson, J. A. T. *The Priority of John*. London: SCM, 1985.

Rosenberg, Roy A. "Yahweh Becomes King." *Journal of Biblical Literature* 85 (1966): 297–307.

Rudolph, Wilhelm. *Micha, Nahum, Habakuk, Zephanja*. Kommentar zum Alten Testament 13/3. Gütersloh: Gerd Mohn, 1975.

Ryou, Daniel Hojoon. *Zephaniah's Oracles against the Nations: A Synchronic and Diachronic Study of Zephaniah 2:1–3:8*. Biblical Interpretation Series 13. Leiden: Brill, 1995.

Sabottka, Liudger. *Zephanja: Versuch einer Neuübersetzung mit philogischen Kommentar*. Biblica et orientalia 25. Rome: Pontifical Biblical Institute, 1972.

Salier, Willis Hedley. *The Rhetorical Impact of the Sēmeia in the Gospel of John*. Wissenschaftliche Untersuchungen zum Neuen Testament, 2nd ser., 186. Tübingen: Mohr Siebeck, 2004.

Samely, Alexander. *Rabbinic Interpretation of Scripture in the Mishnah*. New York: Oxford University Press, 2002.

Sanders, James A. "A New Testament Hermeneutic Fabric: Psalm 119 in the Entrance Narrative." In *Early Jewish and Christian Exegesis: Studies in Memory of William Hugh Brownlee*, edited by Craig A. Evans and William Franklin, 177–90. Homage Series 10. Atlanta: Scholars Press, 1987.

Sandmel, Samuel. "Parallelomania." *Journal of Biblical Literature* 81 (1962): 1–13.

Schart, Aaron. "Putting the Eschatological Visions of Zechariah in Their Place: Malachi as a Hermeneutical Guide for the Last Section of the Book of the Twelve." In *Bringing Out the Treasure: Inner Biblical Allusion in Zechariah 9–14*, edited by Mark J. Boda and Michael H. Floyd, 333–43. Sheffield: Sheffield Academic Press, 2003.

Schnackenburg, Rudolf. *The Gospel according to St John*. Translated by K. Smyth, C. Hastings, F. McDonagh, D. Smith, R. Foley, and G. A. Kon. 3 vols. Herders Theological Commentary on the New Testament. New York: Crossroad, 1980–82.

Schnelle, Udo. "Cross and Resurrection in the Gospel of John." In *The Resurrection of Jesus in the Gospel of John*, edited by Craig R. Koester and Reimund Bieringer, 127–51. Translated by Roy A. Harrisville and Reimund Bieringer. Wissenschaftliche Untersuchungen zum Neuen Testament 222. Tübingen: Mohr Siebeck, 2008.

Schreiner, Thomas R. *Interpreting the Pauline Epistles*, 2nd ed. Grand Rapids: Baker Academic, 2011.

Schuchard, Bruce G. *Scripture within Scripture: The Interrelationship of Form and Function in the Explicit Old Testament Citations in the Gospel of John*. Society of Biblical Literature Dissertation Series 133. Atlanta: Scholars Press, 1992.

Schultz, Richard L. *The Search for Quotation: Verbal Parallels in the Prophets*. Edited by David J. A. Clines and Philip R. Davies. Journal for the Study of the Old Testament Supplement Series 180. Sheffield: Sheffield Academic Press, 1999.

Scott, Martin. *Sophia and the Johannine Jesus*. Journal for the Study of the Old Testament Supplement Series 71. Sheffield: JSOT Press, 1992.

Segal, A. F. "Ruler of This World: Attitudes about Mediator Figures and the Importance of Sociology for Self-Definition." In *Aspects of Judaism, in the Greco-Roman Period*, edited by E. P. Sanders, A. I. Baumgartner, and Alan Mendelson, vol. 2, *Jewish and Christian Self-Definition*, edited by E. P. Sanders, A. I. Baumgartner, Alan Mendelson, and Ben F. Meyer, 245–68. Philadelphia: Fortress, 1981.

Shaw, David A. "Converted Imaginations? The Reception of Richard Hays's Intertextual Method." *Currents in Biblical Research* 11 (2013): 234–45.

Sheridan, Ruth. *Retelling Scripture: 'The Jews' and the Scriptural Citations in John 1:19–12:15*. Biblical Interpretation Series 110. Leiden: Brill, 2012.

Simoens, Yves. *Selon Jean*. 3 vols. Collection d'Institut d'Études Théologiques 17. Brussels: Éditions de l'Institut d'Études Théologiques, 1997.

Smith, Craig A. "Criteria for Biblical Chiasms: Objective Means for Distinguishing Chiasm of Design from Accidental and False Chiasm." PhD diss., University of Bristol, 2009.

Smith, D. Moody. *The Fourth Gospel in Four Dimensions: Judaism and Jesus, the Gospels and Scripture*. Columbia, SC: University of South Carolina Press, 2008.

———. *Johannine Christianity: Essays on Its Setting, Sources, and Theology*. Columbia, SC: University of South Carolina Press, 1984.

———. *John among the Gospels*. 2nd ed. Columbia, SC: University of South Carolina Press, 2001.

Smith, John M. P. "Zephaniah." In *A Critical and Exegetical Commentary on Micah, Zephaniah, Nahum, Habakkuk, Obadiah and Joel*, 159–263. International Critical Commentary 24. New York: Scribner's, 1911.

Smith, Ralph L. *Micah–Malachi*. Word Biblical Commentary 32. Waco, TX: Word, 1984.

Smolar, Leivy, and Moses Aberbach. *Studies in Targum Jonathan to the Prophets*. Library of Biblical Studies. New York: KTAV, 1983.

Snodgrass, Klyne. "The Use of the Old Testament in the New." In *The Right Doctrine from the Wrong Texts? Essays on the Use of the Old Testament in the New*, edited by G. K. Beale, 29–51. Grand Rapids: Baker, 1994.

Sommer, Benjamin D. *A Prophet Reads Scripture: Allusion in Isaiah 40–66*. Stanford: Stanford University Press, 1998.

Sonne, Isaiah. Preface to *The Palestinian Triennial Cycle: Leviticus and Numbers to Seder 106*, by Jacob Mann and Isaiah Sonne, vol. 2, *The Bible As Read and Preached in the Old Synagogue*. Cincinnati:

Mann-Sonne Publication Committee, Hebrew Union College, 1966.

Sproston, Wendy E. "Satan in the Fourth Gospel." In *Studia Biblica 1978*, vol. 2, *Papers on the Gospels*, edited by E. A. Livingstone, 307–11. Journal for the Study of the New Testament Supplement Series 2. Sheffield: JSOT, 1980.

Stendahl, Krister. *The School of St. Matthew, and Its Use of the Old Testament*. Acta Seminarii Neotestamentici Upsaliensis. Uppsala: Gleerup, 1954.

Stinespring, W. F. "No Daughter of Zion: A Study of the Appositional Genitive in Hebrew Grammar." *Encounter* 26 (1965): 133–41.

Stuart, Douglas K. *Studies in Early Hebrew Meter*. Harvard Semitic Monographs 13. Missoula, MT: Scholars Press, 1976.

Stuhlmueller, Carroll. *Rebuilding with Hope: A Commentary on the Books of Haggai and Zechariah*. International Theological Commentary. Grand Rapids: Eerdmans; Edinburgh: Handsel Press, 1988.

Sweeney, Marvin A. "Dating Prophetic Texts." *Hebrew Studies* 48 (2007): 55–73.

———. "A Form-Critical Reassessment of the Book of Zephaniah." *Catholic Biblical Quarterly* 53 (1991): 388–408.

———. "Synchronic and Diachronic Concerns in Reading the Book of the Twelve Prophets." In *Perspectives on the Formation of the Book of the Twelve: Methodological Foundations, Redactional Processes, Historical Insights*, edited by Rainer Albertz, James D. Nogalski, and Jakob Wöhrle, 21–34. Beihefte zur Zeitschrift für die alttestamentliche Wissenschaft 433. Berlin: de Gruyter, 2012.

———. "Twelve, Book of the." In *Dictionary of the Old Testament Prophets*, edited by Mark J. Boda and J. Gordon McConville, 788–806. Downers Grove, IL: InterVarsity Press, 2012.

———. *Zephaniah: A Commentary*. Edited by Paul D. Hanson. Hermeneia: A Critical and Historical Commentary on the Bible. Minneapolis: Fortress Press, 2003.

———. "Zephaniah: A Paradigm for the Study of the Prophetic Books." *Currents in Research: Biblical Studies* 7 (1999): 119–45.

Széles, Mária Eszenyei. *Wrath and Mercy: A Commentary on the Books of Habakkuk and Zephaniah*. Translated by George A. F. Knight. International Theological Commentary. Grand Rapids: Eerdmans, 1987.

Tabb, Brian J. "Jesus's Thirst at the Cross: Irony and Intertextuality in John 19:28." *Evangelical Quarterly* 85 (2013): 338–51.

Tan, Kim Huat. *The Zion Traditions and the Aims of Jesus*. Society for New Testament Studies Monograph Series 91. New York: Cambridge University Press, 1997.

Tanna debe Eliyyahu. Translated by W. G. Braude and I. J. Kapstein. Philadelphia: Jewish Publication Society of America, 1981.

Theobald, M. *Das Evangelium nach Johannes: Kapitel 1–12*. Regensburger Neues Testament. Regensburg: Friedrich Pustet, 2009.

Thyen, Hartwig. *Das Johannesevangelium*. Handbuch zum Neuen Testament 6. Tübingen: Mohr Siebeck, 2005.

Timmer, Daniel C. *The Non-Israelite Nations in the Book of the Twelve: Thematic Coherence and the Diachronic-Synchronic Relationship in the Minor Prophets*. Biblical Interpretation Series 135. Leiden: Brill, 2015.

Tomson, P. J. "'Jews' in the Gospel of John as Compared with the Palestinian Talmud, the Synoptics, and Some New Testament Apocrypha." In *Anti-Judaism and the Fourth Gospel*, edited by Reimund Bieringer, Didier Pollefeyt, and Frederique Vandecasteele-Vanneuville, 176–212. Louisville: Westminster John Knox, 2001.

Tov, Emanuel. "The Septuagint." In *Mikra: Text, Translation, Reading and Interpretation of the Hebrew Bible in Ancient Judaism and Early Christianity*, edited by Martin Jan Mulder, 161–88. Compendia Rerum Iudaicarum ad Novum Testamentum 2.1. Assen: Van Gorcum; Philadelphia: Fortress, 1988.

Trost, Travis D. *Who Should Be King in Israel? A Study on Roman Imperial Politics, the Dead Sea Scrolls, and the Fourth Gospel*. Society of Biblical Literature 139. New York: Lang, 2010.

Tsuchido, Kiyoshi. "Tradition and Redaction in John 12:1–43." *New Testament Studies* 30 (1984): 609–19.

Udoekpo, Michael Ufok. *Re-thinking the Day of YHWH and Restoration of Fortunes in the Prophet Zephaniah: An Exegetical and Theological Study of 1:14–18; 3:14–20*. Edited by Michael Fieger and Sigrid

Hodel-Hoenes. Das Alte Testament Im Dialog 2. Bern: Lang, 2010.

Vander Hoek, G. W. "The Function of Ps 82 in the Fourth Gospel and History of the Johannine Community: A Comparative Midrash Study." PhD diss., Claremont Graduate School, 1988.

VanGemeren, Willem A. *Interpreting the Prophetic Word: An Introduction to the Prophetic Literature of the Old Testament.* Grand Rapids: Zondervan, 1990.

———. "Oracles of Salvation." In *Cracking Old Testament Codes*, edited by D. B. Sandy and R. L. Giese Jr., 139–55. Nashville: Broadman & Holman, 1995.

Vlaardingerbroek, Johannes. *Zephaniah.* Historical Commentary on the Old Testament. Leuven: Peeters, 1999.

Wacholder, Ben Zion. "Prolegomenon." In *The Palestinian Triennial Cycle: Genesis and Exodus*, by Jacob Mann, vol. 1, *The Bible As Read and Preached in the Old Synagogue*, xi–lxxxvi. Library of Biblical Studies. Repr. with new matter, New York: KTAV, 1971.

Wahlde, Urban C. von. *The Earliest Version of John's Gospel: Recovering the Gospel of Signs.* Good News Studies 30. Wilmington, DE: Glazier, 1989.

———. *The Gospel and Letters of John: Commentary on the Gospel of John.* 3 vols. Eerdmans Critical Commentary. Grand Rapids: Eerdmans, 2010.

Walker, Larry L. "Zephaniah." In *Daniel—Malachi*, edited by Tremper Longman III and David E. Garland. Revised Expositor's Bible Commentary 8. Grand Rapids: Zondervan, 2008.

Wallace, Daniel B. *Greek Grammar beyond the Basics: An Exegetical Syntax of the New Testament.* Grand Rapids: Zondervan, 1996.

Waltke, Bruce K., and Michael O'Connor. *An Introduction to Biblical Hebrew Syntax.* Winona Lake, IN: Eisenbrauns, 1990.

Watts, John D. *The Books of Joel, Obadiah, Jonah, Nahum, Habakkuk, and Zephaniah.* Cambridge Bible Commentary. New York: Cambridge University Press, 1975.

Weissenberg, Hanne von. "'Aligned' or 'Non-Aligned'? The Textual Status of the Qumran Cave 4 Manuscripts of the Minor Prophets." In *Perspectives on the Formation of the Book of the Twelve:*

Methodological Foundations, Redactional Processes, Historical Insights, edited by Rainer Albertz, James D. Nogalski, and Jakob Wöhrle, 381–96. Beihefte zur Zeitschrift für die alttestamentliche Wissenschaft 433. Berlin; Boston: de Gruyter, 2012.

Wendland, Ernst R. *The Discourse Analysis of Hebrew Prophetic Literature: Determining the Larger Textual Units of Hosea and Joel*. Mellen Biblical Press Series 40. Lewiston: Mellen Biblical Press, 1995.

Wendland, Ernst R., and David J. Clark. "Zephaniah: Anatomy and Physiology of a Dramatic Prophetic Text." *Journal of Translation and Textlinguistics* 16 (2003): 1–44.

Wengst, Klaus. *Das Johannesevangelium*. 2 vols. Theologischer Handkommentar zum Neuen Testament 4. Stuttgart: Kohlhammer, 2000–2001.

Weren, Wilhelmus J. C. "Jesus' Entry into Jerusalem: Mt 21, 1–17 in the Light of the Hebrew Bible and the Septuagint." In *The Scriptures in the Gospels*, 117–41. Biblioetheca Ephemeridum theologicarum Lovaniensium 131. Louvain: Leuven University Press, 1997.

Werner, Eric. "'Hosanna' in the Gospels." *Journal of Biblical Literature* 65 (1946): 97–122.

Westermann, Claus. *Basic Forms of Prophetic Speech*. Translated by H. C. White. Louisville: Westminster John Knox, 1991.

———. *Praise and Lament in the Psalms*. Translated by Keith R. Crim and Richard N. Soulen. Atlanta: John Knox, 1981.

Wilckens, Ulrich. *Das Evangelium nach Johannes*. Das Neue Testament Deutsch 4. Göttingen: Vandenhoeck & Ruprecht, 1998.

Wilcox, Max. "The 'Prayer' of Jesus in John XI.41b–42." *New Testament Studies* 24 (1977): 128–32.

Willett, Michael E. *Wisdom Christology in the Fourth Gospel*. San Francisco: Mellen Research University Press, 1992.

Williams, Catrin H. *I Am He: The Interpretation of 'Anî Hû' in Jewish and Early Christian Literature*. Wissenschaftliche Untersuchungen zum Neuen Testament, 2nd ser., 113. Tübingen: Mohr Siebeck, 2000.

———. "The Testimony of Isaiah and Johannine Christology." In *"As Those Who Are Taught": The Interpretation of Isaiah from the LXX to the SBL*, edited by C. Mathews McGinnis and P. K. Tull, 107–24.

Society of Biblical Literature Symposium Series 27. Atlanta: Society of Biblical Literature, 2006.

Williams, Donald Leigh. "Zephaniah: A Re-interpretation." PhD diss., Duke University, 1962.

Williams, Ronald J., and John C. Beckman. *Williams' Hebrew Syntax*. 3rd ed. Toronto: University of Toronto Press, 2007.

Winsor, Ann Roberts. *A King Is Bound in the Tresses: Allusions to the Song of Songs in the Fourth Gospel*. Studies in Biblical Literature 6. New York: Lang, 1999.

Wise, Michael Owen. "Accidents and Accidence." In *Studies in Qumran Aramaic*, edited by T. Muraoka, 124–67. Abr-Nahrain Supplement Series 3. Louvain: Peeters, 1992.

Wise, Michael Owen, Martin G. Abegg, and Edward M. Cook. *The Dead Sea Scrolls: A New Translation*. San Francisco: Harper San Francisco, 1996.

Witherington, Ben, III. *John's Wisdom: A Commentary on the Fourth Gospel*. Louisville: Westminster John Knox, 1995.

Witmer, Stephen E. "Approaches to Scripture in the Fourth Gospel and the Qumran Pesharim." *Novum Testamentum* 48 (2006): 313–28.

Wright, N. T. *New Testament and the People of God*, vol. 1, *Christian Origins and the Question of God*. Minneapolis: Fortress, 1992.

Wright, R. B. "Psalms of Solomon: A New Translation and Introduction." In *The Old Testament Pseudepigrapha*, edited by James H. Charlesworth, 2:639–70. Garden City, NY: Doubleday, 1985.

Zeitlin, Solomon. "The Hallel: A Historical Study of the Canonization of the Hebrew Liturgy." *Jewish Quarterly Review* 53 (1962): 22–29.

Ziegler, Joseph, ed. *Duodecim Prophetae*, vol. 14, *Septuaginta: Vetus Testamentum Graecum Auctoritate Academiae Scientiarum Gottingensis Editum*. Göttingen: Vandenhoeck & Ruprecht, 1943.

Index of Scripture

Jeremiah

Lamentations

Ezekiel

Daniel

Haggai

Zechariah

Other Rabbinic Material

Early Christian Literature

Index of Subjects and Names

Christopher S. Tachick (MA, Gordon-Conwell Theological Seminary; ThM, Bethlehem College & Seminary) is adjunct professor of Hebrew at Bethlehem College & Seminary and a member of Wycliffe Bible Translators serving as a translation consultant with Seed Company. He has assisted several Bible translation teams around the world but mostly consults in English-speaking and French-speaking Africa. He resides in St. Paul, Minnesota, with his wife and three children.

Available in the Reformed Academic Dissertation Series

◆

It Has Not Yet Appeared What We Shall Be: A Reconsideration of the Imago Dei *in Light of Those with Severe Cognitive Disabilities*, by George C. Hammond

How Should We Treat Detainees? An Examination of "Enhanced Interrogation Techniques" under the Light of Scripture and the Just War Tradition, by J. Porter Harlow

Marks of Saving Grace: Theological Method and the Doctrine of Assurance in Jonathan Edwards's A Treatise Concerning Religious Affections, by Eric J. Lehner

The Doctrine of the Spirituality of the Church in the Ecclesiology of Charles Hodge, by Alan D. Strange

From Inscrutability to Concursus: Benjamin B. Warfield's Theological Construction of Revelation's Mode from 1880 to 1915, by Jeffrey A. Stivason

Preaching with Biblical Motivation: How to Incorporate the Motivation Found in the Inspired Preaching of the Apostles into Your Sermons, by Ray E. Heiple Jr.

The Triune God of Unity in Diversity: An Analysis of Perspectivalism, the Trinitarian Theological Method of John Frame and Vern Poythress, by Timothy E. Miller

A Development, Not a Departure: The Lacunae in the Debate of the Doctrine of the Trinity and Gender Roles,
by Hongyi Yang

The Trinity, Language, and Human Behavior: A Reformed Exposition of the Language Theory of Kenneth L. Pike,
by Pierce Taylor Hibbs

Free to Be Sons of God
by Geoffrey M. Ziegler

"King of Israel" and "Do Not Fear, Daughter of Zion": The Use of Zephaniah 3 in John 12,
by Christopher S. Tachick

Forthcoming

I See Dead People: The Function of the Resurrection of the Saints in Matthew 27:51–54,
by Raymond M. Johnson

Do Good to All People as You Have Opportunity: A Biblical Theology of the Good Deeds Mission of the New Covenenat Community,
by John Wind

A Strategy for Incorporating Biblical Counseling in North American Church Plants,
by Rush Witt